Subject Headings for
School and Public Libraries

Subject Headings for School and Public Libraries

An LCSH/Sears Companion

Second Edition

Joanna F. Fountain

1996
LIBRARIES UNLIMITED, INC.
Englewood, Colorado

Libraries Unlimited, Inc.
P.O. Box 6633
Englewood, CO 80155-6633
(800) 237-6124

Production Editor: Stephen Haenel
Proofreader: Barbara Schmidt
Typesetter: Michael Florman

Library of Congress Cataloging-in-Publication Data

Fountain, Joanna F.
    Subject headings for school and public libraries : an LCSH/Sears
companion / Joanna F. Fountain. -- 2nd ed.
    xxxii, 171 pp. 22x28 cm.
    Rev. ed. of: Headings for children's materials. 1993.
    ISBN 1-56308-360-4
    1. Subject headings, Library of Congress. 2. Sears, Minnie Earl,
1873-1933. Sears list of subject headings. 3. Public libraries--
United States. I. Fountain, Joanna F. Headings for children's
materials. II. Title.
Z695.Z8L5235 1996
025.4′68088′99282--dc20   96-6784
                                                            CIP

Contents

PREFACE

As school and public librarians automate their catalogs and receive a higher and higher percentage of their cataloging from MARC records, it becomes more and more feasible to use the *Library of Congress Subject Headings* ([LCSH]; Washington, DC: Library of Congress, 1994 [18th ed.]) instead of the *Sears List of Subject Headings* (New York: H. W. Wilson, 1994 [15th ed.]). In fact, the American Library Association (ALA) encourages libraries to standardize subject access across types of libraries ("Guidelines for Standardized Cataloging of Children's Materials," *Top of the News* [Fall 1983]: 49-55). The Library of Congress (LC) publishes a list of the headings used in its Annotated Card Program (ACP) in the first volume of LCSH, an immense four-volume listing. Catalogers who wish to convert to LC face a major task in checking and rechecking every heading: Is the heading a true LCSH heading? Is the heading an AC heading? Is the heading used the same way in AC usage as in LCSH or *Sears* practice?

Subject Headings for School and Public Libraries: An LCSH/Sears Companion has been created to assist in the conversion and standardization of headings for both automated and card catalogs. It is based on the 18th edition of LCSH, and includes the most-used headings and subdivisions in LCSH and its Annotated Card Program. The list also includes many names of authors, other individuals, corporate bodies, characters, and geographical names that would otherwise need to be verified in the Library of Congress Name Authority File. This list of *Subject Headings* will serve as a "first check" source, eliminating much of the time spent checking the AC list against the main LCSH list and searching the LC Name Authority File.

Background

The first version of this list was published in 1993 as *Headings for Children's Materials: An LCSH/Sears Companion* (Englewood, CO: Libraries Unlimited), and was based on the more than 20,000 bibliographic records in the union catalog of the Eanes Independent School District (Westlake Hills, Tex.), a public school system recognized for its excellent education program. Their collection includes book and nonbook materials for all areas of interest among children and young adult readers, as well as curriculum support areas for its five elementary, two middle, and one high school. Their shared online catalog consists of records derived largely from the Library of Congress and reflects many years of high-quality acquisitions by the librarians of that district.

The compilation has been retitled to reflect the addition of several thousand headings used in the catalogs of many types of libraries using Marcive, Inc.'s bibliographic services as well as the full subject authority list of the Kemp Public Library of Wichita Falls (Tex.), a large regional library serving a general population.

In the past, each of these libraries used the headings suggested by the *Sears List of Subject Headings*. However, when they automated their catalogs, they followed the recommendations of the American Library Association and other library agencies to use the headings provided by the Library of Congress in its Annotated Card Program. Each entry has been reconciled with the current (18th) edition of LCSH, modifications for the Annotated Card Program, and changes published through the Fall 1995 issue of the *Cataloging Service Bulletin* (Washington, DC: Library of Congress, quarterly).

Although the manual processes involved in making a change of this magnitude are time consuming and labor intensive, they have been undertaken many times in the past by individual libraries—notably by college and university libraries. However, the results have always been only for local use, so the procedure has necessarily been repeated each time another library decides to use LCSH as its subject authority. Because *Subject Headings for School and Public Libraries* is based on careful authority work at many libraries, it will ease the burden of libraries undertaking future projects of this type.

Acknowledgments

I am grateful to all the librarians in the Eanes Independent School District, the Kemp Public Library, and Marcive, for sharing their authority files as a basis for this work. I have greatly appreciated the encouragement and comments of librarians in the El Paso ISD, the Texas Education Agency, and the Smith [public] Memorial Library (Chautauqua, N.Y.). Faculty at the Graduate School of Library and Information Science at The University of Texas at Austin, where I teach part-time, have also been very supportive in my development of this revised compilation.

The task of updating the list has been greatly eased by the very able and careful assistance of my writer-daughter, Stacey, who has been amazed at the kinds of animals that might be viewed "as pets!" I am grateful for the careful work of my teaching assistant, Kyung-Sun Kim, who verified the authorized forms of hundreds of names in LC's Name Authority File. I extend special thanks to Dr. David Loertscher, formerly of Libraries Unlimited, who has provided me with materials, suggestions, and invaluable feedback as I developed plans for this work, and to editor Steve Haenel for his careful attention to the many details of this publication. I am grateful to all the wonderful people in my greater family for always "being there" for me. Most of all, I acknowledge and appreciate the unending support of my husband, Ray, who takes up a lot of slack for me and gives me the kind of space this kind of work requires.

INTRODUCTION

Subject Headings for School and Public Libraries features headings established by the Library of Congress (LC) for its use in cataloging library materials. This book provides headings for topics, for literary and organizational form, and for names of individuals, corporate bodies, places, works, and so on, that might be needed to catalog a *general collection* used by children and readers or viewers interested in popular topics. It expands the first edition, *Headings for Children's Materials: An LCSH/Sears Companion* (Englewood, CO: Libraries Unlimited, 1993), and was compiled in response to the needs of school and public librarians who wish to use in their own cataloging the same headings supplied on bibliographic records purchased from various vendors for the catalogs of most college and university libraries. It is particularly useful for libraries wishing to migrate from the *Sears List of Subject Headings* (New York: H. W. Wilson, 1994 [15th ed.]) to *Library of Congress Subject Headings* ([LCSH]; Washington, DC: Library of Congress, 1994 [18th ed.]) and for those using LC's modifications for its Annotated Card Program (ACP).

In libraries replacing *Sears* with LCSH as subject authority, headings can be checked against this book's list for either a matching (boldface) term or a cross-reference (in light type) to another term. Boldface terms followed by the *[S]* or *[AC, S]* notation will require no change; unauthorized terms (in light type) will require changes in the existing catalog.

Libraries that use standard LCSH headings will find this headings list a help in day-to-day application of the Annotated Card (AC) modifications of topical headings, as well as in identifying the standard ("main") headings and subdivisions they replace. In addition, the list includes names of many authors and other individuals, corporate bodies, and characters, all of which have been verified in the Library of Congress's Name Authority File to minimize the amount of name-authority work that must be done at the local level. Any name not included should be formulated according to the appropriate rules in *Anglo-American Cataloguing Rules*, 2nd edition, as amended in 1993 (Chicago: American Library Association, 1993), which is also the basis for names in LC's authority file.

Preceding the main listing is a list of the free-floating subdivisions used most often by catalogers. The introduction to this list on p. xi provides instructions on using subdivisions not printed in the main list.

Library of Congress's Annotated Card Program

For most titles, the catalogers at the Library of Congress use the same subject headings and subdivisions as those found in the full, four-volume LCSH. However, for materials likely to be cataloged for general populations, including younger and less sophisticated readers, certain headings and subdivisions have been modified as a part of the Annotated Card Program. This list of modifications, which is based in part on *Sears* usage of subject terminology, is published in the front of the first volume of each edition of the LCSH, along with instructions for use at the local level. Users will recognize the AC headings as those found in the bracketed area of Cataloging in Publication (CIP) supplied by the Library of Congress. Modifications include: 1) common terms (replacing scientific terms), 2) spelling modifications, 3) terms long used in school and general catalogs and based on various editions of the *Sears* listing, and 4) other words and phrases that are likely to be sought by the general reading public. Subdivision practice is also somewhat modified, with a small number of replacements and some changes in usage. Some examples are:

Standard LCSH Usage	AC Usage
Lights	**Light**
Social reformers	**Reformers**
Kings and rulers; Queens; Regency	**Kings, queens, rulers, etc.**
Basketball stories	**Basketball—Fiction**

Format of the Subject Headings List

The subject headings list follows current standards for headings and thesauri:

Boldface type indicates authorized terms and names;
normal (light) type indicates unused terms;
italic type is used for information or instructions to the cataloger.

Cross-references to other headings and to subdivisions also appear in standard thesaurus form and conform to those used in LCSH.

LC and AC Headings. Terms authorized for use as headings by LC, as in most standard headings lists, appear in boldface type. The headings in this list are taken from the 18th edition of the *Library of Congress Subject Headings* (LCSH) and the Name Authority File of the Library of Congress. Headings that have been modified for the Annotated Card Program are identified by the letters *[AC]* in brackets following the heading.

AC only Headings. Terms with the designation *[AC only]* are unique to the AC list, that is, they are not in the main LCSH list or in *Sears*, or they are applied in a different way in AC usage.

Sears Headings. If a heading in the list is followed by *[S]*, the LC/AC heading is identical to the heading used in the 15th edition of *Sears*.

Subdivisions. Terms authorized as subdivisions in LCSH, but for which a modification in usage has been made for children's materials, are identified by the bracketed letters *[AC]*.

To recapitulate:

Term *[S]* means that the term is identical in LCSH and in *Sears*.

Term *[AC only]* means that it is neither an LCSH term nor a *Sears* term—it appears only in the AC list. This means that a similar LCSH term has been modified.

Term *[AC, S]* means that the term is identical in both the AC list and the *Sears* list. It is a modification of a term in LCSH.

Term with *no designation* means that this is a standard LCSH term that is not found in *Sears* and has not been modified for the AC list.

The standard thesaurus-style references (USE, UF, BT, RT, NT, and SA) make it easy to follow concepts from broad to narrow and across through related terminology. LCSH explains this system further in its full introduction. References used in the subject headings list are similar to those in both LCSH and the *Sears* list.

USE   Use the name or term(s) following *USE* instead of the name or listed term.

UF   The name or term listed is **U**sed **F**or (in place of) the name or term(s) following *UF*.

RT   In addition to the name or term(s) listed, the cataloger may wish to use **R**elated **T**erms such as those suggested following *RT*.

BT   **B**roader **T**erms refer to more inclusive concepts. For example, **Dogs** is a broader term than **Collies**.

NT   Narrower **T**erms refer to more specific concepts. For example, **Cosmology** is a narrower term than **Universe**.

SA   In addition to the usage of the term as a heading, the cataloger may wish to use some terms as subdivisions; the SA

reference points the user to alternate terms, and also to the list of free-floating subdivisions.

See "Key to Subject Headings" on p. 2.

Using the Subject Headings List

Although it is not the purpose of this introduction to instruct the user in the rudiments of subject cataloging practice, a few basic practices that might be useful are discussed here. Normally, catalogers have followed Cutter's practice of assigning to a work one to three subject headings of the most specific nature that describe the work in hand. Following that style of cataloging, the cataloging record for a book on collies would have only the subject heading **Collies**, and not the broader heading **Dogs**. One of the most important modifications introduced by the Annotated Card Program is the use of *both* the most specific terms and broad terms that include the specific. For example, a book on collies will be assigned both the term **Collies** and the term **Dogs**. This is done when the cataloger determines that the general reader might not look up the specific term and would be more likely to find the work under a more general term. Catalogers are also encouraged to increase the number of subject headings assigned to a work. The practice of assigning a very few headings saved time when catalog cards were handwritten or typed. In automated systems, however, the number of access points can be increased greatly. LC catalogers have been assigning an increasing number of subject headings since they automated their own catalog and since the inception of the Annotated Card Program.

Using Free-floating Phrase Headings

In addition to the headings actually listed, LCSH authorizes the cataloger to compose and apply certain types of headings as needed. The following types of headings, called *free-floating phrase headings*, are allowed:

[Personal name]	**in fiction, drama, poetry, etc.**
[Topic or place]	**in literature**
[Topic or place]	**in art**
[Name of city]	**Metropolitan Area** ([Geographic qualifier])
[Name of city]	**Region** ([Geographic qualifier])
[Name of city]	**Suburban Area** ([Geographic qualifier])
[Name of river]	**Region** ([Geographic qualifier])
[Name of river]	**Watershed** ([Geographic qualifier])
[Name of river]	**Valley** ([Geographic qualifier])
[Name of geographic feature]	**Region** ([Geographic qualifier])

Using Free-floating Subdivisions

Long ago, subject catalogers determined that adding subdivisions to subject headings would help patrons find desired materials when the library contained many sources on the same subject. For example, if there were 50 general books on **Biology**, the patron could be assisted if this heading were broken down further by form, by geography, or by time. Thus, headings such as **Biology—France** or **Biology—Periodicals** are quite useful. Because catalogers found that such subdivisions were used repeatedly, the Library of Congress created a list of "Free-floating Subdivisions," which may be used whenever they are needed to narrow the catalog user's search.

Free-floating subdivisions cannot be used indiscriminately under any subject heading because they often don't make sense and because they may be reserved for special categories of headings only. For example, **Biology—Adjective** is a senseless use of a subdivision. LC applies the subdivision **—Adjective** under names of languages, e.g., **French language—Adjective**.

Types of Subdivisions

LC has established four broad types of free-floating subdivisions, all of which are interfiled in the following list. Detailed instructions for using each of the subdivisions is given in the *Subject Cataloging Manual: Subject Headings* (SCM:SH), 4th edition (Washington, DC: Library of Congress, 1991). A summary of these is also provided in the annual supplementary publication titled *Free-floating Subdivisions: An Alphabetical Index,* 7th edition (Washington, DC: Library of Congress, 1995). Together with the four-volume LCSH, these works complete the print version of the Library of Congress subject authority system. A list of free-floating subdivisions is included in the section titled "Free-floating Subdivisions," beginning on page xv. Instructions for using these subdivisions are included in each listing.

Topical Subdivisions. Topical subdivisions further elaborate assigned subject headings, making them narrower in meaning. A few examples are **University of Denver—Admission**; **Hospitals—Administration**; and **World War, 1939-1945—Aerial operations**. For example, **—Accidents** may be used as a subdivision under general topics and names of industries: **Transportation—Accidents**; **Construction industry—Accidents**. Follow the instructions given and inspect the examples for guidance. Most free-floating subdivisions are topical.

Geographical Subdivisions. Many subjects become more useful when a geographic subdivision is added such as **Bicycle racing—France**. Authority to add this type of subdivision is given in the main list as well as in the free-floating list. For example, **Music trade** *(May add geog subd)* means that the cataloger may add the name of any geographical entity—such as the name of a country, state, region, county, or city—as a subdivision of the heading, using the guidance of *Anglo-American Cataloguing Rules*, 2nd edition, amended 1993. AC usage limits the use of the subdivision **—United States** (and headings including the word "American") to subjects that are universal in nature. However, it can be useful to add geographical subdivisions for other parts of the world, e.g., **Monuments—Mexico**.

Sometimes a geographical subdivision can be used after another subdivision. Consider the example: **Boxing—Law and legislation—Alabama**. ("Boxing—Alabama—Law and legislation" would be incorrect.) The MARC entry for these two subdivisions would read

650 _0 **Boxing $xLaw and legislation $zAlabama**

A heading found only in the AC listing with the same subdivisions would be tagged

650 _1 **Runaways $xLaw and legislation $zCalifornia**

LC's Name Authority File can be checked when the authorized form of a geographical entity or name is in question. Additional geographic names may be taken from a recent edition of the *Commercial Atlas and Marketing Guide* (Chicago: Rand McNally, annual), which is the reference source used by catalogers at the Library of Congress.

Chronological or Period Subdivisions. Chronological subdivisions are used to limit a subject heading to a particular time period. Almost all such subdivisions are given in the main list (the full four-volume compilation) under the actual subject rather than in this book. Examples include **France—Revolution, 1789-1799**; **France—1945-1958**. At the beginning of the free-floating list, there are a few broad chronological headings listed, but note that their use is severely restricted. For example, **—16th century** may be used as a free-floating subdivision only under names of music compositions. These same period subdivisions, however, may be used as second subdivisions under the topical subdivision **—History** when appropriate, e.g., **—History—16th century**. A convenient list for use in cataloging collections with a substantial historical emphasis is *LC Period Subdivision Under Names of Places,* 5th edition (Washington, DC: Library of Congress, 1994).

Form Subdivisions. Form subdivisions are used to indicate the form in which the material on a subject is organized and presented. Almost all form subdivisions refer to the forms that books or other *textual* materials—such as databases or microfilms—take. Examples of frequently used form subdivisions include: **—Catalogs**; **—Dictionaries**; **—Pictorial works**; **—Tables**. Check SCM:SH for assistance if the usage of the subdivisions in the list below is still in question.

Form subdivisions are not applied as *topical* subdivisions when they represent the physical form of an item, such as a motion picture. Instead, the cataloger adds genre terms as separate headings, entering them in field 655 of the USMARC record.

A very useful list of genre terms that are in accord with LCSH is available to further designate content: *Guidelines on Subject Access to Individual Works of Fiction, Drama, Etc.* (Chicago: American Library Association, 1990).

Pattern Headings

In addition to the free-floating subdivisions, the subdivisions of many headings in the LCSH main list are also considered to be free-floating under specific categories. Each category is represented by one term that serves as a pattern heading for all terms in that category.

Thus, any of the subdivisions of **Cattle** (**—Anatomy**; **—Breeding**; **—Diseases**; etc.) can be used as subdivisions under any LCSH term in the category "domestic animals."

The Table of Pattern Headings is provided as a general guideline to the cataloger. The full LCSH edition must be consulted to find complete listings of subdivisions available for each category named.

Table of Pattern Headings

Pattern Heading	*Category*
Literatures and Languages	
English language	Languages and groups of languages
French language	A second pattern for languages and groups of languages
Romance languages	A third pattern for languages and groups of languages
English literature	Literatures including individual genres
Authors, English	Groups of literary authors
Shakespeare, William, 1564-1616	Individual literary authors
Shakespeare, William, 1564-1616. Hamlet	Literary works entered under author
Beowulf	Literary works entered under title
Wars and Military Topics	
World War, 1939-1945	Wars
United States—History—Civil War, 1861-1865	A second pattern for wars
United States—Armed Forces	Military services in general
United States. Air Force	Air forces
United States. Army	Armies
United States. Marine Corps	Marine forces
United States. Navy	Navies
Governments, Institutions, Industries, and Legal Matters	
United States. Congress	Legislative bodies
Great Britain—Colonies	Colonies
Universities and colleges	Types of educational institutions
Harvard University	Names of educational institutions
Construction industry	Industries
Retail trade	A second pattern for industries
Labor laws and legislation	Legal topics
Animals, Humans, and Natural Things	
Fishes	Animals in general
Cattle	Domestic animals
Metals	Materials
Concrete	A second pattern for materials
Copper	Chemicals
Insulin	A second pattern for chemicals
Cancer	Diseases
Tuberculosis	A second pattern for diseases
Heart	Organs and regions of the body
Foot	A second pattern for organs and regions of the body
Corn	Plants and crops
Religion	
Bible	Sacred works
Catholic Church	Christian denominations
Buddhism	Religions in general
Jesuits	Religious and monastic orders
Salvation	Theological topics
Miscellaneous	
Operas	Music compositions
Piano	Musical instruments
Newspapers	Newspapers
Soccer	Sports
Automobiles	Land vehicles

Categories with No Pattern Headings

Pattern headings are no longer provided for individual names, classes (category groupings) of persons, or geographic (place) names, although complete lists of suitable subdivisions are printed in the related sections of SCM:SH. Additionally, all subdivisions that can be used freely under any type of heading are listed in alphabetical order in the annual publication *Free-floating Subdivisions: An Alphabetical Index*.

Nevertheless, some guidance is available under such typical headings as **Jesus Christ** or **Lincoln, Abraham, 1809-1865**, which use many of the free-floating subdivisions allowed under personal names. For subdivisions typically found under headings for classes of persons, see such terms as **Teachers**, **Hockey—Coaches**, or **Youth**. For geographic names, see such place names as **Chicago** or **London** for cities, **New York** for states, **Appalachian Region** for regions, or **United States** for countries.

A Few Caveats

Care must be taken when using subdivisions. Do not use one subject heading from the main list as a subdivision of another subject heading from the main list without authority to do so. For example, one would not create the heading "Actors and actresses—Afro-American women" because neither term in the main list gives instructions that allow this combination. On the other hand, the term **Periodicals** (used as a heading for works *about* periodicals) may be used as a subdivision to indicate the form of the work, as in **Geography—Periodicals**.

Some headings in the main list have been modified slightly for AC usage. For example, the AC list includes the heading **Kings, queens, rulers, etc.**; however, the corresponding subdivision is **—Kings and rulers**, which is standard LCSH usage.

Format of the Free-floating Subdivision List

Free-floating subdivisions appear in standard thesaurus form.

Boldface type indicates authorized subdivisions; normal (light) type indicates unused subdivisions; *italic* type is used for information or instructions to the cataloger or catalog user.

All subdivisions begin with a dash (—) because they are to be used only as subdivisions, not as headings.

Subdivisions followed by the code *[S]* are also subdivisions in *Sears*.

Subdivisions followed by the code *[AC usage]* are used by LC in the Annotated Card Program.

Subdivisions followed by the code *[AC, S]* are used in both *Sears* and the AC list.

Subdivisions with *no designation* are used by LCSH as needed, including children's and popular works.

Underlined subdivisions indicate the form or format of works and are usually used *last* when more than one subdivision is used, e.g., **French literature—18th century—Adaptations**.

USE   indicates the authorized subdivision that should be used instead of the unauthorized subdivision.

UF   means the authorized subdivision is **U**sed **F**or (in place of) the unauthorized subdivision following *UF*.

See also refers to related subdivisions.

See "Key to Free-floating Subdivisions" on p. xiv.

KEY TO FREE-FLOATING SUBDIVISIONS

Dash (—) indicates terms are subdivisions

—Nest May be used as a subdivision under kinds of animals, e.g., **Ants—Nest**

Subdivisions in *Sears* as well as LCSH

—Nutrition *[S]* May be used as a subdivision under classes of persons; ethnic groups; kinds of animals; domestic animals; Indian tribes; and plants and crops, e.g., **Teenage mothers—Nutrition**

Indicates the form or format of works; subdivision must be used last when more than one subdivision is used

Example of subdivision usage

—Observers' manuals May be used as a subdivision under general topics, e.g., **Astronomy—Observers' manuals**

—Photographs May be used as a subdivision under general topics; classes of persons; and ethnic groups, e.g., **Mountains—Photographs**

Used for

    UF —Pictures

    See also **—Pictorial works; —Portraits**

Used in both *Sears* and AC list

See other subdivisions

—Pictorial works *[AC, S]* May be used under general topics and all subjects presented exclusively or predominantly through pictorial matter, e.g., **Reptiles—Pictorial works**

    See also **—Art collections**

Unauthorized subdivision

—Pictures

    USE **—Photographs; —Pictorial works; —Portraits**

Used by LC as a subdivision for children's materials

Use authorized subdivision

—Wit and humor *[AC usage]* May be used as a subdivision under general topics and topical wit and humor, including jokes and riddles, e.g., **Camping—Wit and humor**

    See also **—Humor**

FREE-FLOATING SUBDIVISIONS

Each subdivision preceded by a dash (—) may be used as needed to describe the nature or content of a work. While these subdivisions are "free-floating," they should be used only under the types of headings specified.

Some subdivisions may in turn be "subdivided" by adding a geographic name after a second dash, *e.g.*, **Transportation—Accidents—Maine**.

Subdivisions followed by the code *[S]* are also free-floating in *Sears*. Subdivisions specified by LC as ACP replacements for regular LCSH subdivisions are indicated by the term *[AC usage]*.

Underlined subdivisions indicate the form or format of works, and will normally be used *last* when more than one subdivision is used, *e.g.*, **French literature—18th century—Adaptations**.

Subdivisions

—16th century May be used as a subdivision only under names of music compositions, *e.g.*, **Carols—16th century**
See also **—History—16th century**

—17th century May be used as a subdivision under drama and names of music compositions, *e.g.*, **Songs—17th century**
See also **—History—17th century**

—18th century May be used as a subdivision under names of groups of literary authors; literatures (language or country); drama; and types of music compositions, *e.g.*, **Poets—18th century**
See also **—History—18th century**

—19th century May be used as a subdivision under names of groups of literary authors; literatures (language or country); drama; and types of music compositions, *e.g.*, **Mexican literature—19th century**
See also **—History—19th century**

—20th century May be used as a subdivision under names of groups of literary authors; literatures (language or country); drama; and types of music compositions, *e.g.*, **Plays—20th century**
See also **—History—20th century**

—Abuse of *(May add geog subd)* May be used as a subdivision under names of classes of persons, *e.g.*, **Homeless persons—Abuse of**

—Accidents *[S] (May add geog subd)* May be used as a subdivision under topical headings and names of industries, *e.g.*, **Transportation—Accidents; Construction industry—Accidents**

—Adaptations May be used as a subdivision under names of individual persons and individual literary authors; titles of literary works; and literatures (language or country), *e.g.*, **Cinderella—Adaptations; Twain, Mark, 1835-1910—Adaptations**
See also **—Film and video adaptations**

—Adjective May be used as a subdivision under languages, *e.g.*, **French language—Adjective**

—Administration *[S]* May be used as a subdivision under topical headings; names of corporate bodies; chemicals; colonies; individual schools; and types of schools, *e.g.*, **Hospitals—Administration; Voice of America (Organization)—Administration**

—Admission May be used as a subdivision under names of individual schools and types of schools. *e.g.*, **University of Denver—Admission**
See also **—Entrance requirements**

—Aerial operations May be used as a subdivision under names of wars, *e.g.*, **World War, 1939-1945—Aerial operations**

—Aerial operations, American, [British, etc.] May be used as a subdivision under names of wars, *e.g.*, **World War, 1914-1918—Aerial operations, British**

—Air conditioning *[S] (May add geog subd)* May be used as a subdivision under topical headings and names of land vehicles. *e.g.*, **Theaters—Air conditioning; Taxicabs—Air conditioning**

—Alcohol use *[S]* May be used as a subdivision under names of individual persons, *e.g.*, **Nero, Emperor of Rome, 37-68—Alcohol use**

—Alcohol use *[S] (May add geog subd)* May be used as a subdivision under classes of persons and ethnic groups, *e.g.*, **Legislators—Alcohol use**

—Alphabet May be used as a subdivision under names of languages, *e.g.*, **Spanish language—Alphabet**

—Amphibious operations May be used as a subdivision under names of wars, *e.g.*, **Normandy (France), Attack on, 1944—Amphibious operations**

—**Anatomy** *[S]* May be used as a subdivision under kinds of animals; organs/regions of the body; plants & crops, *e.g.*, **Cats—Anatomy**

—**Anecdotes** *[S]* May be used as a subdivision under topical headings; classes of persons; ethnic groups; corporate bodies; individual persons; places; types of schools; individual literary authors; and sacred works, *e.g.*, **Broadcasting—Anecdotes; Buffalo Bill, 1846-1917—Anecdotes**

—**Anniversaries, etc.** May be used as a subdivision under topical headings; classes of persons; ethnic groups; corporate bodies; individual persons; places; individual literary authors; Christian denominations; and wars, *e.g.*, **Crusades—Anniversaries; Baptists—Anniversaries**

—**Antiquities** *[S]* May be used as a subdivision under names of ethnic groups; places; sacred works; and wars, *e.g.*, **London (England)—Antiquities**

—**Appropriations and expenditures** May be used as a subdivision under names of corporate bodies; places; legislative bodies; and military services, *e.g.*, **Florida—Appropriations and expenditures**

—**Armed Forces** *(May add geog subd)* May be used as a subdivision under names of places, *e.g.*, **Nicaragua—Armed Forces**

—**Art** May be used as a subdivision under topical headings; individual persons; and individual literary authors, *e.g.*, **Flowers—Art**

—**Art collections** May be used as a subdivision under names of corporate bodies; individual persons; and families, *e.g.*, **Harvard University—Art collections**
   See also —**Collectibles; —Collectors and collecting**

—**Assassination** *[S]* May be used as a subdivision under names of individual persons, *e.g.*, **Kennedy, Robert F., 1925-1968 —Assassination**

—**Atlases** *[S]* May be used as a subdivision under topical headings, *e.g.*, **Zoology—Atlases**

—**Attitudes** *[S]* May be used as a subdivision under classes of persons; and ethnic groups, *e.g.*, **Vietnamese Americans—Attitudes**

—**Audio adaptations** May be used as a subdivision under names of individual literary authors and literatures (language or country), *e.g.*, **Frost, Robert, 1874-1963—Audio adaptations**
   See also —**Audio-visual aids; —Film and video adaptations**

—**Audio-visual aids** May be used as a subdivision under topical headings, *e.g.*, **Levers—Audio-visual aids**
   See also —**Audio adaptations; —Film and video adaptations; —Software**

—**Authorship** May be used as a subdivision under topical headings; individual persons; individual literary authors; and titles of literary and sacred works, *e.g.*, **Literary recreations—Authorship; Beowulf—Authorship**

—**Automation** *[S]* May be used as a subdivision under topical headings; corporate bodies; and industries, *e.g.*, **Measurement—Automation; Energy industries—Automation**
   See also —**Computer programs**

—Behavior [of animals]
   USE —**Habits and behavior**

—**Bibliography** *[S]* May be used as a subdivision under topical headings; classes of persons; ethnic groups; corporate bodies; individual persons; individual literary authors; and literatures (language or country), *e.g.*, **Best books—Bibliography; Carroll, Lewis, 1832-1898—Bibliography**
   See also —**Bio-bibliography; —Discography**

—**Bio-bibliography** *[S]* May be used as a subdivision under topical headings; names of ethnic groups; places; religious orders; and Christian denominations, *e.g.*, **Athletics—Bio-bibliography; Methodists—Bio-bibliography**
   See also —**Bibliography; —Discography**

—**Biography** *[AC, S]* Used for both collected and individual biographies under names of ethnic groups; also use under subject fields where *no specific term* designates the profession or contributions of the biographee, *e.g.*:
   Aeronautics—Biography
   Hispanic Americans—Biography
   Indians of North America—Biography
Do *not* use this subdivision, however, where a term designates the profession, such as **Musicians**.
   See also —**Personal narratives**

—**Biological control** *(May add geog subd)* May be used as a subdivision under names of animals; and plants & crops, *e.g.*, **Weeds—Biological control**

—**Black authors** May be used as a subdivision under names of literatures (language or country), *e.g.*, **English literature—Black authors**

—**Blockades** May be used as a subdivision under names of wars, *e.g.*, **Persian Gulf War, 1991—Blockades**

—**Bodies** May be used as a subdivision under names of land vehicles, *e.g.*, **Sports cars—Bodies**

—**Books and reading** *[S]* May be used as a subdivision under classes of persons; ethnic groups; individual persons; and individual literary authors, *e.g.*, **Criminals—Books and reading**

—**Boundaries** *(May add geog subd)* May be used as a subdivision under names of places and colonies, *e.g.*, **Louisiana—Boundaries**

—**Breeding** *(May add geog subd)* May be used as a subdivision under kinds of animals; and plants & crops, *e.g.*, **Gerbils—Breeding**

—**Buildings, structures, etc,** May be used as a subdivision under names of places, *e.g.*, **Washington (D.C.)—Buildings, structures, etc.**

—**Calendars** May be used as a subdivision under topical headings; corporate bodies; places; and individual literary authors, *e.g.*, **Libraries—Calendars; Washington, D.C.—Calendars**

—Camouflage   May be used as a subdivision under names of wars, *e.g.*, **Canadian Invasion, 1775-1776—Camouflage**

—Campaigns *(May add geog subd)*   May be used as a subdivision under names of wars, *e.g.*, **Iran-Iraq War, 1980-1988—Campaigns**

—Capital and capitol   May be used as a subdivision under names of places, *e.g.*, **Bolivia—Capital and capitol**

—Captivity, [dates]   May be used as a subdivision under names of individual persons, *e.g.*, **Jacobsen, David (David P.)—Captivity, 1985-1986**

—Care *[S] (May add geog subd)*   May be used as a subdivision under names of classes of persons, *e.g.*, **Diabetics—Care**
   See also —**Care and hygiene**; —**Dental care**; —**Hospital care**; —**Institutional care**

—Care and hygiene *[S] (May add geog subd)*   May be used as a subdivision under names of organs/regions of the body, *e.g.*, **Ear—Care and hygiene**
   See also —**Care**; —**Dental care**; —**Hospital care**; —**Treatment**

—Cartoons and comics *[AC, S]*   May be used as a subdivision under topical headings; classes of persons; ethnic groups; corporate bodies; individual persons; individual literary authors; sacred works; and families, *e.g.*, **Jungles—Cartoons and comics**; **Musicians—Cartoons and comics**
   UF   —Caricatures and cartoons

—Case studies *[S]*   May be used as a subdivision under topical headings; classes of persons; ethnic groups; and corporate bodies, *e.g.*, **Justice—Case studies**; **Consumers—Case studies**

—Cases   May be used as a subdivision under legal topical headings, *e.g.*, **Family violence—Cases**

—Catalogs *[S]*   May be used as a subdivision under topical headings; corporate bodies; and individual persons, *e.g.*, **Games—Catalogs**; **Museum of New Mexico—Catalogs**
   See also —**Catalogs and collections**; —**Film catalogs**

—Catalogs and collections *(May add geog subd)*   May be used as a subdivision under topical headings; animals; musical instruments; and plants & crops, *e.g.*, **Dolls—Catalogs and collections**; **Clarinet—Catalogs and collections**
   See also —**Catalogs**; —**Film catalogs**

—Causes   May be used as a subdivision under names of wars, *e.g.*, **Crimean War, 1853-1856—Causes**

—Censorship *[S] (May add geog subd)*   May be used as a subdivision under topical headings; and individual literary authors, *e.g.*, **Television—Censorship**; **Sendak, Maurice—Censorship**

—Census *(May add , [date])*   May be used as a subdivision under names of ethnic groups; and places, *e.g.*, **Navajo Indians—Census**; **Abilene (Tex.)—Census, 1990**

—Ceremonies
   USE —**Rites and ceremonies**

—Certification *(May add geog subd)*   May be used as a subdivision under topical headings; classes of persons; and industries, *e.g.*, **Air quality—Certification**; **Psychologists—Certification**

—Characters   May be used as a subdivision under names of individual literary authors and titles of literary works, *e.g.*, **Miller, Arthur, 1915- —Characters**

—Charities   May be used as a subdivision under names of ethnic groups; corporate bodies; religions; and Christian denominations, *e.g.*, **Catholic Church—Charities**

—Chemical warfare *(May add geog subd)*   May be used as a subdivision under names of wars, *e.g.*, **World War, 1914-1918—Chemical warfare**

—Children *(May add geog subd)*   May be used as a subdivision under names of wars, *e.g.*, **World War, 1939-1945—Children—France**

—Chronology *[S]*   May be used as a subdivision under topical headings; individual persons; groups of literary authors; individual literary authors; literatures (language or country); sacred works; and wars, *e.g.*, **Architecture—Chronology**; **Canadian literature—Chronology**

—Church history *(May add —[-th] century)*   May be used as a subdivision under names of places, *e.g.*, **Germany—Church history—15th century**

—Citizen participation *[S]*   May be used as a subdivision under topical headings, *e.g.*, **Environmental protection—Citizen participation**

—Civil rights *[S] (May add geog subd)*   May be used as a subdivision under names of classes of persons and ethnic groups, *e.g.*, **Employees—Civil rights**

—Civilian relief *(May add geog subd)*   May be used as a subdivision under names of wars, *e.g.*, **Zulu War, 1879—Civilian relief**

—Civilization *(May add —[-th] century)*   May be used as a subdivision under names of places, *e.g.*, **Peru—Civilization—16th century**

—Claims   May be used as a subdivision under names of ethnic groups; places; and wars, *e.g.*, **Koasati Indians—Claims**

—Classification   May be used as a subdivision under topical headings; classes of persons; animals; languages; and plants & crops, *e.g.*, **Vehicles—Classification**; **Insects—Classification**

—Clergy   May be used as a subdivision under names of Christian denominations, *e.g.*, **Baptists—Clergy**

—Climate   May be used as a subdivision under names of places, *e.g.*, **Bahamas—Climate**

—Clubs
   USE —**Societies and clubs**; —**Societies, etc.**

—**Collectibles** *[S] (May add geog subd)* May be used as a subdivision under topical headings; classes of persons; ethnic groups; corporate bodies; individual persons; and wars, *e.g.*, **Glassware—Collectibles; Los Angeles Rams (Football team)—Collectibles**
See also —**Art collections; —Collection and preservation**

—**Collection and preservation** *[S]* May be used as a subdivision under topical headings and animals, *e.g.*, **Photographs—Collection and preservation; Ostriches—Collection and preservation**
See also —**Art collections; —Collectors and collection**

—**Collections** *[AC, S]* Use under topical headings, for publications containing works by more than one author, *e.g.*, **Cheerleading—Fiction—Collections**.
See also —**Art collections; —Literary collections**

—**Collectors and collecting** *[S] (May add geog subd)* May be used as a subdivision under topical headings; and land vehicles, *e.g.*, **Postcards—Collectors and collecting; Corvette automobile—Collectors and collecting**
See also —**Art collections; —Collection and preservation**

—**Colonies** *[S]* May be used as a subdivision under names of places, *e.g.*, **France—Colonies**

—**Colonization** May be used as a subdivision under names of places, *e.g.*, **Cuba—Colonization**

—**Color** *[S]* May be used as a subdivision under kinds of animals; and plants & crops, *e.g.*, **Snakes—Color**
See also —**Coloring**

—**Coloring** May be used as a subdivision under names of chemicals and materials, *e.g.*, **Plastics—Coloring**
See also —**Color**

—**Comedies** May be used as a subdivision under names of individual literary authors, *e.g.*, **Shakespeare, William, 1564-1616—Comedies**

—**Commerce** *(May add geog subd)* May be used as a subdivision under names of ethnic groups; places; and colonies, *e.g.*, **Scandinavia—Commerce**

—**Commercial policy** May be used as a subdivision under names of places, *e.g.*, **Japan—Commercial policy**

—**Comparison** May be used as a subdivision under names of languages, *e.g.*, **Romance languages—Comparison**

—**Competitions** *[S] (May add geog subd)* May be used as a subdivision under topical headings, *e.g.*, **Mathematics—Competitions**

—**Complications** *(May add geog subd)* May be used as a subdivision under names of diseases, *e.g.*, **Nutrition disorders—Complications**

—**Composition** *[S]* May be used as a subdivision under topical headings; kinds of animals; and plants & crops, *e.g.*, **Food—Composition; Cactus—composition**
See also —**Composition and exercises**

—**Composition and exercises** May be used as a subdivision under names of languages, *e.g.*, **English language—Composition and exercises**
See also —**Composition; —Problems, exercises, etc.**

—**Compound words** May be used as a subdivision under names of languages, *e.g.*, **Spanish language—Compound words**

—**Computer programs** *[S]* May be used as a subdivision under topical headings and plants & crops, *e.g.*, **Research—Computer programs; Vegetables—Computer programs**
See also —**Programmed instruction; —Programming; —Software**

—**Computer-assisted instruction** *[S]* May be used as a subdivision under topical headings and languages, *e.g.*, **Repairing—Computer-assisted instruction; German language—Computer-assisted instruction**

—**Concordances** *[S]* May be used as a subdivision under topical headings; individual persons; individual literary authors; literatures (language or country); and sacred works, *e.g.*, **Music—Concordances; Bible—Concordances**

—**Congresses** *[S]* May be used as a subdivision under topical headings; classes of persons; ethnic groups; corporate bodies; individual persons; places; individual literary authors; literary works/author entry; titles of literary works; Christian denominations; wars; and families, *e.g.*, **AIDS (Disease)—Congresses; King, Martin Luther, Jr., 1929-1968—Congresses**

—**Conservation** *(May add geog subd)* May be used as a subdivision under names of materials *e.g.*, **Balsa wood—Conservation**
See also —**Conservation and restoration**

—**Conservation and restoration** *[S]* May be used as a subdivision under topical headings; and land vehicles, *e.g.*, **Books—Conservation and restoration; Rolls-Royce automobile—Conservation and restoration**
See also —**Collection and preservation; —Conservation**

—**Constitution** May be used as a subdivision under names of corporate bodies and places, *e.g.*, **South Carolina—Constitution**

—**Constitution—Amendments** May be used as a subdivision under names of places, *e.g.*, **Utah—Constitution—Amendments**

—**Constitution—Amendments—1st, [2nd, 3rd, etc.]** May be used as a subdivision under names of places, *e.g.*, **United States—Constitutions—Amendments—1st**

—**Constitution—Signers** May be used as a subdivision under names of places, *e.g.*, **Kansas—Constitution—Signers**

—**Constitutional history** May be used as a subdivision under names of places and colonies, *e.g.*, **Great Britain—Constitutional history**

—**Constitutional law** May be used as a subdivision under names of places; and colonies, *e.g.*, **Argentina—Constitutional law**

—**Constitutional law—Amendments—1st, [2nd, 3rd, etc.]** May be used as a subdivision under names of places, *e.g.*, **Texas—Constitutional law—Amendments—3rd**

—**Control** [S] (*May add geog subd*)   May be used as a subdivision under kinds of animals; and plants & crops, *e.g.*, **Coyotes—Control**

—<u>**Conversation and phrase books**</u>   May be used as a subdivision under names of languages, *e.g.*, **Hopi language—Conversation and phrase books**

—<u>**Correspondence**</u> [S]   May be used as a subdivision under classes of persons; ethnic groups; individual persons; individual literary authors; and families, *e.g.*, **Alcott family—Correspondence**

—**Costume** [S] (*May add geog subd*)   May be used as a subdivision under classes of persons and ethnic groups, *e.g.*, **Gypsies—Costume**

—**Counseling of** (*May add geog subd*)   May be used as a subdivision under classes of persons and names of ethnic groups, *e.g.*, **Alcoholics—Counseling of**

—**Court and courtiers**   May be used as a subdivision under names of places, *e.g.*, **France—Court and courtiers**

—**Criticism and interpretation**   May be used as a subdivision under names of individual persons and individual literary authors, *e.g.*, **Golding, William, 1911- —Criticism and interpretation**
   See also —**Criticism and interpretation—History;** —**Criticism, interpretation, etc.—History and criticism**

—**Criticism and interpretation—History**   May be used as a subdivision under names of individual literary authors, *e.g.*, **Hemingway, Ernest, 1899-1961—Criticism and interpretation—History**
   See also —**History and criticism**

—**Criticism, interpretation, etc.** (*May add geog subd*)   May be used as a subdivision under names of sacred works, *e.g.*, **Bible—Criticism, interpretation, etc.**
   See also —**Criticism and interpretation;** —**History and criticism**

—**Cross-cultural studies**   May be used as a subdivision under topical headings, *e.g.*, **Herbs—Cross-cultural studies**

—<u>**Curricula**</u> [S]   May be used as a subdivision under topical headings; individual schools; and types of schools, *e.g.*, **Engineering—Curricula; Nursery schools—Curricula**

—**Customizing** (*May add geog subd*)   May be used as a subdivision under names of musical instruments and land vehicles, *e.g.*, **Guitar—Customizing**

—**Customs and practices**   May be used as a subdivision under religions; religious orders; and Christian denominations, *e.g.*, **Mormons—Customs and practices**
   See also —**Social life and customs**

—**Data processing** [S]   May be used as a subdivision under topical headings and corporate bodies, *e.g.*, **Business—Data processing; Miami Dolphins (Football team)—Data processing**
   See also —**Computer programs**

—<u>**Databases**</u>   May be used as a subdivision under topical headings; places; and names of corporate bodies, *e.g.*, **Agriculture—Databases; United States. Bureau of the Census—Databases**
   See also —**Computer programs**

—**Death and burial**   May be used as a subdivision under names of individual persons and individual literary authors, *e.g.*, **Nixon, Richard M. (Richard Milhous), 1913- —Death and burial.**

—**Decision making**   May be used as a subdivision under topical headings, *e.g.*, **Youth—Decision making**

—**Defenses**   May be used as a subdivision under names of places and colonies, *e.g.*, **Puerto Rico—Defenses**

—**Dental care** (*May add geog subd*)   May be used as a subdivision under classes of persons; ethnic groups; and military services, *e.g.*, **Children—Dental care—Michigan**
   See also —**Care;** —**Care and hygiene**

—**Description and travel**   May be used as a subdivision under names of places and colonies, *e.g.*, **Mississippi River Valley—Description and travel**
   See also —**Travel**

—**Design** [S]   May be used as a subdivision under topical headings and chemicals, *e.g.*, **Furniture—Design; Antibiotics—Design**

—**Design and construction** [S]   May be used as a subdivision under topical headings and names of land vehicles, *e.g.*, **Architecture, Domestic—Design and construction; Automobiles—Design and construction**

—**Development**   May be used as a subdivision under kinds of animals and plants & crops, *e.g.*, **Horses—Development**

—<u>**Diaries**</u>   May be used as a subdivision under classes of persons; ethnic groups; individual persons; individual literary authors; military services; and families, *e.g.*, **Columbus, Christopher, 1449-1506—Diaries**

—<u>**Dictionaries**</u> [S]   May be used as a subdivision under topical headings; ethnic groups; corporate bodies; individual persons; languages; and names of individual authors, *e.g.*, **Psychology—Dictionaries; Hebrew language—Dictionaries**
   See also —**Encyclopedias;** —**Lexicography**

—**Dictionaries—French, [Italian, etc.]**   May be used as a subdivision under languages, *e.g.*, **Spanish language—Dictionaries—French**

—**Diet therapy** [S]   May be used as a subdivision under names of diseases, *e.g.*, **Diabetes—Diet therapy**

—**Diplomatic and consular service** (*May add geog subd*)   May be used as a subdivision under places, *e.g.*, **Israel—Diplomatic and consular service**

—<u>**Directories**</u> [S]   May be used as a subdivision under topical headings; classes of persons; ethnic groups; corporate bodies; places; and families, *e.g.*, **Foreign study—Directories; Wisconsin—Directories**
   See also —**Telephone directories**

—**Discipline**   May be used as a subdivision under topical headings; classes of persons; corporate bodies; religions; and Christian denominations, *e.g.*, **Athletics—Discipline**

—<u>Discography</u> *[S]* May be used as a subdivision under topical headings; classes of persons; ethnic groups; corporate bodies; individual persons; individual literary authors; and types of music compositions, *e.g.*, **Success in business—Discography; Sandburg, Carl, 1878-1967—Discography**
See also —**Bibliography;** —**Bio-bibliography**

—**Discovery and exploration** May be used as a subdivision under names of places and colonies, *e.g.*, **West (U.S.)—Discovery and exploration**

—**Diseases** *[S] (May add geog subd)* May be used as a subdivision under classes of persons; ethnic groups; kinds of animals; and organs/regions of the body, *e.g.*, **Lungs—Diseases**
See also —**Diseases and pests**

—**Diseases and pests** *[S] (May add geog subd)* May be used as a subdivision under names of plants & crops, *e.g.*, **Corn—Diseases and pests**

—**Dispersal** *(May add geog subd)* May be used as a subdivision under names of animals and plants & crops, *e.g.*, **Dandelions—Dispersal**

—**Drama** *[S]* May be used as a subdivision under topical headings; classes of persons; ethnic groups; corporate bodies; individual persons; places; and individual literary authors, *e.g.*, **Slavery—Drama; Sullivan, Anne, 1866-1936—Drama**
UF —Juvenile drama

—**Drug use** *[S]* May be used as a subdivision under names of individual persons, *e.g.*, **Phoenix, River—Drug use**

—**Drying** May be used as a subdivision under topical headings; materials; and plants & crops, *e.g.*, **Buildings—Drying; Flowers—Drying**

—**Dwellings** May be used as a subdivision under classes of persons and ethnic groups, *e.g.*, **Eskimos—Dwellings**

—**Ecology** *(May add geog subd)* May be used as a subdivision under kinds of animals and plants & crops, *e.g.*, **Succulent plants—Ecology**

—**Economic aspects** *(May add geog subd)* May be used as a subdivision under topical headings, *e.g.*, **Trees—Economic aspects**

—**Economic conditions** *[S]* May be used as a subdivision under classes of persons; ethnic groups; places; and colonies, *e.g.*, **Aged—Economic conditions**

—**Economic policy** May be used as a subdivision under names of places and colonies, *e.g.*, **Puerto Rico—Economic policy**

—**Education** *[S] (May add geog subd)* May be used as a subdivision under classes of persons; ethnic groups; religious orders; and Christian denominations, *e.g.*, **Automobile drivers—Education**

—**Education (Higher)** *(May add geog subd)* May be used as a subdivision under classes of persons and ethnic groups, *e.g.*, **Working class—Education (Higher)—Missouri**

—**Eggs** *(May add geog subd)* May be used as a subdivision under kinds of animals, *e.g.*, **Birds—Eggs**

—**Embryos** May be used as a subdivision under names of animals and plants & crops, *e.g.*, **Chickens—Embryos**

—**Emigration and immigration** May be used as a subdivision under names of places and colonies, *e.g.*, **Ireland—Emigration and immigration**

—**Employees** May be used as a subdivision under topical headings; corporate bodies; individual persons; individual schools; types of schools; industries; and Christian denominations, *e.g.*, **Postal service—Employees; Universities and colleges—Employees**

—**Employment** *[S] (May add geog subd)* May be used as a subdivision under classes of persons and ethnic groups, *e.g.*, **College graduates—Employment**

—<u>Encyclopedias</u> May be used as a subdivision under topical headings; ethnic groups; individual persons; individual literary authors, *e.g.*, **Sports—Encyclopedias; Asimov, Isaac, 1920- —Encyclopedias**
See also —**Dictionaries**

—<u>Entrance examinations</u> May be used as a subdivision under names of individual schools and types of schools, *e.g.*, **Boarding schools—Entrance examinations**
See also —**Examinations, questions, etc.**

—**Entrance requirements** *[S]* May be used as a subdivision under names of individual schools and types of schools, *e.g.*, **Berry Schools (Berry, Ga.)—Entrance requirements**
See also —**Admission**

—**Environmental aspects** May be used as a subdivision under military services, *e.g.*, **United States. Army—Environmental aspects**
See also —**Environmental aspects** *(May add geog subd)*

—**Environmental aspects** *[S] (May add geog subd)* May be used as a subdivision under topical headings; chemicals; diseases; industries; materials; land vehicles; and wars, *e.g.*, **Acid rain—Environmental aspects; Chlorofluorocarbons—Environmental aspects**
See also —**Ecology;** —**Environmental aspects** *(Not subd geog)*

—**Equipment** May be used as a subdivision under military services, *e.g.*, **United States. Coast Guard—Equipment**

—**Equipment and supplies** *[S]* May be used as a subdivision under topical headings; corporate bodies; animals; industries; plants & crops; land vehicles; and wars, *e.g.*, **Diving, Submarine—Equipment and supplies**
See also —**Materials**

—**Errors of usage** May be used as a subdivision under names of languages, *e.g.*, **Spanish language—Errors of usage**

—**Eruption, [date]** May be used as a subdivision under names of places, *e.g.*, **Krakatoa (Indonesia)—Eruption, 1883**

—**Ethnic relations** May be used as a subdivision under names of places, *e.g.*, **South Africa—Ethnic relations**
See also —**Race relations**

—**Ethnobotany** May be used as a subdivision under names of ethnic groups and Indian tribes, *e.g.*, **Ojibwa Indians—Ethnobotany**

—**Etymology** May be used as a subdivision under names of languages, *e.g.*, **English language—Etymology**

—**Etymology—Names** May be used as a subdivision under names of languages, *e.g.*, **Hebrew language—Etymology—Names**

—**Evacuation of civilians** (*May add geog subd*) May be used as a subdivision under names of wars, *e.g.*, **World War, 1939-1945—Evacuations of civilians**

—**Evaluation** May be used as a subdivision under topical headings; corporate bodies; and types of schools, *e.g.*, **Water quality—Evaluation; Middle schools—Evaluation**
See also —**Entrance examinations; —Examinations, questions, etc.; —Medical examinations; —Testing**

—**Evolution** May be used as a subdivision under kinds of animals; chemicals; organs/regions of the body; and plants & crops, *e.g.*, **Vertebrates—Evolution**

—**Examinations** [S] May be used as a subdivision under topical headings; classes of persons; corporate bodies; individual schools; types of schools; and military services, *e.g.*, **Universities and colleges—Examinations**
See also — **Entrance examinations; —Evaluation; —Examinations, questions, etc.; —Medical examinations**

—**Examinations, questions, etc.** May be used as a subdivision under topical headings; classes of persons; ethnic groups; and sacred works, *e.g.*, **Medicine—Examinations, questions, etc.**
See also —**Entrance examinations; —Evaluation; —Examinations; —Medical examinations; Problems, exercises, etc.**

—**Exhibitions** [S] May be used as a subdivision under topical headings; classes of persons; ethnic groups; corporate bodies; individual persons; and individual literary authors, *e.g.*, **Books—Exhibitions; Amon Carter Museum of Western Art—Exhibitions**

—**Experiments** [S] May be used as a subdivision under topical headings, *e.g.*, **Aeronautics—Experiments**

—**Faculty** May be used as a subdivision under names of individual schools and types of schools, *e.g.*, **Juilliard School—Faculty**

—**Family** May be used as a subdivision under names of individual persons, and individual literary authors, *e.g.*, **Njeri, Itabari—Family**

—**Family relationships** May be used as a subdivision under classes of persons, *e.g.*, **Adoptees—Family relationships**

—**Fiction** [S] AC usage: May be used under all subjects for individual or collected works of fiction on identifiable topical headings, *e.g.*, **Selfishness—Fiction; McDuck, Scrooge (Fictitious character)—Fiction**
    UF   —Juvenile fiction

—**Field work** May be used as a subdivision under topical headings, *e.g.*, **Comparative linguistics—Field work**

—**Film and video adaptations** May be used as a subdivision under names of individual literary authors; literatures (language or country); and music compositions, *e.g.*, **Steinbeck, John, 1902-1968—Film and video adaptations**
See also —**Adaptations** and headings of the type **[...] films**, *e.g.* **Amateur films**

—**Film catalogs** May be used as a subdivision under topical headings; classes of persons; ethnic groups; corporate bodies; and individual persons, *e.g.*, **Computer crimes—Film catalogs; Jones, Indiana (Fictitious character)—Film catalogs**
See also —**Catalogs; —Catalogs and collections; —Video catalogs**

—**Finance** [S] May be used as a subdivision under topical headings; corporate bodies; individual schools; types of schools; industries; military services; and Christian denominations, *e.g.*, **Corporations—Finance; Girl Scouts—Finance**
See also —**Finance** (*May add geog subd*); —**Finance, Personal**

—**Finance** (*May add geog subd*) May be used as a subdivision under names of wars, *e.g.*, **World War, 1914-1918—Finance—Great Britain**
See also —**Finance** (*Not subd geog*)

—**Finance, Personal** May be used as a subdivision under classes of persons; ethnic groups; and individual persons, *e.g.*, **Lee, Robert E., 1807-1870—Finance, Personal**
See also —**Finance**

—**Fires and fire prevention** [S] (*May add geog subd*) May be used as a subdivision under topical headings; industries; and land vehicles, *e.g.*, **Agricultural chemicals—Fires and fire prevention; Motorcycles—Fire and fire prevention**

—**Folklore** [S] May be used as a subdivision under topical headings; classes of persons; ethnic groups; places; and sacred works, *e.g.*, **Dragons—Folklore; Cowboys—Folklore; Navajos—Folklore**

—**Food** [S] May be used as a subdivision under names of ethnic groups; and animals, *e.g.*, **Marine animals—Food**
See also —**Nutrition**

—**Forecasting** May be used as a subdivision under topical headings and places, *e.g.*, **Population—Forecasting; Russia—Forecasting**
See also —**Prophecies**

—**Foreign countries** May be used as a subdivision under names of ethnic groups; languages; literatures (language or country); and military services, *e.g.*, **Americans—Foreign countries**

—**Foreign economic relations** (*May add geog subd*) May be used as a subdivision under names of places, *e.g.*, **Poland—Foreign economic relations**

—**Foreign public opinion** May be used as a subdivision under names of places and wars, *e.g.*, **China—Foreign public opinion**
See also —**Public opinion**

—**Foreign relations** *(May add geog subd)* May be used as a subdivision under names of places, *e.g.*, **Arab countries—Foreign relations**

—**Foreign words and phrases** May be used as a subdivision under names of languages, *e.g.*, **English language—Foreign words and phrases**

—**Forgeries** *(May add geog subd)* May be used as a subdivision under topical headings; individual persons; and individual literary authors, *e.g.*, **Money—Forgeries; Degas, Edgar, 1834-1917—Forgeries**

—**Games** May be used as a subdivision under names of ethnic groups, *e.g.*, **Indians of Central America—Games**
   See also —**Recreation**

—**Gazetteers** May be used as a subdivision under names of places, *e.g.*, **New England—Gazeteers**
   See also —**Geography**

—**Genetic aspects** *[S]* May be used as a subdivision under names of diseases, *e.g.*, **Alzheimer's disease—Genetic aspects**

—**Geography** May be used as a subdivision under names of places; colonies; and sacred works, *e.g.*, **Alaska—Geography**
   See also —**Gazeteers; —Historical geography; —Maps**

—**Glossaries, vocabularies, etc.** May be used as a subdivision under names of languages, *e.g.*, **Swahili language—Glossaries, vocabularies, etc.**

—**Gold discoveries** May be used as a subdivision under names of places, *e.g.*, **California—Gold discoveries**

—**Government policy** *[S] (May add geog subd)* May be used as a subdivision under topical headings; classes of persons; ethnic groups; and industries, *e.g.*, **Religion—Government policy; Creek Indians—Government policy**

—**Government relations** May be used as a subdivision under names of ethnic groups, *e.g.*, **Indians of North America—Government relations**

—**Grammar** May be used as a subdivision under names of languages, *e.g.*, **Italian language—Grammar**

—**Growth** *[S]* May be used as a subdivision under kinds of animals; organs/regions of the body; and plants and crops, *e.g.*, **Hair—Growth**

—**Guides** *[AC usage]* May be used as a subdivision under topical headings; corporate bodies; and places, *e.g.*, **Historic sites—Guides; Austin (Tex.)—Guides**
   UF —**Guidebooks**

—**Gypsies** *(May add geog subd)* May be used as a subdivision under names of wars, *e.g.* **World War, 1939-1945—Gypsies**

—**Habitat** May be used as a subdivision under kinds of animals; and plants & crops, *e.g.*, **Amphibians—Habitat**

—**Habitations** May be used as a subdivision under kinds of animals, *e.g.*, **Mammals—Habitations**

—**Habits and behavior** *[AC usage]* May be used as a subdivision under any kind of animal, bird, reptile, or fish, *e.g.*, **Ants—Habits and behavior**.
   UF —Behavior

—**Handbooks, manuals, etc.** *[S]* May be used as a subdivision under topical headings; classes of persons; corporate bodies; places; individual literary authors; and sacred works, *e.g.*, **Astronomy—Handbooks, manuals, etc.; Boy Scouts—Handbooks, manuals, etc.**

—**Health and hygiene** *[S] (May add geog subd)* May be used as a subdivision under classes of persons; and ethnic groups, *e.g.*, **Infants—Health and hygiene**

—**Hibernation** *(May add geog subd)* May be used as a subdivision under kinds of animals, *e.g.*, **Bears—Hibernation**

—**Historical geography** May be used as a subdivision under names of places, *e.g.*, **Scotland—Historical geography**
   See also —**Geography**

—**Historiography** *[S]* May be used as a subdivision under topical headings; classes of persons; ethnic groups; corporate bodies; places; and sacred works, *e.g.*, **Dwellings—Historiography; Clergy—Historiography**

—**History** *[S]* May be used as a subdivision under topical headings; classes of persons; ethnic groups; corporate bodies; places; colonies; languages; military services; and sacred works, *e.g.*, **Insurance, Health—History; Hindi language—History**

—**History—16th century** May be used as a subdivision under topical headings; classes of persons; ethnic groups; corporate bodies; military services; and Christian denominations, *e.g.*, **Education—History—16th century; Athletes—History—16th century**
   See also —**16th century**

—**History—17th century** May be used as a subdivision under topical headings; classes of persons; ethnic groups; corporate bodies; military services; and Christian denominations, *e.g.*, **Clothing and dress—History—17th century; Women—History—17th century**
   See also —**17th century**

—**History—18th century** May be used as a subdivision under topical headings; classes of persons; ethnic groups; corporate bodies; military services; and Christian denominations, *e.g.*, **Music—History—18th century; Presbyterians—History—18th century**
   See also —**18th century**

—**History—19th century** May be used as a subdivision under topical headings; classes of persons; ethnic groups; corporate bodies; military services; and Christian denominations, *e.g.*, **Transportation—History—19th century; Slaves—History—19th century**
   See also —**19th century**

—**History—20th century** May be used as a subdivision under topical headings; classes of persons; ethnic groups; corporate bodies; military services; and Christian denominations, *e.g.*, **Communication—History—20th century; Librarians—History—20th century**
   See also —**20th century**

—History, Local   May be used as a subdivision under names of places, *e.g.*, **Plymouth (Mass.)—History, Local**

—History, Military   May be used as a subdivision under names of places, *e.g.*, **Greece—History, Military**
   See also **—Regimental histories**

—History, Naval   May be used as a subdivision under names of places, *e.g.*, **Great Britain—History, Naval**

—History and criticism *[S]*   May be used as a subdivision under topical headings; literatures (language or country); and music compositions, *e.g.*, **Cartoons and comics—History and criticism; Afro-American literature—History and criticism**
   See also **—Criticism and interpretation; —Criticism, interpretation, etc.; —Stage history**

—History of Biblical events   May be used as a subdivision under titles of sacred works, *e.g.*, **Bible. New Testament—History of Biblical events**

—Homes and haunts *(May add geog subd)*   May be used as a subdivision under classes of persons; ethnic groups; individual persons; individual literary authors; and families, *e.g.*, **Jefferson, Thomas, 1743-1826—Homes and haunts**

—Homonyms   May be used as a subdivision under names of languages, *e.g.*, **Spanish language—Homonyms**

—Hospital care *(May add geog subd)*   May be used as a subdivision under classes of persons and ethnic groups, *e.g.*, **Poor—Hospital care**
   See also **—Care; —Institutional care; —Patients**

—Hospitals *(May add geog subd)*   May be used as a subdivision under classes of persons; ethnic groups; diseases; and wars, *e.g.*, **Tuberculosis—Hospitals**
   See also **—Institutional care; —Patients**

—Housing *[S] (May add geog subd)*   May be used as a subdivision under classes of persons; ethnic groups; and animals, *e.g.*, **Eskimos—Housing**

—Humor *[S]*   May be used as a subdivision under topical headings *[except AC]*; names of classes of persons; ethnic groups; corporate bodies; individual persons; places; individual literary authors; and sacred works, *e.g.*, **Fields, W.C., 1879-1946—Humor**
   UF **—Juvenile humor**
   See also **—Wit and humor**

—Hunting   May be used as a subdivision under names of ethnic groups, *e.g.*, **Iriquois Indians—Hunting**

—Identification *[S]*   May be used as a subdivision under topical headings; classes of persons; kinds of animals; and plants & crops, *e.g.*, **Grasses—Identification**

—Idioms   May be used as a subdivision under names of languages, *e.g.*, **French language—Idioms**

—Illustrations
   USE **—Pictorial works**

—Immunology   May be used as a subdivision under kinds of animals; chemicals; and organs/regions of the body, *e.g.*, **Dogs—Immunology**
   See also **—Vaccination**

—Impeachment   May be used as a subdivision under names of individual persons, *e.g.*, **Johnson, Andrew, 1808-1875—Impeachment**

—Implements   May be used as a subdivision under names of ethnic groups, *e.g.*, **Zuni Indians—Implements**

—Indexes *[S]*   May be used as a subdivision under topical headings; classes of persons; ethnic groups; corporate bodies; individual persons; and individual literary authors, *e.g.*, **Science—Indexes; Twain, Mark, 1835-1910—Indexes**

—Industries   May be used as a subdivision under names of ethnic groups; places; and colonies, *e.g.*, **Korea—Industries**

—Infancy   May be used as a subdivision under kinds of animals, *e.g.*, **Cattle—Infancy**

—Institutional care *[S] (May add geog subd)*   May be used as a subdivision under classes of persons and ethnic groups, *e.g.*, **Mentally ill—Institutional care**
   See also **—Care; —Hospital care; —Patients**

—Instruction and study *(May add geog subd)*   May be used as a subdivision under musical compositions and musical instruments, *e.g.*, **Piano—Instruction and study**

—Intellectual life *[S]*   May be used as a subdivision under classes of persons; ethnic groups; and places, *e.g.*, **Europe—Intellectual life**

—Interpretation   May be used as a subdivision under individual tests and types of tests, *e.g.*, **Scholastic Aptitude Test—Interpretation**

—Interviews   May be used as a subdivision under classes of persons; ethnic groups; individual persons; and individual literary authors, *e.g.*, **Authors—Interviews**

—Jargon *[S]*   May be used as a subdivision under languages, *e.g.*, **English language—Jargon**
   See also **—Language; —Language (New words, slang, etc.); —Terminology; —Terms and phrases**

—Jews *(May add geog subd)*   May be used as a subdivision under names of wars, *e.g.*, **Israel-Arab War, 1948-1949—Jews**

—Journeys *(May add geog subd)*   May be used as a subdivision under names of individual persons; groups of literary authors; and individual literary authors, *e.g.*, **Dyson, John, 1943- —Journeys—America**
   See also **—Travel**

—Judging   May be used as a subdivision under kinds of animals; and plants & crops, *e.g.*, **Horses—Judging**

—Juvenile drama
   USE **—Drama**

—Juvenile fiction
USE —**Fiction**

—Juvenile films **Do not use.**
RT —**Film and video adaptations**

—Juvenile humor
USE —**Humor**; —**Wit and humor**

—Juvenile literature **Do not use.**
RT —**Collections**

—Juvenile poetry
USE —**Poetry**

—Juvenile software
USE —**Software**

—Juvenile sound recordings **Do not use.**
RT —**Audio adaptations**; —**Audio-visual aids**

—**Kidnapping, [date]** May be used as a subdivision under names of individual persons, *e.g.*, **Harrison, William—Kidnapping, 1660**

—**Kings and rulers** May be used as a subdivision under ethnic groups; and places, *e.g.*, **Britons—Kings and rulers**

—**Laboratory manuals** *[S]* May be used as a subdivision under scientific and technical topical headings, *e.g.*, **Chemistry—Laboratory manuals**

—**Land tenure** May be used as a subdivision under names of ethnic groups, *e.g.*, **Ojibwa Indians—Land tenure**

—**Language** *[S]* May be used as a subdivision under topical headings; classes of persons; corporate bodies; individual persons; legal topical headings; individual literary authors; and titles of literary works and newspapers, *e.g.*, **Gardening—Language; Teachers—Language**
See also —**Language (New words, slang, etc.)**; —**Jargon**; —**Noun**; —**Number**; —**Onomatopoeic words**; —**Possesives**; —**Prepositions**; —**Pronunciation**; —**Provincialism**; —**Rhetoric**; —**Sentences**; —**Slang**; —**Spelling**; —**Synonyms and antonyms**; —**Terminology**; —**Terms and phrases**; —**Verb**

—**Language (New words, slang, etc.)** May be used as a subdivision under classes of persons; individual schools; and wars, *e.g.*, **Students—Language (New words, slang, etc.)**.
See also —**Jargon**; —**Language**; —**Slang**; —**Terminology**; —**Terms and phrases**

—**Law and legislation** *[S] (May add geog subd)* May be used as a subdivision under kinds of animals; chemicals; diseases; types of schools; industries; materials; plants and crops; land vehicles; and wars, *e.g.*, **Drugs—Law and legislation**
See also —**Legal status, laws, etc.**

—**Legal status, laws, etc.** *(May add geog subd)* May be used as a subdivision under classes of persons and ethnic groups, *e.g.*, **Wives—Legal status, laws, etc.**
See also —**Law and legislation**

—**Legends** May be used as a subdivision under topical headings; individual persons; individual literary authors; and sacred works, *e.g.*, **Bison—Legends; Alabama Indians—Legends**

—**Lexicography** May be used as a subdivision under topical headings and languages, *e.g.*, **Technology—Lexicography**
See also —**Dictionaries**

—**Libraries** May be used as a subdivision under names of corporate bodies; and wars, *e.g.*, **AFL-CIO—Libraries**
See also —**Library**

—**Library** May be used as a subdivision under names of corporate bodies; individual persons; individual literary authors; and families, *e.g.*, **Edison, Thomas Alva, 1847-1931—Library**
See also —**Libraries**

—**Librettos** May be used as a subdivision under types of music compositions, *e.g.*, **Musical revues, comedies, etc.—Librettos**

—**Life cycles** May be used as a subdivision under kinds of animals; and plants & crops, *e.g.*, **Oak—Life cycles**

—**Life skills guides** May be used as a subdivision under classes of persons and ethnic groups, *e.g.*, **Teenagers—Life skills guides**

—**Lighting** *[S] (May add geog subd)* May be used as a subdivision under topical headings and land vehicles, *e.g.*, **Theaters—Lighting**

—**Literary collections** May be used as a subdivision under topical headings; classes of persons; ethnic groups; corporate bodies; individual persons; places; and individual literary authors, *e.g.*, **Zoology—Literary collections; Witches—Literary collections**
See also —**Collections**

—**Longitudinal studies** May be used as a subdivision under topical headings; classes of persons; and ethnic groups, *e.g.*, **Psychology—Longitudinal studies; Women—Longitudinal studies**
See also —**Research**

—**Maintenance and repair** *[S]* May be used as a subdivision under topical headings; and land vehicles, *e.g.*, **Computers—Maintenance and repair; Ford automobile—Maintenance and repair**
See also —**Repairing**

—**Management** *[S]* May be used as a subdivision under topical headings; corporate bodies; industries; and military services, *e.g.*, **Natural resources—Management; Computer industry—Management**
See also headings incorporating such words as **administration** and **management**, *e.g.*, **Water quality management**

—**Maps** *[S]* May be used as a subdivision under topical headings; ethnic groups; corporate bodies; and places, *e.g.*, **Rivers—Maps; China—Maps**

—**Marketing** *[S]* May be used as a subdivision under topical headings; animals; plants & crops; and land vehicles, *e.g.*, **Farm produce—Marketing; BMW automobile—Marketing**
See also —**Geography**

—**Marking** *(May add geog subd)* May be used as a subdivision under animals, *e.g.*, **Cattle—Marking**

—Mascots May be used as a subdivision under names of individual schools and military services, *e.g.*, **University of Texas at Austin—Mascots**

—Materials *[S]* May be used as a subdivision under topical headings and land vehicles, *e.g.*, **Boatbuilding—Materials; Fire engines—Materials**
See also **—Equipment and supplies**

—Mathematical models *[S]* May be used as a subdivision under topical headings; industries; and organs/regions of the body, *e.g.*, **Social sciences—Mathematical models; Heart—Mathematical models**
See also **—Models**

—Mathematics *[S]* May be used as a subdivision under topical headings; and ethnic groups, *e.g.*, **Physics—Mathematics; Cuban Americans—Mathematics**
See also **—Problems, exercises, etc.; —Statistics**

—Medical care *(May add geog subd)* May be used as a subdivision under classes of persons; ethnic groups; military services; and wars, *e.g.*, **Teenage girls—Medical care**

—Medical examinations *(May add geog subd)* May be used as a subdivision under sstopics; classes of persons; ethnic groups; and military services, *e.g.*, **Digestive organs—Medical examinations; Men—Medical examinations**
See also **—Evaluation; —Examinations, questions, etc.**

—Medicine May be used as a subdivision under names of ethnic groups, *e.g.*, **Apache Indians—Medicine**

—Metallurgy May be used as a subdivision under names of chemicals, *e.g.*, **Chlorofluorocarbons—Metallurgy**

—Methodology *[S]* May be used as a subdivision under topical headings where theory or practice May be followed, *e.g.*, **Archaeology—Methodology**
See also **—Technique**

—Migration *(May add geog subd)* May be used as a subdivision under kinds of animals, *e.g.*, **Birds—Migration**

—Military aspects *(May add geog subd)* May be used as a subdivision under names of industries, *e.g.*, **Petroleum industry and trade—Military aspects**
See also **—Strategic aspects**

—Military life May be used as a subdivision under names of military services, *e.g.*, **United States. Air Force—Military life**
See also **—Officers**

—Military policy May be used as a subdivision under names of places, *e.g.*, **Nicaragua—Military policy**

—Military relations *(May add geog subd)* May be used as a subdivision under places, *e.g.*, **Iraq—Military relations—Iran**

—Militia May be used as a subdivision under names of places, *e.g.*, **Texas—Militia**

—Milling *(May add geog subd)* May be used as a subdivision under names of plants & crops, *e.g.*, **Grain—Milling**

—Missions *(May add geog subd)* May be used as a subdivision under names of ethnic groups; religions; religious orders; and Christian denominations, *e.g.*, **Catholic Church—Missions**

—Models *[S]* May be used as a subdivision under types of objects, *e.g.*, **Airplanes—Models; Leg—Models**
See also **—Mathematical models**

—Moral and ethical aspects May be used as a subdivision under topical headings and wars, *e.g.*, **Medical care—Moral and ethical aspects; Persian Gulf War, 1991—Moral and ethical aspects**
See also **—Religious aspects**

—Moral conditions May be used as a subdivision under names of places, *e.g.*, **California—Moral conditions**

—Mortality May be used as a subdivision under classes of persons; ethnic groups; animals; and diseases, *e.g.*, **Infants—Mortality**
See also **—Statistics, Medical**

—Motors May be used as a subdivision under names of land vehicles, *e.g.*, **Automobiles—Motors**

—Museums *[S]* May be used as a subdivision under corporate bodies, *e.g.*, **University of Texas at El Paso—Museums**
See also **—Museums** *(May add geog subd)*

—Museums *[S] (May add geog subd)* May be used as a subdivision under topical headings; classes of persons; ethnic groups; individual persons; individual literary authors; Christian denominations; wars; and families, *e.g.*, **Natural history—Museums; Truman, Harry S., 1884-1972—Museums**
See also **—Museums** *(Not subd geog)*

—Music May be used as a subdivision under ethnic groups, *e.g.*, **Afro-Americans—Music**
See also **—Songs and music**

—Mythology
USE **—Religion** and the heading **Mythology**

—Names May be used as a subdivision under topical headings; animals; and types of schools, *e.g.*, **Cities and towns—Names; Parrots—Names**

—Naval operations May be used as a subdivision under names of wars, *e.g.*, **United States—History—Revolution, 1775-1783—Naval operations**

—Navigation May be used as a subdivision under names of bodies of water, *e.g.*, **Mississippi River—Navigation**

—Nests May be used as a subdivision under kinds of animals, *e.g.*, **Ants—Nests**

—Noise *[S]* May be used as a subdivision under topical headings and industries, *e.g.*, **Automobile industry and trade—Noise**

—Noun May be used as a subdivision under names of languages, *e.g.*, **Yiddish language—Noun**
See also **—Language**

—Number May be used as a subdivision under names of languages, *e.g.*, **Chinese language—Number**
　See also **—Language**

—Numerals May be used as a subdivision under names of languages, *e.g.*, **Spanish language—Numerals**

—Nursing *[S] (May add geog subd)* May be used as a subdivision under diseases, *e.g.*, **Alzheimer's disease—Nursing**

—Nutrition *[S]* May be used as a subdivision under classes of persons; ethnic groups; animals; and plants and crops, *e.g.*, **Teenage mothers—Nutrition**

—Observers' manuals May be used as a subdivision under topical headings, *e.g.*, **Astronomy—Observers' manuals**

—Occupations May be used as a subdivision under names of religious orders, *e.g.*, **Ursulines—Occupations**

—Officers May be used as a subdivision under names of military services, *e.g.*, **United States. Army—Officers**
　See also **—Military life**

—Officials and employees *[S]* May be used as a subdivision under topical headings; corporate bodies; colonies; legislative bodies; and military services, *e.g.*, **State governments—Officials and employees; United States. Congress—Officials and employees**

—Onomatopoeic words May be used as a subdivision under names of languages *e.g.*, **Spanish language—Onomatopoeic words**
　See also **—Language**

—Oratory May be used as a subdivision under names of individual persons, *e.g.*, **Clinton, Bill, 1946- —Oratory**

—Ordnance and ordnance stores May be used as a subdivision under military services, *e.g.*, **France. Army. Foreign legion—Ordnance and ordnance stores**

—Origin *[S]* May be used as a subdivision under names of ethnic groups; animals; plants & crops; and religions, *e.g.*, **Cactus—Origin; Taino Indians—Origin**

—Orthography and spelling
　USE **—Spelling**

—Outlines, syllabi, etc. *[S]* May be used as a subdivision under topical headings; classes of persons; ethnic groups; individual persons; individual literary authors; and sacred works, *e.g.*, **History—Outlines, syllabi, etc.; Stein, Gertrude, 1866-1946—Outlines, syllabi, etc.**
　See also **—Writing**

—Parachute troops May be used as a subdivision under military services, *e.g.*, **Great Britain. Armed Forces—Parachute troops**

—Parodies, imitations, etc. May be used as a subdivision under topical headings; individual persons; individual literary authors; and titles of literary works, *e.g.*, **Politicians—Parodies, imitations, etc.; Moore, Clement Clarke, 1779-1863—Parodies, imitations, etc.**
　See also **—Writing**

—Patients *(May add geog subd)* May be used as a subdivision under names of diseases, *e.g.*, **Leprosy—Patients—Iran**
　See also **—Hospital care; —Hospitals; —Institutional care**

—Parturition *(May add geog subd)* May be used as a subdivision under names of animals, *e.g.*, **Cows—Parturition**

—Peace May be used as a subdivision under names of wars, *e.g.*, **World War, 1914-1918—Peace**
　See also **—Wars**

—Performances *(May add geog subd)* May be used as a subdivision under names of corporate bodies, individual persons, and musical compositions, *e.g.*, **Nutcracker (Choreographic work)—Performances**

—Periodicals *[S]* May be used as a subdivision under topical headings; classes of persons; ethnic groups; corporate bodies; individual persons; and individual literary authors, *e.g.*, **Woodwork—Periodicals; Chrysler Corporation—Periodicals**
　UF **—Yearbooks**

—Personal narratives May be used as a subdivision under topical headings and wars, *e.g.*, **Cancer—Personal narratives; World War, 1939-1945—Personal narratives**
　See also **—Biography**

—Personal narratives, American, [French, etc.] May be used as a subdivision under names of wars, *e.g.*, **World War, 1914-1918—Personal narratives, Polish**
　See also **—Personal narratives; —Personal narratives, Jewish**

—Personal narratives, Jewish May be used as a subdivision under names of wars, *e.g.*, **World War, 1914-1918—Personal narratives, Jewish**
　See also **—Personal narratives; —Personal narratives, American, [French, etc.]**

—Philosophy *[S]* May be used as a subdivision under topical headings; individual persons; groups of literary authors; sacred works; and sports, *e.g.*, **Euthanasia—Philosophy; Melville, Herman, 1819-1891—Philosophy**

—Photographs May be used as a subdivision under topical headings; classes of persons; and ethnic groups, *e.g.*, **Mountains—Photographs**
　UF **—Pictures**
　See also **—Pictorial works; —Portraits**

—Photographs from space *[S]* May be used as a subdivision under topical headings and names of places, *e.g.*, **Rivers—Photographs from space; New Zealand—Photographs from space**

—Physiological aspects May be used as a subdivision under types of activities and mental conditions for works on the relationship between people's activities, mental state, etc., and their physiology
　See also **—Physiology**

—Physiological effect *[S]* May be used as a subdivision under topical headings; chemicals; materials; and plants & crops, *e.g.*, **Cold—Physiological effect; Alcohol—Physiological effect**

—**Physiology**   May be used as a subdivision under names of classes of persons; ethnic groups; animals; organs/regions of the body; and plants & crops, *e.g.*, **Mammals—Physiology**

—<u>**Pictorial works**</u> *[AC, S]* May be used under topical headings and all subjects presented exclusively or predominantly through pictorial matter, *e.g.*, **Reptiles—Pictorial works**
   See also —**Art collections**

—Pictures
   USE   —**Photographs;** —**Pictorial works;** —**Portraits**

—Plays
   USE   —**Drama**; *see also* the heading **Plays**

—Plots
   USE   —**Stories, plots, etc.;** —**Themes, motives**

—<u>**Poetry**</u> *[S]* May be used as a subdivision under topical headings; classes of persons; ethnic groups; corporate bodies; individual persons; and individual literary authors, *e.g.*, **Rain and rainfall—Poetry; Santa Claus—Poetry**
   UF   —Juvenile poetry

—**Political activity** *[S]* May be used as a subdivision under topical headings; classes of persons; corporate bodies; industries; groups of literary authors; individual literary authors; military services; and Christian denominations; and names of families, *e.g.*, **Minorities—Political activity**

—**Political aspects** *(May add geog subd)* May be used as a subdivision under topical headings and names of religions, *e.g.*, **Abortion—Political aspects; Islam—Political aspects**

—**Politics and government**   May be used as a subdivision under names of ethnic groups and places, *e.g.*, **India—Politics and government**

—<u>**Popular works**</u>   May be used as a subdivision under topical headings; legal topical headings; and land vehicles, *e.g.*, **Law—Popular works; Sexual harassment of women—Popular works**

—**Population**   May be used as a subdivision under ethnic groups; places; and colonies, *e.g.*, **Developing countries—Population**

—<u>**Portraits**</u> *[S]* May be used as a subdivision under classes of persons; ethnic groups; individual persons; individual schools; individual literary authors; religious orders; wars; and families, *e.g.*, **Springsteen, Bruce, 1949- —Portraits**
   See also —**Photographs**

—**Possessives**   May be used as a subdivision under languages, *e.g.*, **English language—Possessives**

—**Prepositions**   May be used as a subdivision under languages, *e.g.*, **Spanish language—Prepositions**

—**Preservation** *[S]* May be used as a subdivision under topical headings; organs/regions of the body; and plants & crops, *e.g.*, **Food—Preservation; Ferns—Preservation**

—**Press coverage** *(May add geog subd)* May be used as a subdivision under names of wars, *e.g.*, **Iraq-Kuwait Crisis, 1990-1991—Press coverage—Israel**

—**Prevention** *[S]* May be used as a subdivision under topical headings and diseases, *e.g.*, **Substance abuse—Prevention; Heart—Diseases—Prevention**

—**Prices** *[S] (May add geog subd)* May be used as a subdivision under topical headings; chemicals; industries; materials; plants & crops; and land vehicles, *e.g.*, **Stocks—Prices; Porsche automobile—Prices**

—**Prisoners and prisons**   May be used as a subdivision under names of wars, *e.g.*, **World War, 1939-1945—Prisoners and prisons**

—<u>**Problems, exercises, etc.**</u> *[S]* May be used as a subdivision under topical headings
   See also —**Composition and exercises;** —**Examinations, questions, etc.**

—**Programmed instruction** *[S]* May be used as a subdivision under topical headings, *e.g.*, **Furniture repairing—Programmed instruction**
   See also —**Computer programs**

—**Programming**   May be used as a subdivision under topical headings for computers and calculators, *e.g.*, **Macintosh (Computer)—Programming**
   See also —**Computer programs**

—**Pronunciation**   May be used as a subdivision under names of languages, *e.g.*, **French language—Pronunciation**
   See also —**Language**

—**Propaganda**   May be used as a subdivision under names of wars, *e.g.*, **Cuban Missile Crisis, 1962—Propaganda**

—<u>**Prophecies**</u> *[S]* May be used as a subdivision under topical headings; classes of persons; ethnic groups; individual persons; individual literary authors; sacred works; and wars, *e.g.*, **Elections—Prophecies; Bible—Prophecies**
   See also —**Forecasting**

—**Protection** *[S] (May add geog subd)* May be used as a subdivision under topical headings; classes of persons; organs/ regions of the body; plants & crops; and land vehicles, *e.g.*, **Birds—Protection; Refugees—Protection**

—**Provincialisms** *(May add geog subd)* May be used as a subdivision under names of languages, *e.g.*, **English language—Provincialisms—New York (N.Y.)**.
   See also —**Language**

—**Psychological aspects** *[S]* May be used as a subdivision under topical headings; animals; diseases; and wars, *e.g.*, **Grief—Psychological aspects; Diabetes—Psychological aspects**

—**Psychology** *[S]* May be used as a subdivision under topical headings; classes of persons; ethnic groups; individual persons; animals; individual literary authors; religions; and sacred works, *e.g.*, **Music—Psychology; Prisoners of war—Psychology**

—**Public opinion** *[S]* May be used as a subdivision under topical headings; classes of persons; ethnic groups; corporate bodies; individual persons; and wars, *e.g.*, **Firearms—Public opinion; Vietnamese Conflict, 1961-1975—Public opinion**
   See also —**Foreign public opinion**

—**Publishing** *(May add geog subd)* May be used as a subdivision under topical headings; corporate bodies; and Christian denominations, *e.g.*, **Picture books—Publishing; Baptists—Publishing—Tennessee**

—<u>**Quotations**</u> *[S]* May be used as a subdivision under classes of persons; ethnic groups; individual persons; individual literary authors; and sacred works, *e.g.*, **Presidents—United States—Quotations**
  See also —**Quotations, maxims, etc.**

—<u>**Quotations, maxims, etc.**</u> May be used as a subdivision under topical headings and names of places, *e.g.*, **Health—Quotations, maxims, etc.; Ireland—Quotations, maxims, etc.**
  See also —**Quotations**

—**Race relations** May be used as a subdivision under names of places and colonies, *e.g.*, **Africa, Central—Race relations**
  See also —**Ethnic relations**

—Recordings
  USE —**Audio adaptations; —Audio-visual aids; —Film and video adaptations**

—**Recreation** *[S]* May be used as a subdivision under classes of persons and ethnic groups, *e.g.*, **Children—Recreation**
  See also —**Games**

—**Recreational use** May be used as a subdivision under topical headings and names of bodies of water, *e.g.*, **Seashore—Recreational use; Brazos River (Tex.)—Recreational use**

—**Recycling** *[S]* May be used as a subdivision under names of chemicals and materials, *e.g.*, **Plastic scrap—Recycling**

—**Refining** May be used as a subdivision under names of materials, *e.g.*, **Petroleum—Refining**

—**Refugees** May be used as a subdivision under names of wars, *e.g.*, **World War, 1939-1945—Refugees**

—**Regimental histories** *(May add geog subd)* May be used as a subdivision under names of wars, *e.g.*, **Vietnamese Conflict, 1961-1975—Regimental histories**
  See also —**History, Military**

—**Rehabilitation** *[S] (May add geog subd)* May be used as a subdivision under classes of persons and ethnic groups, *e.g.*, **Physically handicapped—Rehabilitation**

—**Relations** May be used as a subdivision under names of religions and Christian denominations, *e.g.*, **Judaism—Relations—Catholic Church**
  See also —**Relations** *(May add geog subd)*

—**Relations** *(May add geog subd)* May be used as a subdivision under names of places, *e.g.*, **Arab countries—Relations—Israel**
  See also —**Foreign relations; —Relations**

—**Religion** *[S]* May be used as a subdivision under topical headings; ethnic groups; corporate bodies; individual persons; places; colonies; types of schools; and individual literary authors, *e.g.*, **Byzantine Empire—Religion; Bolivia—Religion**
  See also —**Religious aspects** and the heading **Mythology**

—**Religion—16th, [17th, 18th, etc.] century** May be used as a subdivision under names of places, *e.g.*, **Portugal—Religion—20th century**

—**Religious aspects** May be used as a subdivision under animals; diseases; languages; materials; organs/regions of the body; plants & crops; musical instruments; and wars, *e.g.*, **Bread—Religious aspects**
  See also —**Moral and ethical aspects; —Religion**

—**Religious life** *[S]* May be used as a subdivision under classes of persons; and military services, *e.g.*, **Youth—Religious life**

—**Religious life and customs** May be used as a subdivision under names of places and colonies, *e.g.*, **Mexico—Religious life and customs**

—**Repairing** *[S]* May be used as a subdivision under topical headings, *e.g.*, **Clothing and dress—Repairing**
  See also —**Maintenance and repair**

—**Reproduction** May be used as a subdivision under kinds of animals; and plants & crops, *e.g.*, **Roses—Reproduction**

—<u>**Research**</u> *[S] (May add geog subd)* May be used as a subdivision under topical headings; classes of persons; ethnic groups; corporate bodies; places; legal topical headings; and plants & crops, *e.g.*, **Social sciences—Research; North Pole—Research**
  See also —**Longitudinal studies; —Study and teaching**

—<u>**Reviews**</u> *[S]* May be used as a subdivision under topical headings, *e.g.*, **Books—Reviews**
  See also —**Writing**

—**Rhetoric** May be used as a subdivision under names of languages, *e.g.*, **English language—Rhetoric**
  See also —**Language**

—**Rhyme** May be used as a subdivision under names of languages, *e.g.*, **Hebrew language—Rhyme**
  See also —**Language**

—**Rites and ceremonies** May be used as a subdivision under names of ethnic groups, *e.g.*, **Caddo Indians—Rites and ceremonies**
  UF —Ceremonies

—**Romances** May be used as a subdivision under topical headings and names of individual persons, *e.g.*, **Adolescence—Romances; Cid, ca. 1043-1099—Romances**

—<u>**Rules**</u> May be used as a subdivision under topical headings and names of religious orders, *e.g.*, **Badminton—Rules**

—**Rural conditions** May be used as a subdivision under names of places and colonies, *e.g.*, **Luna County (N.M.)—Rural conditions**

—**Safety measures** *[S]* May be used as a subdivision under topical headings; types of schools; industries; and military services, *e.g.*, **Outdoor recreation—Safety measures; Nuclear power plants—Safety measures**
  See also —**Security measures**

—**Scientific applications**   May be used as a subdivision under topical headings, *e.g.*, **Photography—Scientific applications**

—**Secret service** *(May add geog subd)*   May be used as a subdivision under names of wars, *e.g.*, **World War, 1914-1918—Secret service**

—**Security measures** *[S]*   May be used as a subdivision under topical headings; corporate bodies; industries; and military services, *e.g.*, **Airports—Security measures; Retail trade—Security measures**
  See also —**Safety measures**

—**Sentences**   May be used as a subdivision under names of languages, *e.g.*, **Navajo language—Sentences**
  See also —**Language**

—**Services for**   May be used as a subdivision under types of schools, *e.g.*, **Middle schools—Services for**
  See also —**Services for** *(May add geog subd)*

—**Services for** *(May add geog subd)*   May be used as a subdivision under classes of persons; ethnic groups; and animals, *e.g.*, **Abused children—Services for**
  See also —**Services for** *(Not subd geog)*

—**Sexual behavior** *[S]*   May be used as a subdivision under classes of persons; ethnic groups; individual persons; and individual literary authors, *e.g.*, **Athletes—Sexual behavior**

—**Shorelines**   May be used as a subdivision under names of bodies of water, *e.g.*, **Rhine River—Shoreline**

—**Slang**   May be used as a subdivision under topical headings and languages, *e.g.*, **Boys—Slang; Italian language—Slang**
  See also —**Jargon;** —**Language;** —**Language (New words, slang, etc.);** —**Terminology;** —**Terms and phrases**

—**Slides**   May be used as a subdivision under topical headings; and names of individual persons and places, *e.g.*, **Hawaii—Slides**

—**Social aspects** *[S] (May add geog subd)*   May be used as a subdivision under topical headings; industries; languages; and wars, *e.g.*, **Computers—Social aspects; Motion picture industry—Social aspects**

—**Social conditions** *[S]*   May be used as a subdivision under classes of persons; ethnic groups; places; and colonies, *e.g.*, **Cambodia—Social conditions**

—**Social life and customs** *[S]*   May be used as a subdivision under classes of persons; ethnic groups; places; and colonies, *e.g.*, **Mennonites—Social life and customs**
  See also —**Customs and practices**

—**Societies and clubs**   May be used as a subdivision under classes of persons, *e.g.*, **Restaurateurs—Societies and clubs**
  UF —**Clubs**
  See also —**Societies, etc.**

—**Societies, etc.,**   May be used as a subdivision under topical headings; classes of persons; ethnic groups; corporate bodies; individual persons; individual literary authors; and sacred works, *e.g.*, **Environmental protection—Societies, etc.; Harley-Davidson motorcycle—Societies, etc.**
  See also —**Societies and clubs**

—**Software**   May be used as a subdivision under topical headings, *e.g.*, **Computer graphics—Software**
  See also —**Audio-visual aids;** —**Computer programs**

—**Songs and music**   May be used as a subdivision under topical headings; classes of persons; ethnic groups; corporate bodies; individual persons; places; individual literary authors; and military services, *e.g.*, **Family life—Songs and music; Fishers—Songs and music**
  See also —**Music**

—Sound recordings
  USE —**Audio adaptations;** —**Sound recordings for French, [Spanish, etc.] speakers**

—**Sound recordings for French, [Spanish, etc.] speakers**   May be used as a subdivision under languages, *e.g.*, **Spanish language—Sound recordings for English speakers**

—**Sources** *[S]*   May be used as a subdivision under topical headings; individual persons; individual literary authors; literatures (language or country); and wars, *e.g.*, **History, Modern—Sources; Arthur, King—Sources**

—**Specimens**   May be used as a subdivision under topical headings, *e.g.*, **Insects—Specimens**

—**Spelling**   May be used as a subdivision under names of languages, *e.g.*, **French language—Spelling**
  UF —**Orthography and spelling**
  See also —**Language**

—**Stage history** *(May add geog subd)*   May be used as a subdivision under names of individual literary authors, *e.g.*, **Shakespeare, William, 1564-1616—Stage history**
  See also —**History and criticism**

—**Standardization**   May be used as a subdivision under names of languages, *e.g.*, **Spanish language—Standardization**

—**Standards** *(May add geog subd)*   May be used as a subdivision under topical headings; chemicals; types of schools; and industries, *e.g.*, **Middle schools—Standards; Food industry and trade—Standards**

—**States**   May be used as a subdivision under headings of the type **[topic]—[country]** for works discussing collectively the states of a country in relation to the topic, *e.g.*, **Festivals—Mexico—States**

—**Statistical methods**   May be used as a subdivision under topical headings; and industries, *e.g.*, **Economics—Statistical methods; Horse industry—Statistical methods**

—**Statistics** *[S]*   May be used as a subdivision under topical headings; classes of persons; ethnic groups; corporate bodies; and places, *e.g.*, **Aging—Statistics; Hispanic Americans—Statistics**
  See also —**Mathematics;** —**Statistics, Medical;** —**Tables**

—**Statistics, Medical**   May be used as a subdivision under names of places, *e.g.*, **Oklahoma—Statistics, Medical**
  See also —**Mortality;** —**Statistics;** —**Tables**

—<u>Stories, plots, etc.</u> *[S]* May be used as a subdivision under names of individual persons; individual literary authors; literatures (language or country); and music compositions, *e.g.*, **Opera—Stories, plots, etc.**
See also **—Themes, motives**

—**Strategic aspects** May be used as a subdivision under names of places, *e.g.*, **Middle East—Strategic aspects**
See also **—Military aspects**

—**Study and teaching** *[S] (May add geog subd)* May be used as a subdivision under topical headings; ethnic groups; corporate bodies; individual persons; places; languages; individual literary authors; and sacred works, *e.g.*, **Biology—Study and teaching; Russian language—Study and teaching**
See also **—Instruction and study; —Research; —Training**

—**Study and teaching—Foreign speakers** May be used as a subdivision under languages, *e.g.*, **English language—Study and teaching—Foreign speakers**
    UF   English as a second language
            ESL
            ESOL
            Teaching English as a second language
            TESL

—**Study and teaching—Foreign speakers—Audio-visual aids** May be used as a subdivision under languages, *e.g.*, **Spanish language—Study and teaching—Foreign speakers**
    UF   Spanish as a second language
            SSL

—**Study and teaching (Early childhood)** *(May add geog subd)* May be used as a subdivision under topical headings; ethnic groups; corporate bodies; and places, *e.g.*, **Counting—Study and teaching (Early childhood)**

—**Study and teaching (Elementary)** *(May add geog subd)* May be used as a subdivision under topical headings; ethnic groups; corporate bodies; places; and languages, *e.g.*, **Science—Study and teaching (Elementary)**

—**Study and teaching (Higher)** *(May add geog subd)* May be used as a subdivision under topical headings; ethnic groups; corporate bodies; places; and languages, *e.g.*, **Biochemistry—Study and teaching (Higher); South Carolina—Study and teaching (Higher)**

—**Study and teaching (Preschool)** *(May add geog subd)* May be used as a subdivision under topical headings; ethnic groups; corporate bodies; and places, *e.g.*, **Alphabet—Study and teaching (Preschool)**

—**Study and teaching (Primary)** *(May add geog subd)* May be used as a subdivision under topical headings; ethnic groups; corporate bodies; and places, *e.g.*, **Color—Study and teaching (Primary)**

—**Study and teaching (Secondary)** *(May add geog subd)* May be used as a subdivision under topical headings; ethnic groups; corporate bodies; places; and languages, *e.g.*, **History—Study and teaching (Secondary); Chinese Americans—Study and teaching (Secondary)**

—**Study and teaching (Secondary)—German, [Spanish, etc.]** *(May add geog subd)* May be used as a subdivision under topical headings; ethnic groups; corporate bodies; places; and languages, *e.g.*, **History—Study and teaching (Secondary)—Spanish**

—**Study guides** May be used as a subdivision under topical headings, *e.g.*, **Literature—Study guides**

—**Style** May be used as a subdivision under languages; names of individual literary authors; and titles of literary works, *e.g.*, **Poe, Edgar Allan, 1800-1849—Style**

—**Submarine forces** May be used as a subdivision under military forces, *e.g.*, **Japan—Navy—Submarine forces**

—**Suffrage** *(May add geog subd)* May be used as a subdivision under classes of persons and ethnic groups, *e.g.*, **Women—Suffrage**

—**Suicidal behavior** *(May add geog subd)* May be used as a subdivision under classes of persons and ethnic groups, *e.g.*, **Terminally ill—Suicidal behavior**

—**Surgery** *[S] (May add geog subd)* May be used as a subdivision under classes of persons; ethnic groups; animals; diseases; and organs/regions of the body, *e.g.*, **Kidneys—Surgery**

—**Synonyms and antonyms** May be used as a subdivision under names of languages, *e.g.*, **Danish language—Synonyms and antonyms**
See also **—Language**

—<u>Tables</u> *[S]* May be used as a subdivision under topical headings, *e.g.*, **Weather—Tables**
See also **—Statistics; —Statistics, Medical**

—<u>Technique</u> *[S]* May be used as a subdivision under topical headings and names of individual literary authors, *e.g.*, **Comedy—Technique; Twain, Mark, 1835-1910—Technique**
See also **—Methodology**

—<u>Telephone directories</u> *[S]* May be used as a subdivision under topical headings; classes of persons; ethnic groups; corporate bodies; places; and industries, *e.g.*, **Publishers and publishing—Telephone directories**
See also **—Directories**

—**Terminology** *[S]* May be used as a subdivision under topical headings; classes of persons; and sacred works, *e.g.*, **Education—Terminology**
See also **—Jargon; —Language; —Language (New words, slang, etc.); —Slang**

—**Terms and phrases** May be used as a subdivision under names of languages, *e.g.*, **Latin language—Terms and phrases**
See also **—Jargon; —Language; —Language (New words, slang, etc.); —Terminology; —Slang**

—**Territorial expansion** May be used as a subdivision under names of places, *e.g.*, **United States—Territorial expansion**

—**Territories and possessions** May be used as a subdivision under names of places, *e.g.*, **Great Britain—Territories and possessions**

—Tests
  USE —Examinations; —Examinations, questions, etc.

—Testing *[S]* May be used as a subdivision under topical headings; animals; chemicals; and materials, *e.g.*, **Textile fibers—Testing**
See also —**Evaluation**

—Textbooks for foreign speakers May be used as a subdivision under languages, *e.g.*, **English language—Textbooks for foreign speakers**
See also —**Texts**

—Texts *[S]* May be used as a subdivision under topical headings and languages, *e.g.*, **Geometry—Texts; Russian language—Texts**
See also —**Textbooks for foreign speakers**

—Themes, motives May be used as a subdivision under topical headings; names of individual persons; and literatures (language or country), *e.g.*, **Motion pictures—Themes, motives; Cartoons and comics—Themes, motives**
See also —**Stories, plots, etc.**

—Therapeutic use *[S]* May be used as a subdivision under topical headings; animals; chemicals; and plants & crops, *e.g.*, **Books—Therapeutic use; Dopa—Therapeutic use**

—Tomb May be used as a subdivision under names of individual persons and individual literary authors, *e.g.*, **Tutankhamen, King of Egypt—Tomb**

—Toxicology *[S] (May add geog subd)* May be used as a subdivision under topical headings; animals; chemicals; materials; and plants & crops, *e.g.*, **Drugs—Toxicology; Plants, Ornamental—Toxicology**

—Tragedies May be used as a subdivision under names of individual literary authors, *e.g.*, **Shakespeare, William, 1564-1616—Tragedies**

—Training *[S] (May add geog subd)* May be used as a subdivision under animals; and plants & crops, *e.g.*, **Bonsai—Training**
See also —**Study and teaching; —Training of**

—Training of *(May add geog subd)* May be used as a subdivision under names of classes of persons, *e.g.*, **Teachers of gifted children—Training of**
See also —**Study and teaching; —Training**

—Translations May be used as a subdivision under topical headings; names of individual literary authors; titles of literary works; and literatures (language or country), *e.g.*, **Andersen, Hans Christian, 1805-1875—Translations; French drama—Translations**
See also —**Translations into**

—Translations into French [German, etc.] May be used as a subdivision under topical headings for collections of translated works; names of individual literary authors; titles of literary works; and literatures (language or country), *e.g.*, **Marketing—Translations into Russian; American poetry—Translations into German**
See also —**Translations**

—Transplantation *[S] (May add geog subd)* May be used as a subdivision under names of organs/regions of the body, *e.g.*, **Liver—Transplantation**

—Transportation *[S]* May be used as a subdivision under topical headings; classes of persons; ethnic groups; animals; materials; military services; plants & crops; land vehicles; and wars, *e.g.*, **Space and time—Transportation; Students—Transportation**
See also —**Travel**

—Travel *(May add geog subd)* May be used as a subdivision under classes of persons and ethnic groups, *e.g.*, **Sales personnel—Travel**
See also —**Description and travel; —Journeys; —Transportation**

—Treatment *(May add geog subd)* May be used as a subdivision under names of diseases, *e.g.*, **Measles—Treatment**
See also —**Care and hygiene; —Vaccination**

—Trials, litigation, etc. May be used as a subdivision under names of corporate bodies; individual persons; and places, *e.g.*, **Salem (Mass.)—Trials, litigation, etc.**

—Underground movements *(May add geog subd)* May be used as a subdivision under names of wars, *e.g.*, **World War, 1939-1945—Underground movements**

—Uniforms May be used as a subdivision under classes of persons; corporate bodies; military services; and sports, *e.g.*, **Nurses—Uniforms**

—Usage May be used as a subdivision under names of languages, *e.g.*, **Arabic language—Usage**
See also —**Language**

—Vaccination May be used as a subdivision under diseases and animals, *e.g.*, **Chicken pox—Vaccination**
See also —**Immunology; —Treatment**

—Variation *(May add geog subd)* May be used as a subdivision under animals and languages, *e.g.*, **Horses—Variation**

—Verb May be used as a subdivision under names of languages, *e.g.*, **Eskimo language—Verb**
See also —**Language**

—Versions May be used as a subdivision under titles of sacred works, *e.g.*, **Bible—Versions**

—Veterans *(May add geog subd)* May be used as a subdivision under names of wars, *e.g.*, **Greco-Turkish War, 1921-1922—Veterans**

—Videos
  See —**Film and video adaptations; —Audio-visual aids**

—Video catalogs May be used as a subdivision under general topics; ethnic groups; corporate bodies; and individual persons, *e.g.*, **Rain forests—Video catalogs**
See also —**Film catalogs**

—Vocabulary May be used as a subdivision under names of languages

—**Vocational guidance** *[S] (May add geog subd)*   May be used as a subdivision under topical headings; classes of persons; corporate bodies; industries; languages; and military services, *e.g.*, **Accounting—Vocational guidance; Teenage parents—Vocational guidance**

—**Wars** *(May add geog subd)*   May be used as a subdivision under names of ethnic groups, *e.g.*, **Apache Indians—Wars**
 See also —**Peace**

—Weather
 USE —**Climate**

—**Wintering**   May be used as a subdivision under animals, *e.g.*, **Cattle—Wintering**

—**Wit and humor** *[AC usage]*   May be used as a subdivision under topical headings and topical wit and humor, including jokes and riddles, *e.g.*, **Camping—Wit and humor**
 See also —**Humor**

—**Women**   May be used as a subdivision under military services, *e.g.*, **Israel—Armed forces—Women**
 See also —**Women** *(May add geog subd)*

—**Women** *(May add geog subd)*   May be used as a subdivision under names of wars, *e.g.*, **World War, 1914-1918—Women**
 See also —**Women** *(Not subd geog)*

—**Women authors**   May be used as a subdivision under names of literatures (language or country), *e.g.*, **American fiction—Women authors**

—**Wounds and injuries** *(May add geog subd)*   May be used as a subdivision under classes of persons; names of ethnic groups; animals; organs/regions of the body; and plants & crops, *e.g.*, **Cats—Wounds and injuries**

—**Writing**   May be used as a subdivision under names of languages, *e.g.*, **Pueblo Indians—Writing**
 See also —**Outlines, syllabi, etc.; —Parodies, imitations, etc.; —Reviews**

—Yearbooks
 USE —**Periodicals**

SUBJECT HEADINGS

KEY TO SUBJECT HEADINGS

Authorized Term ——————— **Local Government** *[S] (May add geog subd)* ———————— Term is identical in *LCSH* and *Sears*

Term can be subdivided geographically

Broader Term ——————— *BT*   Political science

Related Terms ——————— *RT*   Cities and towns

Villages

Narrower Term ——————— *NT*   Municipal government

Term is identical in *Sears* and AC lists

Lost and found possessions *[AC, S] (May add geog subd)*

Used For ——————————— *UF*   Finding things

Unauthorized Term ———— Love poetry

Use authorized term——————— *USE*   Love—Poetry *[AC only]* ——————— Term appears only in the AC list

LCSH term that has ——— **Outlines**
been applied to
children's books   *SA*   *the subdivision* —Outlines, syllabi, etc.

See also ——————

2

3-D
  USE *terms beginning with* Three-dimensional
Aachen (Germany)
  —History
  — —Siege, 1944
Aadler, Stella
Aardvark *(May add geog subd)*
Aaron, Hank, 1934-
Aaron Ward (Ship)
Aaronsohn, Sarah
Abacus *[S]*
  UF Soroban
Abandoned children *[S]*
  UF Children, Abandoned
       Homeless children
  RT Orphans
Abandoned towns
  USE Extinct cities
       Ghost towns
Abbeys *[S] (May add geog subd)*
Abbott, Bud
Abbott, Edwin Abbott, 1838-1926
Abbott, Jim, 1967-
Abbreviations *[S] (May add geog subd)*
  UF Contractions
  RT Acronyms
       Ciphers
ABC Wide World of Sports (Television program)
Abdul, Paula
Abdul-Jabbar, Kareem, 1947-
Abel, Rudolf, 1903-1971
Abernathy, Louie
Abernathy, Temple
Abilene (Tex.)
Ability *[S]*
  UF Aptitude
  RT Creative ability
       Leadership
  —Testing *[S]*
     UF Ability testing
          Aptitude tests
          Testing, Ability
     RT Educational tests and measurements
Abnaki Indians
Abnormalities, Human *(May add geog subd)*
  UF Birth defects
  RT Birth injuries
Abolitionists *[S]*
  UF Abolition of slavery—Biography
       Slavery—United States
Abortion *[S] (May add geog subd)*
  RT Pro-choice movement
  —Law and legislation
Abraham (Biblical patriarch)
Abraham Lincoln Brigade *[AC only]*
  UF Lincoln Brigade
       Spain Ejército Popular de la
          República. 15th International Brigade
       Spain Ejército Popular de la
          República. Abraham Lincoln Brigade
       Spain Ejército Popular de la
          República. Brigada Internacional, XV
Abrahams, Harold Maurice, 1899-
Abramson, Manya Polevoi

Abstract photography
  USE Photograms
Abused children
  UF Battered children
       Child abuse victims
       Victims of abuse
Academic freedom *[S] (May add geog subd)*
  UF Educational freedom
       Freedom, Academic
       Intellectual freedom
  RT Church and education
Academy of Motion Picture Arts and Sciences
Acadia National Park (Me.)
Acapulco (Mexico)
Accidents *[S] (May add geog subd)*
  UF Emergencies
       Injuries
  RT Disasters
       Explosions
       Fires
       First aid
       Home accidents
       Poisons
       Shipwrecks
       Traffic accidents
       Wounds and injuries
  —Prevention
     USE Safety *[AC only]*
     SA   *the subdivision* —Accidents
Accordion
  UF Accordeon
Accounting *[S] (May add geog subd)*
Acculturation *[S] (May add geog subd)*
  BT Anthropology
       Civilization
       Culture
       Ethnology
  NT Ethnic relations
       Intercultural education
       Socialization
Achievement motivation
  BT Motivation (Psychology)
Achievement tests
Acid rain *[S] (May add geog subd)*
  UF Rain, Acid
  BT Rain and rainfall
Acids *[S]*
Acne *[S] (May add geog subd)*
  UF Pimples
Acosta, Pablo, d.1987
Acoustical engineering
  UF Sound engineering
  BT Engineering
Acquaintance rape *(May add geog subd)*
Acquired immune deficiency syndrome
  USE AIDS (Disease)
  RT HIV (Viruses)
Acquisitions (Libraries)
Acrobats
Acronyms *(May add geog subd)*
Acrylic painting *(May add geog subd)*
  UF Polymer painting
ACT assessment
  UF American College Testing Assessment

Acting *[S]*
Action in art
Actions and defenses *(May add geog subd)*
Activity programs in education *(May add geog subd)*
Actors
    USE   Actors and actresses *[AC only]*
Actors and actresses *[AC only]*
    UF   Actors
            Actresses
            Motion picture actors and actresses
            Movie stars
            Television actors and actresses
    BT   Motion pictures—Biography
Actresses
    USE   Actors and actresses *[AC only]*
Acupressure *[S] (May add geog subd)*
    UF   Shiatsu
Acupuncture *[S] (May add geog subd)*
Adair, Christia
Adair, Cornelia Wadsworth
Adair, Red
Adam (Biblical figure)
Adams, Abigail, 1744-1818
Adams, Charles Francis, 1807-1886
Adams, Douglas, 1952-
Adams, Grizzly, 1812-1860
Adams, Henry, 1838-1918
Adams, John Quincy, 1767-1848
Adams, John
Adams, John, 1735-1826
Adams, Louisa Catherine, 1775-1852
Adams, Randall
Adams, Samantha (Fictitious character)
Adams, Samuel, 1722-1803
Adams family
Adamson, Joy
Adaptability *(May add geog subd)*
Adaptation (Biology) *(May add geog subd)*
Adaptation (Physiology) *(May add geog subd)*
Addams, Jane, 1860-1935
ADD
    USE   Attention-deficit hyperactivity disorder
Addiction
    USE   Alcoholism
            Drug abuse
            Substance abuse
Addicts
Addition
Addresses
    USE   Speeches, addresses, etc.
Adélie penguin *(May add geog subd)*
Adenauer, Konrad, 1876-1967
Adirondack Mountains (N.Y.)
Adjustment (Psychology) *[S]*
Adler, Mortimer Jerome, 1902-
Administrative agencies *(May add geog subd)*
    UF   Government agencies
Admirals *[S]*
Adobe houses *(May add geog subd)*
Adolescence *[S]*
Adolescence in literature *[S]*
Adolescent behavior
Adolescent boys
    USE   Teenage boys
Adolescent girls
    USE   Teenage girls

Adolescent psychology *[S] (May add geog subd)*
Adoptees
Adoption *[S] (May add geog subd)*
Adoption agencies *(May add geog subd)*
Adult child abuse victims
Adult child sexual abuse victims
Adult children
Adult children of alcoholics *[S]*
Adult children of dysfunctional families
Adult education *(May add geog subd)*
Adultery *[S] (May add geog subd)*
Adulthood *(May add geog subd)*
Adventists
Adventure and adventurers *[S]*
  —Fiction *[AC, S]*
    UF   Adventure stories
Adventure stories
    USE   Adventure and adventurers—Fiction *[AC only]*
Adventurers
    USE   Adventure and adventurers
Advertising *[S] (May add geog subd)*
  —Alcoholic beverages *(May add geog subd)*
  —Beer *(May add geog subd)*
  —Cigarettes *(May add geog subd)*
  —Psychological aspects
    RT   Motivation research (Marketing)
  —Tobacco industry *(May add geog subd)*
Advertising, Direct mail *(May add geog subd)*
Advertising, Outdoor *(May add geog subd)*
Advertising, Political *(May add geog subd)*
Advertising agencies *(May add geog subd)*
Advertising copy *[S] (May add geog subd)*
Advertising layout and typography *[S] (May add geog subd)*
Aebi, Tania, 1966-
Aeneas (Legendary character)
Aerial reconnaissance *[S] (May add geog subd)*
Aerialists
Aerobic dancing *(May add geog subd)*
Aerobic exercises
Aerodynamics *[S]*
Aeronautical sports *[S] (May add geog subd)*
Aeronautics *[S] (May add geog subd)*
    RT   Airplanes
            Airships
            Astronautics
            Balloons
            Rocketry
            Flight
            Navigation (Aeronautics)
            Unidentified flying objects
  —Flights
Aeronautics, Commercial *(May add geog subd)*
Aeronautics, Military *[S] (May add geog subd)*
Aerosol sniffing
Aerospace industries *(May add geog subd)*
Aesthetics *[S]*
Aesthetics, British
  —19th century
  —20th century
Aethelwold, Saint, Bishop of Winchester, ca. 908-984
Affective education *(May add geog subd)*
Affirmative action programs *[S] (May add geog subd)*
Afghan Wars
Afghanistan

Africa *[S]*
—History *[S]*
— —to 1490
— —1960- *[S]*
Africa, Central
Africa, East
Africa, Eastern
Africa, French-speaking Equatorial
Africa, French-speaking West
Africa, North
Africa, Southern
Africa, Sub-Saharan
Africa, West
    RT   West Africans
African Americans
    USE   Afro-Americans
African buffalo *(May add geog subd)*
African elephant *(May add geog subd)*
African literature
African literature (English) *[S]*
African National Congress
African poetry
Africanized honeybee *(May add geog subd)*
Africans *[S]*
Afrikaners *[S]*
Afro-American agriculturists
Afro-American air pilots
Afro-American astronauts
Afro-American athletes
Afro-American authors
Afro-American basketball players
Afro-American churches *(May add geog subd)*
Afro-American clergy
Afro-American dance
Afro-American entertainers
Afro-American families
Afro-American intellectuals
Afro-American journalists
Afro-American lawyers
Afro-American leadership *(May add geog subd)*
Afro-American literature
    USE   American literature—Afro-American authors
Afro-American men
Afro-American musicians
Afro-American outlaws
Afro-American periodicals *(May add geog subd)*
Afro-American physicians
Afro-American poets
Afro-American scholars
Afro-American scientists
Afro-American singers
Afro-American soldiers
Afro-American songs
    USE   Afro-Americans—Music
Afro-American students
Afro-American surgeons
Afro-American teachers
Afro-American teenagers
Afro-American theater *(May add geog subd)*
Afro-American universities and colleges *(May add geog subd)*
Afro-American women
Afro-American women athletes
Afro-American women authors
Afro-American women in literature

Afro-American youth
Afro-Americans
    UF   African Americans
—Folklore
    USE   Folklore, Afro-American *[AC only]*
—**Dancing**
—**Segregation**
Afro-Americans in art
Afro-Americans in business
Afro-Americans in motion pictures
    Use for works discussing the portrayal of Afro-Americans in motion pictures. Works discussing all aspects of Afro-American involvement in motion pictures are entered under: Afro-Americans in the motion picture industry. Works discussing specific aspects of Afro-American involvement are entered under the specific subject, e.g., Afro-American motion picture actors and actresses.
Afro-Americans in television
Afro-Americans in television broadcasting
Afro-Americans in the motion picture industry
Agamemnon (Greek mythology)
Agassiz, Elizabeth Cabot Cary, 1822-1907
Agassiz, Louis, 1807-1873
Age and employment *[S] (May add geog subd)*
Aged
    UF   Elderly
    RT   Old age
          Aging
—**Abuse of**
    UF   Elder abuse
—**Health and hygiene**
    RT   Geriatrics
Aged as consumers
Aged as offenders
Aged volunteers
Ageism *(May add geog subd)*
Agelenidae
    USE   Funnel-web spiders *[AC only]*
Agent orange *[S]*
Aggressive behavior in animals
Aggressiveness (Psychology) *(May add geog subd)*
Agincourt, Battle of, 1415
Aging *(May add geog subd)*
    RT   Aged
          Old age
Aging parents
Agkistrodon piscivorus
    USE   Water moccasin *[AC only]*
Agnew, Spiro T., 1918-
Agoraphobia *(May add geog subd)*
Agricultural chemicals *(May add geog subd)*
Agricultural ecology *(May add geog subd)*
Agricultural education *(May add geog subd)*
Agricultural implements *(May add geog subd)*
Agricultural industries *[S] (May add geog subd)*
Agricultural laborers *[S]*
Agricultural laws and legislation *(May add geog subd)*
Agricultural machinery *[S] (May add geog subd)*
Agricultural pests *[S] (May add geog subd)*
Agriculture *[S] (May add geog subd)*
    NT   Aquaculture
          Food industry and trade
          Produce trade
Agriculture and state *(May add geog subd)*
Agriculturists
Ahab, Captain (Fictitious character) *(Not subd geog)*

AIDS (Disease) *[S] (May add geog subd)*
 RT Immune system
    Immunology
 —Prevention
  RT Safe sex in AIDS prevention
AIDS phobia *(May add geog subd)*
Ailurus fulgens
 USE Lesser panda *[AC only]*
Ainu
 BT Ethnology
 —Japan
Air *[S]*
Air conditioning
 SA *the subdivision* —Air conditioning
Air defenses *[S]*
Air Force Academy
Air pilots
 NT Women air pilots
Air pilots, Military
Air power *[S] (May add geog subd)*
Air quality *(May add geog subd)*
Air quality management *(May add geog subd)*
Air traffic control *(May add geog subd)*
Air traffic controllers
Air travel *(May add geog subd)*
 SA *specific types, e.g.,* Transatlantic flights
Air warfare
Airbrush art *(May add geog subd)*
Aircraft
 USE Airplanes
 NT Ultralight aircraft
 SA *names of specific aircraft and uses, e.g.,* Research aircraft
Aircraft carriers *[S] (May add geog subd)*
Aircraft industry *(May add geog subd)*
Airlift, Military *(May add geog subd)*
Airlines *[S] (May add geog subd)*
Airplane racing *[S] (May add geog subd)*
Airplanes *[S] (May add geog subd)*
 SA *specific types of aircraft and airplanes, e.g.,* Rocket planes
 —Motors
 —Piloting *[S]*
 —Safety
  USE Aeronautics—Safety measures
 —Turbojet engines
Airplanes, Experimental
 USE Research aircraft
Airplanes, Home-built *(May add geog subd)*
Airplanes, Military *[S] (May add geog subd)*
 —Camouflage
 —Markings
Airplanes, Private *(May add geog subd)*
Airplanes in art *[S]*
Airports *[S] (May add geog subd)*
Airships *[S] (May add geog subd)*
Ajjer (African people)
 BT Tuaregs
Akchurin, Marat
Akhenaton, King of Egypt
Akhetaton (Ancient city)
Akihito, Emperor of Japan, 1933-
Akita dogs *(May add geog subd)*
 BT Dogs
Alabama
 —Social life and customs
 — —1865-1918 *[AC only]*

Alabama Indians
Alabama-Coushatta Indians
 USE Koasati Indians
Alamo (San Antonio, Tex.)
Alaska
 —Discovery and exploration
  NT Bering's Expedition, 1st, 1725-1730 *[AC only]*
Albatrosses *(May add geog subd)*
Albert, Carl Bert, 1908-
Albert, Prince Consort of Victoria, Queen of Great Britain, 1819-1861
Alberta
Albright, Ivan, 1897-
Alcatraz Island (Calif.)
Alchemy *[S] (May add geog subd)*
Alcibiades
Alcohol *[S]*
 UF Alcohol and youth *[AC only]*
 SA *the subdivision* —Alcohol use
Alcohol and youth
 USE Alcohol *[AC only]*
    Alcoholism *[AC only]*
Alcoholic beverages
 —Law and legislation
  RT Prohibition
Alcoholics *[S]*
Alcoholics Anonymous
Alcoholism *[AC, S] (May add geog subd)*
 UF Alcohol and youth
Alcoholism and employment *(May add geog subd)*
Alcott, Louisa May, 1832-1888
Alcott family
Alday family
Aleuts
Alexander, Sally Hobart
Alexander II, Emperor of Russia, 1818-1881
Alexander VI, Pope, 1431-1503
Alexander, the Great, 356-323 B.C.
Alexandra, Empress, consort of Nicholas II, Emperor of Russia, 1872-1918
Alexandria (Egypt) *(Not subd geog)*
Alfalfa *[S] (May add geog subd)*
Alfalfa as feed *(May add geog subd)*
Alford, Ed, 1901-
Alfred, King of England, 849-899
Algae *[S] (May add geog subd)*
Algebra *[S]*
Algebra, Abstract
Algebra, Boolean *[S]*
Algeria
Algiers, Battle of, 1816
Algonquian Indians
Alhambra (Granada, Spain)
Ali, Muhammad, 1942-
Aliav, Ruth, 1914-
Alien beings
 USE Extraterrestrial beings *[AC only]*
Alien labor, Mexican
Alienation (Social psychology)
 UF Rebellion
Aliens *[S]*
Aliens, Illegal
 USE Illegal aliens
Aline, Countess of Romanones, 1923-

All Souls' Day *(May add geog subd)*
    UF Day of the Dead
    BT Fasts and feasts
All-Star Baseball Game
All terrain bicycles *(May add geog subd)*
    UF Mountain bikes
All terrain cycling *(May add geog subd)*
All terrain vehicles *[S] (May add geog subd)*
Allagash River (Me.)
Allegiance, Pledge
    USE Pledge of Allegiance *[AC only]*
Allegories *[S]*
    RT Fables
           Parables
Allegory
Allen, Ethan, 1738-1789
Allen, Marcus, 1960-
Allen, Richard, 1760-1831
Allen, Woody
Allende Gossens, Salvador, 1908-1973
Allergens *(May add geog subd)*
Allergy *[S] (May add geog subd)*
    UF Hypersensitivity
    RT Immunity
Allergy products *(May add geog subd)*
Alliance for Progress
Allied health personnel *[S]*
    RT Paramedical education
Alligators *[S] (May add geog subd)*
Alliluyeva, Svetlana, 1925-
Allinger, Jean
Alliteration
Allosaurus
Alloys *[S]*
Allusions *[S]*
Almanacs *[S]*
    UF Almanacs, American *[AC only]*
Almedingen, E. M. (Edith Martha), 1898-1971
Almond *[S] (May add geog subd)*
Alonso, Alicia
Alopiidae
    USE Thresher sharks *[AC only]*
Alpha Centauri
Alphabet *[AC, S]*
    UF Alphabet books
    SA *the subdivision* —Alphabet
Alphabet books
    USE Alphabet *[AC, S]*
Alphabet rhymes
Alphabets *[S]*
Alphabets in art *[S]*
Alpine animals
    USE Mountain animals
Alpine fauna
    USE Mountain animals
Alpine flora
    USE Alpine plants *[AC only]*
Alpine mountain goat
    USE Ibex
Alpine plants *[AC only] (May add geog subd)*
    UF Alpine flora
Alps
ALS
Alston, Theodosia (Burr), 1783-1813
Altai (Turkic people)
  —Folklore

    USE Folklore, Altai *[AC only]*
Altdorfer, Albrecht, ca. 1480-1538. Battle of Alexander and Darius at Issus *(Not subd geog)*
    UF Alexander's battle (Painting)
Alternative medicine *[S] (May add geog subd)*
    NT Homeopathy
Altruism *(May add geog subd)*
Alvarez, Luis W., 1911-
Alvin Ailey American Dance Theater
Alyeska Pipeline Service Company
Alzheimer's disease *[S] (May add geog subd)*
Amadeus (Motion picture)
Amaryllis (Hippeastrum) *[AC only]*
    UF Hippeastrum
Amateur films *[S] (May add geog subd)*
Amateur plays *(May add geog subd)*
Amateur radio stations *(May add geog subd)*
Amateur theater *[S] (May add geog subd)*
  —Production and direction
Amazon River
Amazon River Region
Amazon River Valley
Amazons
Ambassadors
Amenhotep II, King of Egypt
Amerasians
America *[S]*
  —Discovery and exploration
  — —Pre-Columbian
  —History *[S]*
  — —to 1810
American Airlines, Inc.
American alligator *(May add geog subd)*
American Association of Community and Junior Colleges
American Basketball Association
American Battle Monuments Commission
American bison *(May add geog subd)*
    UF Bison, American
American bison in art
    UF Bison, American, in art
American Broadcasting Company
American Camping Association
American chameleon
    USE Anoles *[AC only]*
American Civil Liberties Union
American College Testing Assessment
    USE ACT Assessment
American drama *[S] (May add geog subd)*
    RT Plays
  —Afro-American authors
American essays *[S] (May add geog subd)*
American Express Company
American fiction *[S] (May add geog subd)*
  —Afro-American authors
American heritage (Periodical)
American Indians
    USE Indians
           Indians of Mexico
           Indians of North America
           Indians of South America
           Indians of the West Indies
American letters *[S]*
American literature *[S] (May add geog subd)*
  —19th century
  —20th century

—**Afro-American authors**
   UF   Afro-American literature (English)
          Black literature (American)
—**Asian American authors**
—**Indian authors**
   UF   Indian literature (American)
   BT   American literature—Minority authors
—**Mexican American authors**
   UF   Mexican American literature
—**Minority authors**
   UF   Ethnic literature
          Minority literature (American)
American Loyalists
American marten *(May add geog subd)*
American newspapers *[S] (May add geog subd)*
American periodicals *[S] (May add geog subd)*
American [Danish, English, etc.] poetry *[AC, S] (May add geog subd)*
   Use for single poems or collections of poetry by individual American [Danish, English, etc.] authors. Collections of poetry by several authors of the same nationality are entered under American [Danish, English, etc.] poetry—Collections *[AC, S]*.
—**19th century**
—**20th century**
—**Afro-American authors**
—**Indian authors**
—**Jewish authors**
American prose literature *[S] (May add geog subd)*
American Red Cross
American Revolution
   USE   United States—History—Revolution, 1775-1783
American Revolution Bicentennial, 1776-1976 *[S]*
American Samoa
American Sign Language *(May add geog subd)*
American Society for the Prevention of Cruelty to Animals
American wit and humor
   USE   Wit and humor *[AC only]*
Americana *[S] (May add geog subd)*
Americanisms *[S] (May add geog subd)*
Americanization *[S]*
Americans *[S]*
America's Cup races
Amish *[S]*
Amish in art
Amistad (Schooner)
Amityville (N.Y.)
Amnesia *[S] (May add geog subd)*
Amon Carter Museum of Western Art
Amory, Cleveland
Amos 'n' Andy (Radio program)
Amos 'n' Andy (Television program)
Amnesty International
Amphetamines *[S] (May add geog subd)*
Amphibians *[S] (May add geog subd)*
   SA   *the names of specific amphibious animals*
Amphibians, Fossil *(May add geog subd)*
Amphibians as pets
Amphibious assault ships
   SA   *the subdivision* —Amphibious operations
Amphibious warfare
Amputees
—**Psychology**
—**Rehabilitation**
Amsterdam (Netherlands)
Amundsen, Roald, 1872-1928

Amusement parks *[S] (May add geog subd)*
Amusement rides *(May add geog subd)*
Amusements *[AC, S] (May add geog subd)*
—**Medieval period**
   NT   Literary recreations
Amycus (Greek mythology)
Amyotrophic lateral sclerosis *(May add geog subd)*
Anabolic steroids
   RT   Steroids
Anaconda *[S] (May add geog subd)*
Analgesics *(May add geog subd)*
Anansi (Legendary character)
Anastasia Nikolaevna, Grand duchess, daughter of Nicholas II, Emperor of Russia, 1901-1918
Anatomy *[S]*
   RT   Physiology
          Preservation of organs, tissues, etc.
   SA   *the subdivision* —Anatomy
Anatomy, Artistic *[S]*
Anatomy, Comparative *[S]*
Anatomy, Human
   USE   Human anatomy
Anchorage (Alaska)
Ancient Roman Empire
   USE   Rome
Ancient science
   USE   Science, Ancient
Andersen, H.C. (Hans Christian), 1805-1875
Andersen, H.C. (Hans Christian), 1805-1875. Steadfast tin soldier
Anderson, Anna
Anderson, Elizabeth Garrett, 1836-1917
Anderson, Marian, 1902-
Anderson, Poul, 1926-
Anderson, Sherwood, 1876-1941
Anderson, Sparky, 1934-
Anderson, Susan, 1870-1960
Anderson, Terry A., 1949-
Andersonville (Ga.)
Andersonville Military Prison (Ga.)
Andes
Andes Region *(Not subd geog)*
Andre, John, 1751-1780
Andrea Doria (Steamship)
Andreas, Dwayne, 1918-
Andretti, Mario, 1940-
Andrews, Benjamin Koo
Andrews, Roy Chapman, 1884-1960
Androids
   USE   Robots *[AC only]*
Anecdotes *[S] (May add geog subd)*
   SA   *the subdivision* —Anecdotes
Angel fish *[S]*
Angelico, fra, ca. 1400-1455
Angelou, Maya
Angel dust
   USE   Phyncyclidine
Angels *[S]*
Anger *(May add geog subd)*
Anger, Per, 1913-
Angiosperms *(May add geog subd)*
   UF   Flowering plants
   RT   Flowers
Angle
Anglican communion *(May add geog subd)*
Anglicans

Anglo-Saxons *[S]*
Angola
Angouleme, Marie-Therese Charlotte, duchesse d',
  1778-1851
Animal abuse
   USE   Animals—Treatment *[AC only]*
Animal attacks *[S] (May add geog subd)*
   UF   Attacks by animals
   RT   Dangerous animals
Animal behavior *(May add geog subd)*
Animal breeding *(May add geog subd)*
Animal culture *(May add geog subd)*
Animal communication *[S]*
Animal communities *(May add geog subd)*
Animal defenses *[S]*
Animal distribution *[AC only] (May add geog subd)*
   UF   Biogeography
           Geographical distribution of animals and plants
           Zoogeography
Animal ecology *(May add geog subd)*
Animal experimentation *[S] (May add geog subd)*
Animal fighting
Animal health *(May add geog subd)*
Animal husbandry
   USE   Domestic animals
           Livestock
Animal illustration
   USE   Animals in art
Animal intelligence *[S]*
Animal introduction *(May add geog subd)*
Animal locomotion *[S]*
Animal migration *(May add geog subd)*
Animal painting and illustration
   USE   Animals in art
Animal navigation *(May add geog subd)*
Animal populations *(May add geog subd)*
Animal rights *[S] (May add geog subd)*
Animal sculpture *(May add geog subd)*
Animal societies
Animal sounds *[AC only] (May add geog subd)*
   UF   Sound production by animals
Animal specialists
Animal tracks *[S] (May add geog subd)*
Animal trainers
Animal weapons
Animal welfare
   USE   Animals—Treatment *[AC only]*
Animals *[S] (Not subd geog; general works only)*
   RT   Zoology *[S] (May add geog subd)*
   NT   Urban animals *[AC only]*
   SA   *names of specific animals and types of animals, and*
           habitats of animals, e.g., Marine animals
—Age
—Air transportation
—Courtship *[AC only]*
   UF   Courtship of animals
—Food habits
—Grooming behavior *[AC only]*
   UF   Grooming behavior in animals
—Illustration
   USE   Animal painting and illustration
—Migration *[S]*
—Play behavior *[AC only]*
   UF   Play behavior in animals

—Sleep behavior *[AC only]*
   UF   Sleep behavior in animals
—Training *[S]*
—Treatment *[AC only]*
   UF   Animal welfare
   RT   Laboratory animals
Animals, Mythical *(May add geog subd)*
   NT   Mermaids
           Mermen
   RT   Ocean—Folklore
           Ocean—Mythology
Animals, Poisonous
   USE   Poisonous animals
Animals, Predatory
   USE   Predatory animals
Animals, Prehistoric
   USE   Prehistoric animals
Animals, Rare
   USE   Rare animals *[AC only]*
Animals, Urban
   USE   Urban animals
Animals and civilization
Animals as artists
Animals in art *[S]*
   RT   Zoological illustration
Animals in literature *[S]*
Animals in motion pictures *[S] (May add geog subd)*
Animals in the Bible
Animated films *[AC only] (May add geog subd)*
   RT   Animation (Cinematography)
Animation (Cinematography) *[AC, S] (May add geog subd)*
   RT   Animated films
Animators
Annapurna
Anne Boleyn, Queen, consort of Henry VIII, King of
  England, 1507-1536
Anne, consort of Richard III, King of England, 1456-1485
Anne, Queen of Great Britain, 1665-1714
Annelida
   USE   Annelids *[AC only]*
Annelids *[AC only]*
   UF   Annelida
Anning, Mary, 1799-1847
Anniversaries
   SA   *the subdivision* —Anniversaries, etc.
Annuities *(May add geog subd)*
Anoles *[AC only] (May add geog subd)*
   UF   American chameleon
           Anolis carolinensis
           Chameleon, American
   RT   Chameleons
Anolis carolinensis
   USE   Anoles *[AC only]*
Anonymous writings
Anonyms and pseudonyms
Anorexia *(May add geog subd)*
Anorexia nervosa *[S] (May add geog subd)*
Answers
   USE   Questions and answers
   RT   Examinations
Antarctic regions
   USE   Antarctica
Antarctica
   UF   Antarctic regions

Anteaters *[AC, S] (May add geog subd)*
  UF Anteater, Giant
         Anteater, Great
         Anteaters, American
         Myrmecophaga
         Myrmecophagidae
Anteus (Greek mythology)
Antelopes *[S] (May add geog subd)*
Anthony, Susan B. (Susan Brownell), 1820-1906
Anthropologists
Anthropology *[S] (May add geog subd)*
  RT National characteristics
  SA *names of specific types*
Anthropology, Historic *(May add geog subd)*
Anti-apartheid movements *(May add geog subd)*
Anti-communist movements *(May add geog subd)*
Antibiotics *[S]*
  NT Penicillin
Antietam, Battle of, 1862
Antigone (Legendary character)
Antihistamines
Antilles, Lesser
Antinuclear movement *[S] (May add geog subd)*
Antioxidants
Antiques *[S] (May add geog subd)*
Antiques, Victorian *(May add geog subd)*
Antiquities *[S]*
  SA *the subdivision* —Antiquities
Antislavery movements
  UF Slavery—Anti-slavery movements
  RT Underground railroad
Antisemitism *[S] (May add geog subd)*
Antisocial personality disorders *(May add geog subd)*
Antitank weapons
Antlers
Antonetty, Evelina, 1922-1984
Antoninus, Marcus, 83?-30 B.C.
  USE Antony, Mark, 83?-30 B.C. *[AC only]*
Antony, Mark, 83?-30 B.C. *[AC only]*
  UF Antoninus, Marcus, 83?-30 B.C.
Antonyms
  SA *the subdivision* —Synonyms and antonyms
Antrim, Henry (Billy the Kid)
  USE Billy, the Kid
Ants *[S] (May add geog subd)*
Ants as pets *(May add geog subd)*
Anxiety *(May add geog subd)*
Anza, Juan Bautista de, 1735-1788
Apache Indians
Apartheid *[S] (May add geog subd)*
  RT Race discrimination
         Segregation
Apartment houses *[S] (May add geog subd)*
Apatosaurus *(May add geog subd)*
Apes *[S] (May add geog subd)*
Aphasia *(May add geog subd)*
Aphasic persons
Aphididae
  USE Aphids *[AC only]*
Aphids *[AC, S]*
  UF Aphididae
Aphorisms and apothegms
  UF Apothegms
         Sayings
  RT Proverbs

Aphrodite (Greek deity)
Apollo (Greek deity)
Apollo Soyuz Test Project
  UF Soyuz Test Project
Apollo Theatre (New York, N.Y.)
Apologetics *[S]*
Apostles *[S]*
Apothegms
  USE Aphorisms and apothegms
Appalachian Mountains
Appalachian Region
Appalachian Region, Southern
Appalachian Trail
Appaloosa horse *[S]*
Appetite disorders *(May add geog subd)*
Appetizers *(May add geog subd)*
Apples *(May add geog subd)*
Apple CD 150 (CD-ROM player)
Apple Computer, Inc.
Apple growers
Apple II (Computer)
Apple II Plus (Computer)
Apple IIc (Computer)
Apple IIe (Computer)
Apple IIGS (Computer)
Apple III (Computer)
Appleseed, Johnny, 1774-1845
AppleTalk (Computer program)
Appleworks (Computer program)
Applications for positions *[S]*
  RT Job hunting
Applied psychology
  USE Psychology, Applied
Appliqué *(May add geog subd)*
Appomattox Campaign, 1865
Apprentices *[S] (May add geog subd)*
April Fools' Day *[S]*
Aptitude
  USE Ability
Aptitude tests
  USE Ability—Testing
Aquaculture *[S] (May add geog subd)*
  UF Ocean Farming
         Sea farming
  BT Agriculture
  NT Fish culture
Aquarium fishes *(May add geog subd)*
Aquariums *[S] (May add geog subd)*
Aquariums, Public *(May add geog subd)*
Aquarius (Astrology) *(May add geog subd)*
Aquatic animals *(May add geog subd)*
Aquatic ecology *(May add geog subd)*
Aquatic exercises *(May add geog subd)*
Aquatic insects *(May add geog subd)*
  UF Insects, Aquatic
Aquatic mammals *(May add geog subd)*
Aquatic plants *(May add geog subd)*
Aquatic sports *(May add geog subd)*
Aquino, Corazon Cojuangco
Arab Americans *(May add geog subd)*
Arab countries *[S]*
Arabesques
Arabian horse *[S] (May add geog subd)*
Arabian Peninsula *[S]*

Arabic language *[S] (May add geog subd)*
—**Readers** *[AC only]*
　　Use for reading texts in Arabic containing materials for instruction and practice in reading that language.
　　RT　Arabic language materials *[AC only]*
Arabic language materials *[AC only]*
　　Use for works written in Arabic intended primarily for general information or recreational reading. Such works with text also given in English are further subdivided by the subdivision —Bilingual.
　　RT　Aramaic language—Readers *[AC only]*
—**Bilingual** *[AC only]*
Arabic literature *[S] (May add geog subd)*
—**20th century**
Arabs *[S]*
　　NT　Palestinian Arabs
—**Folklore** *[AC, S]*
　　UF　　Folklore, Arab
Arachnida
　　USE　Arachnids *[AC only]*
Arachnids *[AC, S]*
　　UF　Arachnida
Arafat, Yasir, 1929-
Aramaic language *[S] (May add geog subd)*
—**Readers** *[AC only]*
　　Use for reading texts in Aramaic containing materials for instruction and practice in reading that language.
　　RT　　Aramaic language materials *[AC only]*
Aramaic language materials *[AC only]*
　　Use for works written in Aramaic intended primarily for general information or recreational reading. Such works with text also given in English are further subdivided by the subdivision —Bilingual.
　　RT　Aramaic language—Readers *[AC only]*
—**Bilingual** *[AC only]*
Arapaho Indians
Arawak Indians
Arbitration, Industrial *[S] (May add geog subd)*
Arbitration and award *[S] (May add geog subd)*
Arbor Day *(May add geog subd)*
Archaeologists
Archaeology *(May add geog subd)*
　　NT　Underwater archaeology
Archeologists
　　USE　Archaeologists
Archeology
　　USE　Archaeology
Archer County (Tex.)
Archer Daniels Midland Company
Archer M. Huntington Gallery
Archer, Jules
Archer, Isabel (Fictitious character)
Archery *[S] (May add geog subd)*
Archimedes
Archimedes' principle
Architects *[S]*
　　NT　Women architects
Architectural drawing *[S] (May add geog subd)*
　　BT　Drawing
Architectural ironwork *(May add geog subd)*
Architecture *[S] (May add geog subd)*
—**Composition, proportion, etc.** *[S]*
Architecture, American *[S] (May add geog subd)*
Architecture, Ancient *[S] (May add geog subd)*
Architecture, Baroque *(May add geog subd)*
Architecture, Classical *(May add geog subd)*
Architecture, Colonial *(May add geog subd)*

Architecture, Domestic *(May add geog subd)*
　　UF　Houses
　　RT　Dwellings
Architecture, Early Christian *(May add geog subd)*
Architecture, Egyptian
Architecture, Gothic *[S] (May add geog subd)*
Architecture, Greek *[S] (May add geog subd)*
Architecture, Indian
　　USE　Indian architecture
Architecture, Islamic *(May add geog subd)*
Architecture, Italian *(May add geog subd)*
Architecture, Medieval *[S] (May add geog subd)*
Architecture, Modern *[S] (May add geog subd)*
—**19th century**
—**20th century**
Architecture, Postmodern *(May add geog subd)*
Architecture, Primitive
Architecture, Rococo *(May add geog subd)*
Architecture, Roman *[S] (May add geog subd)*
Architecture, Romanesque *(May add geog subd)*
Architecture, Vernacular
　　USE　Vernacular architecture
Architecture, Victorian *(May add geog subd)*
Architecture and society *(May add geog subd)*
Arco Publishing Company
Arctic circle
　　USE　Arctic regions
Arctic fox *[S] (May add geog subd)*
Arctic Ocean
Arctic peoples
　　NT　Tunguses
Arctic regions *[S]*
　　NT　Northwest Passage
Arctic Star (Offshore cruiser)
Arden, Elizabeth, 1878-1966
Ardennes, Battle of the, 1944-1945 *[S]*
Ardshiel (Ship)
Area measurement
　　BT　Geometry, Plane
　　　　Surveying
Argentina
Argonauts (Greek mythology)
Argüello y Morago, María de Concepción, d. 1857
Argyoneta *(May add geog subd)*
　　BT　Spiders
Arid regions *(May add geog subd)*
Arias Sánchez, Oscar
Aries (Astrology) *(May add geog subd)*
Arion
Aristocracy
　　USE　Aristocracy (Political science)
　　　　Aristocracy (Social class)
Aristocracy (Political science) *(May add geog subd)*
Aristocracy (Social class) *(May add geog subd)*
Aristotle
Arithmetic *[S]*
　　NT　Average
Arithmetic, Mental
　　USE　Mental arithmetic *[S]*
Arizona (Battleship)
Arizona
Arkansas
Arlington National Cemetery (Va.)
Arm
Armada, 1588

Armaments
    USE Military weapons
Armadillos
Armed forces *[S]*
    RT Armies
           Military service, Voluntary
    NT Infantry
    SA *the subdivision* —Armed forces
Armenian Americans
Armenian massacres, 1915-1923
Armenians *[S]*
Armes, Jay J.
Armies *[S] (May add geog subd)*
    RT Armed forces
Arminianism *(May add geog subd)*
Armor *(May add geog subd)*
Armored animals *(May add geog subd)*
Armored vehicles, Military *(May add geog subd)*
Arms and armor
    USE Armor
           Weapons
           Ordnance
           Rifles
           Shotguns
Arms control *[S] (May add geog subd)*
Arms race *[S]*
Armstrong, Louis, 1900-1971
Armstrong, Neil, 1930-
Armstrong, Penny
Army ants *[S] (May add geog subd)*
Arnez, Desi, 1917-1986
Arnhem, Battle of, 1944
Arnold, Benedict, 1741-1801
Arnold, Margaret Shippen, 1760-1804
Arnold, Rosanne
Aromatherapy *(May add geog subd)*
Aronson, Henry M.
Arquette, Kaitlyn Clare, 1970-1989
Arrowheads *(May add geog subd)*
    RT Bow and arrow
Arroyo, Tomás
Arson *(May add geog subd)*
Art *[S] (May add geog subd)*
    SA *specific forms of art, names of artistic periods, and*
           the subdivisions —Art *and* —Art collections
  —**Awards** *(May add geog subd)*
Art, Abstract *[S] (May add geog subd)*
Art, African *[S] (May add geog subd)*
Art, American *[S] (May add geog subd)*
Art, Ancient *[S] (May add geog subd)*
Art, Asian *[S] (May add geog subd)*
Art, Baroque *[S] (May add geog subd)*
Art, British *(May add geog subd)*
Art, Buddhist *(May add geog subd)*
Art, Burmese *(May add geog subd)*
Art, Byzantine *(May add geog subd)*
Art, Celtic *(May add geog subd)*
    BT Art, Irish
Art, Chinese *[S] (May add geog subd)*
Art, Classical *(May add geog subd)*
Art, Colonial *(May add geog subd)*
Art, Early Christian *(May add geog subd)*
Art, Early Renaissance *(May add geog subd)*
Art, East Asian *(May add geog subd)*
Art, Egyptian *[S] (May add geog subd)*
Art, English *[S] (May add geog subd)*

Art, Etruscan *[S] (May add geog subd)*
Art, European *(May add geog subd)*
Art, Flemish *[S] (May add geog subd)*
Art, French *[S] (May add geog subd)*
Art, German *[S] (May add geog subd)*
Art, Gothic *(May add geog subd)*
Art, Greco-Roman *(May add geog subd)*
Art, Greek *[S] (May add geog subd)*
Art, Indian
    USE Indian art
Art, Indic *(May add geog subd)*
Art, Iranian *[S] (May add geog subd)*
Art, Irish *(May add geog subd)*
Art, Islamic *[S] (May add geog subd)*
Art, Italian *[S] (May add geog subd)*
Art, Japanese *[S] (May add geog subd)*
Art, Korean *(May add geog subd)*
Art, Latin American *[S] (May add geog subd)*
Art, Medieval *[S] (May add geog subd)*
Art, Mexican *[S] (May add geog subd)*
Art, Modern *[S] (May add geog subd)*
    RT Modernism (Art)
  —**17th-18th centuries**
  —**19th century**
  —**20th century**
Art, Oriental *(May add geog subd)*
Art, Philippine *[S] (May add geog subd)*
Art, Polish *(May add geog subd)*
Art, Prehistoric *[S] (May add geog subd)*
Art, Primitive *(May add geog subd)*
Art, Regional *(May add geog subd)*
Art, Renaissance *[S] (May add geog subd)*
Art, Rococo *(May add geog subd)*
Art, Roman *[S] (May add geog subd)*
Art, Romanesque *[S] (May add geog subd)*
Art, Russian *[S] (May add geog subd)*
Art, Scandinavian *[S] (May add geog subd)*
Art, Spanish *[S] (May add geog subd)*
Art, Viking *(May add geog subd)*
Art, Wildlife
    USE Wildlife art
Art and mythology
Art and nature
    USE Nature (Aesthetics)
Art and religion *[S] (May add geog subd)*
Art and science
Art and society *[S] (May add geog subd)*
Art appreciation *[S] (May add geog subd)*
Art criticism *[S] (May add geog subd)*
Art deco *(May add geog subd)*
Art glass *(May add geog subd)*
Art Institute of Chicago
Art metalwork *[AC, S] (May add geog subd)*
    UF Art metal-work
    RT Decorative cast-ironwork
Art museum attendance *(May add geog subd)*
    UF Art museums—Visitors
Art museums *(May add geog subd)*
    SA *the subdivision* —Art collections
  —**Visitors**
    USE Art museum attendance
Art objects *[S] (May add geog subd)*
Art objects, American *(May add geog subd)*
Art objects, Chinese *(May add geog subd)*
Art pottery *(May add geog subd)*

Art thefts *[S] (May add geog subd)*
Art therapy *(May add geog subd)*
Artagnan, Charles de Batz-Castelmore, Comte d',
   1613-1673
Arteriosclerosis *[S] (May add geog subd)*
Arthritis *[S] (May add geog subd)*
   NT Rheumatoid arthritis
Arthropoda
   USE Arthropods *[AC only]*
Arthropoda, Poisonous
   USE Arthropods, Poisonous *[AC only]*
Arthropods *[AC only] (May add geog subd)*
   UF Arthropoda
Arthropods, Poisonous *[AC only] (May add geog subd)*
   UF Arthropoda, Poisonous
Arthur, Chester Alan, 1829-1886
Arthur, King
Arthurian romances *[S]*
Artificial flowers *[S]*
Artificial insemination, Human *(May add geog subd)*
Artificial intelligence *[S]*
Artificial limbs *[S]*
   RT Prosthesis
Artificial organs *[S]*
   RT Prosthesis
Artificial satellites *[S]*
Artificial satellites, Russian *[S]*
Artificial satellites in telecommunication *[S] (May add geog subd)*
Artillery *[S] (May add geog subd)*
Artisans
Artists *[S]*
   UF Painters *[AC only]*
      Portrait painters *[AC only]*
   NT Women artists
Artists' materials
Artists' models *[S]*
   UF Models, Artists'
Artists' studios *(May add geog subd)*
Artists' tools *(May add geog subd)*
Arts *[S] (May add geog subd)*
Arts, American *[S] (May add geog subd)*
Arts, Black *(May add geog subd)*
Arts, Modern *(May add geog subd)*
   NT Art, Modern
      Literature, Modern
  —**20th century**
     NT Dadaism
        Pop art
        Surrealism
Arts and crafts
   USE Handicraft *[AC, S]*
Arts fund raising *(May add geog subd)*
Arts publicity *(May add geog subd)*
Asbestos industry *(May add geog subd)*
Ash, Mary Kay
Ashabranner, Brent K., 1921-
Ashanti (African people)
  —**Folklore**
     USE Folklore, Ashanti *[AC only]*
Ashanti (Kingdom)
Ashbery, John
Ashe, Arthur
Ashford, Evelyn
Asia *[S]*
Asia, Southeastern
Asia, Southern

Asian American women
Asian Americans
Asian and Pacific Council countries
   USE Pacific Area
Asian elephant
   USE Asiatic elephant
Asian wild horse
   USE Przewalski's horse
Asimov, Isaac, 1920-
Aspley, Keith
Asoka, King of Magadha, fl. 259 B.C.
Assassination *[S] (May add geog subd)*
   SA *the subdivision* —Assassination
Assassins
Assateague Island National Seashore (Md. and Va.)
Assembler language (Computer program language)
Assembly, Right of *(May add geog subd)*
Assertiveness (Psychology) *[S]*
Assisi (Italy)
Assisted suicide *(May add geog subd)*
Associations
   USE Associations, institutions, etc.
Associations, institutions, etc. *(May add geog subd)*
Assyria
Asteroids
Asthma *[S] (May add geog subd)*
Astor, John Jacob, 1763-1848
Astor, Nancy Witcher Langhorne Astor, Viscountess,
   1879-1964
Astral projection *(May add geog subd)*
Astrogeology *[S]*
Astrology *[S]*
   RT Zodiac
   NT Horary astrology
   SA *the names of individual astrological signs*
Astrology and psychology
Astrology, Chinese
Astronautics *[S] (May add geog subd)*
Astronautics, Military *(May add geog subd)*
Astronautics and religion
   USE Religion and astronautics
Astronautics in astronomy *(May add geog subd)*
Astronauts *[S]*
   NT Women astronauts
Astronomers *[S]*
   NT Women astronomers
Astronomical instruments *[S] (May add geog subd)*
Astronomical museums *(May add geog subd)*
Astronomical observatories *[S] (May add geog subd)*
Astronomy *[S] (May add geog subd)*
   NT Planets
      Radio astronomy
   SA *the subdivision* —Astronomy
Astronomy, Ancient
Astronomy, Medieval
Astronomy, Prehistoric *(May add geog subd)*
Astronomy in the Bible
Astronomy projects *(May add geog subd)*
Astrophysics *[S] (May add geog subd)*
Asturias (Spain) *(Not subd geog)*
Aswan High Dam (Egypt)
Atari computer
Ataturk, Kemal, 1881-1938
Athapascan Indians
Atheism *[S] (May add geog subd)*
Athena (Greek deity)

Athens (Greece)
Atherton, Gertrude Franklin Horn, 1857-1948
Athletes *[S]*
    NT Women athletes
Athletes, Black
    RT Afro-American athletes
Athletes, Indian
Athlete's foot *(May add geog subd)*
Athletes in art *[S]*
Athletic clubs *(May add geog subd)*
Athletic injuries
    USE Sports injuries
Athletics *[S] (May add geog subd)*
Atlanta (Ga.)
Atlanta Braves (Baseball team)
Atlanta Campaign, 1864
Atlanta Falcons (Football team)
Atlanta Hawks (Basketball team)
Atlantic bottlenosed dolphin *(May add geog subd)*
Atlantic City (N.J.)
Atlantic Coast (Canada)
Atlantic Coast (U.S.)
Atlantic Ocean *[S]*
Atlantic ridley turtle *[AC only]*
    UF Kemp's loggerhead turtle
          Kemp's turtle
          Lepidochelys kempii
Atlantic States *[S]*
Atlantic salmon *(May add geog subd)*
    BT Salmon
Atlantis
Atlases *[S]*
    UF World atlases
    SA Maps
Atmosphere *[S]*
Atmospheric ozone *(May add geog subd)*
Atmospheric physics *(May add geog subd)*
Atmospheric pressure *(May add geog subd)*
Atocha (Shipwreck)
Atomic bomb *[S] (May add geog subd)*
  —Blast effect
Atomic bomb victims
Atomic mass
Atomic theory *[S]*
Atomic volume
Atoms *[S]*
Attack planes *(May add geog subd)*
Attacks by animals
    USE Animal attacks
Attention *[S] (May add geog subd)*
Attention deficit disorder
    USE Attention-deficit hyperactivity disorder
Attention-deficit hyperactivity disorder *(May add geog subd)*
Attila, d. 453
Attitude (Psychology) *[S] (May add geog subd)*
Attitude change
    SA *the subdivision* —Attitudes
Attlee, C.R. (Clement Richard), 1883-1967
Attorney and client *(May add geog subd)*
Aubrey, Jack (Fictitious character)
Auden, W.H. (Wystan Hugh), 1907-1973
Audio equipment industry *(May add geog subd)*
Audio-visual education *(May add geog subd)*
Audio-visual equipment
    RT Overhead projection
Audio-visual library service *(May add geog subd)*

    RT Media programs (Education)
Audio-visual materials *(May add geog subd)*
    SA *the subdivision* —Audio-visual aids
Audiocassettes
    SA *the subdivision* —Audio adaptations
Audiocassettes in education *(May add geog subd)*
Audiovisual ...
    USE Audio-visual ...
Audiology *(May add geog subd)*
Audubon, John James, 1785-1851
Audubon, Lucy Green Bakewell, 1788-1874
Auerbacher, Inge, 1934-
Augustus, Emperor of Rome, 63 B.C.-14 A.D.
Aunts
Auroras *[S] (May add geog subd)*
Auschwitz (Poland : Concentration camp)
Austen, Jane, 1775-1817
Austen, Jane, 1775-1817.   Pride and prejudice
Austin, James H., 1925-
Austin, Moses, 1761-1821
Austin (Tex.)
Austin, Stephen F. (Fuller), 1793-1836
Austin, Tracy, 1962-
Austin City Limits (Television program)
Austin County (Tex.)
Austin Region (Tex.)
Australasia
Australia
  —Zoology
Australian aborigines *[S]*
  —Folklore
      USE Folklore, Australian aborigine *[AC only]*
  —Legends
      USE Folklore, Australian aborigine *[AC only]*
Australian poetry *(May add geog subd)*
Australian prose literature *(May add geog subd)*
Austria
Authors *[S]*
    SA *the subdivisions* —Black authors *and* —Women authors
    NT Women authors
Authors, Afro-American
    USE Afro-American authors
Authors, American *[S]*
Authors, Austrian *[S]*
Authors, Black
    RT Afro-American authors
Authors, Canadian
Authors, Cuban
Authors, Danish *[S]*
Authors, English *[S]*
  —18th century
  —19th century
  —20th century
Authors, European
Authors, French *[S]*
Authors, German *[S]*
Authors, Greek *[S]*
Authors, Irish *[S]*
Authors, Jamaican
Authors, Latin
Authors, Latin American
Authors, Mexican *[S]*
  —17th century
Authors, Russian *[S]*
Authors, Scottish

Authors, South African *[S]*
Authors, Spanish *[S]*
Authors, Swedish *[S]*
Authors, Women
    USE Women authors
Authors, Yiddish
Authors and publishers *[S]*
Authors' spouses
Authorship *[S]*
    RT Literature
    SA the subdivision —Authorship
  —Style manuals
      UF Style manuals
Autism *[S] (May add geog subd)*
Autistic children
Autobiographies *(May add geog subd)*
    Use for collections of autobiographies.
Autobiography
AutoCAD (Computer program)
Autogiros
Autograph albums *(May add geog subd)*
Autographs *[S] (May add geog subd)*
Autoharp music
Automata *[AC only]*
    Use for works on robots which do not take human form.
    RT Robots *[AC only]*
Automatic pistols *(May add geog subd)*
Automation *[S] (May add geog subd)*
    SA the subdivision —Automation
Automobile driver education *(May add geog subd)*
Automobile drivers *[S]*
Automobile driving *(May add geog subd)*
    UF Driving, Automobile
Automobile engineers
Automobile industry and trade *(May add geog subd)*
Automobile license plates *(May add geog subd)*
Automobile mechanics
Automobile racing *[S] (May add geog subd)*
Automobile trade
    USE Automobile industry and trade
Automobile travel *(May add geog subd)*
Automobiles *[S] (May add geog subd)*
    NT Sports cars
    SA the names of specific makes or manufacturers
  —Service stations
      USE Service stations
Automobiles, Foreign *(May add geog subd)*
Automobiles, Racing *(May add geog subd)*
    RT Sports cars
    NT Hot rods
Autonomy
Autumn *[S] (May add geog subd)*
    UF Fall
Autumn in art *[S]*
Avalanches *(May add geog subd)*
Avarice
    USE Greed *[AC only]*
Ave Maria (Music)
    USE Hail Mary *[AC only]*
Average *[S]*
    BT Arithmetic
Aversion therapy *(May add geog subd)*
Avery, Cheryl
Avery, Dennis
Avery, Ephraim K., d. 1869
Avocado *[S] (May add geog subd)*

Avogadro's hypothesis
Awards *(May add geog subd)*
    UF Prizes (Rewards, etc.)
          Rewards (Prizes, etc.)
    SA the names of specific awards and prizes in various fields, e.g.,
          Newbery medal books; Nobel Prizes
    NT Literary prizes
Aware, Inc.
Aylor, Joy
Aylward, Gladys
Azalea *[S] (May add geog subd)*
Aztec language
    USE Nahuatl language
Aztecs *[S]*
B-17 bomber
B-29 bomber
Baba Yaga (Legendary character)
Babbage, Charles, 1791-1871
Babel, Tower of
    UF Tower of Babel
Babies
    UF Infants
          Infants (Newborn)
    BT Test tube babies
    RT Brothers and sisters *[AC only]*
Babington, Anthony, 1561-1586
Baboons *(May add geog subd)*
Baby boom generation *(May add geog subd)*
Baby sitters
    USE Babysitters
Babylon (Ancient city)
Baby Peggy, 1918-
    SA Cary, Diana Serra
Babysitters *[S]*
Babysitting *[S]*
Baca, Elfego, 1864-1945
Bacall, Lauren, 1924-
Bach, Johann Sebastian, 1685-1750
Bach, Richard
Bachelors
Back
Backache *[S] (May add geog subd)*
Backgammon
Backpacking *[S] (May add geog subd)*
Bacon, Francis, 1561-1626
Bacon, Nathaniel, 1648-1676
Bacteria *(May add geog subd)*
Bacterial diseases *(May add geog subd)*
Bacteriologists
Bacteriology *[S] (May add geog subd)*
Baden-Powell of Gilwell, Robert Stephenson Smyth,
    Baden-Powell, Baron, 1857-1941
Badgers *[S]*
Badlands National Park (S.D.)
Badminton (Game) *[S] (May add geog subd)*
Baeck, Leo, 1873-1956
Baekeland, L.H. (Leo Hendrick), 1863-1944
Baez, Joan
Baghdad (Iraq)
Bagley, Sarah G.
Bagpipe *[S]*
Bahamas
Bahamas in art *[S]*
Bahrain
Baikal-Amur Railroad *[AC only]*
    UF Baikalo-Amurskaia magistral

Baikalo-Amurskaia magistral
    USE   Baikal-Amur Railroad *[AC only]*
Bail *(May add geog subd)*
Bailey, F. Lee (Francis Lee), 1933-
Bailey, Mollie, d. 1918
Bailey, Pearl
Bain, Catherine
Bainbridge Island (Wash.)
Bait fishing *(May add geog subd)*
Baja California (Mexico)
Baker, Ella, 1903-1986
Baker, Florence, Lady
Baker, John, d. 1970
Baker, Josephine, 1906-1975
Baker, LaFayette C. (LaFayette Charles), 1826-1868
Baker, Robert Gene
Baker, Russell, 1925-
Baker, Samuel White, Sir, 1821-1893
Bakeries
    USE   Bakers and bakeries
Bakers and bakeries
Baking *[S] (May add geog subd)*
Balaklava, Battle of, 1854
Balance
Balance of trade *[S] (May add geog subd)*
    UF   Trade, Balance of
    BT   Commerce
          Economics
Balboa, Vasco Núñez de, 1475-1519
Balchen, Bernt, 1899-
Bald eagle *[S] (May add geog subd)*
Baldness *(May add geog subd)*
Baldwin, James, 1924-
Bali Island (Indonesia)
Balkan peninsula
Ball games *[S] (May add geog subd)*
Ball, Lucille, 1911-
Ballads *[S] (May add geog subd)*
Ballads, English *(May add geog subd)*
Ballads, Scots *(May add geog subd)*
Ballerinas
Ballet *[S] (May add geog subd)*
Ballet dancers *[S]*
Ballet dancing
Ballets
    Use for musical works composed for ballet.
Ballistic missiles *[S] (May add geog subd)*
Balloon ascensions
Balloon sculpture
Balloons *[S] (May add geog subd)*
Balloons, Sounding
Balloons in astronomy
Ballroom dancing *(May add geog subd)*
Balls (Sporting goods)
Balsa wood
Balsa wood craft *(May add geog subd)*
Baltic States *(Not subd geog)*
Baltimore (Md.)
Baltimore Orioles (Baseball team)
Balto (Dog)
Balukas, Jean
Balzac, Honore de, 1799-1850
Bambara (African people)
Bananas *[S] (May add geog subd)*
Bancroft, Anne, 1931-
Band music *[S]*

Band saws
Bandicoots *[AC only]*
    UF   Peramelidae
Bands (Music) *[S] (May add geog subd)*
Banking
    USE   Banks and banking
Bangladesh
Banjo *(May add geog subd)*
Bank failures *[S] (May add geog subd)*
Banking law *(May add geog subd)*
Bankruptcy *[S] (May add geog subd)*
Bankhead, Tallulah, 1902-1968
Banks, Ernie, 1931-
Banks, Graham
Banks, Lynne Reid, 1929-
Banks and banking *[S] (May add geog subd)*
Banned books
    USE   Prohibited books
Banneker, Benjamin, 1731-1806
Bannock Indians
Banting, Frederick Grant, Sir, 1891-1941
Bantu speaking peoples
    —Folklore
        USE   Folklore, Bantu *[AC only]*
Baobab *[S] (May add geog subd)*
    BT   Plants
Baptists *[S]*
    —Clergy
Bar coding
    USE   Product coding
Bar mitzvah
Barbados
Barbecue cookery
Barbed wire
Barber, Walter Lanier
    USE   Barber, Red, 1908-
Barber, Red, 1908-
Barbers
Barbie, Klaus, 1913-
Barbiturates *(May add geog subd)*
Barcelona (Spain) *(Not subd geog)*
Bar coding of products
    USE   Product coding
Bargaining
    USE   Negotiation
Barlowe, Wayne Douglas
Barn owl *[S] (May add geog subd)*
Barnard, Christiaan, 1922-
Barnett, Ida B. Wells, 1862-1931
Barns *[S] (May add geog subd)*
Barnum, P.T. (Phineas Taylor), 1810-1891
Barometer *(May add geog subd)*
Barr, Rosanne
Barracudas *[S]*
Barringer, Emily Dunning, 1876-1961
Barry, Stephen P., 1948-
Barrymore, Drew
Barrymore, Ethel, 1879-1959
Bartending *(May add geog subd)*
Barter *[S] (May add geog subd)*
Barth, John.   Giles, goat-boy
Bartholdi, Frederic Auguste, 1834-1904
Bartlett, John Frederick, 1892-1947
Bartlett family
Bartok, Bela, 1881-1945
Barton, Clara, 1821-1912

Baryshnikov, Mikhail, 1948-
Basal reading instruction
Base running (Baseball)
Baseball [S] (May add geog subd)
—Fiction [AC only]
    UF   Baseball stories
    BT   Sports—Fiction
Baseball bats
Baseball cards (May add geog subd)
Baseball players
Baseball stories
    USE   Baseball—Fiction [AC only]
Bashfulness [S]
Bashkiroff, Anne
Bashkiroff, Sasha
BASIC (Computer program language)
Basic education [S] (May add geog subd)
    UF   Basic skills education
    BT   Education
—Ability testing
Basket making [S] (May add geog subd)
    BT   Handicraft
    RT   Raffia
Basketball [S] (May add geog subd)
—Fiction
    UF   Basketball stories
    BT   Sports—Fiction
Basketball players
    NT   Women basketball players
Basketball stories
    USE   Basketball—Fiction
Baskets (May add geog subd)
Basketwork (May add geog subd)
Bass, Rick, 1958-
Bass, Sam, 1851-1878
Bassoon [S]
Bastille (Paris, France)
Bastrop County (Tex.)
Bataan, Battle of, 1942
Bataan (Philippines : Province)
Bateman, Hester, 1709-1794
Bathing beaches (May add geog subd)
Bathrooms
Baths [AC, S]
    BT   Cleanliness [AC only]
Batik [S] (May add geog subd)
Batman (Fictitious character)
Baton twirling [S] (May add geog subd)
Bats [S] (May add geog subd)
    BT   Mammals
Batting (Baseball)
Battles [S] (May add geog subd)
Battleships (May add geog subd)
Battlestar Galactica (Television program)
Baucis (Greek mythology)
Baudelaire, Charles, 1821-1867
Bauer, Marion Dane
Bauhaus
    BT   Art, Modern—20th century
Bavaria (Germany)
Baxter, Anne
Bayeux tapestry
Baylor, Byrd
Baylor, Don
Bayous (May add geog subd)

Beaches [S] (May add geog subd)
Bead flowers
Beadwork [S] (May add geog subd)
Beagle expedition (1831-1836)
Beagles (Dogs)
    BT   Dogs
Beale, Thomas Jefferson
Bean, Alan, 1932-
Bean, Roy, d. 1903
Beans (May add geog subd)
Bear's Heart, 1851-1882
Beard, Daniel Carter, 1850-1941
Bearden, Romare, 1911-1988
Bears [S] (May add geog subd)
Beat generation (May add geog subd)
    RT   Bohemianism
Beatles
Beatrice, consort of Lodovico Sforza il Moro, Duke of
    Milan, 1475-1497
Beatty, Warren, 1937-
Beauty contestants
Beaumont, William, 1785-1853
Beaumont (Tex.)
Beauty, Personal
Beauty contests (May add geog subd)
Beauty operators
Beaver, Tony (Legendary character)
Beavers [S]
Becket, Thomas à, Saint, 1118?—1170
Beckett, Samuel, 1906- . Innommable
    USE   Beckett, Samuel, 1906- . Unnamable [AC only]
Beckett, Samuel, 1906- . Malone dies [AC only]
    UF   Beckett, Samuel, 1906- . Malone meurt
Beckett, Samuel, 1906- . Malone meurt
    USE   Beckett, Samuel, 1906- . Malone dies [AC only]
Beckett, Samuel, 1906- . Unnamable [AC only]
    UF   Beckett, Samuel, 1906- . Innommable
Beckwourth, James Pierson, 1798-1866
Bed and breakfast accommodations (May add geog subd)
    RT   Hotels, motels, etc
Bedichek, Roy, 1878-1959
Bedouins [S]
Bedrooms (May add geog subd)
Beds (May add geog subd)
Bedtime [AC, S]
    RT   Night [AC only]
           Sleep [AC only]
Bedwetting [AC only]
    UF   Enuresis
    BT   Urinary incontinence [AC only]
Bee culture (May add geog subd)
Bee hunting
Beebe, Charles William, 1877-1962
Beef cattle [S]
Beef industry (May add geog subd)
Bees [S] (May add geog subd)
Beethoven, Ludwig van, 1770-1827
Beetles [S] (May add geog subd)
Beetles as pets (May add geog subd)
Befana (Legendary character)
Begin, Menachem, 1913-
Begley, Kathleen A.
Behavior [AC only]
    RT   Conduct of life [AC only]
           Etiquette [AC only]

Behavior disorders in children *(May add geog subd)*
Behavior evolution
Behavior modification *[S] (May add geog subd)*
Behavior therapy *(May add geog subd)*
Behavioral assessment *(May add geog subd)*
Behaviorism (Psychology) *[S] (May add geog subd)*
Beirut (Lebanon) *(Not subd geog)*
Belgian Americans
Belgium
Belief and doubt in literature
Bell, Alexander Graham, 1847-1922
Bell, Terrel Howard, 1921-
Bell founders
    BT   Metalworkers *[AC only]*
Bellamy, Francis.   Pledge of allegiance to the flag
    USE   Pledge of Allegiance *[AC only]*
Belleau Wood, Battle of, 1918
Bellerophon (Greek mythology)
Bellini, Giovanni, d. 1516
Bellow, Saul
Bells *[S] (May add geog subd)*
Belly button *[AC only]*
    UF   Navel
           Umbilicus
Belly dance
Belushi, John
Ben & Jerry's (Firm)
Ben-Gurion, David, 1886-1973
Ben-Yehuda, Eliezer, 1858-1922
Bench, Johnny, 1947-
Bender, David L. 1936-
Beneficial insects *[S] (May add geog subd)*
    UF   Insects, Injurious and beneficial
Beneke, George J.
Benelux countries
Benet, Stephen Vincent, 1898-1943
Bengali (South Asian people)
   —Folklore
    USE   Folklore, Bengali *[AC only]*
Bengali language *[S] (May add geog subd)*
   —Readers *[AC only]*
       Use for reading texts in Bengali containing materials for instruction
       and practice in reading that language.
    RT   Bengali language materials *[AC only]*
Bengali language materials *[AC only]*
       Use for works written in Bengali intended primarily for general
       information or recreational reading. Such works with text also given
       in English are further subdivided by the subdivision —Bilingual.
    RT   Bengali language—Readers *[AC only]*
   —Bilingual *[AC only]*
Benin
Benoit, Joan
Benson, Arthur Christopher, 1862-1925
Benton, Thomas Hart, 1889-1975
Benton, William, 1900-1943
Bent's Fort (Colo.)
Beothuk Indians
Beowulf
Berardelli, Alessandro, d. 1920
Berbers
    NT   Tuaregs
Bereavement *[S]*
Beregovo (Ukraine)
Berendzen, Richard
Berenstain, Jan, 1923-
Berenstain, Stan, 1923-

Berg Collection
Berg, Patty, 1918-
Bergen-Belsen (Germany : Concentration camp)
Bergh, Henry, 1811-1888
Bergman, Ingrid, 1915-
Berig, Karen
Bering's Expedition, 1st, 1725-1730 *[AC only]*
    UF   Kamchatskaia ekspeditsiia
    BT   Alaska—Discovery and exploration
Berkowitz, David Richard, 1953-
Berlin question
    USE   Berlin (Germany)—History—1945-1990
Berle, Milton
Berlin (Germany)
   —Blockade, 1948-1949
   —History
   — —1945-1990
Berlin, Irving, 1888-
Berlin, Irving N., 1917-
Berlin Wall, Berlin, Germany, 1961-1989
Bermuda Islands
Bermuda petrel
    BT   Sea birds
Bermuda Triangle *[S]*
Bernadette, Saint, 1844-1879
Bernard, Claude, 1813-1878
Bernards, Neal, 1963-
Bernbaum, Israel
Bernhardt, Sarah, 1844-1923
Bernini, Gian Lorenzo, 1598-1680
Bernstein, Carl, 1944-
Bernstein, Leonard, 1918-
Berra, Yogi, 1925-
Berry, Martha, 1866-1942
Berry Schools (Mount Berry, Ga.)
Beshoar, Michael, 1833-1907
Bessemer, Henry, 1813-1898
Best books
       For lists of recommended books on specific topics, assign this
       heading and a second heading in the form (topic)—Bibliography.
Best sellers *(May add geog subd)*
Bet ha-halim "Hadasah" (Jerusalem)
Bethlehem (Pa.)
Bethune, Mary McLeod, 1875-1955
Bets
    USE   Wagers
Betta *(May add geog subd)*
    UF   Fighting fishes
Better Homes and Gardens Books (Firm)
Beverages *[S]*
Bewick's swan *[S] (May add geog subd)*
Bhutto, Benazir
Bianco, Margery Williams, 1880-1944
Bias, Len, 1963-1986
Bible *[S]*
       This heading is used only with subdivisions.
    RT   Nature in the Bible
           Sacred books
   —Prayers
    USE   Lord's prayer
   —Selections *[AC only]*
Bible. N.T. *[S]*
       This heading is used only with subdivisions.
Bible. N.T. Matthew [etc.] *[S]*
       This heading is used only with subdivisions.

Bible. O.T. *[S]*
　　This heading is used only with subdivisions.
Bible. O.T. Genesis [etc.] *[S]*
　　This heading is used only with subdivisions.
Bible and science *[S]*
Bible as literature *[S]*
Bible colleges *(May add geog subd)*
Bible records
　　UF　Family Bible records
Bible stories *[S]*
Bible stories, English
Biblical costume *(Not subd geog)*
Bibliography *[S] (May add geog subd)*
　　RT　Best books
　　SA　*the subdivisions* —Bibliography *and* —Bio-bibliography
Bibliotherapy *(May add geog subd)*
Bickerdyke, Mary Ann, 1817-1901
Bicycle motocross *[S] (May add geog subd)*
Bicycle racing *[S] (May add geog subd)*
Bicycle touring *(May add geog subd)*
Bicycles and bicycling *[AC, S] (May add geog subd)*
　　UF　Cycling
　　　　　Tricycles
Bicycling
　　USE　Bicycles and bicycling
Bicyclists *[AC only]*
　　UF　Cyclists
Bierce, Ambrose, 1842-1914
Big Apple Circus
Big bands *(May add geog subd)*
Big bang theory
　　RT　Universe
Big Basin State Park (Calif.)
Big books
　　USE　Oversize books
Big Bend Region (Tex.)
Big business *(May add geog subd)*
Big game hunting *(May add geog subd)*
Big Thicket National Preserve (Tex.)
Bighorn sheep *[S] (May add geog subd)*
Biko, Steve, 1946-1977
Bilingual books *[S] (May add geog subd)*
Bilingual education
　　USE　Education, Bilingual
Bill of rights (United States Constitution)
　　USE　United States—Constitution—Amendments—1st-10th
Bilingualism *[S] (May add geog subd)*
Billboards *(May add geog subd)*
Billiards *[S] (May add geog subd)*
Billings, Frederick, 1823-1890
Billington, John
Billion (The number)
Billy, the Kid
　　UF　Antrim, Henry (Billy the Kid)
　　　　　Bonney, William H.
Biloxi Indians
Binary system (Mathematics) *[S]*
Binoculars *(May add geog subd)*
Bio-bibliography
Biochemistry *[S] (May add geog subd)*
Biodegradation
Bioelectricity
　　USE　Electrophysiology
Bioethics *[S] (May add geog subd)*
Biofeedback training *[S]*
Biogeography

　　USE　Animal distribution *[AC only]*
　　　　　Plant distribution *[AC only]*
Biographers
Biography *[S]*
　　NT　Military biography
　　　　　Oral biography
　　SA　*the subdivisions* —Biography *and* —Personal narratives.
　　　　　When used as a subdivision, do not use geographic
　　　　　subdivisions
　　—11th [12th, etc.] century
Biography as a literary form
　　BT　Literary form
　　RT　Literature
Biological diversity conservation *(May add geog subd)*
Biological rhythms *[S]*
Biological physics
　　USE　Biophysics
Biological specimens
Biological systems
Biological warfare *[S] (May add geog subd)*
Biologists *[S]*
　　NT　Physiologists
　　　　　Women biologists
Biology *[S] (May add geog subd)*
　　NT　Photobiology
　　　　　Seashore biology
　　　　　Space biology
Biology, Experimental
　　NT　Vivisection
Biology, Molecular
　　USE　Molecular biology
Bioluminescence *[S] (May add geog subd)*
　　BT　Photobiology
Biomass energy *[S] (May add geog subd)*
Biomechanics
Biomedical engineering *(May add geog subd)*
Biomes
　　USE　Biotic communities
Biometry
Bionics *[S]*
Biophysics *[S] (May add geog subd)*
　　UF　Biological physics
　　BT　Physics
Biosphere
Biosphere 2 (Project)
Biotechnology *[S] (May add geog subd)*
Biotechnology industries *(May add geog subd)*
Biotic communities *(May add geog subd)*
Bird, Larry, 1956-
Bird, Roland T., 1899-
Bird feeders *(May add geog subd)*
Bird pests *(May add geog subd)*
Bird refuges *(May add geog subd)*
Bird song *[AC, S] (May add geog subd)*
　　UF　Birdsongs
Bird watchers
Bird watching *[S] (May add geog subd)*
Birdhouses *(May add geog subd)*
Birds *[S] (May add geog subd)*
　　RT　Ornithology
　　SA　*the names of specific birds*
　　—Attracting *[AC only]*
　　—Flight *[S]*
　　—Protection *[AC, S]*
　　　　UF　Birds, Protection of

Birds, Extinct
    USE   Extinct birds
Birds, Fossil *(May add geog subd)*
Birds, Protection of
    USE   Birds—Protection *[AC only]*
Birds, Rare
    USE   Rare birds
Birds as pets *[AC only]*
    BT   Pets
Birds of prey *(May add geog subd)*
Birmingham (Ala.)
Birth *[AC only]*
    Use for works on birth in general or on animal birth in particular. Works on human birth are entered under Childbirth.
    UF   Parturition
    BT   Reproduction
    RT   Childbirth
Birth, Multiple
    USE   Multiple birth
Birth certificates *(May add geog subd)*
Birth control *[AC, S]* *(May add geog subd)*
    UF   Contraception
Birth control clinics *(May add geog subd)*
Birth defects
    USE   Abnormalities, Human
            Birth injuries
Birth injuries *(May add geog subd)*
    RT   Abnormalities, Human
Birth stones
    UF   Birthstones
Birthday books
Birthdays *[S]*
Birthparents *[S]*
Birthstones
    UF   Birth stones
Bishop, Elizabeth, 1911-1979
Bismarck, Otto, Furst von, 1815-1898
Bismarck (Battleship)
Bison *[S]* *(May add geog subd)*
Bison, American
    USE   American bison
Bison, American, in art
    USE   American bison in art
Bisque dolls *(May add geog subd)*
Bissell, Alfred Elliott, 1903-1975
Bites and stings *(May add geog subd)*
Bitters, Stan
Bizet, Georges, 1838-1875
Black bear *[S]* *(May add geog subd)*
Black death *[S]* *(May add geog subd)*
Black Elk, 1863-1950
Black-footed ferret *[S]*
Black Gold (Race horse)
Black Hawk, Sauk chief, 1767-1838
Black Hawk War, 1832 *[S]*
Black Hills (S.D. and Wyo.)
Black history
    USE   Afro-Americans—History
            Blacks—History [non-U.S. residents]
Black Hole (Motion picture)
Black Hole Incident, Calcutta, India, 1756
Black holes (Astronomy) *[S]*
Black literature (American)
    USE   American literature—Afro-American authors
Black Muslims *[S]*

Black nationalism *[S]* *(May add geog subd)*
Black Panther Party
Black poetry
    USE   Poetry—Black authors
Black power *[S]* *(May add geog subd)*
Black rhinoceros *(May add geog subd)*
Black skimmer *(May add geog subd)*
    UF   Scissors bill
Black-tailed prairie dog *[AC only]*
    UF   Black-tailed prairie marmot
            Cynomys ludovicianus
            Plains prairie dog
Black-tailed prairie marmot
    USE   Black-tailed prairie dog *[AC only]*
Black widow spider *(May add geog subd)*
    BT   Spiders
Black women
    USE   Women, Black
Blackbeard, d. 1718 *[AC only]*
    UF   Teach, Edward, d. 1718
Blackjack (Game) *(May add geog subd)*
Blacklisting of entertainers *(May add geog subd)*
Blacks *[S]*
    Use for works on blacks as an element in the population. Works on black people in countries whose racial composition is predominantly black are assigned headings appropriate for the country as a whole without the use of the heading Blacks. This heading is used only if the work discusses blacks apart from other groups in the country.
    UF   Negroes
    RT   Afro-Americans
  —Dancing
    USE   Dance, Black
  —Folklore *[AC, S]*
    UF   Folklore, Black
Blacks in art *[S]*
    UF   Negroes in art
Blacks in literature *[S]*
    UF   Negroes in literature
Blacksmithing *[S]*
Blacksmiths
Blackwell, Elizabeth, 1821-1910
Bladder
Blake, Eubie, 1883-
Blake, William, 1757-1827
Blakey, Art, 1919-
Blanc, Mel
Blanch, Lesley
Blankets *(May add geog subd)*
Blavatsky H.P. (Helena Petrovna), 1831-1891
Blegvad, Erik
Bleriot, Louis, 1872-1936
Blessing and cursing
Bligh, William, 1754-1817
Blind *[S]*
    RT   Visually handicapped
Blind-deaf
Blindness *(May add geog subd)*
Bliss, Charles Kasiel
Blizzards *[S]* *(May add geog subd)*
Block printing
Blocks (Toys) *(May add geog subd)*
Blood *[S]*
    NT   Leucocytes
  —Circulation *[S]*
  —Transfusion *[S]*
Blood banks *(May add geog subd)*

Blood cholesterol *(May add geog subd)*
   RT Cholesterol
Blood pressure *[S] (May add geog subd)*
Bloodhounds *(May add geog subd)*
Bloodsucking animals *(May add geog subd)*
Blos, Joan W.
Blue Jacket, Shawnee chief, b. ca. 1752
Blue Nile River (Ethiopia and Sudan)
Blue-streaked cleaner wrasse
   USE Cleaner fish *[AC only]*
Blue tit
   BT Birds
Blue whale *[S]*
Blueberries *[S] (May add geog subd)*
Bluebirds *[S] (May add geog subd)*
Bluebonnets (Lupines) *(May add geog subd)*
Bluefish *[S] (May add geog subd)*
Bluegrass music *(May add geog subd)*
Blueprints *[S] (May add geog subd)*
Blues (Music) *(May add geog subd)*
   RT Rhythm and blues music
Bluford, Guion Stewart, 1942-
Blum, Leon, 1872-1950
Blume, Judy
Bly, Nellie, 1867-1922
BMW automobile
Boa constrictor *[S] (May add geog subd)*
Boadicea, Queen, d. 62
Board games *(May add geog subd)*
Board of Governors of the Federal Reserve System (U.S.)
Boarding schools *(May add geog subd)*
Boards of trade *(May add geog subd)*
   UF Chambers of commerce
Boastfulness in literature
   RT Pride and vanity
Boat names *(May add geog subd)*
Boatbuilding *[S] (May add geog subd)*
Boating
   USE Boats and boating
Boatright, Mody Coggin, 1896-1970
Boats and boating *[S] (May add geog subd)*
Boats in art *[S]*
Bobbin lace *(May add geog subd)*
Bobcat *[S]*
Bobsledding *(May add geog subd)*
Bobwhite *[S]*
Boccioni, Umberto, 1882-1916
Bode, Elroy, 1931-
Body, Human *(May add geog subd)*
   UF Human body
Body covering (Anatomy)
Body image
Body size
Body temperature *[S]*
Bodybuilding *[S] (May add geog subd)*
Bodybuilding for women *(May add geog subd)*
Boeing Company
Boetticher, Bud, 1916-
Boetticher, John, 1900-1950
Bogart, Humphrey, 1899-1957
Bohemia (Czech Republic)
   —History
   — —Hussite Wars, 1419-1436
Bohemianism
   RT Beat generation
Bohr, Niels Henrik David, 1885-1962

Bolivar, Simon, 1783-1830
Bolivia
Böll, Heinrich, 1917-
Boller, Paul F.
Bombers *[S] (May add geog subd)*
   RT Airplanes, Military
Bombing, Aerial *(May add geog subd)*
Bombings *(May add geog subd)*
Bon Homme Richard (Ship)
Bon Jovi (Musical group)
Bonaparte, Elizabeth Patterson, 1785-1879
Bond, Horace Mann, 1904-1972
Bonds *[S] (May add geog subd)*
Bone carving *(May add geog subd)*
Bones *[S]*
   —Diseases
     RT Osteoporosis
     NT Osteogenesis imperfecta
Bonham, James Butler, 1807-1836
Bonheur, Rosa, 1822-1899
Bonn (Germany)
Bonneville, Benjamin Louis Eulalie de, 1796-1878
Bonney, William H.
   USE Billy, the Kid
Bonnie, 1910-1934
Bonsai *[S] (May add geog subd)*
Book collecting *[S] (May add geog subd)*
Book industries and trade *(May add geog subd)*
Book of Mormon
   RT Church of Jesus Christ of Latter-Day Saints
Book reviewing *(May add geog subd)*
Book selection *[S]*
Book talks *(May add geog subd)*
Book trade
   USE Book industries and trade
           Booksellers and bookselling
Bookbinding *[S] (May add geog subd)*
Bookkeeping *[S] (May add geog subd)*
Bookmarks
Bookmobiles *[S] (May add geog subd)*
Books *[S] (May add geog subd)*
   RT Literature
   NT Paperbacks
   —Class sets
     RT Children's literature
           Printing
           Publishers and publishing
Books and reading *[S] (May add geog subd)*
   SA *the subdivision* —Books and reading
Booksellers and bookselling *[S]*
   BT Selling
   RT Publishers and publishing
Booksellers' catalogs
   USE Catalogs, Booksellers'
Boomerangs
Boone, Daniel, 1734-1820
Boone family *(Not subd geog)*
Booth, Evangeline, 1865-1950
Booth family *(Not subd geog)*
Booth, John Wilkes, 1838-1865
Booth, Junius Brutus, 1796-1852
Boots *(May add geog subd)*
   BT Shoes
   RT Spurs
Borchgrave, Jacques de, Baron

Borchgrave, Sheri de, Baroness
Borden, Gail, 1801-1874
Borden, Lizzie, 1860-1927
Border collies
Boredom
Borg, Bjorn, 1956-
Borgia, Cesare, 1476?-1507
Borgia, Lucrezia, 1480-1519
Borgia family
Borglum, Gutzon, 1867-1941
Boring [S] (May add geog subd)
Boris Fyodorovich Godunov, Czar of Russia, 1551 or
    2-1605
Borland, Hal, 1900-1978
Borman, Frank, 1928-
Bormann, Martin, 1900-1945
Borneo
Borrowing
    USE   Borrowing and lending [AC only]
Borrowing and lending [AC only]
    UF   Borrowing
          Lending
    RT   Loans
          Mortgages
Bosch, Hieronymus, d. 1516
Bosnia and Hercegovina
Boston (Mass.)
Boston Braves (Baseball team)
Boston Celtics (Basketball team)
Boston Marathon
Boston Massacre, 1770
Boston Pops Orchestra
Boston Red Sox (Baseball team)
Boston Tea Party, 1773
Botanical gardens [S] (May add geog subd)
Botanical illustration (May add geog subd)
Botanical literature
    NT   Herbals
Botanists [S]
Botany [S] (May add geog subd)
    BT   Plants
    RT   Plant names, Popular
—Anatomy
    NT   Bulbs
Botany, Economic [S] (May add geog subd)
Botany, Medical [S] (May add geog subd)
Botany projects (May add geog subd)
Botswana
Botticelli, Sandro, 1444 or 5-1510
Bottlenosed dolphins [S]
Bottles (May add geog subd)
Botulism (May add geog subd)
Boucher, François, 1703-1770
Boulogne-Sur-Mer (France)
Bounty (Ship)
Bounty Mutiny, 1789
Bourke-White, Margaret, 1904-1971
Bovidae
Bow and arrow [S]
Bow and arrow making (May add geog subd)
Bowditch, Nathaniel, 1773-1838
Bowhunting (May add geog subd)
Bowie, James, d. 1836
Bowling [S] (May add geog subd)
Boxers (Sports)
Boxes [S] (May add geog subd)

Boxing [S] (May add geog subd)
—Fiction [AC only]
    UF   Boxing stories
    RT   Sports—Fiction
Boxing stories
    USE   Boxing—Fiction [AC only]
Boy George, 1961-
Boy Scouts [S]
    BT   Scouts and scouting
Boy Scouts of America
Boyce, Christopher John
Boyd, Belle, 1844-1900
Boyd, William, 1895-1972
    UF   Cassidy, Hopalong, 1895-1972
Boyington, Gregory
Boyle, Robert, 1627-1691
Boys [S]
Brachiosaurus (May add geog subd)
    BT   Dinosaurs
Brackenridge, George Washington, 1832-1921
Bradbury, Ray, 1920-
Bradford, William, 1590-1657
Bradley, Bill, 1943-
Bradshaw, Terry
Bradstreet, Anne, 1612?-1672
Brady, Mathew B., 1823 (ca.)-1896
Brahms, Johannes, 1833-1897
Braid (May add geog subd)
Braille, Louis, 1809-1852
Braille books
    USE   Blind—Books and reading
Braille system
    USE   Blind—Printing and writing systems
Brain [S]
    NT   Neurophysiology
Brain-damaged children
Brainwashing [S] (May add geog subd)
Braithwaite, Edward Ricardo
Bramwell-Booth, Catherine, 1883-1987
Brand, Joel, 1906-
Brand name products [S] (May add geog subd)
Brando, Marlon
Brandeis, Louis Dembitz, 1856-1941
Brandley, Clarence
Brandt, Willy, 1913-
Branson, Richard
Brant, Joseph, 1742-1807
Brass rubbing (May add geog subd)
Brasses [S] (May add geog subd)
Brassi, Battista, 1854-1925
Brasswork (May add geog subd)
Brazil
Brazos River (Tex.)
Brazza, Pierre Savorgnan de, 1852-1905
Bread [S] (May add geog subd)
Bread dough craft (May add geog subd)
Break dancing [S] (May add geog subd)
Breakfasts [S]
Breast
Breast feeding [S] (May add geog subd)
Breast implants (May add geog subd)
Breast milk
    UF   Milk, Human
Breckingridge, Mary, 1881-1965
Brendan, Saint, The voyager, ca. 483-577
Brett, George

Brewing
Brezhnev, Leonid Il'ich, 1906-
Brian's Song (Motion picture)
Bricklaying *[S] (May add geog subd)*
Brickmaking *(May add geog subd)*
Bricks *[S] (May add geog subd)*
Bridge (Game) *[AC only]*
   UF Bridge whist
         Contract bridge
Bridge whist
   USE Bridge (Game) *[AC only]*
Bridger, Jim, 1804-1881
Bridges *[S] (May add geog subd)*
   SA names of specific bridges and types of bridges
Bridges, Concrete *(May add geog subd)*
Bridgman, Laura Dewey, 1829-1889
Brigands and robbers
   USE Robbers and outlaws *[AC only]*
Brinkley, David
Britain, Battle of, 1940
Britannia (Rowboat)
British
British Americans
British Antarctic Expedition, 1910-1913
British Columbia
British Isles
British literature
British Museum
Britons
   BT Celts
Broadcast journalism *[S] (May add geog subd)*
Broadcasting *[S] (May add geog subd)*
   RT Journalism
   NT Radio broadcasting
Broadway (New York, N.Y.)
Broca, Paul, 1824-1880
Brodie, William, 1741-1788
Brokers
Bromeliaceae
   USE Bromeliads *[AC only]*
Bromeliads *[AC only]*
   UF Bromeliaceae
Bronchitis *(May add geog subd)*
Brontë, Anne, 1820-1849
Brontë, Charlotte, 1816-1855. Jane Eyre
Brontë, Emily, 1818-1848. Wuthering Heights
Brontë, Patrick Branwell, 1817-1848
Brontë family
Bronx (New York, N.Y.)
Bronze age *[S] (May add geog subd)*
Bronze founding *(May add geog subd)*
Bronze sculpture *(May add geog subd)*
Bronzes *[S] (May add geog subd)*
Bronzes, Chinese *(May add geog subd)*
Bronzes, Renaissance *(May add geog subd)*
Brookings Institution
Brooklyn (New York, N.Y.)
Brooklyn Bridge (New York, N.Y.)
Brooklyn Dodgers (Baseball team)
Brooklyn Museum
Brooks, Gwendolyn, 1917-
Brooks, Mel
Brooms and brushes *(May add geog subd)*
   UF Brushes
Brotherhood of Sleeping Car Porters
Brothers

   RT Brothers and sisters
        Sisters
Brothers and sisters *[AC, S]*
   UF Siblings
   RT Babies *[AC only]*
        Brothers
        Sisters
Broun, Heywood, 1888-1939
Brown, Barnum
Brown, Charles P., b. 1879
Brown, Claude, 1937-
Brown County (Tex.)
Brown, Elaine, 1943-
Brown, Helen Gurley
Brown, Helene
Brown, Jacob, 1775-1828
Brown, James, 1928-
Brown, Jim, 1936-
Brown, John, 1800-1859
Brown, Louise, 1978-
Brown, Marcia
Brown, Margaret Tobin, 1867-1932
   USE Brown, Molly, 1867-1932
Brown, Molly, 1867-1932
Brown pelican *[S]*
Brownies (Cookery)
Browning, Elizabeth Barrett, 1806-1861
Browning, Robert, 1812-1889
Brownstein, Karen Osney
Bruce, David, 1855-1931
Bruce, James, 1730-1794
Bruce, Shelley
Bruegel, Pieter, ca. 1525-1569
Bruegel, Pieter, 1564-1638.   Fair
Brunei
Brushes
   USE Brooms and brushes
Bryan, Sophia Wyers, 1837-1904
Bryan, William Jennings, 1860-1925
Bryant, Louise, 1885-1936
Bryant, Paul W.
Bryant, William Cullen, 1794-1878
Bryce Canyon National Park (Utah)
Bubble gum
Bubbles
Buber, Martin, 1878-1965
Buchanan, Edna
Buchanan, James, 1791-1868
Buchwald, Ann
Buchwald, Art
Buck, Pearl S. (Pearl Sydenstricker), 1892-1973
Budapest (Hungary)
Buddha *[AC only]*
   UF Gautama Buddha
Buddhism *[S] (May add geog subd)*
   BT Religions
   NT Zen Buddhism
Buddhist saints
   USE Saints *[AC only]*
Budgerigar
   USE Parakeets *[AC only]*
Budget *[S] (May add geog subd)*
Budget deficits *(May add geog subd)*
Buenoano, Judias
Buffalo (N.Y.)
Buffalo Bill Historical Center

Buffalo Bill, 1846-1917
Buffalo Bills (Football team)
Buffalo Zoo
Buffaloes *[S] (May add geog subd)*
Buffets (Cookery)
    USE Cookery—Buffets *[AC only]*
Bugle and drum corps
    USE Drum and bugle corps *[AC only]*
Building *[S] (May add geog subd)*
    NT Floors
Building, Adobe *(May add geog subd)*
Building, Brick *(May add geog subd)*
Building, Wooden *(May add geog subd)*
Building failures *[S] (May add geog subd)*
Building laws *(May add geog subd)*
Building layout
Building materials *[S] (May add geog subd)*
Building stones *(May add geog subd)*
Building trades *(May add geog subd)*
Buildings *[S] (May add geog subd)*
    RT Structural engineering
    SA *the subdivision* —Buildings, structures, etc.
Buildings in art *[S]*
Bukusu (African people)
    USE Kusu (African people) *[AC only]*
Bulbs *[S] (May add geog subd)*
    BT Flower gardening
    NT Corms
Bulgaria
Bulimia *[S] (May add geog subd)*
Bull Run, 1st Battle of, Va., 1861
Bulla, Clyde Robert
Bulletin boards *[S]*
Bullfights *[S]*
Bullies *[AC only]*
    UF Bully
Bulls *[S] (May add geog subd)*
Bully
    USE Bullies *[AC only]*
Bullying *(May add geog subd)*
Bumblebees *(May add geog subd)*
Bunche, Ralph J. (Ralph Johnson), 1904-1971
Bundy, Theodore Robert
Bunker Hill, Battle of, 1775
Bunyan, Paul (Legendary character)
Burch, Jennings Michael
Bureaucracy *[S] (May add geog subd)*
Burger, Warren E., 1907-
Burgess, Abbie, 1839-1892
Burgess, Anthony, 1917-
Burgess, Anthony, 1917- . Clockwork orange
Burglary *(May add geog subd)*
Burglary protection *[S] (May add geog subd)*
Burgoyne, John, 1722-1792
Burial *[S] (May add geog subd)*
Burial laws *(May add geog subd)*
Buried treasure *[AC, S] (May add geog subd)*
    UF Sunken treasure
        Treasure trove
Burke, Edmund, 1729-1797. Reflections on the revolution in France
Burlesque (Theater) *(May add geog subd)*
Burma
Burma-Siam Railroad
Burne-Jones, Edward Coley, Sir, 1833-1898

Burnet, David Gouverneur, 1789-1870
Burnet County (Tex.)
Burnet, Thomas, 1635?-1715
Burnett, Carol
Burnett, Frances Hodgson, 1849-1924
Burningham, John
Burns, Anthony, 1834-1862
Burns and scalds
Burr, Aaron, 1756-1836
Burr Conspiracy, 1805-1807
Burrell, Kenny
Burroughs, Edgar Rice, 1875-1950
Burroughs, John, 1837-1921
Burroughs, William S., 1914-
Burrowing animals *(May add geog subd)*
Burrowing owl *(May add geog subd)*
Burton, Richard Francis, Sir, 1821-1890
Burundi
Buscaglia, Rocco Bartolomeo
Buses *[S] (May add geog subd)*
Bush, Barbara, 1925-
Bush, George, 1924-
Bush babies
    USE Bushbabies
Bushbabies *(May add geog subd)*
    UF Bush babies
    BT Primates
Business *[S]*
    RT Commercial correspondence
        Success in business
   —Information services
       USE Business information services
Business communication *(May add geog subd)*
Business cycles *[S] (May add geog subd)*
Business education *[S] (May add geog subd)*
Business enterprises *(May add geog subd)*
Business enterprises, Foreign
Business ethics *[S] (May add geog subd)*
Business etiquette *(May add geog subd)*
Business failures *(May add geog subd)*
Business forecasting *[S]*
Business information services *(May add geog subd)*
    UF Business—Information services
Business intelligence *(May add geog subd)*
Business libraries *[S] (May add geog subd)*
Business literature *(May add geog subd)*
Business mathematics
Business names *(May add geog subd)*
    UF Trade names
    RT Trademarks
Business presentations *(May add geog subd)*
Business psychology
    USE Psychology, Industrial
Business report writing
Business travel *(May add geog subd)*
Business women
    USE Businesswomen *[AC only]*
Business writing *(May add geog subd)*
Businessmen *[S]*
Businesswomen *[AC, S]*
    UF Business women
        Entrepreneurs, Women
        Women entrepreneurs
        Women in business
    BT Women

Busing for school integration *(May add geog subd)*
 BT School integration
 RT Segregation in education
Butcher, Solomon D. (Solomon Devore), 1856-1927
Butchers
Butter *[S]*
Butterflies *[S]*
 NT Monarch butterfly
Butterfly farming *(May add geog subd)*
Butterworth, Emma Macalik
Buttons *[S] (May add geog subd)*
Buying
 USE Purchasing
Buzzards *[S]*
Byars, Betsy Cromer
Bylot Island (N.W.T.)
Byrd, Dennis
Byrd, Richard Evelyn, 1888-1957
Byrd Antarctic Expedition, 2nd, 1933-1935
Byron, George Gordon Noel Byron, Baron, 1788-1824
Bywater, Hector C. (Hector Charles), 1884-1940
Byzantine Empire *[S]*
 —History
 — —**Constantine XI Dragases, 1448-1453**
C. Fred (Dog)
CD-ROMs *(May add geog subd)*
 UF CDROM
Cabeza de Vaca, Alvar Núñez, 16th cent. *[AC only]*
 UF Núñez Cabeza de Vaca, Alvar, 16th cent.
Cabinet officers *[S]*
Cabinetwork *(May add geog subd)*
Cable cars *[AC only]*
 BT Railroads, Cable
Cable News Network
Cables, Submarine *[S]*
Cabot, John, d. 1498?
Cabot, Sebastian, ca. 1474-1557
Cabrillo, Juan Rodríguez, d. 1543
Cacao *[S] (May add geog subd)*
Cactus *[S] (May add geog subd)*
CAD
 USE Computer-aided design
Caddis flies *[AC only]*
 UF Caddisflies
Caddo Indians
Cadmus (Greek mythology)
Caesar, Julius
Caffeine *[S]*
Cage birds *[S]*
Caillaux, Henriette
Caillaux, Joseph, 1863-1944
Caito, Fred
Cajuns
Cairo (Egypt) *(Not subd geog)*
Cairo (Ill.) *(Not subd geog)*
Caithness (Scotland)
Cake *[S] (May add geog subd)*
Cake decorating *[S]*
Calcium
Calculating machines
 USE Calculators *[AC only]*
Calculators *[AC, S]*
 UF Calculating machines
   Pocket calculators
 RT Computers

Calculus *[S] (May add geog subd)*
Calcutta (India)
Caldecott Medal
 UF Caldecott Medal books
Caldecott, Randolph, 1846-1886
Calder, Alexander, 1898-1976
Calderone, Antonino, 1935-
Calendar *(May add geog subd)*
 SA the subdivision —Calendar
Calendar, Gregorian *(May add geog subd)*
Calendars *[S] (May add geog subd)*
 SA the subdivision —Calendars
Calhoun, John C. (Caldwell), 1782-1850
California
 —History
 — —**To 1846**
 — —**1846-1850**
 — —**1850-1950**
 — —**1950-**
California, Northern
California, Southern
California Angels (Baseball team)
Caliphs
 USE Kings, queens, rulers, etc. *[AC only]*
Caligula, Emperor of Rome, 12-41
Callahan, Steven
Callas, Maria, 1923-1977
Calligraphy *[S] (May add geog subd)*
 RT Lettering
Calmette, Gaston, 1858-1914
Calvert family
Calves *[S] (May add geog subd)*
Calvin, Jean, 1509-1564
Calvinism *[S] (May add geog subd)*
Calydonian boar (Greek mythology)
Calypso (Music)
Calypso (Ship)
Cambodia
 NT Khmers
Cambodian Americans
Cambodian-Vietnamese Conflict, 1977- *(May add geog subd)*
Camellia *[S] (May add geog subd)*
Camels *[S] (May add geog subd)*
Cameras *[S] (May add geog subd)*
Cameroon
Camouflage (Biology) *[S]*
 UF Mimicry (Biology) *[AC only]*
 SA the subdivision —Camouflage
Camp counselors
Camp sites, facilities, etc. *(May add geog subd)*
 UF Campgrounds
Campaign management *(May add geog subd)*
Campaign paraphernalia *(May add geog subd)*
Campanella, Roy, 1921-
Campbell, Arthur, 1742-1811
Campbell, Earl
Campbell, John Wood, 1910-1971
Campbell, Joseph, 1904-
Campgrounds
 USE Camp sites, facilities, etc.
Camping *[S] (May add geog subd)*
Camps *[S] (May add geog subd)*
Camps, Music
 USE Music camps *[AC only]*
Camus, Albert, 1913-1960

Camus, Albert, 1913-1960. Etranger
   USE   Camus, Albert, 1913-1960.   Stranger *[AC only]*
Camus, Albert, 1913-1960.   Stranger *[AC only]*
   UF   Camus, Albert, 1913-1960.   Etranger
Canada *[S]*
   —History *[S]*
   — —To 1763 (New France)
Canada. Royal Canadian Mounted Police
Canada, Western
Canada goose *[S] (May add geog subd)*
Canadian-American Challenge Cup
Canadian Invasion, 1775-1776
Canadian literature *[S]*
Canadian poetry
Canadians *[S]*
Canal Zone
Canals *[S] (May add geog subd)*
Canaries *[S]*
Canary Islands
Canby, Peter
Cancer *[S] (May add geog subd)*
   BT   Tumors
   NT   Leukemia
Cancer patients
   USE   Cancer—Patients
Cancer (Astrology) *(May add geog subd)*
Cancún (Mexico)
Candleholders
   USE   Candlesticks
Candlemaking *(May add geog subd)*
Candles *[S]*
Candlesticks *(May add geog subd)*
   UF   Candleholders
Candy *[S] (May add geog subd)*
Canidae *(May add geog subd)*
   BT   Carnivores *[AC only]*
Cannes Film Festival
Cannibalism *[S] (May add geog subd)*
Canning and preserving *[S] (May add geog subd)*
Canoes and canoeing *[S] (May add geog subd)*
   RT   Kayaks and kayaking *[AC only]*
   NT   White-water canoeing
Canseco, Jose, 1964-
Canton (China) *(Not subd geog)*
Canute I, King of England, 995?-1035
Canutt, Yakima, 1895-
Canvas embroidery
   UF   Needlepoint
   BT   Needlework
Canyon animals
   UF   Canyon fauna
Canyon de Chelly (Ariz.)
   USE   Chelly, Canyon de (Ariz.)
Canyon fauna
   USE   Canyon animals *[AC only]*
Canyons *(May add geog subd)*
Cape Cod (Mass.)
Capital punishment *[S] (May add geog subd)*
   RT   Executions and executioners
Capitalism *[S] (May add geog subd)*
Capitalists and financiers *[S]*
Capitals (Cities) *[S] (May add geog subd)*
   SA   *the subdivision* —Capital and capitol
Capitols *[S]*
   SA   *the subdivision* —Capital and capitol
Capone, Al, 1899-1947

   UF   Capone, Alphonse
Capote, Truman, 1924-1984
Capra, Frank, 1897-
Capreolus
   USE   Roe deer
Captain America (Comic strip)
Captive lizards *(May add geog subd)*
Captive mammals *(May add geog subd)*
Captive snakes *(May add geog subd)*
Captive wild animals *(May add geog subd)*
Capuchin monkeys
Caputo, Philip
Capybaras *[S]*
Car pools *(May add geog subd)*
Caras, Roger A.
Caravaggio, Michelangelo Merisi da, 1573-1610
Carbon *[S]*
Carbonated beverages
Carcinogens *(May add geog subd)*
Card games *[S] (May add geog subd)*
Card tricks *[AC, S]*
   RT   Magic tricks *[AC only]*
Cardiac arrest *(May add geog subd)*
   UF   Heart arrest
Cardiff giant
Cardiff (N.Y.)
Cardigan, Jake (Fictitious character) *(Not subd geog)*
   UF   Cardinal-birds
Cardinal (Bird) *[AC only]*
Cardinals *[S]*
   BT   Catholic Church—Clergy
Cardiology *(May add geog subd)*
Cardiovascular system
   USE   Circulatory system *[AC only]*
Career changes *[S] (May add geog subd)*
Career development *(May add geog subd)*
Career education *(May add geog subd)*
   RT   Vocational guidance
Career guidance
   USE   Vocational guidance
Careers
   USE   Occupations
           Professions
           Vocational guidance
Caregivers *[S]*
Carib Indians
Caribbean Area
Caribbean Sea
Caribou *[S] (May add geog subd)*
Caricature *(May add geog subd)*
Caricatures and cartoons
   USE   Cartoons and comics *[AC only]*
Caring
Carl Karcher Enterprises
Carle, Eric
Carlos, the Jackal
Carlota, Empress, consort of Maximilian, Emperor of
    Mexico, 1840-1927
Carlsbad Caverns National Park (N.M.)
Carlton, Steve, 1944-
Carmichael, Stokely
Carnegie, Andrew, 1835-1919
Carnegie Hero Fund Commission
Carnival
   USE   Mardi Gras *[AC only]*
Carnival glass *(May add geog subd)*

Carnivals *(May add geog subd)*
Carnivora
   USE   Carnivores *[AC only]*
Carnivores *[AC, S] (May add geog subd)*
   UF   Carnivora
   NT   Canidae
          Mustelidae
Carnivorous plants *(May add geog subd)*
Caroline, consort of George II, 1683-1737
Caroline Mathilde, Queen, consort of Christian VII, King of Denmark, 1741-1775
Carols *[S] (May add geog subd)*
   UF   Christmas carols
Carols, English *(May add geog subd)*
Carols, French *(May add geog subd)*
Carpal tunnel syndrome *(May add geog subd)*
Carpenter, Liz
Carpenters' square
Carpentry *[S] (May add geog subd)*
   RT   Industrial arts
          Woodwork
Carpets *[S] (May add geog subd)*
Carriages and carts *[S] (May add geog subd)*
Carrighar, Sally
Carroll, Lewis, 1832-1898
Carrots *(May add geog subd)*
Cars
   USE   Automobile industry and trade
          Automobiles
Carson, Ben
   UF   Carson, Benjamin S.
Carson, Johnny, 1925-
Carson, Kit, 1809-1868
Carson, Rachel, 1907-1964
Carson, Rachel, 1907-1964.   Silent spring
Carter, Alden R.
Carter, Forrest
Carter, Grady L.
Carter, Howard, 1873-1939
Carter, Jimmy, 1924-
Carter, Robert, 1663-1732
Carter, Rosalynn
Carter's Grove (Va.)
Carthage (Extinct city)
   RT   Phoenicians
Cartier, Jacques, 1491-1557
Cartilaginous fishes *[AC only]*
   UF   Chondrichthyes
   BT   Fishes
Cartographers
Cartography
Cartooning
Cartoonists
Cartoons and comics *[AC only]*
   For fictional cartoons and comics, an additional entry is made under the heading [topic]—Fiction. *[AC only]* For nonfiction cartoons and comics, an additional entry is made under the heading [topic]—Cartoons and comics. *[AC only]*
   UF   Caricatures and cartoons
          Comic books, strips, etc.
          Comics and cartoons
   NT   Goofy (Fictitious character)
          McDuck, Scrooge (Fictitious character)
   SA   *the subdivision* —Cartoons and comics
Carts
   USE   Carriages and carts

Cartwright, Jim
Carver, George Washington, 1864?-1943
Carving (Decorative arts) *(May add geog subd)*
Carwardine, Mark
Cary, Diana Serra
   SA   Baby Peggy, 1918-
Casablanca (Motion Picture)
Cascade Range
Casey, Joan Frances
Cash, Johnny
Casimir, H.B.G. (Hendrik Brugt Gerhard), 1909-
Cassatt, Mary, 1844-1926
Casserole cookery
Cassidy, Butch, b. 1866
   UF   Parker, George Leroy, b. 1866
Cassidy, Hopalong, 1895-1972
   USE   Boyd, William, 1895-1972
Cassino (Italy), Battle of, 1944
Castaneda, Carlos, 1931-
Castellano, Constantino Paul, 1915-1985
Castilleja
   UF   Indian paintbrush (Plant)
Castillo de San Marcos National Monument (Saint Augustine, Fla.)
Casting
   USE   Plaster casts
Castles *[S] (May add geog subd)*
Castro, Fidel, 1927-
Cat breeds
   USE   Cats
Cataloging *[S] (May add geog subd)*
   RT   Subject headings
Cataloging of archival material
Cataloging of audio-visual materials *(May add geog subd)*
Cataloging of children's literature
Catalogs, Booksellers' *(May add geog subd)*
   UF   Booksellers' catalogs
Catalogs, Card *[S]*
   SA   *the subdivisions* —Catalogs *and* —Catalogs and collections
Catalogs, Publishers' *(May add geog subd)*
   UF   Publishers' catalogs
Catalogs, Classified *[S]*
Catalogs, Subject *[S]*
   SA   *the subdivisions* —Catalogs *and* —Catalogs and collections
Catalogs, Union *(May add geog subd)*
   UF   Union catalogs
Cataract *(May add geog subd)*
Catastrophes (Geology)
Catastrophes (Mathematics)
Catbird *[S]*
Catchup
   USE   Ketchup *[AC only]*
Caterers and catering
Caterpillars *[S] (May add geog subd)*
Catfishes *(May add geog subd)*
Catharine Howard, Queen, consort of Henry VIII, King of England, d. 1542
Catharine of Aragon, Queen, consort of Henry VIII, King of England, 1485-1536
Catharine of Braganza, Queen, consort of Charles II, King of England, 1638-1705
Catharine Parr, Queen, consort of Henry VIII, King of England, 1512-1548
Cathedral of St. John the Divine (New York, N.Y.)
Cathedrals *[S] (May add geog subd)*
Cather, Willa, 1873-1947

Catherine de Medicis, Queen, consort of Henry II, King of France, 1519-1589
Catherine II, Empress of Russia, 1729-1796
Catherwood, Frederick
Catholic Church *[S] (May add geog subd)*
   RT Inquisition
Catholic literature *[S] (May add geog subd)*
Catholics *[S]*
Catiline, ca. 108-62 B.C.
Catlin, George, 1796-1872
Cats *[S] (May add geog subd)*
   UF Kittens *[AC only]*
Cats in art *[S]*
Cats in literature *[S]*
Catskill Mountains (N.Y.)
Catsup
   USE Ketchup *[AC only]*
Cattails *[AC only]*
   UF Typha
Cattle *[S] (May add geog subd)*
   NT Texas longhorn cattle
Cattle drives *(May add geog subd)*
Cattle egret *(May add geog subd)*
   BT Herons
Cattle trade *(May add geog subd)*
Caughley porcelain
Caulfield, Holden (Fictitious character) *(Not subd geog)*
Cauthen, Steve, 1960-
Cavalry *(May add geog subd)*
Cavasos, Juana, d. 1906
Cave animals *(May add geog subd)*
   UF Cave fauna
Cave bears *(May add geog subd)*
Cave drawings *[AC, S] (May add geog subd)*
   UF Cave-drawings
   RT Picture-writing
Cave dwellers *[S]*
   UF Cave-dwellers
Cave dwellings
   UF Cave-dwellings
Cave fauna
   USE Cave animals *[AC only]*
Cave paintings *(May add geog subd)*
Caves *[S] (May add geog subd)*
   RT Speleology
Caving *(May add geog subd)*
   UF Spelunking
Cayce, Edgar, 1877-1945
Caylor, H.W., 1867-1932
Cayuga Indians
Cayuse Indians
CDROM
   USE CD-ROMs
Cedar *(May add geog subd)*
Ceilings *(May add geog subd)*
Celebrations
   USE Holidays
Celebrities *[S] (May add geog subd)*
Celia, d. 1855
Celine, Louis-Ferdinand, 1894-1961
Cellini, Benvenuto, 1500-1571
Cells *[S]*
   RT Cytology
Celtic folklore
   USE Folklore, Celtic *[AC only]*

Celtic literature
Celts *[S]*
   —**Folklore**
     USE Folkore, Celtic *[AC only]*
Cement *[S] (May add geog subd)*
Cemeteries *[S] (May add geog subd)*
Censorship *[S] (May add geog subd)*
   RT Prohibited books
   SA *the subdivision* —Censorship
Census *[S]*
   SA *the subdivision* —Census
Centers (Basketball)
Centers for Disease Control
Centipedes *[S] (May add geog subd)*
Central African Republic
Central America *[S]*
Central Americans
Central Europe *[S]*
   UF Europe, Central
Central High School (Little Rock, Ark.)
Central Pacific Railroad
Cepeda, Orlando
Cephalapoda
   USE Cephalapods *[AC only]*
Cephalopods *[AC only] (May add geog subd)*
Ceramic materials *[S] (May add geog subd)*
Ceramic sculpture *(May add geog subd)*
Ceramic teapots *(May add geog subd)*
Ceramics *[S]*
Cercopithecus *(May add geog subd)*
   BT Primates
Cerberus (Greek mythology)
Cerebral dominance *(May add geog subd)*
   UF Dominance, Cerebral
Cerebral palsied
Cerebral palsy *[S] (May add geog subd)*
Cerebrovascular disease *(May add geog subd)*
Ceremonies
   USE Rites and ceremonies
   SA *the subdivision* —Rites and ceremonies
Ceres (Roman deity)
Cervantes Saavedra, Miguel de, 1547-1616
Cervantes Saavedra, Miguel de, 1547-1616. Don Quixote
Cervidae
Cesarean section *(May add geog subd)*
Cesnola, Luigi Palma di, 1832-1904
Cetacea
   USE Cetaceans *[AC only]*
Cetaceans *[AC only] (May add geog subd)*
   UF Cetacea
Cetewayo, King of Zululand, ca. 1826-1884
Cézanne, Paul, 1839-1906
Chad *(Not subd geog)*
Chaga (African people)
Chagall, Marc, 1887-
Chain saws
Chain stores *[S] (May add geog subd)*
Chair caning *[S] (May add geog subd)*
Chairs *(May add geog subd)*
Chaka, Zulu chief, 1787?-1828
Chalk-talks
Challenger (Spacecraft)
Challenger, Professor (Fictitious character) *(Not subd geog)*
Chamberlain, Henrietta
Chamberlain, Wilt, 1936-

Chambers, Whittaker
Chambers of commerce
 USE Boards of trade
Chameleons *[S]*
 RT Anoles
Champion, Don F.
Champlain, Samuel de, 1567-1635
Chancellorsville, Battle of, 1863
Chaney, John
Change
Chanson de Roland
Chaotic behavior in systems
Chapelle, Dickey, 1919-1965
Chaplin, Charlie, 1889-1977
Chapman, John
 USE Appleseed, Johnny, 1774-1845
Character jugs *(May add geog subd)*
Character steins *(May add geog subd)*
Characters and characteristics in literature *[S]*
 SA *the subdivision* —Characters
Charades *[S]*
Charcoal drawing *(May add geog subd)*
Chardin, Jean Baptiste Siméon, 1669-1779
Charitable uses, trusts, and foundations *(May add geog subd)*
Charities *[S] (May add geog subd)*
 SA *the subdivision* —Charities
Charity *[S]*
Charlemagne, Emperor, 742-814
Charles, Edward, 1757-1828
Charles, Prince of Wales, 1948-
Charles, Ray, 1930-
Charles Edward, Prince, grandson of James II, King of England, 1720-1788
Charles I, Emperor of Austria, 1887-1922
Charles I, King of England, 1600-1649
Charles II, King of England, 1630-1685
Charles V, Holy Roman Emperor, 1500-1558
Charleston (S.C.)
Charlottesville (Va.)
Charms *[S] (May add geog subd)*
Charrière, Henri, 1906-1973
Chartres (France)
Charts, diagrams, etc.
Chase County (Kan.)
Chasmosaurus *(May add geog subd)*
 BT Dinosaurs
Château-Thierry, Battle of, 1918
Chaucer, Geoffrey, d. 1400
Chaucer, Geoffrey, d. 1400. Canterbury tales
Chavez, Cesar, 1927-
Checkers *[S]*
Chee, Jim (Fictitious character) *(Not subd geog)*
Cheerleading *[S]*
Cheese *[S] (May add geog subd)*
Cheesecake (Cookery)
Cheetah
Cheever, John
Chekhov, Anton Pavlovich, 1860-1904. Cherry orchard *[AC only]*
 UF Chekhov, Anton Pavlovich, 1860-1904. Vishnevyi sad
Chekhov, Anton Pavlovich, 1860-1904. Vishnevyi sad
 USE Chekhov, Anton Pavlovich, 1860-1904. Cherry orchard *[AC only]*
Chelly, Canyon de (Ariz.)
 UF Canyon de Chelly (Ariz.)

Chelm (Chelm, Poland) *[AC only]*
Chelsea porcelain
Chemical bonds
Chemical elements *[S]*
Chemical engineering *[S] (May add geog subd)*
Chemical industry *[S] (May add geog subd)*
Chemical reactions *[S]*
 NT Polymerization
Chemical warfare *[S] (May add geog subd)*
 SA *the subdivision* —Chemical warfare
Chemicals *[S] (May add geog subd)*
Chemistry *[S] (May add geog subd)*
Chemistry, Organic *[S] (May add geog subd)*
Chemistry, Physical and theoretical
Chemistry, Technical *[S]*
 NT Workshop recipes
Chemistry experiments
Chemists *[S]*
 NT Women chemists
Chemotherapy *[S] (May add geog subd)*
 UF Drug therapy
Chennault, Claire Lee, 1890-1958
Cher, 1946-
Chernobyl Nuclear Accident, Chornobyl', Ukraine, 1986
Cherokee County, (Tex.)
Cherokee Indians
Cherokee Removal, 1838
 USE Trail of Tears, 1838
Cherry *[S] (May add geog subd)*
Cherry, Fred V.
Chesapeake Bay (Md. and Va.)
Chesapeake Bay Region (Md. and Va.)
Chess *[S] (May add geog subd)*
Chest pain *(May add geog subd)*
Chests *(May add geog subd)*
Chevrolet automobile *(May add geog subd)*
Cheyenne Indians
Ch'i (Chinese philosophy)
Ch'i kung *(May add geog subd)*
 BT Exercise
Chiang, Kai-shek, 1887-1975
Chicago (Ill.) *[S]*
—Fire, 1871
Chicago American Indian Center
Chicago Bears (Football team)
Chicago Bulls (Basketball team)
Chicago Cubs (Baseball team)
Chicago Historical Society
Chicago Tribune
Chicago White Sox (Baseball team)
Chicken pox
 USE Chickenpox
    Varicella
Chickenpox *(May add geog subd)*
Chickens *[S] (May add geog subd)*
 UF Chicks *[AC only]*
    Hens
 RT Poultry
Chicks
 USE Chickens *[AC only]*
Chief executive officers
Child, Lydia Maria Francis, 1802-1880
Child abuse *[S] (May add geog subd)*
 BT Family violence
 RT Child sexual abuse
    Incest

Child analysis *(May add geog subd)*
Child and parent
   USE Parent and child
Child care *[S] (May add geog subd)*
Child care centers
   USE Day care centers
Child care services *(May add geog subd)*
Child development *[S] (May add geog subd)*
Child health services *(May add geog subd)*
Child molesting
   USE Child sexual abuse
   RT Child abuse
         Incest
Child prostitution *(May add geog subd)*
   UF Juvenile prostitution
         Prostitution, Juvenile
Child psychiatry *[S] (May add geog subd)*
Child psychology *[S] (May add geog subd)*
Child psychopathology *(May add geog subd)*
Child psychotherapy *(May add geog subd)*
Child rearing *[S] (May add geog subd)*
   UF Children—Management
Child sexual abuse *[S] (May add geog subd)*
   UF Child molesting
Child support *[S] (May add geog subd)*
Child welfare *[S] (May add geog subd)*
Childbirth *[S] (May add geog subd)*
   Use for works on human birth. Works on birth in general or on animal birth in particular are entered under Birth. *[AC only]*
   BT Reproduction
   RT Birth
Childbirth at home *(May add geog subd)*
Children *[S]*
   SA *the subdivision* —Children
   —Foreign countries
      UF Children in foreign countries
   —Growth
   —Health and hygiene
      USE Pediatrics
   —Management
      USE Child rearing
   —Preparation for medical care
Children, Abandoned
   USE Abandoned children
Children, Adopted
Children, Blind
Children, Deaf
Children, Missing
   USE Missing children
Children, Poor
   USE Poor children
Children, Problematic
   USE Problem children
Children and adults *[S]*
   RT Parent and child
Children and death
   RT Bereavement
         Death
Children and mothers
   USE Mother and child
Children and politics
Children and strangers
   USE Strangers *[AC only]*
Children as actors
Children as artists

Children as authors
Children in art *[S] (Not subd geog)*
Children of alcoholics *[S]*
Children of divorced parents *[S]*
Children of entertainers
Children of handicapped parents
Children of Holocaust survivors
Children of immigrants
Children of interracial marriage
Children of military personnel
Children of narcotic addicts
Children of the mentally ill
Children of presidents
Children of working parents *[S]*
   NT Latchkey children
Children's clothing *[S]*
Children's Crusade, 1212
Children's drama
   USE Plays
   SA *the subdivision* —Drama
Children's encyclopedias
   USE Encyclopedias and dictionaries
Children's libraries *(May add geog subd)*
   UF Libraries, Children's
   —Book selection
Children's literature *[S] (May add geog subd)*
   UF Children's stories
   BT Literature
   RT Books—Class sets
   —Technique
Children's literature, American *(May add geog subd)*
Children's literature, Canadian *(May add geog subd)*
Children's literature, Danish *(May add geog subd)*
Children's literature, English *(May add geog subd)*
Children's literature, French *(May add geog subd)*
Children's literature, Latin American *(May add geog subd)*
Children's literature in series
Children's parties
   USE Parties *[AC only]*
Children's plays
   USE Plays *[AC only]*
   SA *the subdivision* —Drama
Children's poems
   USE Poetry *[AC only]*
Children's poetry
   USE Poetry *[AC only]*
Children's rights
Children's songs
   USE Songs *[AC only]*
Children's stories
   USE Children's literature
Children's Theatre Company (Minneapolis, Minn.)
Children's writings *[S]*
Chile
Chilean poetry *(May add geog subd)*
Chileans
Chimera (Greek mythology)
Chimney sweeps
Chimney swift
   UF Swallow, Chimney
   BT Swifts
Chimneys *[S] (May add geog subd)*
Chimpanzees *[S] (May add geog subd)*
Chimpanzees as laboratory animals
Chimpanzees as pets *[AC only]*
Chin, Tiffany, 1967-

China [S]
—Description and travel
— —To 1900 (Not subd geog)
—History [S]
— —221 B.C.-960 A.D.
— —Ch'in dynasty, 221-207 B.C.
— —Yuan dynasty, 1260-1368
— —Ming dynasty, 1368-1644
— —Li Tzu ch'eng Rebellion, 1628-1645
— —Tatar Conquest, 1643-1644
— —Ch'ing dynasty, 1644-1912
— —Taiping Rebellion, 1850-1864
— —Boxer Rebellion, 1899-1901
— —20th century
— —Revolution, 1911-1912
— —Republic, 1912-1949
— —1937-1945
— —1949- [S]
— —1949-1976 [S]
— —1976- [S]
— —Tiananmen Square Incident, 1989
—Politics and government
— —1949-
— —1976-
China Air Force American Volunteer Group
China painting [S] (May add geog subd)
China trade art (May add geog subd)
China trade porcelain (May add geog subd)
Chinatown (New York, N.Y.)
Chinatown (San Francisco, Calif.)
Chinchillas (May add geog subd)
Chincoteague Island (Va.)
Chincoteague pony (May add geog subd)
Chinese
Chinese American women
Chinese Americans [S]
—Folklore
USE Folklore, Chinese American [AC only]
Chinese characters (May add geog subd)
Chinese language [S] (May add geog subd)
—Readers [AC only]
Use for reading texts in Chinese containing materials for instruction and practice in reading that language.
RT Chinese language materials [AC only]
Chinese language materials [AC only]
Use for works written in Chinese intended primarily for general information or recreational reading. Such works with text also given in English are further subdivided by the subdivision —Bilingual.
RT Chinese language—Readers [AC only]
—Bilingual [AC only]
Chinese literature (May add geog subd)
Chinese medicine
USE Medicine, Chinese
Chinese New Year (May add geog subd)
Chinese poetry (May add geog subd)
Ching, Lucy
Chinook salmon [S] (May add geog subd)
Chipmunks [S]
Chippewa Indians
USE Ojibwa Indians
Chippewa language [S] (May add geog subd)
—Readers [AC only]
Use for reading texts in Chippewa containing materials for instruction and practice in reading that language.
RT Chippewa language materials [AC only]

Chippewa language materials [AC only]
Use for works written in Chippewa intended primarily for general information or recreational reading. Such works with text also given in English are further subdivided by the subdivision —Bilingual.
RT Chippewa language—Readers [AC only]
—Bilingual [AC only]
Chiropractic [S] (May add geog subd)
Chisholm, Jesse
Chisholm, Shirley, 1924-
Chisholm Trail
Chisum, John Simpson, 1824-1884
Chivalry [S]
Use for nonfiction works only. Works of fiction are entered under Knights and knighthood—Fiction. [AC only]
—Fiction
USE Knights and knighthood—Fiction [AC only]
Chivington, John M. (Milton), 1821-1894
Chlorofluorocarbons
Chocolate [S] (May add geog subd)
Choctaw Indians
Choice [AC only]
UF Choice (Psychology)
Choice of college
USE College, Choice of
Choirs (Music) [S] (May add geog subd)
Cholera [S] (May add geog subd)
Cholesterol
RT Blood cholesterol
Cholistan Desert (Pakistan)
Chonrichthyes
USE Cartilaginous fishes [AC only]
Chopin, Frédéric, 1810-1849
Chopin, Kate, 1851-1904
Chopstix Dim Sum Café
Choral music [S] (May add geog subd)
Choral recitations
Choral speaking [S]
Chordata
USE Chordates [AC only]
Chordates [AC only]
UF Chordata
Choreographers
Choruses, Sacred
Chou, En-lai, 1898-1976
Chow chows (Dogs)
BT Dogs
Chowcilla (Calif.)
Christ
USE Jesus Christ
Christian art and symbolism [S] (May add geog subd)
Christian biography
USE Religious leaders
RT Missionaries
Christian education [S] (May add geog subd)
Christian ethics [S] (May add geog subd)
Christian fiction
USE Christian life—Fiction [AC only]
Christian life [S]
Use for works on the effect of Christian religions on everyday life. [AC only]
—Fiction [AC only]
UF Christian fiction
Christian literature (May add geog subd)
Christian martyrs
Christian poetry

Christian saints
　　USE　Saints [AC only]
Christian Science [S] (May add geog subd)
Christian sects
　　USE　Sects [AC only]
Christianity [S] (May add geog subd)
　　BT　Religions
　—History
　　　UF　Church history [AC only]
　— —**Primitive and early church, ca. 30-600**
　— —**Middle ages, 600-1500**
Christianity and culture
Christianity and other religions
Christianity and politics [S] (May add geog subd)
Christie, Agatha, 1890-1976
Christmas [S] (May add geog subd)
　—**Drama** [AC only]
　　　UF　Christmas plays
　—**Fiction** [AC only]
　　　UF　Christmas stories
　—**Poetry** [AC only]
　　　UF　Christmas poetry
　—**Prayer books and devotions** [AC only]
Christmas carols
　　USE　Carols
　　　　　Christmas music
Christmas plays
　　USE　Christmas—Drama [AC only]
Christmas poetry
　　USE　Christmas—Poetry [AC only]
Christmas stories
　　USE　Christmas—Fiction [AC only]
Christmas cookery
Christmas decorations [S] (May add geog subd)
Christmas in art
Christmas music
Christmas plays (May add geog subd)
Christmas trees [S] (May add geog subd)
Christ's Hospital (London, England)
Chromium in human nutrition
Chronic diseases (May add geog subd)
Chronic fatigue syndrome (May add geog subd)
Chronic renal failure (May add geog subd)
Chronically ill
Chronobiology (May add geog subd)
Chronologies
　　USE　Chronology, Historical
Chronology [AC, S]
　　RT　Chronology, Historical
　　NT　Morning
　　SA　the subdivision —Chronology
Chronology, Historical
　　UF　Chronologies
　　　　　Dates, Historical
　　　　　Timelines
Chrysler Corporation
Chumash Indians (May add geog subd)
Chumash language (May add geog subd)
Chung, Connie
Church
Church and education [S] (May add geog subd)
　　RT　Religion in the public schools
Church and state [S] (May add geog subd)
Church architecture (May add geog subd)
Church buildings (May add geog subd)

　　UF　Churches
Church controversies
Church decoration and ornament (May add geog subd)
Church history
　　USE　Christianity—History [AC only]
　　SA　the subdivision —Church history
Church membership (May add geog subd)
Church of England [S] (May add geog subd)
Church of God (May add geog subd)
Church of Jesus Christ of Latter-Day Saints [S] (May add geog subd)
　　BT　Mormon Church
　　RT　Book of Mormon
Church of Scientology (Los Angeles, Calif.)
Church pennants
Church records and registers (May add geog subd)
Church renewal
Church schools (May add geog subd)
　　NT　Sunday schools
Church work with the poor (May add geog subd)
Church work with youth [S] (May add geog subd)
Church year (May add geog subd)
Churches
　　USE　Church buildings
Churchill, Clementine, Lady, 1885-1977
Churchill, Randolph Spencer, Lady, 1854-1921
Churchill, Sarah, 1914-1981
Churchill, Winston, Sir, 1620?-1688
Churchill, Winston, Sir, 1874-1964
Churchill family
Ciardi, John, 1916-
Cibola, Seven cities of
Cicada [S]
Cicero, Marcus Tullius
Cid, ca. 1043-1099
Cigarette habit (May add geog subd)
Cigarette industry (May add geog subd)
Cigarette smokers (May add geog subd)
Cigarettes [S]
Ciliata
　　USE　Ciliates [AC only]
Ciliates [AC only]
　　UF　Ciliata
Cincinnati Bengals (Football team)
Cincinnati (Ohio)
Cincinnati Reds (Baseball team)
Cinco de Mayo, Battle of, 1862
Cinco de Mayo (Mexican holiday)
Cinderella (Tale) (May add geog subd)
Cinematography
Cipher and telegraph codes [S]
Ciphers [S]
　—**Fiction** [AC only]
　　　UF　Cipher stories
　　　　　Code and cipher stories
　　　　　Code stories
　　　　　Cryptogram stories
　　　BT　Mystery and detective stories [AC only]
Circle songs
Circle
Circuit training (May add geog subd)
Circulatory system [AC only]
　　UF　Cardiovascular system
Circumcision (May add geog subd)

Circus *[S] (May add geog subd)*
  —**Fiction** *[AC only]*
     UF   Circus stories
Circus stories
    USE   Circus—Fiction *[AC only]*
Circus animals *(May add geog subd)*
Circus owners
Circus in art
Cisneros, Henry
Cities and towns *[S] (May add geog subd)*
    RT   Local government
Cities and towns, Ancient
    USE   Extinct cities
Cities and towns, Medieval *(May add geog subd)*
Cities and towns, Ruined, extinct, etc.
    USE   Extinct cities
          Ghost towns
Cities and towns in art
Cities and towns in literature
Citizen GSX-140 Plus dot matrix printer
Citizen Kane (Motion picture)
Citizens band radio *[S] (May add geog subd)*
Citizenship *[S] (May add geog subd)*
    RT   Civics
    SA *the subdivision* —Citizen participation
City and town life *(May add geog subd)*
City council members
City halls *(May add geog subd)*
City planners
City planning *[S] (May add geog subd)*
City traffic *[S] (May add geog subd)*
Civics
    RT   Citizenship
          Political science
Civil defense *[S]*
Civil engineering *[S] (May add geog subd)*
Civil law *(May add geog subd)*
Civil procedure *(May add geog subd)*
Civil rights *[S] (May add geog subd)*
    SA *the subdivision* —Civil rights
Civil rights movements *(May add geog subd)*
Civil rights workers
Civil service *[S] (May add geog subd)*
Civil service positions *(May add geog subd)*
Civil War
    USE   United States—History—Civil War, 1861-1865
Civilization *[S]*
    RT   Animals and civilization
          Science and civilization
    SA *the subdivision* —Civilization
  —**Indian influences**
Civilization and technology
    USE   Technology and civilization
Civilization, Aegean
Civilization, Ancient *[S]*
Civilization, Anglo-Saxon
Civilization, Arab *[S]*
Civilization, Assyro-Babylonian
Civilization, Celtic
Civilization, Christian
Civilization, Classical
Civilization, Greco-Roman
Civilization, Islamic
Civilization, Medieval *[S]*
    NT   Twelfth century
Civilization, Modern *[S]*

  —**Roman influences**
  —**1950-** *[S]*
  —**20th century**
Civilization, Mycenaean
Civilization, Oriental
Civilization, Western
  —**Roman influences**
Clairmont, Clara Mary Jane, 1798-1879
Clairvoyance *[S]*
Clallam Indians
Clams *(May add geog subd)*
Clans *[S] (May add geog subd)*
Clapton, Eric, 1945-
Clarinet *[S]*
Clarisworks (Computer program)
Clark, Charlotte Moon, Mrs., 1829-1895
    USE   Clay, Charles M., 1829-1895
Clark, Eugenie, 1917-
Clark, George Rogers, 1752-1818
Clark, Kenneth, 1903-1983
Clark, Septima Poinsette, 1898-1987
Clark, William, 1770-1838
Clarke, Arthur Charles, 1917-
Clarke, Bobby, 1949-
Classical antiquities *[S]*
Classical drama *(May add geog subd)*
Classical geography
Classical literature *[S]*
    BT   Literature
Classicism *(May add geog subd)*
Classicism in art *(May add geog subd)*
Classification
    SA *the subdivision* —Classification
  —**Books** *[S]*
    RT   Subject headings
Classification, Dewey decimal
Classroom environment *(May add geog subd)*
Classroom management *[S] (May add geog subd)*
Claudius, Emperor of Rome, 10 B.C.-54 A.D.
Clay *[S] (May add geog subd)*
Clay, Charles M., 1829-1895
    UF   Clark, Charlotte Moon, Mrs., 1829-1895
Clay, Henry, 1777-1852
Clay industries *[S] (May add geog subd)*
Clay modeling *[AC only]*
    BT   Modeling
Clayton, Billy
Cleaner fish *[AC only]*
    UF   Blue-streaked cleaner wrasse
          Labroides dimidiatus
Cleaning *[S]*
Cleanliness *[AC only]*
    UF   Dirtiness
          Hygiene
          Messiness
          Neatness
          Tidiness
          Untidiness
    BT   Health *[AC only]*
          Sanitation *[AC only]*
    RT   Grooming *[AC only]*
          Orderliness *[AC only]*
    NT   Baths *[AC only]*
Cleary, Beverly
Cleft lip *(May add geog subd)*

Cleft palate *(May add geog subd)*
Clemenceau, Georges, 1841-1929
Clemens, Roger
Clemens, Samuel Langhorne, 1835-1910
   USE Twain, Mark, 1835-1910
Clemens, Susy, 1872-1896
Clemente, Roberto, 1934-1972
Cleopatra, Queen of Egypt, d. 30 B.C.
Clergy *[S]*
   SA the subdivision —Clergy
Clerical ability and aptitude tests
Clerks of court
Cleveland, Barbara Villiers Palmer, Duchess of, 1641-1709
Cleveland, Grover, 1837-1908
Cleveland Browns (Football team)
Cleveland Cavaliers (Basketball team)
Cleveland Indians (Baseball team)
Cleverness
   USE Problem solving
Cliburn, Van, 1934-
Clicquot-Ponsardin, Barbe-Nicole, 1777-1866
Cliff dwellers *[AC only]*
   UF Cliff-dwellers
Cliff-dwellers
   USE Cliff dwellers *[AC only]*
Cliff dwellings *[AC usage] (May add geog subd)*
   UF Cliff-dwellings
Cliff-dwellings
   USE Cliff dwellings *[AC only]*
Clift, Montgomery
Climatic changes *(May add geog subd)*
Climatology
   UF Climate
   SA the subdivision —Climate
Climate
   USE Climatology
Climbing plants *[S] (May add geog subd)*
Clinton, Bill, 1946-
Clip art *(May add geog subd)*
Clipper ships *[AC, S] (May add geog subd)*
   UF Clipper-ships
Clipper-ships
   USE Clipper ships *[AC only]*
Cloaks
Clock and watch makers
Clock and watch making *(May add geog subd)*
Clocks and watches *[S] (May add geog subd)*
Cloisonné
   BT Art metalwork *[AC only]*
       Enamel and enameling
Clones of IBM computers
   USE IBM-compatible computers
Clones of Macintosh computers
   USE Macintosh-compatible computers
Cloning
   BT Genetic engineering
Close air support
Close corporations *(May add geog subd)*
Closed captioned video recordings
   USE Video recordings for the hearing impaired
Closed ecological systems (Space environment)
Closing of factories
   USE Plant shutdowns
Clothing and dress *[S]*
Clothing trade *[S] (May add geog subd)*
Clouds *[S] (May add geog subd)*

Clowning *(May add geog subd)*
Clowns *[S]*
Clubs *[S] (May add geog subd)*
   SA the subdivisions —Clubs, —Societies and clubs, *and* —Societies, etc.
Clum, John Philip, 1851-1932
Clyde, 1909-1934
Coast changes *(May add geog subd)*
Coast Guard
   USE United States. Coast Guard
Coast Salish Indians
Coastal surveillance *(May add geog subd)*
Co-dependence (Psychology)
   USE Codependency
Codependency
   UF Co-dependence (Psychology)
Coaching (Athletics) *[S]*
   SA the subdivisions —Coaches *and* —Coaching
Coal *[S] (May add geog subd)*
Coal mines and mining *[S] (May add geog subd)*
Coal miners
   —Pennsylvania
       NT Molly Maguires
Coalbrookdale (England)
Coastal ecology *(May add geog subd)*
Coastal zone management *(May add geog subd)*
Coasts *(May add geog subd)*
Coatis *[S]*
Coats
Cobb, Ty, 1886-1961
COBOL (Computer program language)
Cobras *[S] (May add geog subd)*
Coca-Cola Company
Cocaine *[S]*
Cocaine habit *(May add geog subd)*
Cocaine industry *(May add geog subd)*
Cochise, Apache chief, d. 1874
Cochiti Indians
Cochiti Pueblo (N.M.)
Cochran, Jacqueline
Cochrane, Elizabeth, 1867-1922
Cockatiel *[S]*
Cockatoos
   BT Parrots
Cocker spaniels *[S]*
Cockroaches *[S] (May add geog subd)*
Cocoa Beach (Fla.)
Code and cipher stories
   USE Ciphers—Fiction *[AC only]*
Code stories
   USE Ciphers—Fiction *[AC only]*
Codependence
   USE Codependency
Codependency *[S] (May add geog subd)*
   UF Codependence
Coding, Product
   USE Product coding
Coelacanth
Coelenterata
   USE Coelenterates *[AC only]*
Coelenterates *[AC only] (May add geog subd)*
   UF Coelenterata
Coeur, Jacques, 1395-1456
Coffee *[S] (May add geog subd)*
Coffin, John (Fictitious character) *(Not subd geog)*

Cognition
  UF Theory of knowledge
  NT Cognitive styles
  RT Intellect
      Personality and cognition
Cognition in animals
Cognitive learning *(May add geog subd)*
Cognitive psychology *(May add geog subd)*
Cognitive styles
  UF Learning styles
  BT Cognition
      Intellect
      Personality and cognition
Cognitive therapy *(May add geog subd)*
Cohen, S.T.
Coincidence
Coinage *[S] (May add geog subd)*
Coins *[S]*
  UF Numismatics
 —Collectors and collecting *[AC only]*
Coins, Greek *(May add geog subd)*
Coins as an investment
Colbert, Edwin Harris, 1905-
Cold *[S] (May add geog subd)*
Cold (Disease) *[S] (May add geog subd)*
  UF Common cold
Cold-blooded animals *[AC only]*
  UF Poikilotherms
Cold Comfort Farm Society
Cold Harbor, Battle of, 1864
Cold War
Cole, Nat King, 1917-1965
Cole, Richie
Cole, Thomas, 1801-1848
Coleman, Thomas, 1945-
Coleman, Wayne Carl
Coleridge, Samuel Taylor, 1772-1834
Coleridge, Samuel Taylor, 1772-1834.   Rime of the ancient mariner
Colette, 1873-1954
Collage *[S] (May add geog subd)*
Collagen diseases
Collared peccary *(May add geog subd)*
Collectibles *(May add geog subd)*
Collecting of accounts *[S] (May add geog subd)*
Collection agents *(May add geog subd)*
Collection laws *(May add geog subd)*
Collective bargaining *[S] (May add geog subd)*
Collective settlements *[AC, S] (May add geog subd)*
  RT Kibbutzim
 —China
    UF Communes (China)
Collectors and collecting *[S] (May add geog subd)*
  SA the subdivision —Collectors and collecting
College, Choice of
  USE College choice
College administrators
College applications *[S] (May add geog subd)*
College choice *[S] (May add geog subd)*
  UF College, Choice of
College admission
  USE Universities and colleges—Admission
College and school drama *[S]*
College costs *[S] (May add geog subd)*
College Entrance Examination Board.   College-Level Examination Program

College graduates
College-level examinations *(May add geog subd)*
College readers
College sports *[S] (May add geog subd)*
College stories
  USE Universities and colleges—Fiction *[AC only]*
College student orientation *(May add geog subd)*
College students *[S]*
College teaching *(May add geog subd)*
  BT Teaching
Colleges and universities
  USE Universities and colleges
  SA the names of specific universities and colleges
Collies *[S] (May add geog subd)*
Collin County (Tex.)
Collingsworth County (Tex.)
Collins, Judy, 1939-
Collins, Michael, 1930-
Collins, Wilkie, 1824-1889
Collinsworth, Millicent
Collisions (Physics)
Collodi, Carlo, 1826-1890
Colombia
Colomoncagua (Honduras : Refugee camp)
Colón, Fernando, 1488-1539
  USE Columbus, Ferdinand, 1488-1539
Colonial Williamsburg, Inc.
Colonization *[S]*
  SA the subdivisions —Colonies and —Colonization
Color *[AC, S] (May add geog subd)*
  UF Colors
  SA the subdivisions —Color and —Coloring
Color computer graphics
Color drawing *(May add geog subd)*
Color in art *[S]*
Color of animals
Color of man
Color photography *[S]*
Color prints *[S]*
Color variation (Biology) *[AC only]*
  UF Color-variation (Biology)
Color-variation (Biology)
  USE Color variation (Biology) *[AC only]*
Color vision *(May add geog subd)*
Colorado
 —Social life and customs
 — —19th century *[AC only]*
Colorado River
Colorado River Watershed (Colo.-Mex.)
Colors
  USE Color *[AC only]*
Colostomy *(May add geog subd)*
Colt, Samuel, 1814-1862
Colt firearms
Columba, Saint, 521-597
Columban, Saint, 543-615
Columbo, Lieutenant (Fictitious character) *(Not subd geog)*
Columbus, Christopher
Columbus, Ferdinand, 1488-1539
  UF Colón, Fernando, 1488-1539
Columbus Day
Coma *(May add geog subd)*
Comanche County (Okla.)
Comanche Indians
Comaneci, Nadia, 1961-
Combat

Combs, Ann, 1935-
Comedians *[S]*
Comedy *[S]*
    SA *the subdivision* —Comedies
Comedy films *[S] (May add geog subd)*
Comedy programs *(May add geog subd)*
Comets *[S]*
Comic art paraphernalia *(May add geog subd)*
Comic books, strips, etc.
    USE Cartoons and comics *[AC only]*
Coming out (Sexual orientation) *(May add geog subd)*
Commemorative porcelain *(May add geog subd)*
Commemorative pottery *(May add geog subd)*
Commerce *[S]*
    SA *the subdivisions* —Commerce *and* —Commercial policy
Commercial art *[S] (May add geog subd)*
Commercial crimes *(May add geog subd)*
Commercial correspondence
Commercial geography
Commercial law *[S] (May add geog subd)*
Commercial loans *(May add geog subd)*
Commercial photography *(May add geog subd)*
    UF Photography, Commercial
Commercial products *[S] (May add geog subd)*
Commercial products in art
Commercial statistics
Commodore computers
Commodore VIC 20 computer
Commodore 64 (Computer)
Common cold
    USE Cold (Disease)
Commonwealth countries *[S]*
    UF Commonwealth of Nations
Commonwealth of Nations
    USE Commonwealth countries
Commonwealth literature (English)
Communal living *(May add geog subd)*
    UF Counter culture
Communes (China)
    USE Collective settlements—China *[AC only]*
Communicable diseases *[S] (May add geog subd)*
Communication *[S] (May add geog subd)*
    NT Nonverbal communication (Psychology)
          Oral communication
Communication in art *[S]*
Communication in marriage *(May add geog subd)*
Communication in politics *(May add geog subd)*
Communication in sex *(May add geog subd)*
Communication in the family *(May add geog subd)*
Communications software
Communicative disorders in old age *(May add geog subd)*
Communism *[S] (May add geog subd)*
    RT Socialism
Communism and religion *[S]*
Communist Party of the United States of America
Communists
Community
Community colleges *(May add geog subd)*
    RT Junior colleges
Community development *[S]*
Community health services *[S] (May add geog subd)*
Community leadership *(May add geog subd)*
Community life *[S]*
Community services
    USE Municipal services
Compact disc players *[S] (May add geog subd)*

Comparative education
Comparative government *[S]*
Comparative grammar
    USE Grammar, Comparative and general
Comparative government *[S]*
Comparative linguistics
    SA *the subdivision* —Comparison
Comparative literature
    USE Literature, Comparative
Comparative psychology
    USE Psychology, Comparative
Compass *[S]*
Compensation management *(May add geog subd)*
Competition (Psychology)
    SA *the subdivision* —Competitions
Competition, International
    UF International competition
Complex carbohydrate diet *(May add geog subd)*
Composers *[S]*
Composition (Art) *[S]*
Composition (Language arts)
    UF works in or about more than one language
          Composition (Rhetoric)
          Writing (Composition)
          Written composition
    SA *the subdivision* —Composition and exercises *under*
          individual languages, and the heading Written
          communication
Composition (Music) *[S]*
Composition (Rhetoric)
    USE Composition (Language arts)
Compost *[S] (May add geog subd)*
Compson, Caddy (Fictitious character) *(Not subd geog)*
Compulsive behavior *[S] (May add geog subd)*
Compulsive eaters
Compulsive shopping *(May add geog subd)*
Computer-aided design *(May add geog subd)*
Computer animation
Computer art *[S] (May add geog subd)*
Computer-assisted instruction *(May add geog subd)*
Computer bulletin boards *[S]*
Computer crimes *[S] (May add geog subd)*
Computer drawing
Computer engineers
Computer engineering *(May add geog subd)*
Computer files
Computer furniture *(May add geog subd)*
Computer games *[S] (May add geog subd)*
Computer graphics *[S]*
Computer industry *(May add geog subd)*
Computer input-output equipment *(May add geog subd)*
Computer integrated manufacturing systems *(May add geog subd)*
Computer interfaces *[S]*
Computer literacy *[S] (May add geog subd)*
Computer managed instruction *(May add geog subd)*
Computer music *[S] (May add geog subd)*
Computer networks *[S] (May add geog subd)*
Computer programmers
Computer programs
    BT Computer software
    NT Electronic spreadsheets
          Emulators (Computer programs)
          Integrated software
          Word processing

SA *the names of specific computer programs and the sub-
divisions* —Computer programs *and* —Programming
Computer science *[S] (May add geog subd)*
Computer science literature *(May add geog subd)*
Computer security *(May add geog subd)*
Computer software *[S]*
   NT Computer programs
         Integrated software
Computer storage devices *[S]*
Computer sound processing *[S]*
Computer viruses *[S]*
Computerized instruments *(May add geog subd)*
Computerized typesetting
ComputerLand (Firm)
Computers *[S] (May add geog subd)*
   UF Electronic digital computers *[AC only]*
   RT Automation
         Calculators
         Data processing
         Robotics
  —Programming
     USE Programming (Computers)
Computers and civilization *[S]*
Comstock Lode (Nev.)
Concentration camps *[S] (May add geog subd)*
Conception
Concepts *[S]*
Concessions *(May add geog subd)*
Concerts *[S] (May add geog subd)*
Concord, Battle of, 1775
Concord (Mass.)
Concrete *[S]*
Concrete construction *[S] (May add geog subd)*
  —Formwork
Condensation
Condensed matter
Condiments *(May add geog subd)*
Condominiums *[S] (May add geog subd)*
Condoms *(May add geog subd)*
Condors *[S] (May add geog subd)*
Conduct of life *[AC only]*
    Use for works on moral and ethical values in everyday life.
   BT Ethics
         Life skills
   RT Behavior *[AC only]*
   NT Selfishness *[AC only]*
Conductors (Music) *[S]*
Cone
   BT Geometry, Solid
Confectionery *[S] (May add geog subd)*
Confederate States of America *[S]*
Confederate States of America. Army
Confession
   USE Forgiveness of sin
Confidential communications *(May add geog subd)*
Conflict (Psychology)
Conflict management *(May add geog subd)*
   BT Negotiation
Conflict of generations *[S] (May add geog subd)*
   UF Counter culture
Confucianism *[S] (May add geog subd)*
Confucius
Conglomerate corporations *[S] (May add geog subd)*
Congo (Brazzaville)
Congo River
Conjuring

   USE Magic tricks *[AC only]*
Conic sections
   RT Ellipse
         Parabola
   NT Hyperbola
Conifers *(May add geog subd)*
Conjugal violence *(May add geog subd)*
Connally, John Bowden, 1917-
Connecticut
Conniff, George, d. 1935
Connor, Brian Joseph
Connors, Jimmy, 1952-
Conquerors
Conrad, Joseph, 1857-1924
Conscientious objectors
Consciousness *[S]*
Conservation of natural resources *[AC, S] (May add geog subd)*
   UF Nature conservation
Conservation of water
   USE Water conservation
Conservationists
Conservatism *[S] (May add geog subd)*
Conservatories *(May add geog subd)*
Consolation *[S]*
Consolidation and merger of corporations *(May add geog subd)*
   UF Corporate mergers
Conspiracies *(May add geog subd)*
Conspiracy *(May add geog subd)*
Constable, John, 1776-1837
Constellations
Constitution (Frigate)
Constitution (U.S.)
   USE United States—Constitution
   SA *the subdivision* —Constitution
Constitutional history *[S]*
   SA *the subdivision* —Constitutional history
Constitutional law *[S]*
   SA *the subdivision* —Constitutional law
Construction equipment *(May add geog subd)*
Construction industry *(May add geog subd)*
   NT Underground construction
Constructivism (Education)
Consultants *[S]*
Consumer behavior *(May add geog subd)*
Consumer credit *[S] (May add geog subd)*
Consumer education *[S] (May add geog subd)*
Consumer goods *[S] (May add geog subd)*
Consumer price indexes *[S] (May add geog subd)*
Consumer protection *[S] (May add geog subd)*
Consumer satisfaction *(May add geog subd)*
Consumers *[S]*
Consumption (Economics) *(May add geog subd)*
Contact lenses *[S] (May add geog subd)*
Container gardening *[S] (May add geog subd)*
Containers *(May add geog subd)*
   NT Parfleches
         Pitchers
Contemporary Christian music *(May add geog subd)*
Contests *[S] (May add geog subd)*
Continental drift *[S]*
   BT Plate tectonics
Continental shelf *[S]*
Continents *[S] (May add geog subd)*
Continuing education *[S] (May add geog subd)*
Contraception
   USE Birth control *[S, AC]*

Contraceptives *(May add geog subd)*
Contract bridge
   USE   Bridge (Game) *[AC only]*
Contract labor *[S]*
Contractors
Contracts *[S] (May add geog subd)*
Controlled fusion *(May add geog subd)*
Convection (Meteorology) *(May add geog subd)*
Convenience foods *[S] (May add geog subd)*
Convents *[S] (May add geog subd)*
Conversation *[S]*
   SA   *the subdivision* —Conversation and phrase books
Converts from Judaism
Conveying machinery *[S] (May add geog subd)*
Convulsions *(May add geog subd)*
Conway, Jill K., 1934-
Cook, James, 1728-1779
Cook, Stephani, 1944-
Cooke, Alistair, 1908-
Cookery *[AC, S] (May add geog subd)*
   NT   Barbecue cookery
         Brownies (Cookery)
         Casserole cookery
         Cheesecake (Cookery)
         Christmas cookery
         Easter cookery
         Hanukkah cookery
         Holiday cookery
         Microwave cookery
         Passover cookery
         Quantity cookery
         Quick and easy cookery
         Thanksgiving cookery
         Vegetarian cookery
         Wok cookery
—**Apples** *[AC only]*
—**Appetizers** *[AC only]*
—**Bananas** *[AC only]*
—Bean curd *[AC only]*
   USE   Cookery—Tofu *[AC only]*
—**Beans** *[AC only]*
—**Beef** *[AC only]*
—**Buffets** *[AC only]*
   UF   Buffets (Cookery)
—**Butter** *[AC only]*
—**Cereals** *[AC only]*
—**Cheese** *[AC only]*
—**Chicken** *[AC only]*
—**Chocolate** *[AC only]*
—**Coconut** *[AC only]*
—**Coffee** *[AC only]*
—**Cold dishes** *[AC only]*
—**Crabs** *[AC only]*
—**Dairy products** *[AC only]*
—**Desserts** *[AC only]*
—**Ducks** *[AC only]*
—**Eggs** *[AC only]*
—**Fish** *[AC only]*
—**Frankfurters** *[AC only]*
—**Frozen foods** *[AC only]*
—**Fruit** *[AC only]*
—**Garlic** *[AC only]*
—**Garnishes** *[AC only]*

—**Greens** *[AC only]*
—Health foods
   USE   Cookery—Natural foods
—**Herbs** *[AC only]*
—**Honey** *[AC only]*
—**Hot peppers** *[AC only]*
—**Lamb and mutton** *[AC only]*
—Macaroni
   USE   Cookery—Pasta
—**Meat** *[AC only]*
—**Molasses** *[AC only]*
—**Natural foods** *[AC, S]*
   UF   Cookery—Natural foods
         Cookery—Organic foods
—Noodles
   USE   Cookery—Pasta
—Organic foods
   USE   Cookery—Natural foods
   RT   Organic farming
—**Pasta** *[AC only]*
   UF   Cookery—Macaroni
         Cookery—Noodles
         Cookery—Spaghetti
         Cookery—Vermicelli
   RT   Pasta products
—**Peanut butter** *[AC only]*
—**Peanuts** *[AC only]*
—**Potatoes** *[AC only]*
—**Pork** *[AC only]*
—**Poultry** *[AC only]*
—**Pumpkin** *[AC only]*
—**Rice** *[AC only]*
—**Seafood** *[AC only]*
—Spaghetti
   USE   Cookery—Pasta
—**Sprouts** *[AC only]*
—**Tea** *[AC only]*
—**Tofu** *[AC only]*
   UF   Cookery—Bean curd
—**Turkeys** *[AC only]*
—**Veal** *[AC only]*
—**Vegetables** *[AC, S]*
—**Venison** *[AC only]*
—Vermicelli
   USE   Cookery—Pasta
—**Wild foods** *[AC only]*
—**Wine** *[AC only]*
Cookery, African
Cookery, Algerian
Cookery, American
Cookery, Austrian
Cookery, Belgian
Cookery, British
Cookery, Bulgarian
Cookery, Cajun
Cookery, Canadian
Cookery, Caribbean
Cookery, Chinese
Cookery, Cuban
Cookery, Easy
   USE   Quick and easy cookery
Cookery, English
Cookery, European

Cookery, French
Cookery, Georgian (Transcaucasian)
Cookery, German
Cookery, Greek
Cookery, Guatemalan
Cookery, Hungarian
Cookery, Indian
Cookery, Indic
Cookery, Indonesian
Cookery, International
Cookery, Israeli
Cookery, Italian
Cookery, Japanese
Cookery, Jewish
    NT   Passover cookery
Cookery, Korean
Cookery, Latin American
Cookery, Lebanese
Cookery, Maya
Cookery, Mediterranean
Cookery, Mexican
Cookery, Middle Eastern
Cookery, Moroccan
Cookery, Norwegian
Cookery, Oriental
Cookery, Philippine
Cookery, Polish
Cookery, Portuguese
Cookery, Quantity
    USE   Quantity cookery
Cookery, Romanian
Cookery, Russian
Cookery, Scandinavian
Cookery, Southeast Asian
Cookery, Spanish
Cookery, Swiss
Cookery, Thai
Cookery, Tunisian
Cookery, Vietnamese
Cookery for one
Cookery for the sick *(May add geog subd)*
Cookery for two
Cookies
Cooking
    USE   Cookery
Cooks
Coolidge, Calvin, 1872-1933
Cooney, Barbara, 1917-
Cooper, Adrianne
Cooper, Gary, 1901-1961
Cooper, Peter, 1791-1883
Cooper, Susan
Cooperation *[S] (May add geog subd)*
Cope, E.D. (Edward Drinker), 1840-1897
Copernicus, Nicolaus, 1473-1543
Copland, Aaron, 1900-
Copley, John Singleton, 1738-1815
Copp, Joseph (Fictitious character)
Copper *[S] (May add geog subd)*
Copper enameling
Copper Miners' Strike, Ariz., 1917
Copperheads
Copperwork *[S] (May add geog subd)*
Copy art *(May add geog subd)*
Copying machine industry *(May add geog subd)*
Copying processes

Copyright *[S] (May add geog subd)*
    BT   Intellectual property
Coral reef animals *[AC only] (May add geog subd)*
    UF   Coral reef fauna
Coral reef biology *(May add geog subd)*
Coral reef ecology *(May add geog subd)*
Coral reef fauna
    USE   Coral reef animals *[AC only]*
Coral reefs and islands *[S] (May add geog subd)*
Coral Sea, Battle of the, 1942
Coral snakes *[AC only]*
    UF   Micrurus
Corals *[S] (May add geog subd)*
Corcoran family
Cordobes, 1936-
Corfu Island (Greece)
Cormier, Robert
Cormorants *(May add geog subd)*
    BT   Sea birds
Corms *(May add geog subd)*
    BT   Bulbs
Corn *[S] (May add geog subd)*
Cornhusk craft *(May add geog subd)*
Cornell, Sarah Maria, 1802-1832
Cornish, Sam
Cornwall (England)
Cornwallis, Charles Cornwallis, Marquis, 1738-1805
Coronado, Francisco Vásquez de, 1510-1554 *[AC only]*
    UF   Vásquez de Coronado, Francisco, 1510-1554
Coronary artery bypass *(May add geog subd)*
Coronary heart disease *(May add geog subd)*
    NT   Silent myocardial ischemia
Coroners
Corporate culture *(May add geog subd)*
Corporate mergers
    USE   Consolidation and merger of corporations
Corporate reorganizations *(May add geog subd)*
Corporate turnarounds *(May add geog subd)*
Corporation law *[S] (May add geog subd)*
Corporations *[S] (May add geog subd)*
Corporations, Foreign *(May add geog subd)*
    NT   Corporations, Japanese
Corporations, Japanese *(May add geog subd)*
    BT   Corporations, Foreign
Correctional institutions *[S] (May add geog subd)*
Corrections *[S] (May add geog subd)*
Corregidor Island (Philippines)
Correspondence school and courses *[S] (May add geog subd)*
Corruption (in politics)
    USE   Political corruption
Corruption investigation *(May add geog subd)*
Cortés, Hernán, 1485-1547
    USE   Cortés, Hernando, 1485-1547 *[AC only]*
Cortés, Hernando, 1485-1547 *[AC only]*
    UF   Cortés, Hernán, 1485-1547
           Cortez, Hernando, 1485-1547
Cortez, Hernando, 1485-1547
    USE   Cortés, Hernando, 1485-1547 *[AC only]*
Cortez, Gregorio, 1875-1916
Corvette automobile
Corvidae *(May add geog subd)*
    BT   Songbirds
Cosby Show (Television program)
Cosby, Bill, 1937-
Cosell, Howard, 1918-

Cosmetics *[S] (May add geog subd)*
Cosmetics industry *(May add geog subd)*
Cosmic rays *[S] (May add geog subd)*
Cosmogony
    USE   Cosmology *[AC only]*
           Universe *[AC only]*
Cosmography
    USE   Cosmology *[AC only]*
           Universe *[AC only]*
Cosmology *[AC only]*
    Use for works on the general science or philosophy of the universe. Works limited to the physical description of the universe are entered under the heading Universe.
    UF   Cosmogony
           Cosmography
    BT   Universe *[AC only]*
Cosmology, Ancient
Cosmology, Babylonian
Cosmopolitan
Cost accounting *[S] (May add geog subd)*
Cost and standard of living *(May add geog subd)*
Costa Rica
Costello, Lou
Costner, Kevin
Costume *[S] (May add geog subd)*
    SA   *the subdivisions* —Costume *and* —Costume and adornment
Costume design *(May add geog subd)*
Costume designers
Côte d'Ivoire
    UF   Ivory Coast
Cotton *[S] (May add geog subd)*
Cotton picking *(May add geog subd)*
Cotton manufacture *[S] (May add geog subd)*
Cotton yarn *(May add geog subd)*
Cottonmouth
    USE   Water moccasin *[AC only]*
Cottontails *[S]*
Coucy, Enguerrand de, 1340-1397
Cougars
    USE   Pumas
Cough
Counseling *[S]*
    SA   *the subdivision* —Counseling of
Counselors
Counter culture
    USE   Communal living
           Conflict of generations
           Life style
Counterfeits and counterfeiting *[S] (May add geog subd)*
    RT   Forgery
           Fraud
           Impostors and imposture
           Quacks and quackery
Counting *[S]*
    RT   Counting-out rhymes *[AC only]*
Counting games *[AC only]*
    BT   Mathematical recreations *[AC only]*
           Number games *[AC only]*
Counting-out rhymes *[AC only] (May add geog subd)*
    Use for works containing rhymes traditionally used to count out or eliminate a player in a child's game. Counting books in rhyme are entered under Counting. *[AC only]*
    RT   Counting *[AC only]*
Country homes *(May add geog subd)*
Country life *[S] (May add geog subd)*
Country music *[S] (May add geog subd)*

Country musicians
County courts *(May add geog subd)*
County services
    UF   Public services
    NT   Municipal services
Courage *[S] (May add geog subd)*
Courbet, Gustave, 1819-1877
Courtesy
    USE   Etiquette *[AC only]*
Courtesy *[S]*
Court records *(May add geog subd)*
Courthouses *(May add geog subd)*
Courts *[S] (May add geog subd)*
    RT   Jurisprudence
           Judges
           Justice
    NT   Criminal courts
           Juvenile courts
Courts and courtiers *[S]*
    SA   *the subdivision* —Court and courtiers
Courts of last resort *(May add geog subd)*
Courtship *(May add geog subd)*
    RT   Love
    NT   Dating (Social customs)
Courtship of animals
    USE   Animals—Courtship *[AC only]*
Cousins
    BT   Family *[AC only]*
Cousins, Norman
Cousteau, Jacques Yves
Covenants *[S] (May add geog subd)*
Cover letters *(May add geog subd)*
Covered bridges *(May add geog subd)*
Coverlets *(May add geog subd)*
Covetousness
    USE   Greed *[AC only]*
Coward, Noel, 1899-1973
Cowart, Donald
Cowboys
Cowboys in art
Cowens, David W., 1948-
Cows *[S] (May add geog subd)*
Cox, Lynn
Coyne, Brady (Fictitious character)
Coyote (Legendary character)
Coyotes *[S] (May add geog subd)*
CPR (First aid) *(May add geog subd)*
Crabbing *(May add geog subd)*
Crabs *[S] (May add geog subd)*
Crabtree & Evelyn (Firm)
Crack (Drug) *[S] (May add geog subd)*
Craft, Robert
Crafts
    USE   Handicraft *[AC,S]*
Cranach, Lucas, 1472-1553
Cranberries *(May add geog subd)*
Cranbrook Academy of Art
Crane, Cheryl
Crane, Hart, 1899-1932
Crane, Stephen, 1871-1900
Cranes, derricks, etc. *[S] (May add geog subd)*
Cranes (Birds) *(May add geog subd)*
Crapper, Thomas, 1837-1910
Craven, Margaret
Crawdads
    USE   Crayfish

Crawfish
   USE Crayfish
Crawford, Christina, 1939-
Crawford, Joan, 1908-1977
Crawford, John S.
Crayfish *(May add geog subd)*
   UF Crawdads
       Crawfish
Crayfish culture *(May add geog subd)*
Crayon drawing *[S] (May add geog subd)*
Crayons
Crazy Horse, ca. 1842-1877
Cream, Thomas Neill, 1850-1892
Creation *[S]*
Creation (Literary, artistic, etc.)
Creationism *[S] (May add geog subd)*
Creative ability *[S] (May add geog subd)*
   UF Creativeness
   NT Genius
Creative ability in business *(May add geog subd)*
Creative ability in science *(May add geog subd)*
Creative activities and seat work
   USE Handicraft *[AC only]*
       Indoor games *[AC only]*
       Mathematical recreations *[AC only]*
       Puzzles *[AC only]*
Creative thinking *[S]*
Creative writing *[S]*
Creative writing (Elementary education)
Creativeness
   USE Creative ability
Creaton, David
Credit *[S] (May add geog subd)*
Credit bureaus *(May add geog subd)*
Credit control *(May add geog subd)*
Creeds *[S]*
Creek Indians
Creighton, Christopher
Crenshaw, Mary Ann
Crests *(May add geog subd)*
   BT Heraldry
Crete (Greece)
Crewelwork *[S] (May add geog subd)*
Crib quilts *(May add geog subd)*
Cricket *[S]*
  —Fiction *[AC only]*
     UF Cricket stories
     BT Sports—Fiction *[AC only]*
Cricket stories
   USE Cricket—Fiction *[AC only]*
Crickets *[S]*
   BT Orthoptera
   NT Mole crickets
Crime *(May add geog subd)*
   RT Criminals
       Victims of crimes
   NT Organized crime
       Political crimes and offenses
       Racketeering
       White collar crimes
Crime and narcotics
   USE Narcotics and crime
Crime and the press *(May add geog subd)*
Crime films
   USE Mystery and detective films *[AC only]*
Crime laboratories *(May add geog subd)*

Crime prevention *[S] (May add geog subd)*
   NT Vigilance committees
Crimean Tatars
Crimean War, 1853-1856 *[S]*
Crimes
   USE Crime
Crimes without victims *[S] (May add geog subd)*
   UF Victimless crimes
Criminal courts *(May add geog subd)*
Criminal investigation *[S] (May add geog subd)*
Criminal justice, Administration of *[S] (May add geog subd)*
Criminal law *[S] (May add geog subd)*
Criminal procedure *[S] (May add geog subd)*
Criminal registers *(May add geog subd)*
Criminal statistics *(May add geog subd)*
Criminally insane
   USE Insane, Criminal and dangerous
Criminals *[S]*
   RT Crime
       Organized crime
   NT Pirates
Criminology *(May add geog subd)*
   RT Crime
Crisis intervention (Psychiatry)
Criswell College
Critical path analysis
Critical thinking *[S] (May add geog subd)*
   RT Thought and thinking
Critically ill
Criticism *[S] (May add geog subd)*
   UF Literary criticism
   RT Literature—Criticism and interpretation
   SA *the subdivisions* —Criticism and interpretation *and*
         —Criticism, interpretation, etc.
Criticism, Personal
Critics
Croatia *(Not subd geog)*
Crocheting *[S] (May add geog subd)*
  —Patterns
Crockett, Davy, 1786-1836
Crocodiles *[S] (May add geog subd)*
Crofutt, George A.
Cromwell, Oliver, 1599-1658
Cronkite, Walter
Crooked Creek (Kan.), Battle of, 1859
Crops *(May add geog subd)*
Crosby County (Tex.)
Cross-cultural studies *(May add geog subd)*
   SA *the subdivision* —Cross-cultural studies
Cross-country skiing *(May add geog subd)*
Cross-stitch
Crossword puzzles *[S]*
Crouch, John Russell, 1916-1976
Crouse, Russel, 1893-1966
Crow Indians
Crown jewels *(May add geog subd)*
Crows *[S] (May add geog subd)*
Cruise ships *(May add geog subd)*
Crusades *[S]*
Crustacea
   USE Crustaceans *[AC only]*
Crustaceans *[AC only] (May add geog subd)*
   UF Crustacea
Crying *(May add geog subd)*
Cryptogram stories
   USE Cliphers—Fiction *[AC only]*

Cryptograms *(May add geog subd)*
Cryptography *[S] (May add geog subd)*
Cryptozoa *(May add geog subd)*
Crystal City (Texas)
Crystal growth *(May add geog subd)*
Crystallography *[S]*
Crystals
Cub Scouts
    BT   Scouts and scouting
    NT   Webelos
Cuba *[S]*
  —History *[S]*
  — —Revolution, 1959
  — —1959- *[S]*
  — —Invasion, 1961
  —Politics and government
  — —1959-
Cuban American literature (Spanish) *(May add geog subd)*
Cuban Americans
    BT   Hispanic Americans
Cuban Missile Crisis, 1962
Cubism *[S] (May add geog subd)*
Cuchulain (Legendary character)
Cuckoos *[S]*
Cuffe, Paul, 1759-1817
Culloden, Battle of, 1746
Cultivated plants
    USE   Plants, Cultivated
Cults *[S] (May add geog subd)*
    RT   Brainwashing
           Religions
           Sects
Culture *[S]*
Culture, Popular
    USE   Popular culture
Culture Club (Musical group)
Cupboards *(May add geog subd)*
Cumberland Mountains
Cummings, E.E. (Edward Estlin), 1894-1962
Cuneiform inscriptions
Curaçao
Curie, Marie, 1867-1934
Curie, Pierre, 1859-1906
Curiosities and wonders *[S] (May add geog subd)*
Curiosity
Current events *[S]*
Curriculum evaluation *(May add geog subd)*
Curriculum planning *(May add geog subd)*
    SA   *the subdivision* —Curricula
Currier & Ives
Curry family *(Not subd geog)*
Cursing
    USE   Blessing and cursing
Curtis, Tony, 1925-
Cushing, Harvey, 1869-1939
Cushions
Cushman, Charlotte, 1816-1876
Custer, Elizabeth Bacon, 1842-1933
Custer, George Armstrong, 1839-1876
Custis, George Washington Parke, 1781-1857
Custody of children *(May add geog subd)*
Customer relations
Customer service *(May add geog subd)*
Customs, Social
    USE   Manners and customs

    SA   *the subdivisions* —Customs and practices *and* —Social life and customs
Cut flowers *(May add geog subd)*
Cut glass *(May add geog subd)*
Cut-out craft *(May add geog subd)*
Cuthbert, Saint, Bishop of Lindisfarne, ca. 635-687
Cutucu Mountains (Ecuador)
Cy Young Award
Cybernetics *[S] (May add geog subd)*
Cycles
    UF   Periodicity
Cycling
    USE   Bicycles and bicycling *[AC only]*
Cycling for women *(May add geog subd)*
Cyclists
    USE   Bicyclists *[AC only]*
Cyclones *[S] (May add geog subd)*
Cyclops (Greek mythology)
Cynomys ludovicianus
    USE   Black-tailed prairie dog *[AC only]*
Cyprus
Cyrano de Bergerac, 1619-1655
Cyrus, The younger, d. 401 B.C.
Cystic fibrosis *(May add geog subd)*
Cystitis *(May add geog subd)*
Cytology *(May add geog subd)*
    RT   Cells
Czech Americans
Czech folklore
    USE   Folklore, Czech *[AC only]*
Czechoslovakia *[S]*
Czechs
  —Folklore
      USE   Folklore, Czech *[AC only]*
Czerny, Carl, 1791-1857
Czolgosz, Leon F., 1873?-1901
D Day
    USE   Normandy (France), Attack on, 1944
D.N.A.
    USE   DNA
Da Terni, Giorgio Maria
    UF   Terni, Giorgio
Dachshunds *[S]*
Dadaism *(May add geog subd)*
    BT   Arts, Modern—20th century
Daddy longlegs *[AC only]*
    UF   Harvestmen
           Opiliones
Daedalus (Greek mythology)
Dahl, Roald
Daily News (New York, N.Y.)
Daimler Company
Dairy cattle *[S] (May add geog subd)*
Dairy farming *(May add geog subd)*
Dairy products *[S] (May add geog subd)*
Dairying *[S] (May add geog subd)*
Daisy Rothschild (Giraffe)
Dakota Indians
Dalai Lama XIV, 1935-
Dale, Sam, 1772-1841
Dali, Salvador, 1904-
Dallas Cowboys (Football team)
Dallas Mavericks (Basketball team)
Dalmatian dog *(May add geog subd)*
Dalton family
Daly, John, 1966-

Daly, Maureen, 1921-
Damien, Father, 1840-1889
Dams *[S] (May add geog subd)*
Damselflies *(May add geog subd)*
Dana, Richard Henry, 1815-1882
Danbury (Conn.)
Dance *(May add geog subd)*
   UF   Dancing
   RT   Movement education
           Physical education and training
   NT   Square dancing
   SA   *the subdivision* —Dances
Dance, Black *(May add geog subd)*
   UF   Blacks—Dancing
Dance music *[S] (May add geog subd)*
Dance Theatre of Harlem
Dance therapy *(May add geog subd)*
Dancers *[S]*
Dancing
   USE   Dance
Dandelions *[S]*
Danes
Dangerous animals *[S] (May add geog subd)*
   RT   Animal attacks
Dangerous fishes *(May add geog subd)*
Dangerous marine animals *(May add geog subd)*
Daniel (Biblical character)
Daniels, Charmian (Fictitious character)
Daniken, Erich von, 1935-
Danish Americans
Danish language *[S] (May add geog subd)*
  —Readers *[AC only]*
      Use for reading texts in Danish containing materials for instruction and practice in reading that language.
     RT   Danish language materials *[AC only]*
Danish language materials *[AC only]*
    Use for works written in Danish intended primarily for general information or recreational reading. Such works with text also given in English are further subdivided by the subdivision —Bilingual.
   RT   Danish language—Readers *[AC only]*
  —Bilingual *[AC only]*
Dante Alighieri, 1265-1321.   Divina commedia
   USE   Dante Alighieri, 1265-1321.   Divine comedy *[AC only]*
Dante Alighieri, 1265-1321.   Divine comedy *[AC only]*
   UF   Dante Alighieri, 1265-1321.   Divina commedia
Danube River (Europe)
Dare, Virginia, b. 1587
Dark matter (Astronomy)
Darlington Stock Car Race
DAR Museum (Denton, Tex.)
Darragh, John
Darrow, Clarence Seward, 1857-1938
Darwin, Charles, 1809-1882
Database management *[S] (May add geog subd)*
Database searching *(May add geog subd)*
Databases *(May add geog subd)*
   SA   *the subdivision* —Databases
Data General Corporation
Data processing *[AC only]*
   UF   Electronic data processing
   RT   Computers
           Programming (Computers)
           Programming languages (Computers)
   SA   *the subdivision* —Data processing
  —Keyboarding *[AC only]*
Data protection *(May add geog subd)*

Data transmission systems *[S] (May add geog subd)*
Date rape
   USE   Dating violence
Dates, Historical
   USE   Chronology, Historical
Dating (Social customs) *[S]*
   BT   Courtship
   RT   Love
   NT   Interethnic dating
           Interracial dating
Dating violence *(May add geog subd)*
   UF   Date rape
Daughters
   RT   Mothers and daughters
Daughters of the American Revolution
Daumier, Honoré, 1808-1879
Davenport, Lucas (Fictitious character)
Davenport, Robert
David, Jacques-Louis, 1748-1825
David, King of Israel
Davis, Benjamin O. (Benjamin Oliver), 1912-
Davis, Bette, 1908-
Davis, Cullen, 1933-
Davis, Jefferson, 1808-1889
Davis, Jim
Davis, Paul Vincent
Davis, Paxton, 1925-
Davis, Sammy, 1925-
Davis, Stuart, 1892-1964
Dawkins, Darryl
Dawson, Charles, 1846-1916
Dawson, Sarah Morgan, 1842-1909
Day *[S]*
   NT   Morning *[AC only]*
Day care centers *(May add geog subd)*
   UF   Child care centers
Day of the Dead
   USE   All Souls' Day
Day, Doris, 1924-
Days
Daytona International Speedway Race
Daytona Literary and Industrial School for Training Negro Girls (Daytona Beach, Fla.)
Daytona 200 Motorcycle Race
dBase IV (Computer program)
De Forest, Lee, 1873-1961
De Mille, Agnes
De Paola, Tomie
De Passe, Suzanne, 1947-
De Rivera, Jose Ruiz, 1904-
De Soto, Hernando, ca.1500-1542 *[AC only]*
   UF   Soto, Hernando de, ca. 1500-1542
De Valera, Eamonn, 1882-1975
Dead
Dead Sea scrolls *[S]*
Deaf *[S]*
  —Means of communication *[S]*
     RT   Nonverbal communication (Psychology)
Deaf, Films for the
   USE   Films for the hearing impaired
Deaf, Teachers of the
   USE   Teachers of the deaf
Deafness *[S]*
Deal, Tara P., 1965-
Dean, Dizzy, 1911-
Dean, James, 1931-1955

Dean, John W. (John Wesley), 1938-
Death *[S]*
    RT Immortality
          Terminal care
          Tragedy
    SA *the subdivision* —Mortality
Death, Apparent
    UF Near-death experiences
Death Valley (Calif. and Nev.)
Death in literature
Death row *(May add geog subd)*
Debates and debating *[S] (May add geog subd)*
Debs, Eugene V. (Victor), 1855-1926
Debt relief *(May add geog subd)*
Debtor and creditor *[S] (May add geog subd)*
Debts, Public *(May add geog subd)*
Debussy, Claude, 1862-1918
Decathlon *[S]*
Decatur, Stephen, 1779-1820
December
Deception
Decimal system
Decision making *[AC, S]*
    UF Decision-making
    SA *the subdivision* —Decision making
Decker, Mary, 1958-
Decks (Architecture, Domestic) *(May add geog subd)*
    RT Patios
Decoration and ornament *[S] (May add geog subd)*
Decoration and ornament, Rustic *(May add geog subd)*
Decorations of honor *[S] (May add geog subd)*
    RT Medals
Decorative arts *[S] (May add geog subd)*
  —Egyptian influences
Decorative arts, Early American *(May add geog subd)*
Decorative arts, Shaker *(May add geog subd)*
Decorative arts, Victorian *(May add geog subd)*
Decorative cast-ironwork *(May add geog subd)*
    RT Art metalwork
Decorative paper *(May add geog subd)*
    BT Paper work
          Handicraft
Decoupage *[S] (May add geog subd)*
Decoys (Hunting) *[S] (May add geog subd)*
Deep diving *(May add geog subd)*
    UF Diving, Submarine
          Submarine diving
Deep-sea fauna *(May add geog subd)*
Deer *[S] (May add geog subd)*
Deer hunting *(May add geog subd)*
Deerfield (Mass.)
Defectors *[S]*
Defence (Ship)
Defense industries *[S] (May add geog subd)*
Defense information, Classified *(May add geog subd)*
Defenses
    USE Actions and defenses
    SA *the subdivision* —Defenses
Deficiency diseases *(May add geog subd)*
Deficit financing *[S] (May add geog subd)*
Defoe, Daniel, 1661?-1731
Deford, Alexandra, 1971-1980
Deforestation *(May add geog subd)*
Degas, Edgar, 1834-1917
Degrees, Academic *(May add geog subd)*
Dehydration (Physiology)

Deirdre (Legendary character)
Deitrick, Frances I.
Delacroix, Eugene, 1798-1863
Delaware
Delaware Indians
Delibes, Leo, 1836-1891
Delius, Frederick, 1862-1934
Delivery of health care
    USE Medical care
Delta Queen (Steamboat)
Deluge
Dementia *(May add geog subd)*
Demeter (Greek deity)
Deming, W. Edwards (William Edwards), 1900-
Democracy *[S] (May add geog subd)*
Democratic Party *[S]*
Demonology *[S] (May add geog subd)*
Demonstrations *(May add geog subd)*
Denali National Park and Preserve (Alaska)
Denmark
Densmore, John
Dental care *(May add geog subd)*
    RT Gums
    SA *the subdivision* —Dental care
Dental hygiene
Dental hygienists
Dental schools *(May add geog subd)*
Dentistry *[S]*
    NT Pedodontics
Dentists
Denver (Colo.)
Denver, John
Denver Broncos (Football team)
Denver Nuggets (Basketball team)
DePalma, Ralph G., 1931-
Department stores *[S] (May add geog subd)*
Dependency (Psychology) *(May add geog subd)*
Depression, Mental *[S] (May add geog subd)*
Depression in adolescence *(May add geog subd)*
Depression in children *(May add geog subd)*
Depressions
  —United States
  — —1929
Dershowitz, Alan M.
Descartes, Rene, 1596-1650
Descriptive cataloging *(May add geog subd)*
Desert animals *[S] (May add geog subd)*
    UF Desert fauna
Desert biology *(May add geog subd)*
Desert ecology *(May add geog subd)*
Desert fauna
    USE Desert animals *[AC only]*
Desert plants *[S] (May add geog subd)*
Desert storm, Operation, 1991
    USE Persian Gulf War, 1991
Desert tortoise *[S]*
Desertification *(May add geog subd)*
Deserts *[S] (May add geog subd)*
Design *[S] (May add geog subd)*
    SA *the subdivisions* —Design *and* —Design and construction
Design, Industrial *(May add geog subd)*
    SA *the subdivision* —Design and construction
Designer drugs *[S] (May add geog subd)*
Designers
Desire (Philosophy)

Desiree, Queen, consort of Charles XIV John, King of Sweden and Norway, 1777-1860
Desktop publishing *[S] (May add geog subd)*
Deskwriter (Computer printer)
Desks *(May add geog subd)*
Desserts *[S] (May add geog subd)*
Detective and mystery films
    USE Mystery and detective films *[AC only]*
Detective and mystery plays
    USE Mystery and detective plays *[AC only]*
Detective and mystery stories
    USE Mystery and detective stories *[AC only]*
Detective and mystery programs
    USE Mystery and detective programs *[AC only]*
Detectives *[S]*
    NT Pinkerton's National Detective Agency
Detectives in literature *(Not subd geog)*
Detectives in mass media *(May add geog subd)*
Detente
Detroit Institute of Arts
Detroit (Mich.)
Detroit Lions (Football team)
Detroit Pistons (Basketball team)
Detroit Tigers (Baseball team)
Developing countries *[S]*
    UF Third World
Developmental biology *(May add geog subd)*
Developmental disabilities *(May add geog subd)*
Developmental psychology *(May add geog subd)*
Developmentally disabled children *(May add geog subd)*
Devereaux (Fictitious character)
Deviant behavior
Devil *[S]*
Devlin, Bernadette, 1947-
Devotional exercises
    USE Prayer books and devotions *[AC only]*
Dewey, John, 1859-1952
Di Maggio, Joe, 1914-
Diabetes *[S] (May add geog subd)*
    UF Diabetes mellitus
    RT Insulin
Diabetes in children *(May add geog subd)*
Diabetes mellitus
    USE Diabetes
Diabetics
Diagnosis *[S]*
    RT Pathology
         Medicine
Diagnosis, Laboratory *(May add geog subd)*
Dialogues
Diamond industry and trade *(May add geog subd)*
Diamonds *[S] (May add geog subd)*
    BT Gems
Diana, Princess of Wales, 1961-
Dianetics
    RT Scientology
Diaries
    UF Diaries (Blank-books) *[AC only]*
    SA *the subdivision* —Diaries
Dickens, Charles, 1812-1870
Dickens, Charles, 1812-1870. **Great expectations**
Dickens County (Tex.)
Dickenson, Susanna
Dickerson, Eric, 1960-
Dickinson, Emily, 1830-1886
Dictators *[S]*

    RT Kings, queens, rulers, etc. *[AC only]*
         Totalitarianism
Dictionaries, Medical
    BT Encyclopedias and dictionaries
Dictionaries, Polyglot
    BT Encyclopedias and dictionaries
Didion, Joan
Diegueño Indians
Diego, Juan, 1474-1548
Diesel motor
Diesel, Rudolf, 1858-1913
Diet *[AC, S] (May add geog subd)*
    RT Weight control *[AC only]*
    NT High-carbohydrate diet
         High-fiber diet
         Low-calorie diet
         Low-fat diet
         Salt-free diet
Diet therapy *[S] (May add geog subd)*
    SA *the subdivision* —Diet therapy
Dietary supplements
Dieters *(May add geog subd)*
Diethylstilbestrol
    BT Estrogen
Dietrich, Marlene
Digestion *[S]*
Digestive system *[AC only]*
Digital communications
Digital electronics *[S] (May add geog subd)*
Diktynna (Greek deity)
Dillard, Annie
Dimensions
Dinah (Dog)
Diners (Restaurants) *(May add geog subd)*
Dingo *[S]*
    BT Dogs
         Wild dogs
  —**Control**
Dinkelsbuhl (Germany)
Dinners and dining *[S]*
Dino, Dorothee, duchesse de, 1793-1862
    UF Talleyrand, Dorothee, duchess of
Dinosaur National Monument (Colo. and Ut.)
Dinosaur Valley State Park (Tex.)
Dinosaurs *[S] (May add geog subd)*
    RT Fossils *[AC only]*
    SA *names of specific dinosaurs, e.g.,* Brachiosaurus
Dioxins *[S]*
Diphtheria *[S] (May add geog subd)*
Diplomacy *[S]*
Diplomatic and consular service *[S] (May add geog subd)*
    SA *the subdivision* —Diplomatic and consular service
Diplomatic Conference on the Protection of the Ozone Layer (1985 : Vienna, Austria)
    UF Vienna Convention for the Protection of the Ozone Layer (1985)
Diplomats *[S]*
Diptera *(May add geog subd)*
    BT Insects
Direct action
Direct marketing *(May add geog subd)*
    BT Marketing
Directories *[S]*
    SA *the subdivisions* —Directories *and* —Telephone directories
Dirtiness
    USE Cleanliness *[AC only]*

Disappointment
    BT   Hope *[AC only]*
Disarmament
Disaster relief *[S] (May add geog subd)*
Disasters *[S] (May add geog subd)*
    RT   Accidents
    SA   *names of specific disasters and types of disaster, e.g.,*
           Shipwrecks
Disc jockeys
Disciples of Christ
Discipline
    RT   Discipline of children
           Punishment
    NT   School discipline
    SA   *the subdivision* —Discipline
Discipline of children *(May add geog subd)*
    RT   Punishment
Disco dancing
Discount brokers *(May add geog subd)*
Discount houses (Retail trade) *(May add geog subd)*
Discounts for the aged *(May add geog subd)*
Discoveries in geography
    SA   *the subdivision* —Discovery and exploration
Discoveries in science *(May add geog subd)*
    RT   Inventions
           Patents
Discrimination *[S]*
    RT   Apartheid
           Segregation
    NT   Discrimination against the handicapped
           Discrimination in education
           Discrimination in employment
           Race discrimination
           Sex discrimination
Discrimination against the handicapped *(May add geog subd)*
    BT   Discrimination
           Handicapped
Discrimination in education *[S] (May add geog subd)*
    BT   Discrimination
Discrimination in employment *[S] (May add geog subd)*
    BT   Discrimination
Discussion
Disease outbreaks
    USE Epidemics
Diseases *[S] (May add geog subd)*
    UF   Illness
    RT   Diagnosis
           Medicine
           Pathology
    SA   *the names of individual diseases and the subdivisions*
           —Diseases *and* —Diseases and pests
Diseases and history *(May add geog subd)*
Disguise *(May add geog subd)*
Disks, Rotating
Disney, Walt, 1901-1966
Disneyland (Calif.)
Disraeli, Benjamin, Earl of Beaconsfield, 1804-1881
Dissection *(May add geog subd)*
Dissenters
Dissertations, Academic *[S] (May add geog subd)*
Dissident art *(May add geog subd)*
Distributive education *(May add geog subd)*
District attorneys
    USE Public prosecutors
Divers
Divination *[S] (May add geog subd)*

Diving *[S]*
Diving, Submarine
    USE Deep diving *(May add geog subd)*
Division
Divorce *[S] (May add geog subd)*
Dix, Dorothea Lynde, 1802-1887
Dixon, Jeane
Dlamar, Mirabeau Buonaparte, 1798-1859
DNA *[S]*
    BT   Nucleic acids
    RT   Genes
    NT   rDNA
Do-it-yourself work
Dobie, J. Frank (James Frank), 1888-1964
Dobu Island (Papua New Guinea)
Dobzhansky, Theodosius Grigorievich, 1900-
Doctor-patient relationship
    USE Physician and patient *(May add geog subd)*
Doctrinal theology
    USE Theology, Doctrinal
Dodge City (Kan.)
Dodge, Grenville Mellen, 1831-1916
Dodgson, Charles Lutwidge, 1832-1898
    USE Carroll, Lewis, 1832-1898
Dodo *(May add geog subd)*
Dods, Mary Diana
Dog breeds *(May add geog subd)*
    SA   *names of specific breeds*
Dog shows *(May add geog subd)*
Dogs *[S] (May add geog subd)*
    UF   Puppies *[AC only]*
    NT   Beagles (Dogs)
           Chow chows (Dogs)
           Hunting dogs
           Police dogs
           Rescue dogs
           Search dogs
           Sled dogs
           Working dogs
    SA   *names of specific breeds of dogs*
Dogs as laboratory animals
Dogs in art *[S]*
Dogs in motion pictures
Dogs in television
Dolch, Edward W. (Edward William), 1889-1961
Dole, Elizabeth Hanford
Dolensek, Emil
Doll clothes
Doll furniture *(May add geog subd)*
Dollar
Dollhouses *[S] (May add geog subd)*
Dollmaking *(May add geog subd)*
Dolls *[S] (May add geog subd)*
Dolomedes *(May add geog subd)*
    UF   Fishing spiders, Giant
Dolphins *(May add geog subd)*
Domenikos Theotokopoulos
    USE El Greco, 1541?-1614
Domestic animals *[S] (May add geog subd)*
    UF   Animal husbandry
           Farm animals
    NT   Livestock
Domestic education *(May add geog subd)*
Domestic employees
    USE Household employees *[AC only]*
Domestic relations *[S] (May add geog subd)*

Domestics
    USE Household employees *[AC only]*
Dominance, Cerebral
    USE Cerebral dominance
Dominican Republic
Dominoes *[S]*
Don Quixote (Fictional character)
Donahue, Phil
Donahue (Television program)
Donald Duck (Cartoon character)
Donaldson, Maureen
Donaldson, Sam
Donkeys *(May add geog subd)*
Donovan, William J. (William Joseph), 1883-1959
Donne, John, 1572-1631
Doo-wop (Music) *(May add geog subd)*
Dooley, Thomas A. (Thomas Anthony), 1927-1961
Doolittle, James Harold, 1896-
Doonesbury (Comic strip)
Doors (Musical group)
Dopa *[S]*
Doping in sports *(May add geog subd)*
    UF Drugs and sports
Dorfman, Ariel
Dormice *[S]*
Dorsett, Tony
DOS (Computer operating system)
DOS device drivers
Dos Passos, John, 1896-1970
Doss, Helen
Dostoyevsky, Fyodor, 1821-1881
Dostoyevsky, Fyodor, 1821-1881.   Crime and punishment
    [AC only]
    UF Dostoyevsky, Fyodor, 1821-1881.   Prestuplenie
            nakazanie
Dostoyevsky, Fyodor, 1821-1881.   Prestuplenie i nakazanie
    USE Dostoyevsky, Fyodor, 1821-1881.   Crime and punishment
            [AC only]
Doubt in literature
    USE Belief and doubt in literature
Dough
Douglas, Margaret, Countess of Lennox, 1515-1578
Douglas, Mike
Douglas, Stephen Arnold, 1813-1861
Douglas, William O. (William Orville), 1898-
Douglass, Frederick, 1817?-1895
Doulton and Company
Dove (Sloop : Lapworth)
Dowling, Father (Fictitious character)
Downie, Jean, 1945-
Downs, Hugh
Down's Syndrome *(May add geog subd)*
Doyle, Arthur Conan, Sir, 1859-1930
Doyle, Charles Altamont
Dr. Jekyll and Mr. Hyde (Motion picture)
Dr. Who (Television program)
Dracula (Motion picture)
Dracula, Count (Fictitious character)
Draft
    UF Military service, Draft
Draft horses *[S] (May add geog subd)*
Draft resisters *[S] (May add geog subd)*
Draft Riot, New York, N.Y., 1863
Drag racing *[S] (May add geog subd)*
Dragonflies *[S] (May add geog subd)*

Dragons *[S] (May add geog subd)*
Dragons in literature *[S]*
Drake, Francis, Sir, 1540?-1596
Drama *[S]*
    —Collections
        USE Plays—Collections *[AC only]*
        BT   Literary form
               Literature
        SA   *the subdivision* —Drama
Drama in education *[S] (May add geog subd)*
Dramatic criticism *[S] (May add geog subd)*
Dramatists *[S]*
    NT Women dramatists
Dramatists, American
Dramatists, Czech
Dramatists, English
Drapery *[S] (May add geog subd)*
Drawing *[S] (May add geog subd)*
    NT Pastel drawing
          Pencil drawing
          Portrait drawing
          Topographical drawing
Drawn-work
Dreadnought (Battleship)
Dreams *[S]*
Dress accessories *[S] (May add geog subd)*
Dressmakers
Dressmaking *[S] (May add geog subd)*
Drew, Charles Richard, 1904-1950
Drexel Burnham Lambert Incorporated
Dreyfus, Alfred, 1859-1935
Dreyfus, Jack, 1913-
Dried flower arrangement *(May add geog subd)*
    BT Flower arrangement
Driftwood
    BT Wood *[AC only]*
Drill (not military)
    USE Marching drills
Drilling platforms *[S] (May add geog subd)*
Drill presses
Drinker family
Drinking of alcoholic beverages *[S] (May add geog subd)*
Drinking water *(May add geog subd)*
Driving, Automobile
    USE Automobile driving
    BT   Motor vehicle driving
Drone aircraft *(May add geog subd)*
Dropouts *[S]*
Droughts *(May add geog subd)*
Drowning *(May add geog subd)*
Drug abuse *[S] (May add geog subd)*
    UF Drugs and youth *[AC only]*
    SA *the subdivision* —Drug use
Drug abuse and crime *(May add geog subd)*
Drug dealers
    USE Narcotics dealers
Drug interactions *(May add geog subd)*
Drug legalization *(May add geog subd)*
Drug-nutrient interactions *(May add geog subd)*
Drug resistance
Drug testing *[S] (May add geog subd)*
Drug therapy
    USE Chemotherapy
Drug traffic *[S] (May add geog subd)*

Drugs *[S] (May add geog subd)*
    UF   Drugs and youth *[AC only]*
    RT   Pharmacology
           Pharmacy
    NT   Psychotropic drugs
           Tranquilizing drugs
Drugs, Nonprescription *(May add geog subd)*
Drugs and employment
    UF   Employees—Drug use
Drugs and sports
    USE   Doping in sports
Drugs and youth
    USE   Drug abuse *[AC only]*
           Drugs *[AC only]*
Druids and Druidism *[S]*
Drum *[S]*
Drum and bugle corps *[AC only]*
    UF   Bugle and drum corps
Drunk driving *[S] (May add geog subd)*
Dry wall
Dryden, John, 1631-1700
Du Bois, W.E.B. (William Edward Burghardt), 1868-1963
Du Pont family
Dual-career families *(May add geog subd)*
Dualism
Du Barry, Jeanne Becu, comtesse, 1743-1793
Dubois, Silvia, 1988 or 9-1889
Duchamp, Marcel, 1887-1968
Duck shooting *(May add geog subd)*
Ducks *[S] (May add geog subd)*
Ducks as pets
Dude ranches *(May add geog subd)*
Dudley, Amy Robsart, Lady, 1532?-1560
Dudley, Robert, Sir, 1574-1649—Fiction
Dudley, William, 1964-
Dufy, Raoul, 1877-1953
Dugong *[S] (May add geog subd)*
    BT   Mammals
Dukakis, Kitty
Dukakis, Michael S. (Michael Stanky), 1933-
Duke, Patty, 1946-
Dull, Christine
Dull, Ralph
Dulles, John Foster, 1888-1959
Dunant, Henry, 1828-1910
Dunbar, Paul Laurence, 1872-1906
Duncan, Isadora, 1878-1927
Duncan, Lois, 1934-
Dundee, John Graham of Claverhouse, Viscount, 1648-1689
Dungee, George Elder
Dunham, Katherine
Duniway, Abigail Scott, 1834-1915
Dunkel, Brian
Dunkerque (France), Battle of, 1940
DuPont, Alfred I (Alfred Irénée), 1864-1935
Dupree, Marcus
Duran Duran (Musical group)
Durante, Jimmy
Durbin, Joseph Walter, 1860-1916
Dürer, Albrecht, 1471-1528
Durham (England)
Durham priory
Durrell, Gerald Malcolm, 1925-
Dust *(May add geog subd)*
Dust storms *[S] (May add geog subd)*

Dutch
Dutch Americans
Duval County (Tex.)
Dwarfs
Dwellings *(May add geog subd)*
    SA   the subdivision —Dwellings
Dwellings in literature
Dye, Charlie, 1906-1973
Dye plants *(May add geog subd)*
Dyer, Mary, d. 1660
Dyes and dyeing *[S]*
    —Wool
Dylan, Bob, 1941-
Dynamic programming
Dynamics *[S]*
Dynamite *[S]*
Dysentery *[S] (May add geog subd)*
Dyslexia *[S] (May add geog subd)*
Dyslexic children
Dyslexics
Dyson, Freeman J.
Dyson, George, 1953-
Dyson, John, 1943-
Eagles *[S] (May add geog subd)*
Eanes Independent School District (Tex.)
Ear *[S]*
Earhart, Amelia, 1897-1937
Early childhood education *(May add geog subd)*
    —Activity programs
Early, Jubal Anderson, 1816-1894
Early retirement *(May add geog subd)*
Earp, Wyatt, 1848-1929
Earrings *(May add geog subd)*
Earth *[S]*
    —Crust *[S]*
    —Internal structure *[S]*
    —Rotation
Earth Day
Earth sciences *[S] (May add geog subd)*
Earth sheltered houses *[S] (May add geog subd)*
Earth stations (Satellite telecommunication)
Earthmoving machinery *(May add geog subd)*
Earthquake prediction *(May add geog subd)*
Earthquakes *[S] (May add geog subd)*
Earthworms *[S] (May add geog subd)*
Easels
East (U.S.)
East, Lorecia
East Asia *[S]*
East Indian Americans
East Indians *[S]*
East Liverpool (Ohio)
Easter *[S] (May add geog subd)*
    —Fiction
        UF   Easter stories *[AC only]*
Easter cookery
Easter decorations *(May add geog subd)*
Easter eggs *(May add geog subd)*
Easter Island
Easter music
Easter stories
    USE   Easter—Fiction *[AC only]*
Eastern Europe
    USE   Europe, Eastern
Eastern grey kangaroo *(May add geog subd)*

UF Grey kangaroo
Eastern Shore (Md. and Va.)
Eastman, Charles Alexander, 1858-1939
Eastman, George, 1854-1932
Eating
   USE Dinners and dining
Eating customs *[AC, S] (May add geog subd)*
   RT Table etiquette
Eating disorders *[S] (May add geog subd)*
Eaton, Ann
Eavesdropping *[S] (May add geog subd)*
Ebal, Mount (West Bank)
Eberly, Angelina Belle Peyton, 1798-1860
Eccentrics and eccentricities *[S]*
Ecclesiastical embroidery
   BT Embroidery
Echidnas *[AC only]*
   UF Spiny anteaters
       Tachyglossidae
   BT Monotremes *[AC only]*
Echinodermata
   USE Echinoderms *[AC only]*
Echinoderms *[AC only]*
   UF Echinodermata
Eclecticism in architecture *(May add geog subd)*
Eclipses, Lunar
   USE Lunar eclipses
Eclipses, Solar
   USE Solar eclipses
Ecologists
Ecology *[S] (May add geog subd)*
   RT Environmental protection
   SA *specific habitats, e.g.,* Mountain ecology, Seashore
       ecology, etc., *and the subdivisions* —Ecology *and*
       —Environmental aspects
Economic assistance *[S] (May add geog subd)*
Economic assistance, Domestic *(May add geog subd)*
Economic conditions
   SA *the subdivision* —Economic conditions
Economic conversion *(May add geog subd)*
Economic development *[S]*
Economic forecasting *[S] (May add geog subd)*
Economic geography *(Not subd geog)*
Economic geology
   USE Geology, Economic
Economic history
Economic indicators *(May add geog subd)*
Economic policy *[S]*
Economic recessions
   USE Recessions
Economics *[S] (May add geog subd)*
   SA *the subdivision* —Economic conditions
Economics in literature
Economists
Ecuador
Edelman, Marian Wright
Edentata
   BT Mammals
Edible plants
   USE Plants, Edible
Edinburgh (Scotland)
Edison, Thomas A. (Thomas Alva), 1847-1931
Editing
Editors
   RT Journalism
       Publishers and publishing

Edmonds, S. Emma E. (Sara Emma Evelyn), 1841-1898
Education *[S] (May add geog subd)*
   RT Learning and scholarship
       Libraries
   NT Basic education
   SA *the subdivision* —Education
—Aims and objectives *[S]*
—Experimental methods *[S]*
—Parent participation
Education, Bilingual *(May add geog subd)*
Education, Elementary *(May add geog subd)*
Education, Graduate
   USE Universities and colleges—Graduate work
Education, Higher *(May add geog subd)*
   SA *the subdivision* —Education (Higher)
Education, Humanistic *(May add geog subd)*
Education, Preschool *(May add geog subd)*
   RT Kindergarten
Education, Primary *(May add geog subd)*
Education, Professional
   USE Professional education
Education, Secondary *(May add geog subd)*
Education, Urban *(May add geog subd)*
Education and church
   USE Church and education
       Religion in the public schools
Education and state *(May add geog subd)*
Educational change *(May add geog subd)*
Educational equalization *(May add geog subd)*
Educational exchanges *(May add geog subd)*
Educational games
Educational innovations *(May add geog subd)*
Educational measurement
   USE Educational tests and measurements
Educational planning *(May add geog subd)*
Educational psychology *[S]*
Educational sociology *[S] (May add geog subd)*
Educational surveys *[S] (May add geog subd)*
Educational technology *(May add geog subd)*
Educational tests and measurements *[S] (May add geog subd)*
Educators *[S]*
Edward I, King of England, 1239-1307
Edward II, King of England, 1284-1327
Edward III, King of England, 1312-1377
Edward IV, King of England, 1442-1483
Edward VI, King of England, 1537-1553
Edward VII, King of Great Britain, 1841-1910
Edward, King of England, ca. 1003-1066
Edwards, Robert Geoffrey
Eels *[S]*
Egg decoration *[S] (May add geog subd)*
Egg-laying mammals
   USE Monotremes *[AC only]*
Eggs *[S] (May add geog subd)*
   SA *the subdivision* —Eggs
—Incubation
Egypt *[S]*
—Civilization
— —To 332 B.C.
—History
— —To 332 B.C.
—Politics and government
— —1970-
—Social life and history
— —To 332 B.C.

Egyptian language *[S]*
Ehmke, Howard
Ehretsmann family
Ehrlich, Paul, 1854-1915
Ehrlichman, John
Eiffel Tower (Paris, France) *[AC only]*
    UF   Tour Eiffel (Paris, France)
Eiger (Switzerland)
Eighteen wheelers
    USE   Tractor trailers *[AC only]*
Eighteenth century *[S]*
    SA   *the subdivisions* —18th century *and* —History—
           18th century
Einstein, Albert, 1879-1955
Eisenhower, Dwight D. (David), 1890-1969
Eisenhower family
Eisner, Michael, 1942-
El Chino (Bong Way Bong)
El Dorado
El Greco (Domenico Theotocopoulos), 1541?-1614
    USE   Greco, 1541?-1614
El Salvador
Elaphe
    USE   Rat snakes *[AC only]*
Elder abuse
    USE   Aged—Abuse of
Elderhostels *(May add geog subd)*
Elderly
    USE   Aged
Eleanor, Queen, consort of Henry II, King of England,
    1122?-1204
Election Day
Election law *(May add geog subd)*
Electioneering *(May add geog subd)*
    UF   Politics
Elections *[S] (May add geog subd)*
    NT   Primaries
Electric apparatus and appliances *[S] (May add geog subd)*
Electric circuits *[S]*
Electric conductors *[S]*
Electric currents *[S]*
Electric drafting
Electric engineering *[S] (May add geog subd)*
Electric eye cameras
Electric generators *[S] (May add geog subd)*
Electric industries *[S]*
Electric kilns
Electric lamps *[S]*
Electric lighting *[S] (May add geog subd)*
Electric motors *[S]*
Electric organs in fishes
Electric power *[S] (May add geog subd)*
Electric power failures *[S] (May add geog subd)*
Electric power plants *[AC, S]*
    UF   Electric power-plants
Electric power plants, Underground *[AC only]*
Electric power production *(May add geog subd)*
Electric power-plants
    USE   Electric power plants *[AC only]*
Electric power plants, Underground
    USE   Underground electric power plants
Electric wiring *[S]*
Electric wiring, Interior
Electricity *[S]*
Electrochemistry *[S]*
Electrolysis

Electromagnetic fields *(May add geog subd)*
Electromagnetic waves *[S]*
    RT   Infrared radiation
Electromagnetism *[S]*
Electron microscopes *(May add geog subd)*
Electron microscopy *(May add geog subd)*
Electronic apparatus and appliances *[S] (May add geog subd)*
Electronic cameras
Electronic circuits *[S]*
Electronic data processing
    USE   Data processing *[AC only]*
Electronic digital computers
    USE   Computers *[AC only]*
Electronic music *[S]*
Electronic publishing *[S] (May add geog subd)*
Electronic spreadsheets *[S] (May add geog subd)*
    BT   Computer programs
Electronic toys *[S]*
Electronics *[S] (May add geog subd)*
Electrons *[S]*
Electrophysiology
    UF   Bioelectricity
Electrostatics
Elementary education
    USE   Education, Elementary
Elementary school libraries *(May add geog subd)*
Elementary school teachers
Elementary school teaching *(May add geog subd)*
Elementary schools *(May add geog subd)*
Elephant man
    USE   Merrick, Joseph Carey, 1862 or 3-1890
Elephant seals *[S] (May add geog subd)*
Elephants *[S] (May add geog subd)*
Elgar, Edward, 1857-1934
Elijah (Biblical prophet)
Eliot, George, 1819-1880
Eliot, T.S. (Thomas Stearns), 1888-1965
Elisha (Biblical prophet)
Elite (Social sciences)
Elizabeth I, Queen of England, 1533-1603
Elizabeth II, Queen of Great Britain, 1926- *[S]*
Elizabeth, consort of Edward IV, King of England,
    1437?-1492
Elizabeth, Empress of Russia, 1709-1762
Elizabeth, Queen, consort of George VI, King of England,
    1900-
Elizabeth, Queen, consort of Henry VII, King of England,
    1465-1503
Elk *[S] (May add geog subd)*
Ellington, Duke, 1899-1974
Ellipse
    RT   Conic sections
Ellis, C. Howard (Charles Howard), 1895-
Ellis Island Immigration Station (New York, N.Y.)
Ellison, Ralph
Ellison lettering machine
Ellsworth, Lincoln, 1880-1951
Elon, Amos
Elsa (Lion)
Elton (Cambridgeshire, England)
Elves
Elway, John, 1960-
Emancipation of slaves
    USE   Slaves, Emancipation
Embarrassment

Emblems, National *(May add geog subd)*
   UF   National emblems
Emblems, State *(May add geog subd)*
   UF   State emblems
Embroidery *[S] (May add geog subd)*
   NT   Ecclesiastical embroidery
Embryology *[S] (May add geog subd)*
   SA   *the subdivision* —Embryos
   —Birds
Emergencies
   USE   Accidents
Emergency medical personnel
Emergency medical services *(May add geog subd)*
Emergency medical technicians
Emergency medicine *[S] (May add geog subd)*
Emergency nursing *(May add geog subd)*
Emergency physicians *(May add geog subd)*
Emergency vehicles *(May add geog subd)*
Emerson, Ralph Waldo, 1803-1882
Emery, Ralph
Emigration and immigration
   SA   *the subdivision* —Emigration and immigration
Emigration and immigration law *(May add geog subd)*
Emmert, Amy
Emotional problems *[AC only]*
   UF   Emotional problems of adolescents
       Emotional problems of children
Emotional problems of adolescents
   USE   Emotional problems *[AC only]*
Emotional problems of children
   USE   Emotional problems *[AC only]*
Emotions *[S]*
   NT   Joy
Empathy
Emperor penguin *[S]*
Emperors
   USE   Kings, queens, rulers, etc. *[AC only]*
Emphysema, Pulmonary *(May add geog subd)*
Empire State Building (New York, N.Y.)
Employee assistance programs *(May add geog subd)*
Employee ownership *(May add geog subd)*
Employee rights *(May add geog subd)*
Employees *[S]*
   SA   *the subdivisions* —Employees *and* —Officials and
       employees
   RT   Age and employment
   —Drug use
      USE   Drugs and employment
   —Dismissal of
   —Rating of
Employees, Professional
   USE   Professional employees
Employer-employee relations
   USE   Industrial relations
Employment
   USE   Work
   RT   Job hunting
   SA   *the subdivision* —Employment
Employment (Economic theory)
   RT   Unemployment
Employment agencies *[S] (May add geog subd)*

Employment forecasting *[S] (May add geog subd)*
   UF   Occupational forecasting
Employment in foreign countries
Employment interviewing
Employment tests *(May add geog subd)*
Emulators (Computer programs)
   BT   Computer programs
Emus *[S] (May add geog subd)*
Enamel and enameling *[S] (May add geog subd)*
Enameled ware *(May add geog subd)*
Encephalitis *[S] (May add geog subd)*
Encopresis in children
   USE   Soiling *[AC only]*
Encyclopedias and dictionaries *[S]*
   UF   Children's encyclopedias and dictionaries
   RT   Lexicographers
   NT   Dictionaries, Medical
       Dictionaries, Polyglot
       Picture dictionaries
   SA   *the subdivisions* —Dictionaries *and* —Encyclopedias
End of the world *[AC, S]*
   UF   End of the world (Astronomy)
       End of the world (Islam)
End of the world (Astronomy)
   USE   End of the world *[AC only]*
End of the world (Islam)
   USE   End of the world *[AC only]*
Endangered animals
   USE   Rare animals *[AC only]*
Endangered plants
   USE   Rare plants
Endangered species *[S]*
Endocrine glands *[S]*
Endocrinology *[S] (May add geog subd)*
Endowments *[S] (May add geog subd)*
Endurance (Ship)
Energy
   USE   Force and energy
       Power (Mechanics)
       Power resources
Energy conservation *[S] (May add geog subd)*
Energy consumption *[S] (May add geog subd)*
   RT   Renewable energy resources
Energy development *[S] (May add geog subd)*
Energy industries *(May add geog subd)*
Energy policy *(May add geog subd)*
Energy resources
   USE   Power resources
Engels, Friedrich, 1820-1895
Engineering *[S] (May add geog subd)*
   NT   Municipal engineering
       Structural engineering
Engineering design *(May add geog subd)*
Engineering mathematics
Engineering models
Engineers *[S]*
Engines *[S]*
   NT   Fire engines
       Internal combustion engines
       Marine engines
   SA   *the subdivision* —Motors

England *[S]*
    —Antiquities
        NT   Lindow Man
    —Civilization
    — —1066-1485
    —History
        USE   Great Britain—History
    —Social life and customs
    — —1066-1485
    — —20th century
English as a second language
    USE   English language—Study and teaching—Foreign speakers
English as a foreign language
    USE   English language—Study and teaching—Foreign speakers
English channel
English drama *[S] (May add geog subd)*
    —17th century
English essays *[S] (May add geog subd)*
English fiction *[S] (May add geog subd)*
    —19th century
English language *[S] (May add geog subd)*
    —Orthography and spelling
        USE   English language—Spelling *[AC only]*
    —Business English *[S]*
    —Composition and exercises
    —Spelling *[AC, S]*
     UF   English language—Orthography and spelling
    —Study and teaching *[S] (May add geog subd)*
    — —Foreign speakers
        UF   English as a second language
            English as a foreign language
            ESL
            ESOL
            Teaching English as a second language
            Teaching English to speakers of other languages
            Teaching English as a foreign language
            TEFL
            TESL
            TESOL
    —Textbooks for foreign speakers
English literature *[S] (May add geog subd)*
    —Middle English, 1100-1500
    —Old English, ca. 450-1100
    —19th century
English poetry *[S] (May add geog subd)*
    —19th century
    —20th century
English prose literature *[S] (May add geog subd)*
English Rose III (Dory)
English sparrow *(May add geog subd)*
English wit and humor
    USE   Wit and humor *[AC only]*
Engraving *[S] (May add geog subd)*
Enlightenment *[S] (May add geog subd)*
Enola Gay (Ship)
Ensor, James, 1860-1949
Entebbe Airport Raid, 1976
Enterprise (Space shuttle)
Enterprise (Television program)
Entertainers *[S]*
Entertaining *[S] (May add geog subd)*
    RT   Parties *[AC only]*
Entomology
    RT   Insects

Entrees (Cookery)
    BT   Cookery
Entrepreneurs
Entrepreneurs, Women
    USE   Businesswomen *[AC only]*
Entrepreneurship *[S] (May add geog subd)*
Enuresis
    USE   Bedwetting *[AC only]*
Environment
    RT   Ecology
          Environmental protection
          Natural resources
    SA   *the subdivision* —Environmental aspects
Environmental degradation *(May add geog subd)*
Environmental education *(May add geog subd)*
    —Activity programs
Environmental engineering *(May add geog subd)*
Environmental ethics *(May add geog subd)*
    UF   Human ecology—Moral and ethical aspects
Environmental health *[S] (May add geog subd)*
Environmental indicators *(May add geog subd)*
Environmental law *(May add geog subd)*
Environmental advertising claims
    USE   Green marketing
Environmental policy *(May add geog subd)*
Environmental pollution
    USE   Pollution
Environmental protection *[S] (May add geog subd)*
Environmental psychology
Environmental sciences *(May add geog subd)*
Environmentalists
Environmentally induced diseases *(May add geog subd)*
Envy
Enzymes *[S]*
EPCOT Center (Fla.)
Epic poetry
Epic poetry, Greek
Epic poetry, Latin
    UF   Latin epic poetry
Epidemics *[S] (May add geog subd)*
    UF   Disease outbreaks
Epidemiologists
Epigrams *[S]*
Epilepsy *[S] (May add geog subd)*
Episcopal Church *[S] (May add geog subd)*
Episcopalians
Eponyms
Epson FX-86e (Computer printer)
Equal pay for equal work *[S] (May add geog subd)*
Equality *[S] (May add geog subd)*
Equality before the law *(May add geog subd)*
Erasmus, Desiderius, d. 1536
Eratosthenes, 276-192 B.C.
Erdstein, Erich
Eric, The Red, fl. 985
Ericson, Leif, d. ca. 1020
    UF   Leif Ericson, d. ca. 1020
          Leiv Eiriksson, d. ca. 1020
Ericsson, John, 1803-1889
Erie, Lake, Battle of, 1813
Erie Canal
Erinyes (Greek mythology)
Eros (Greek deity)
Erosion *[S] (May add geog subd)*
Errors *[S]*
    SA   *the subdivision* —Errors of usage

Errors and blunders, Literary *(May add geog subd)*
Escrows *(May add geog subd)*
Eskimo poetry *(May add geog subd)*
Ervin, Sam J. (Samuel James), 1896-1985
Erving, Julius
Esau (Biblical figure)
Escalante, Jaime
Escapes *[S] (May add geog subd)*
Escher, M.C. (Maurits Cornelis), 1898-1972
Escoffier, A. (Auguste), 1846-1935
Eskimo art
Eskimo language
—**Readers** *[AC only]*
    Use for reading texts in the Eskimo languages containing materials for instruction and practice in reading those languages.
    RT   Eskimo language materials *[AC only]*
Eskimo language materials *[AC only]*
    Use for works written in the Eskimo languages and intended primarily for general information or recreational reading. Such works with text also given in English are further subdivided by the subdivision —Bilingual.
    RT   Eskimo language—Readers *[AC only]*
—**Bilingual** *[AC only]*
Eskimos
    NT   Inuit
—**Legends** *[AC only]*
    UF   Legends
ESL
    USE   English language—Study and teaching—Foreign speakers
ESOL
    USE   English language—Study and teaching—Foreign speakers
Espionage *[AC only]*
    Use for works on the art and techniques of espionage.
    RT   Intelligence service
         Spies
         Trials (Espionage)
—Fiction
    USE   Spies—Fiction *[AC only]*
Essay *[S]*
    BT   Literary form
         Literature
Essayists, American, [French, German, etc.] *[AC only]*
Essays
Essex, Robert Devereux, Earl of, 1566-1601
Essex (Frigate)
Estate planning *[S] (May add geog subd)*
Estefan, Gloria
Estes, Eleanor, 1906-
Estevan, d. 1539
Esther, Queen of Persia
Estimation theory
Estonia
Estrogen
    NT   Diethylstilbestrol
ET, The extra-terrestrial (Motion picture)
Etching *[S] (May add geog subd)*
Ethics *[S] (May add geog subd)*
    NT   Medical ethics
         Political ethics
         Religious ethics
    SA   *the subdivision* —Moral and ethical aspects
Ethics, Medical
    USE   Medical ethics
Ethics, Political
    USE   Political ethics

Ethics, Religious
    USE   Religious ethics
Ethics in the Bible
Ethiopia
Ethnic groups *[S]*
Ethnic literature
    USE   American literature—Minority authors
    NT   American literature
         American literature—Afro-American authors
         American literature—Indian authors
         American literature—Mexican-American authors
Ethnic relations *[S]*
    SA   *the subdivision* —Ethnic relations
Ethnicity *(May add geog subd)*
Ethnobotany *(May add geog subd)*
    SA   *the subdivision* —Ethnobotany
Ethnohistory *(May add geog subd)*
Ethnologists
Ethnology *[S] (May add geog subd)*
—**Syria**
    NT   Phoenicians
Etiquette *[S] (May add geog subd)*
    Use for works on prescribed patterns and conventions of social behavior. *[AC only]*
    UF   Courtesy
    RT   Behavior *[AC only]*
         Manners and customs
    SA   *specific aspects of etiquette, e.g.*, Table etiquette
Etons, Ursula
Etruria
Etruscans
Euclid
Eugenics *[S] (May add geog subd)*
Euphrates River
Europe *[S]*
    UF   Western Europe
—**Economic conditions**
— —**1945-**
—**History** *[S]*
— —**To 476**
— —**476-1492** *[S]*
— —**1492-1648**
— —**1492-1789** *[S]*
— —**1648-1789**
— —**1789-1900** *[S]*
— —**18th century**
— —**1914-1945** *[S]*
— —**1918-1945**
— —**1945-** *[S]*
— —**20th century**
—**Politics and government** *[S]*
— —**1789-1900**
— —**1918-1945**
— —**1945-**
Europe 1992
    BT   European Economic Community countries—Economic policy
Europe, Central
    USE   Central Europe
Europe, Eastern
    UF   Eastern Europe
—**History**
— —**1945-**
— —**20th century**
—**Politics and government**
— —**1989-**

European Americans
European Economic Community *[S]*
European Economic Community countries
 —Economic policy
  NT Europe 1992
European federation *[S]*
European literature
European rabbits *[AC only]*
  UF Oryctolagus cuniculus
European War
  USE World War, 1914-1918
Euthanasia *[S] (May add geog subd)*
Evaluation, Educational
  USE Educational tests and measurements
  SA *the subdivision* —Evaluation
Evangelicalism *(May add geog subd)*
Evangelists
Evans, Arthur, Sir, 1851-1941
Evans, Julian, 1955-
Eve (Biblical figure)
Everest, Frank Kendall, 1920-
Everest, Mount (China and Nepal)
Everglades (Fla.)
Everglades National Park (Fla.)
Evergood, Philip, 1901-1973
Evergreens *[S] (May add geog subd)*
Evil
  USE Good and evil
Evolution *[S]*
  UF Human evolution *[AC only]*
  SA *the subdivision* —Evolution
Evolution and religion
  USE Evolution—Religious aspects
Evolution (Biology)
Ewing, Patrick Aloysius, 1962-
Ex-convicts
Ex-presidents
Examinations *[S] (May add geog subd)*
  RT Questions and answers
  NT Scholastic Aptitude Test
  SA *the subdivision* —Examinations, questions, etc.
Excavation *[S] (May add geog subd)*
Excavations (Archaeology) *[S] (May add geog subd)*
Exceptional children *[S]*
Exchange of persons programs *[S]*
Exchanges, Educational
  USE Educational exchanges
Excretion
  USE Excretory system *[AC only]*
Excretory organs *[AC only]*
  RT Excretory system *[AC only]*
Excretory system *[AC only]*
  UF Excretion
  RT Excretory organs *[AC only]*
Excuses
Executions and executioners
  RT Capital punishment
Executive ability *[S]*
Executive departments *(May add geog subd)*
Executive power *[S] (May add geog subd)*
Executives
  NT Women executives
Executors and administrators *[S]*
Exercise *[S]*
  NT Ch'i kung
   Isometric exercises

Exercise tests
Exercise therapy *(May add geog subd)*
Exhibitions *[S] (May add geog subd)*
Existentialism *[S]*
Existentialism in literature
Exodus, The
Exorcism *[S] (May add geog subd)*
Expatriate painters
Expeditions
  USE Scientific expeditions
  SA *the names of specific exploring and scientific expeditions*
    and the subdivision —Discovery and exploration
Experiential learning *(May add geog subd)*
Experimental aircraft
  USE Research aircraft
Experimental design
Experiments *[AC only]*
  RT Science—Experiments *[AC only]*
  SA *the subdivision* —Experiments
Expert systems (Computer science) *[S] (May add geog subd)*
Exploration
  SA *the subdivision* —Exploring expeditions
Explorers *[S]*
  NT Women explorers
Explosions *[S] (May add geog subd)*
Explosives *[S] (May add geog subd)*
Export marketing *(May add geog subd)*
Exports *(May add geog subd)*
Exposition (Rhetoric)
Express service *[S] (May add geog subd)*
Extinct amphibians
  USE Extinct animals *[AC, S]*
Extinct animals *[S] (May add geog subd)*
  UF Extinct amphibians
   Extinct birds
   Extinct insects
   Extinct mammals
Extinct birds
  USE Extinct animals
Extinct insects
  USE Extinct animals
Extinct mammals
  USE Extinct animals
Extinct animals in art *[S]*
Extinct birds *(May add geog subd)*
  UF Birds, Extinct
Extinct cities *[S] (May add geog subd)*
Extinction (Biology) *(May add geog subd)*
Extrasensory perception *[S] (May add geog subd)*
Extraterrestrial anthropology
Extraterrestrial environment
  USE Space environment
Extraterrestrial beings *[AC only]*
  UF Alien beings
   Interplanetary visitors
Extravehicular activity (Manned space flight)
Extremities, Lower
  USE Leg
Exxon Valdez (Ship)
Eyck, Jan van, 1390-1440
  UF Van Eyck, Jan, ca. 1390-1441
Eye *[S]*
Eyeglasses *[S] (May add geog subd)*
Eyler, Larry
F-16 (Jet fighter plane)

Fabergé (Firm) *[AC only]*
  UF Faberzhe (Firm)
Fabergé, Peter Carl, 1846-1920
Faberzhe (Firm)
  USE Fabergé (Firm) *[AC only]*
Fables *[S]*
  BT Literature
  RT Allegories
       Animals—Fiction
       Animals—Folklore
       Folklore
Fables, Chinese *(May add geog subd)*
Fables, English *(May add geog subd)*
Fables, Greek *(May add geog subd)*
Fables, Japanese *(May add geog subd)*
Fables, Latin *(May add geog subd)*
Fabric flowers
Fabrics
  USE Textiles *[AC only]*
Face *[S]*
  RT Physiognomy
Face in art *[S]*
Face painting *(May add geog subd)*
Facsimile transmission *[S] (May add geog subd)*
  UF Fax
Factorials
Factories *[S] (May add geog subd)*
Factory and trade waste *(May add geog subd)*
Fads *(May add geog subd)*
Failure (Psychology)
Fair use (Copyright) *[S] (May add geog subd)*
Fairchild, Faith Sibley (Fictitious character)
Fairies *[AC, S] (May add geog subd)*
  NT Menehune
  —Poetry *[AC only]*
    UF Fairy poetry
Fairness
Fairs *[S] (May add geog subd)*
Fairs in art *[S]*
Fairy poetry
  USE Fairies—Poetry *[AC only]*
Fairstein, Linda A.
Fairy poetry, English *(May add geog subd)*
Fairy tales *[S] (May add geog subd)*
  BT Literature
  RT Folklore
Faisal, King Of Saudi Arabia, 1906-1975
Faith *[S]*
Falashas
Falconry *[S] (May add geog subd)*
Falcons *[S]*
  NT Kestrels
Falk, Lisanne
Falkland Islands
Fall
  USE Autumn
Fallingwater (Pa.)
Falsehood
  USE Honesty
Falstaff, John, Sir (Fictitious character)
Fame
Familial behavior in animals
Family *[S] (May add geog subd)*
  Use for works stressing the sociological concept and structure of the family. Works stressing the everyday life, interaction, and relationships of family members are entered under Family life. *[AC only]*

  RT Family life *[AC only]*
  NT Cousins *[AC only]*
       Uncles *[AC only]*
       Single-parent family
  —Prayer-books and devotions
    USE Prayer books and devotions *[AC only]*
  SA *the subdivision* —Family
Family Bible records
  USE Bible records
Family circus
Family corporations *(May add geog subd)*
Family festivals *(May add geog subd)*
Family history
  USE Genealogy
Family life *[AC, S] (May add geog subd)*
  Use for works stressing the everyday life, interaction, and relationships of family members. Works stressing the sociological concept and structure of the family are entered under Family.
  RT Family
  SA *the subdivision* —Family relationships
Family life education *(May add geog subd)*
Family medicine *(May add geog subd)*
Family-owned business enterprises *(May add geog subd)*
Family policy *(May add geog subd)*
Family problems *[AC only]*
Family recreation *(May add geog subd)*
Family reunions *[S] (May add geog subd)*
Family size *[S] (May add geog subd)*
Family violence *[S] (May add geog subd)*
  NT Child abuse
       Incest
       Wife abuse
Famine relief
  USE Food relief
Famines *[S] (May add geog subd)*
  UF Potato famine
  BT Food supply
Fancy work
Fannin, James Walker, 1804?-1836
Fans *[S] (May add geog subd)*
Fantastic fiction *[S]*
Fantastic films
  UF Fantasy films
Fantastic Four (Comic strip)
Fantastic literature
Fantastic poetry
Fantastic poetry, English *(May add geog subd)*
Fantasy *[S]*
  RT Fantastic fiction
Fantasy fiction
  USE Fantastic fiction
Fantasy films
  USE Fantastic films
Fantasy games *(May add geog subd)*
Fantasy in art
Fantasy in children
Far East (Russia)
  USE Russian Far East (Russia)
Faraday, Michael, 1791-1867
Farfan, Armando
Farm animals
  USE Domestic animals
Farm buildings *[S] (May add geog subd)*
Farm foreclosures *(May add geog subd)*
Farm life *[S] (May add geog subd)*
Farm life in art

Farm management *[S] (May add geog subd)*
Farm produce *[S] (May add geog subd)*
Farm tenancy *[S] (May add geog subd)*
Farmers *[S]*
    NT   Women farmers
Farmhouses *(May add geog subd)*
Farming
    USE   Agriculture
Farms *[S] (May add geog subd)*
Farnese family
Faroe Islands
Farragut, David Glasgow, 1801-1870
Farrier, Denis, 1921-
Farrow, Mia, 1945-
Fascism *[S] (May add geog subd)*
    UF   Neo-Nazism
    RT   Totalitarianism
Fashion *[S] (May add geog subd)*
Fashion and art
Fashion designers
Fashion drawing
Fashion models
    USE   Models, Fashion
Fashion photography *(May add geog subd)*
Fast food restaurants *(May add geog subd)*
Fasteners
Fasts and feasts *[S] (May add geog subd)*
  —**Judaism**
    RT   Cookery, Jewish
             Passover cookery
    NT   All Souls' Day
Fat persons
    USE   Overweight persons
Father and child *[S] (May add geog subd)*
Father Flanagan's Boys Home
Father's Day
Fathers *[S]*
    RT   Mothers
    NT   Unmarried fathers
Fathers and daughters *[S]*
    RT   Daughters
             Mothers and daughters
Fathers and sons *[S]*
    RT   Mothers and sons
             Sons
Fats and oils
    USE   Oils and fats
Fatuhiva Island
Faulk, John Henry
Faulkner, William, 1897-1962
Faulkner, William, 1897-1962. Sound and the fury
Fauvism
    BT   Art, Modern—20th century
Favorites, Royal
Fear *[S] (May add geog subd)*
    RT   Phobias
    NT   Stage fright
Fear of the dark
Feasts
    USE   Fasts and feasts
Feathers *[S]*
Feature films *(May add geog subd)*
    RT   Motion pictures
Feboldson, Febold (Legendary character)
Fecal incontinence
    RT   Soiling *[AC only]*

Federal aid to education *[S] (May add geog subd)*
Federal aid to higher education *(May add geog subd)*
Federal aid to libraries *[S] (May add geog subd)*
Federal aid to the arts *[S] (May add geog subd)*
Federal government *[S] (May add geog subd)*
    UF   Federalism
Federal Reserve banks
Federalist Party
Federalism
    USE   Federal government
Feedback (Psychology) *[S]*
Feinstein, Dianne, 1933-
Felice, Cynthia
Felidae
    UF   Wild cats
Feller, Robert William Andrew, 1918-
Felt work
    RT   Handicraft
Female offenders
Female reproductive system
    USE   Reproductive system, Female
Femininity (Psychology)
Feminism *[S] (May add geog subd)*
Feminism and literature *(May add geog subd)*
Feminist criticism *(May add geog subd)*
Feminist theory *(May add geog subd)*
    RT   Feminism
Feminists
Fences *(May add geog subd)*
Fencing *[S]*
    UF   Fighting
Fenelon, Fania
Fens, The (England)
Fenway Park (Boston, Mass.)
Feral animals *(May add geog subd)*
    UF   Wild animals
Feral cats *(May add geog subd)*
    UF   Wild cats
Feral children
    UF   Wild children
Ferber, Edna, 1885-1968
Ferdinand V, King of Spain, 1452-1516
Ferguson, Amos, 1920-
Ferguson, James Edward, 1871-1944
Ferland, Carol
Fermat, Pierre, 1601-1665
Fermi, Enrico, 1901-1954
Fernando II, King of Aragon, 1452-1516
Fernea, Elizabeth Warnock
Ferns *[S] (May add geog subd)*
Ferrari automobile
Ferraro, Geraldine
Ferret *[S] (May add geog subd)*
Ferries *(May add geog subd)*
Fertility, Human *[S] (May add geog subd)*
Fertilization in vitro, Human
    USE   Test tube babies *[AC only]*
Fertilization of plants *[S]*
Fertilizers *(May add geog subd)*
Festivals *[S] (May add geog subd)*
Fetal alcohol syndrome *(May add geog subd)*
Fetterman Fight, Wyo., 1866
Fetus *[S]*
Feudalism *[S] (May add geog subd)*
Feuds
    USE   Vendetta

Feynman, Richard Phillips
Fiber optics
Fiberglass craft *(May add geog subd)*
Fiberwork *(May add geog subd)*
    RT Handicraft
Fibers *[S] (May add geog subd)*
    UF Textile fibers
    RT Textiles *[AC only]*
Fiction *[S]*
    BT Literary form
         Literature
    SA *the subdivision* —Fiction
—20th century
Fiction, Gothic
    USE Gothic revival (Literature)
Fiddler (Fictitious character)
Field, Cyrus W. (Cyrus West), 1819-1892
Field, Rachel, 1894-1942
Field hockey *[S]*
Field trips
    USE School field trips
Fields, Mamie Garvin, 1888-
Fields, W.C., 1879-1946
Fifteenth century *[S]*
Fighter pilots
Fighter plane combat *(May add geog subd)*
Fighter planes *(May add geog subd)*
    RT Airplanes, Military
Fighting fishes
    USE Betta
Figure drawing *[S]*
    RT Human figure in art
Figures of speech
    NT Metaphor
Figurines *(May add geog subd)*
File organization (Computer science)
Filing systems
Filipino Americans
Filipinos
Filippo, fra, ca. 1406-1469
Filisola, Vicente
Fillmore, Millard, 1800-1874
Fills (Earthwork)
Film adaptations *[S]*
Film criticism *(May add geog subd)*
Film genres *(May add geog subd)*
Films
    USE Motion pictures
    SA *the subdivisions* —Film and video adaptations *and*
          —Film catalogs
Films for the hearing impaired
    UF Deaf, Films for the
Filmstrips
Fin M'Coul
    USE Finn MacCool *[AC only]*
Finance *[S] (May add geog subd)*
    SA *the subdivision* —Finance
Finance, Personal *(May add geog subd)*
    SA *the subdivision* —Finance, Personal
Finance, International
    USE International finance
Finance, Public *(May add geog subd)*
Financial aid, Student
    USE Student aid
Financial planning, Personal
    USE Finance, Personal

Financial security
    UF Financial planning
Financial services industry *(May add geog subd)*
Financiers
    USE Capitalists and financiers
Finback whale *[S]*
Finches *(May add geog subd)*
    BT Birds
Finding things
    USE Lost and found possessions *[AC only]*
Fine, Joan
Fines (Penalties) *(May add geog subd)*
Fingal, 3rd cent.
    USE Finn MacCool *[AC only]*
Finger calculation
Finger play *[S]*
Fingerprints *[S]*
    RT Thumbprints in art
Fink, Mike, 1770-1823
Finland
Finlay, Carlos Juan, 1833-1915
Finn Mac Cool
    USE Finn MacCool *[AC only]*
Finn mac Cumal
    USE Finn MacCool *[AC only]*
Finn MacCool *[AC only]*
    UF Fin M'Coul
         Fingal, 3rd cent.
         Finn Mac Cool
         Finn mac Cumal
         Finn MacCumal
         Finn MacCumhaill, 3rd cent.
         Finn McCool
         MacCool, Finn
Finn MacCumal
    USE Finn MacCool *[AC only]*
Finn MacCumhaill, 3rd cent.
    USE Finn MacCool *[AC only]*
Finn McCool
    USE Finn MacCool *[AC only]*
Finn, Huckleberry (Fictitious character)
Finnegan, William
Fir *(May add geog subd)*
    BT Trees
Fire *[S]*
Fire alarms *(May add geog subd)*
Fire departments *[S] (May add geog subd)*
    UF Fire-department
         Fire stations
Fire ecology *(May add geog subd)*
Fire engines *[S] (May add geog subd)*
Fire etching
    USE Pyrography
Fire extinction *(May add geog subd)*
Fire fighters *[S]*
Fire investigation *(May add geog subd)*
Fire Island (N.Y.)
Fire prevention *[S] (May add geog subd)*
    UF Fire safety
    SA *the subdivision* —Fires and fire prevention
Fire safety
    USE Fire prevention
Fire stations
    USE Fire departments *[AC only]*

Firearms *[S] (May add geog subd)*
   UF   Guns
   SA   *the names of specific guns and types of firearms*
Firebird (Choreographic work : Béjart)
Fireflies *[S]*
Fireplaces *[S] (May add geog subd)*
Fires *[S] (May add geog subd)*
   SA   *the subdivision* —Fires and fire prevention
Fireworks *[S] (May add geog subd)*
First aid *[AC, S] (May add geog subd)*
   UF   First aid in illness and injury
First aid in illness and injury
   USE   First aid
First century, A.D.
First communion
First ladies *[AC only]*
   UF   Presidents—Wives
           Presidents' wives
Fiscal policy *[S] (May add geog subd)*
Fischer, Bobby, 1943-
Fish as food *[S] (May add geog subd)*
Fish culture *[AC, S] (May add geog subd)*
   UF   Fish-culture
   BT   Aquaculture
Fish habitat improvement *(May add geog subd)*
Fish ponds *(May add geog subd)*
Fish trade *(May add geog subd)*
Fisher spiders *[AC only]*
   UF   Fishing spiders
   NT   Dolomedes
Fisheries *[S] (May add geog subd)*
Fishers
Fishes *[AC, S] (May add geog subd)*
   RT   Aquariums
           Ichthyologists
           Tropical fish
   NT   Cartilaginous fishes
Fishing *[S] (May add geog subd)*
  —Fiction *[AC only]*
   UF   Fishing stories
   BT   Sports—Fiction *[AC only]*
   SA   *types of fishing, and locations, e.g.,* Fly fishing, Ice fishing
Fishing spiders
   USE   Fisher spiders *[AC only]*
Fishing spiders, Giant
   USE   Dolomedes
   BT   Fisher spiders
Fishing stories
   USE   Fishing—Fiction *[AC only]*
Fisk, Carlton, 1947-
Fitness
   USE   Physical fitness
Fitzgerald, Ella
Fitzgerald, F. Scott (Francis Scott), 1896-1940
Fitzgerald, Francis Scott Key, 1896-1940
Fitzgerald, Zelda, 1900-1948
Flack, Roberta
Flags *[S] (May add geog subd)*
  —United States
   RT   Pledge of Allegiance *[AC only]*
  — —States
Flags in art
Flambard, Rannulf, d. 1128
Flamenco
   RT   Dance
Flamenco music

Flamingos *[S] (May add geog subd)*
Flanagan, Edward Joseph, 1886-1948
Flannel boards
   USE   Flannelgraphs
Flannelgraphs
   UF   Flannel boards
   BT   Teaching—Aids and devices
Flashlights
Flatware *(May add geog subd)*
Flatworms *[AC only]*
   UF   Plathelminthes
           Platyhelminthes
Flax *[S] (May add geog subd)*
Flea markets *(May add geog subd)*
Fleas *[S] (May add geog subd)*
Fleischman, Sid
Fleming, Alexander, 1881-1955
Fleming, Peggy
Fletch (Fictitious character)
Flies *[S]*
Flies, Artificial *(May add geog subd)*
Flight *[S]*
Flightless birds *(May add geog subd)*
Flights around the world
Floating bodies
Floods *[S] (May add geog subd)*
Floors *[S] (May add geog subd)*
   BT   Building
Florence (Italy)
Florida
Florida Keys (Fla.)
Flour *[S]*
Flour mills *[S] (May add geog subd)*
Flower arrangement *[S] (May add geog subd)*
   NT   Dried flower arrangement
           Miniature flower arrangement
Flower gardening *[S] (May add geog subd)*
   BT   Gardening
   NT   Bulbs
Flower language
Flower painting and illustration *[S] (May add geog subd)*
Flowering shrubs *(May add geog subd)*
Flowering trees *(May add geog subd)*
Flowers *[S] (May add geog subd)*
   BT   Botany
           Gardens
   RT   Pressed flower pictures
   NT   Perennials
   SA   *the names of specific flowers*
Fluid mechanics *[S]*
Flute *[S]*
Flutie, Doug
Fly casting *[S]*
Fly fishing *(May add geog subd)*
Fly tying
Flying discs (Game)
   UF   Frisbee (Game)
Flying machines *[AC only]*
   UF   Flying-machines
Flynn, Errol, 1909-1959
Foals *[S] (May add geog subd)*
Focke-Wulf 190 (Fighter planes)
Fog *[S] (May add geog subd)*
Folger Shakespeare Library
Folk art *[S] (May add geog subd)*
Folk dancing *[S] (May add geog subd)*

Folk dancing, Mexican *[S] (May add geog subd)*
Folk dancing, Scottish *[S] (May add geog subd)*
Folk drama *[AC, S]*
   UF   Folk-drama
Folk literature *(May add geog subd)*
Folk literature, Irish *(May add geog subd)*
Folk literature, Mexican *(May add geog subd)*
Folk literature, Russian *(May add geog subd)*
Folk medicine
   USE   Traditional medicine
Folk music *[S] (May add geog subd)*
Folk poetry *(Not subd geog)*
Folk poetry, American
Folk songs *(May add geog subd)*
Folk songs, English *(May add geog subd)*
Folk songs, Hebrew *(May add geog subd)*
Folk songs, Irish *(May add geog subd)*
Folk songs, Scots *(May add geog subd)*
Folk songs, Spanish *(May add geog subd)*
Folk tales
   USE   Folk literature
         Folklore
Folklore *[S] (May add geog subd)*
   UF   Legends *[AC only]*
         Folk tales *[AC only]*
         Tales *[AC only]*
   RT   Oral tradition
  —**[country subdivision]** *[AC only]*
       Use for single folktales or collections of folklore originating in a particular country. Single folktales or collections of folklore of ethnic groups *not* limited by country are entered under the heading Folklore, American [Czech, Jewish, etc.].
   SA   *the subdivision* —Folklore
Folklore—Asia *[AC only]*
   UF   Folklore, Oriental
Folklore—Iran *[AC only]*
   UF   Folklore, Persian
Folklore, African *[AC only]*
Folklore, Afro-American *[AC only]*
   UF   Afro-Americans—Folklore
         Folklore, Negro
Folklore, Altai *[AC only]*
   UF   Altai (Turkic people)—Folklore
Folklore, American *[AC only]*
Folklore, Arab
   USE   Arabs—Folklore *[AC, S]*
Folklore, Ashanti *[AC only]*
   UF   Ashanti (African people)—Folklore
   BT   Folklore, African
Folklore, Australian aborigine *[AC only]*
   UF   Australian aborigines—Folklore
Folklore, Bantu *[AC only]*
   UF   Bantu speaking peoples—Folklore
   BT   Folklore, African
Folklore, Bengali *[AC only]*
   UF   Bengali (South Asian people)—Folklore
Folklore, Black
   USE   Blacks—Folklore *[AC, S]*
Folklore, Bukusu
   USE   Folklore, Kusu *[AC only]*
Folklore, Celtic *[AC only]*
   UF   Celtic folklore
         Celts folklore
Folklore, Chinese American *[AC only]*
   UF   Chinese Americans—Folklore
Folklore, Czech *[AC only]*

   UF   Czech folklore
         Czecks—Folklore
Folklore, French-Canadian *[AC only]*
Folklore, Germanic *[AC only]*
   UF   Germanic peoples—Folklore
Folklore, Gypsy *[AC only]*
   UF   Gypsies—Folklore
Folklore, Hmong
   USE   Hmong (Asian people)—Folklore *[AC, S]*
Folklore, Igbo *[AC only]*
   UF   Igbo (African people)—Folklore
   BT   Folklore, African
Folklore, Indian *[AC only]*
Folklore, Jewish *[AC only]*
   UF   Legends, Jewish
Folklore, Kamba *[AC only]*
   UF   Kamba (African people)—Folklore
   BT   Folklore, African
Folklore, Kazakh *[AC only]*
   UF   Kazakhs—Folklore
Folklore, Khoikhoi *[AC only]*
   UF   Khoikhoi (African people)—Folklore
Folklore, Kuzu *[AC only]*
   UF   Folklore, Bukusu
         Kusu (African people)—Folklore
   BT   Folklore, African
Folklore, Malay *[AC only]*
   UF   Malays (Asian people)—Folklore
Folklore, Maori *[AC only]*
   UF   Legends—Maori
         Maori (New Zealand people)—Folklore
         Maori (New Zealand people)—Legends
Folklore, Masai *[AC only]*
   UF   Masai (African people)—Folklore
   BT   Folklore, African
Folklore, Mpongwe *[AC only]*
   UF   Mpongwe (African people)—Folklore
   BT   Folklore, African
Folklore, Navajo *[AC only]*
Folklore, Negro
   USE   Afro-Americans—Folklore *[AC only]*
Folklore, Oriental
   USE   Folklore—Asia *[AC only]*
Folklore, Persian
   USE   Folklore—Iran *[AC only]*
Folklore, San
   USE   Slavs—Folklore *[AC, S]*
   UF   San (African people)—Folklore
   BT   Folklore, African
Folklore, Slavic
   USE   Slavs—Folklore
Folklore, Tonga *[AC only]*
   UF   Tonga (Zambesi people)—Folklore
   BT   Folklore, African
Folklore, Yoruba *[AC only]*
   UF   Yoruba (African people)—Folklore
   BT   Folklore, African
Folklore, Zulu *[AC only]*
   UF   Zulu (African people)—Folklore
   BT   Folklore, African
Folklore and children
Fonda, Henry, 1905-
Fonda, Jane, 1937-
Fonteyn, Margot, Dame, 1919-
Fonts
   USE   Type and type-founding

Food *[S]*
  SA   *the names of specific foods and the subdivision* —Food
Food additives *[S]*
Food adulteration and inspection *[S]*
Food allergy
  RT   Nutritionally induced diseases
Food chains (Ecology) *[S] (May add geog subd)*
Food contamination *[S] (May add geog subd)*
  RT   Legionnaires' disease
Food crops *(May add geog subd)*
Food habits *(May add geog subd)*
Food handling
Food industry and trade *(May add geog subd)*
  UF   Food processing
  RT   Agriculture
  NT   Produce trade
Food poisoning *[S] (May add geog subd)*
Food processor cookery
Food processing
  USE   Food industry and trade
Food relief *[S] (May add geog subd)*
  UF   Famine relief
Food safety
  USE   Food handling
Food service *[S] (May add geog subd)*
Food supply *[S] (May add geog subd)*
  NT   Famines
Foodborne diseases *(May add geog subd)*
Fools Crow, 1890 or 91-
Foot *[S]*
Footbag *[S]*
  BT   Sports
Football *[S] (May add geog subd)*
  —Fiction *[AC only]*
    UF   Football stories
    BT   Sports—Fiction
    RT   Pro Football Hall of Fame (U.S.)
Football cards *(May add geog subd)*
Football players
Football stories
  USE   Football—Fiction *[AC only]*
Footprints, Fossil *(May add geog subd)*
Forbes Magazine
Force and energy *[S]*
  UF   Energy
Ford, Betty, 1918-
Ford, Gerald R., 1913-
Ford, Henry, 1863-1947
Ford, Henry, 1917-
Ford, Robert, 1862-1892
Ford, Whitey, 1928-
Ford automobile *[S]*
Ford family
Ford Motor Company
Ford's Theatre (Washington, D.C.)
Ford's Theatre National Historic Site (Washington, D.C.)
Forecasting *[S]*
  NT   Population forecasting
  SA   *the subdivision* —Forecasting
Forecasting, Population
  USE   Population forecasting
Foreclosure *(May add geog subd)*
Foreign correspondents
Foreign films *(May add geog subd)*
Foreign investments
  USE   Investments, Foreign

Foreign Legion, French
  USE   France. Army. Foreign Legion *[AC only]*
Foreign news *(May add geog subd)*
Foreign study *[S] (May add geog subd)*
Foreman, Michael, 1938-
Forensic accounting
Forensic anthropology
Forensic neurology
Forensic neuropsychology
Forensic pathology
Forensic psychology
  USE   Psychology, Forensic
Forensic psychiatry
Forest animals *[AC, S] (May add geog subd)*
  UF   Forest fauna
Forest birds *(May add geog subd)*
Forest conservation *(May add geog subd)*
Forest dynamics *(May add geog subd)*
Forest ecology *(May add geog subd)*
Forest fauna
  USE   Forest animals *[AC only]*
Forest fires *[S] (May add geog subd)*
Forest flora
  USE   Forest plants *[AC only]*
Forest plants *[AC only]*
  UF   Forest flora
Forest products *[S] (May add geog subd)*
  NT   Timber
Forest rangers
Forest reserves *[S] (May add geog subd)*
Forester, C.S. (Cecil Scott), 1899-1966
Foresters *(May add geog subd)*
Forests and forestry *[S] (May add geog subd)*
Forests, Petrified
  USE   Petrified forests
Forgery *[S] (May add geog subd)*
  RT   Counterfeits and counterfeiting
       Fraud
       Impostors and imposture
  SA   *the subdivision* —Forgeries
Forgery of antiquities
Forgery of manuscripts
Forgiveness of sin
  UF   Confession
Form perception
Former Soviet republics *[S]*
Forms (Law) *(May add geog subd)*
Forms of address *(May add geog subd)*
Formula Atlantic automobiles
Formula One automobiles
Formularies (Diplomatics)
Forster, E.M. (Edward Morgan), 1879-1970
Fort Belknap (Tex.)
Fort Lauderdale (Fla.)
Fort Pillow (Tenn.), Battle of, 1864
Fort Richardson (Tex.)
Fort Sumter (Charleston, S.C.)
Fort Worth (Tex.)
Forten, Charlotte L.
FORTH (Computer program language)
Fortification *[S] (May add geog subd)*
FORTRAN (Computer program language)
Forts
  USE   Fortification
Fortune
  USE   Luck *[AC only]*

Fortune, Amos, 1709 or 10-1801
Fortune telling [AC, S]
    UF   Fortune-telling
Fossey, Dian
Fossil fuels (May add geog subd)
Fossil mammals
    USE   Mammals, Fossil
Fossil man (May add geog subd)
Fossil plants
    USE   Plants, Fossil
Fossil reptiles
    USE   Reptiles, Fossil
Fossil vertebrates
    USE   Vertebrates, Fossil
Fossils [S] (May add geog subd)
    RT   Dinosaurs [AC only]
        Paleontology
        Prehistoric animals [AC only]
  —Collectors and collecting [AC only]
Foster, Rory C.
Foster, Stephen Collins, 1826-1864
Foster children
Foster grandparents [S]
Foster home care [S] (May add geog subd)
Foster parents
Found objects (Art) (May add geog subd)
Foundations [S] (May add geog subd)
Founding
Fourteenth century [S]
Fourth dimension [S]
Fourth grade (Education) (May add geog subd)
Fourth of July [AC, S]
    UF   Fourth of July celebrations
Fourth of July celebrations
    USE   Fourth of July [AC only]
Fouts, Dan
Fowles, John, 1926-
Fox, George, 1624-1691
Fox, Margaret, 1833-1893
Fox, Michael J., 1961-
Foxes [S] (May add geog subd)
    NT   Kit fox
Foyt, A.J., 1935-
Fra Angelico, 1400-1455
    USE   Angelico, fra, ca. 1400-1455
Fra Filippo Lippi, 1406-1469
    USE   Filippo, fra, ca. 1406-1469
Fractals [S]
Fractions [S]
Fractures [S] (May add geog subd)
Fragonard, Jean-Honore, 1732-1806
France [S]
  —Court and courtiers
  —History [S]
  — —Medieval period, 987-1515
  — —House of Valois, 1328-1589
  — —Charles VII, 1422-1461
  — —Bourbons, 1589-1789
  — —18th century
  — —Louis XVI, 1774-1793
  — —Revolution, 1789-1799
  — —1789-1815
  — —1914-1940 [S]
  — —German occupation, 1940-1945
  — —20th century

  —Politics and government
  — —1789-1799
  — —1945-1958
  — —1958-
  —Social life and customs
  — —17th century
  — —18th century
France. Armee. Legion etrangere
    USE   France. Army. Foreign Legion [AC only]
France. Army
France. Army. Foreign Legion [AC only]
    UF   Foreign Legion, French
        France. Armee. Legion etrangere
        French foreign legion
France, Military
France, Northern
France, Peter
Francesco d'Assisi, Saint, 1182-1226
    USE   Francis of Assisi, Saint, 1182-1226
Franchises (Retail trade)
Francis I, King of France, 1494-1547
Francis of Assisi, Saint, 1182-1226
    UF   Francesco d'Assisi, Saint, 1182-1226
Franciscans [S]
Franck, Frederick, 1909-
Franco, Francisco, 1892-1975
Frank, Anne, 1929-1945
Frankenstein (Motion picture)
Frankenthaler, Helen, 1928-
Franklin (Tenn.)
Franklin, Aretha
Franklin, Benjamin, 1706-1790
Franklin, Eileen
Franklin, George
Franklin, John, Sir, 1786-1847
Franks
    BT   Germanic tribes
Franz Ferdinand, Archduke of Austria, 1863-1914
Fraternities
    USE   Greek letter societies
Fraud [S] (May add geog subd)
    RT   Counterfeits and counterfeiting
        Forgery
        Impostors and imposture
        Quacks and quackery
Fraud in science (May add geog subd)
Fraunces, Phoebe
Frazier, Walt, 1945-
Fred Harvey (Firm)
Frederick, Jane
Frederick I, Holy Roman Emperor, ca. 1123-1190
Frederick II, King of Prussia, 1712-1786
Fredericksburg, Battle of, 1862
Fredericksburg (Tex.)
Free enterprise
Free material [S]
Free press and fair trial (May add geog subd)
Free thought [S] (May add geog subd)
Free verse [S]
Free will and determinism [S]
Freedmen
Freedom [AC, S]
    UF   Liberty
    RT   National liberation movements
Freedom of association [S] (May add geog subd)
Freedom of information [S] (May add geog subd)

Freedom of religion *[S] (May add geog subd)*
Freedom of speech *(May add geog subd)*
Freedom of the press *[S] (May add geog subd)*
    RT   Journalism
Freehand technical sketching
Freelance journalism
Freemasonry *(May add geog subd)*
Freight and freightage *[S] (May add geog subd)*
Fremont, Jessie Benton, 1824-1902
Fremont, John Charles, 1813-1890
French
French Americans *[S]*
French Canadians
    UF   French-Canadians
French drama *(May add geog subd)*
French fiction *(May add geog subd)*
French Foreign Legion
    USE France. Army. Foreign Legion *[AC only]*
French Guiana
French drama *(May add geog subd)*
French language *[S] (May add geog subd)*
  —Readers *[AC only]*
       Use for reading texts in French containing materials for instruction and practice in reading that language.
      RT   French language materials *[AC only]*
French language materials *[AC only]*
    Use for works written in French intended primarily for general information or recreational reading. Such works with text also given in English are further subdivided by the subdivision —Bilingual.
French language materials *[AC only] (continued)*
    RT   French language—Readers *[AC only]*
  —Bilingual *[AC only]*
French literature *[S] (May add geog subd)*
  —20th century
French poetry *[S] (May add geog subd)*
French Polynesia
French prose literature *(May add geog subd)*
French Quarter (New Orleans, La.)
    UF New Orleans (La.) Vieux Carre
         Old French Quarter (New Orleans, La.)
         Vieux Carre (New Orleans, La.)
French wit and humor
Fresh air charity *[AC only]*
    UF Fresh-air charity
    RT Child welfare
         Children—Institutional care
         Public welfare
Freshwater animals *[S] (May add geog subd)*
    UF Freshwater fauna
Freshwater fauna
    USE Freshwater animals *[AC only]*
Freshwater biology *[S] (May add geog subd)*
Freshwater ecology *(May add geog subd)*
Freshwater fishes *(May add geog subd)*
Freshwater flora
    USE Freshwater plants
Freshwater invertebrates *(May add geog subd)*
Freshwater plants *[S] (May add geog subd)*
    UF Freshwater flora
Freud, Anna, 1895-
Freud, Sigmund, 1856-1939
Friction
Friedan, Betty
Friedrich, Caspar David, 1774-1840
Friel, Brian
Friends, Imaginary

    USE Imaginary playmates *[AC only]*
Friends of the library *(May add geog subd)*
Friendship *[S] (May add geog subd)*
    NT Imaginary playmates *[AC only]*
Friendship in literature *[S]*
Friendship quilts *(May add geog subd)*
Frigates *(May add geog subd)*
Frisbee (Game)
    USE Flying discs (Game)
Fritz, Jean
Frog hopper
    USE Spittle insects *[AC only]*
Frogs *[S] (May add geog subd)*
Frogs as pets
Frontenac, Louis de Buade, Comte de, 1620-1698
Frontier and pioneer life *[S] (May add geog subd)*
Frost, Benjamin, 1708 or 9-1764
Frost, Jack
    USE Jack Frost *[AC only]*
Frost, Robert, 1874-1963
Frozen foods *[S] (May add geog subd)*
Frugal Gourmet (Television program)
Fruit *[S] (May add geog subd)*
Fruit culture *(May add geog subd)*
    UF Fruit-culture
Fruit juices
Fruit trees *(May add geog subd)*
Fry, Elizabeth Gurney, 1780-1845
Fuchida, Mitsuo, 1902-
Fudge *[S] (May add geog subd)*
Fuel *[S] (May add geog subd)*
    RT Petroleum as fuel
Fuelwood cutting *(May add geog subd)*
Fugitive slaves
Fuller, Margaret, 1810-1850
Fuller, R. Buckminster (Richard Buckminster), 1895-
Fuller, William Marshall
Fulton, Robert, 1765-1815
Functional analysis
Fund raising *[S] (May add geog subd)*
    RT Philanthropists
Fundamentalism *[S]*
Funeral rites and ceremonies *[S] (May add geog subd)*
    UF Funerals
    RT Mourning etiquette
Funerals
    USE Funeral rites and ceremonies
Fungi *[S] (May add geog subd)*
Funnel-web spiders *[AC only]*
    UF Agelenidae
Fur-bearing animals *[S] (May add geog subd)*
Fur trade *[S]*
Fur traders
Furniture *[S] (May add geog subd)*
    SA *headings for specific items and types of furniture, e.g.,* Tables
Furniture, Colonial *(May add geog subd)*
Furniture making *(May add geog subd)*
Furniture painting
Furniture repairing *(May add geog subd)*
Fusion
Future life *[S]*
Future problem solving (Contest)
Futures *(May add geog subd)*
    BT Investments
Futurism (Art) *[S] (May add geog subd)*

Gable, Clark, 1901-1960
Gaelic poetry *(May add geog subd)*
Gafkjen, Carrine
Gag, Wanda
Gagarin, Iurii Alekseevich, 1934-1968
   USE Gagarin, Yuri Alekseyevich, 1934-1968 *[AC only]*
Gagarin, Yuri Alekseyevich, 1934-1968 *[AC only]*
   UF Gagarin, Iuri Alekseevich, 1934-1968
Gage family
Gaia hypothesis
Gainsborough, Thomas, 1727-1788
Galapagos Islands
Galapagos Islands Biosphere Reserve (Galapagos Islands)
   [AC only]
   UF Reserva Biosferica en los Galápagos (Galapagos Islands)
Galatea (Greek deity)
Galaxies *[S]*
Galaxy magazine
Galdikas, Birute
Galdikas, Birute. Marija filomena
Galilei, Galileo, 1564-1642
   USE Galileo, 1564-1642
Galileo, 1564-1642
   UF Galilei, Galileo, 1564-1642
Gall insects *(May add geog subd)*
   BT Insects
Gallaudet, T.H. (Thomas Hopkins), 1787-1851
Galleons *(May add geog subd)*
Gallflies *(May add geog subd)*
   BT Flies
Galls (Botany) *(May add geog subd)*
Galois, Evariste, 1811-1832
Galveston Island (Tex.)
Gálvez, Bernardo de, 1746-1786
Gálvez, Luis
Gama, Vasco da, 1469-1524
Gambling *[S] (May add geog subd)*
Game and game birds *[AC, S] (May add geog subd)*
   UF Game and game-birds
   RT Hunting—Law and legislation
       Hunting law
Game-laws *(May add geog subd)*
Game preserves
   USE Game reserves
Game protection *[S] (May add geog subd)*
Game reserves *[S]*
   UF Game preserves
       Game sanctuaries
       Sanctuaries, Game
   BT Wildlife management areas
Game shows *(May add geog subd)*
Game theory *[S]*
Games *[S] (May add geog subd)*
   RT Educational games
   NT Board games
       Hide-and-seek *[AC only]*
       Music—Games
       Singing games
   SA the names of specific indoor and outdoor games, and the subdivision —Games
Games in art *[S]*
Gamma ray bursts
Gandhi, Indira, 1917-1984
Gandhi, Mahatma, 1869-1948
Gandhi, Rajiv, 1944-

Ganges River (India and Bangladesh)
Gangs *(May add geog subd)*
Gangsters
   USE Gangs
Gannett, Deborah Sampson, 1760-1827
Garages *(May add geog subd)*
Garbage
   USE Refuse and refuse disposal
       Waste products
Garbage Project (University of Arizona)
Garbo, Greta, 1905-
García Lorca, Federico, 1898-1936
García Márquez, Gabriel, 1928- . Cien años de soledad
   USE García Márquez, Gabriel, 1928- . One hundred years of solitude
García Márquez, Gabriel, 1928- . One hundred years of solitude
   UF García Márquez, Gabriel, 1928- . Cien años de soledad
Garden animals *(May add geog subd)*
   UF Garden fauna
Garden ecology *(May add geog subd)*
Garden fauna
   USE Garden animals *[AC only]*
Garden ornaments and furniture *[S] (May add geog subd)*
Garden pests *(May add geog subd)*
Garden rooms *[S] (May add geog subd)*
Garden structures *(May add geog subd)*
Garden tools *(May add geog subd)*
Gardening *[S] (May add geog subd)*
   SA specific types of gardening, e.g., Vegetable gardening
   NT Flower gardening
Gardening for the aged *(May add geog subd)*
Gardening for the physically handicapped *(May add geog subd)*
Gardens *[S] (May add geog subd)*
   NT Flowers
Gardens, Chinese *(May add geog subd)*
Gardens, Japanese *(May add geog subd)*
Gardens, Miniature *[S] (May add geog subd)*
Gardner, Erle Stanley, 1889-1970
Gareth (Legendary character)
Garfield, James A. (James Abram), 1831-1881
Garfield (Cartoon character)
Garibaldi, Giuseppe, 1807-1882
Garland, Hamlin, 1860-1940
Garland, Judy
Garner, John Nance, 1868-1967
Garrison, Jim, 1921-
Garrison, William Lloyd, 1805-1879
Garter snakes
Garvey, Marcus, 1887-1940
Garvey, Steve, 1948-
Garza County (Tex.)
Garza family
Gas *[AC, S]*
   UF Gas, Natural
Gas, Natural
   USE Gas *[AC only]*
Gas industry *(May add geog subd)*
Gases *[S]*
Gastrointestinal system
Gastronomy
Gates *(May add geog subd)*
Gates, Bill, 1956-
Gatzoyiannis, Eleni
Gauch, Patricia Lee

Gauchos
Gaudenzia (Horse)
Gaudi, Antoni, 1852-1926
Gauguin, Paul, 1848-1903
Gaul
Gaulle, Charles de, 1890-1970
Gauss, Karl Friedrich, 1777-1855
Gautama Buddha
    USE   Buddha *[AC only]*
Gawain (Legendary character)
Gay Men's Health Crisis, Inc.
Gay teenagers
Gays
Gazeteers *[S]*
Gaza Strip
Gearing *[S]*
GED tests
    USE   General educational development tests
Geese *[S] (May add geog subd)*
Gehrig, Lou, 1903-1941
Geldof, Bob, 1954-
Gem carving *(May add geog subd)*
Gem cutting *(May add geog subd)*
Gemini (Astrology) *(May add geog subd)*
Gems *[S] (May add geog subd)*
    RT   Precious stones
    SA   *the names of specific gems, e.g.,* Diamonds
Gender role
    USE   Sex role
Gene therapy *[S] (May add geog subd)*
Genealogy *[S]*
    UF   Family history
General Economic Systems
General educational development tests
    UF   GED tests
General Motors Corporation
General relativity (Physics)
General stores *(May add geog subd)*
Generals *[S]*
Generations *(May add geog subd)*
Generative organs, Female
    USE   Reproductive system, Female *[AC only]*
Generative organs, Male
    USE   Reproductive system, Male *[AC only]*
Generosity
Genet, Edmond Charles, 1763-1834
Genetic disorders *(May add geog subd)*
Genetic engineering *[S] (May add geog subd)*
    NT   Test tube babies *[AC only]*
           Cloning
Genetic psychology *(May add geog subd)*
Geneticists
Genetics *[S]*
    RT   DNA
    NT   Population genetics
    SA   *the subdivision* —Genetic aspects
Genghis Khan, 1162-1227
Genius *[S] (May add geog subd)*
    BT   Creative ability
Genocide *(May add geog subd)*
Genre (Literature)
    USE   Literary form
Gentle Jungle (Colton, Calif.)
Geochemistry *[S] (May add geog subd)*
Geodesic domes *(May add geog subd)*
Geoffrey, of Monmouth, Bishop of St. Asaph, 1100?-1154

Geographical distribution of animals and plants
    USE   Animal distribution *[AC only]*
           Plant distribution *[AC only]*
Geography *[S] (May add geog subd)*
    RT   Names, Geographical
    NT   Physical geography
    SA   *the subdivision* —Geography
—Early works to 1800
Geography, Ancient
Geography, Medieval *(May add geog subd)*
Geological specimens
Geological time
Geologists *[S]*
    NT   Women geologists
Geology *[S]*
    NT   Physical geology
Geology, Economic
    UF   Economic geology
Geology, Stratigraphic *[S]*
Geology, Structural
Geometrical drawing *[S]*
Geometry *[S] (May add geog subd)*
    RT   Topology
    NT   Circle
           Quadrilaterals
Geometry, Analytic *[S]*
Geometry, Plane
    UF   Plane geometry
    BT   Geometry
    NT   Area measurement
Geometry, Solid
    UF   Solid geometry
    BT   Geometry
Geomorphology *(May add geog subd)*
Geophysics *[S]*
Geopolitics *[S] (May add geog subd)*
    RT   Political geography
George III, King of Great Britain, 1738-1820
George, Saint, d. 303
George VI, King of Great Britain, 1895-1952
Georgetown Hoyas (Basketball team)
Georgia
  —History
  — —Colonial period, ca. 1600-1775
Georgian S.S.R.
Geothermal engineering
Geothermal resources *[S] (May add geog subd)*
Gerbils *[S]*
Gerbils as pets
Geriatric nursing
Geriatrics
    RT   Aged—Health and hygiene
German Americans
German drama *(May add geog subd)*
German fiction *(May add geog subd)*
German language *[S] (May add geog subd)*
  —Readers *[AC only]*
        Use for reading texts in German containing materials for instruction and practice in reading that language.
    RT   German language materials *[AC only]*
German language materials *[AC only]*
        Use for works written in German intended primarily for general information or recreational reading. Such works with text also given in English are further subdivided by the subdivision —Bilingual.
    RT   German language—Readers *[AC only]*
  —Bilingual *[AC only]*

German literature [S] (May add geog subd)
German poetry (May add geog subd)
German Reunification Question (1949-1990)
German shepherd dogs [S]
Germanic peoples
—Folklore
    USE   Folklore, Germanic [AC only]
Germanic tribes
    NT   Franks
Germans
Germany [S]
—Description and travel
—History [S]
— —To 1517
— —1866-1871
— —20th century
— —Allied occupation, 1918-1930
— —1918-1933 [S]
— —1933-1945 [S]
— —1945-
— —Allied occupation, 1945-1955
    USE   —History—1945-1955
— —1945-1955
— —1945-1990 [S]
— —1990-
—Politics and government
— —1918-1933
— —1933-1945
— —1945-1990
— —1990-
— —Unification, 1990
Germany (East) [S]
Germany (West) [S]
Germination [S]
Germplasm resources, Plant (May add geog subd)
Germs
    USE   Bacteria
Geronimo, Apache Chief, 1829-1909
Gerontology
Gershwin, George, 1898-1937
Geryon (Classical mythology)
Gestalt psychology [S]
Gesture (May add geog subd)
Gethers, Peter
Getty, J. Paul (Jean Paul), 1892-1976
Gettysburg (Pa.), Battle of, 1863
Gettysburg National Military Park (Pa.)
Geysers [S] (May add geog subd)
Ghana
Ghost stories
    USE   Ghosts—Fiction [AC only]
Ghost towns [AC, S] (May add geog subd)
—Fiction
    RT   Cities and towns, Ancient [AC only]
Ghosts [S]
—Fiction [AC, S]
    UF   Ghost stories
Giamatti, A. Bartlett
Giant books
    USE   Oversize books
Giant kelp [S] (May add geog subd)
Giant panda [S] (May add geog subd)
Giant sequoia [S]
Giants [S]
Gibbons (May add geog subd)

Gibbons family
Gibraltar
Gibson, Althea, 1927-
Gibson, Debbie
Gideon, Clarence Earl
Gielgud, John, Sir, 1904-
Gies, Miep, 1909-
Gifford, Kathie Lee, 1953-
Gift wrapping [S]
Gifted children [S]
Gifts [S] (May add geog subd)
Gila monster
Gilbert, W.S. (William Schwenck), 1836-1911
Gilbreth, Frank Bunker, 1868-1924
Gilbreth, Lillian Moller, 1878-1972
Giles, Eugene V. (Eugene Victor), 1884-1974
Gill, Brendan, 1914-
Gilles de la Tourette's syndrome
    USE   Tourette syndrome
Gilmore, Gary
Gilson, Jamie
Ginglymostoma
    USE   Nurse sharks [AC only]
Gingerbread houses
Ginsberg, Allen, 1926-
Giotto, 1266?-1337
Giovanni, Nikki
Gipson, Fred, 1908-
Giraffes [S] (May add geog subd)
Girl Scouts [S]
    BT   Scouts and scouting
Girls [S]
Gish, Dorothy
Gish, Lillian, 1896-
Giverny (France)
Glacial epoch (May add geog subd)
Glacier bear [S]
Glacier National Park (Mont.)
Glaciers [S] (May add geog subd)
Gladstone, W.E. (William Ewart), 1809-1898
Glamour photography
Glands [S]
Glasgow (Scotland)
Glasgow, Ellen Anderson Gholson, 1873-1945
Glasnost
Glass [S]
    NT   Pattern glass
          Pressed glass
Glass, Colored (May add geog subd)
Glass candlesticks (May add geog subd)
Glass craft (May add geog subd)
Glass fruit jars (May add geog subd)
Glass manufacture [S] (May add geog subd)
Glass menagerie (Motion picture)
Glass painting and staining [S] (May add geog subd)
    UF   Stained glass
          Staining glass
Glassware [S]
Glaucoma (May add geog subd)
Glazes [S]
Glazing (Ceramics)
Glees, catches, rounds, etc
    USE   Rounds (Music) [AC only]
Glencoe (Scotland)
Gliders (Aeronautics) [S] (May add geog subd)

Gliding *[AC only] (May add geog subd)*
    UF   Gliding and soaring
Global warming
Globe Theatre (Southwark, London, England)
Globes *[S] (May add geog subd)*
Globetti, Michael
Glomar Challenger (Ship)
Glow-in-the-dark books *(May add geog subd)*
Glue *[S]*
Glyptodon
    BT   Mammals
GMAT
    USE   Graduate Management Admission Test
Gnosticism *[S]*
Gnus *[S] (May add geog subd)*
Goal (Psychology)
Goats *[S] (May add geog subd)*
Gobi Desert (Mongolia and China)
Goblins *(May add geog subd)*
God *[S]*
Goddard, Robert Hutchings, 1882-1945
Godden, Jon, 1906-
Godden, Rumer, 1907-
Goddesses
Gods
Gods, Greek
Godzilla, King of the monsters (Motion picture)
Goethals, George W. (George Washington), 1858-1928
Goethe, Johann Wolfgang von, 1749-1832
Gogh, Vincent van, 1853-1890
    UF   Van Gogh, Vincent
Gold *[S] (May add geog subd)*
Gold coins *(May add geog subd)*
Gold mines and mining *[S]*
    BT   Mines and mineral resources
    SA   *the subdivision* —Gold discoveries
Gold miners
Golden Gate National Recreation Area (Calif.)
Golden eagle *[S] (May add geog subd)*
Golden Gate Bridge (San Francisco, Calif.) *[S]*
Golden hamster *[S] (May add geog subd)*
Golden hamsters as pets *(May add geog subd)*
Golden State Warriors (Basketball team)
Goldfish *[S] (May add geog subd)*
Goldfrank, Lewis R., 1941-
Golding, William, 1911-
Goldman, Emma, 1869-1940
Goldsmith, Oliver, 1728-1774
Goldwater, Barry M. (Barry Morris), 1909-
Goldwork *[S] (May add geog subd)*
Golf *[S] (May add geog subd)*
    NT   Putting (Golf)
Golf courses *[S] (May add geog subd)*
Goliad Massacre, 1836
Goliath (Biblical giant)
Gombe Stream National Park (Tanzania)
Gompers, Samuel, 1850-1924
Gone with the wind (Motion picture)
Gonorrhea *[S] (May add geog subd)*
Gonzales, Elma
Gonzales, Pancho, 1928-
Good and evil *[S]*
    NT   Theodicy
Goodall, Jane, 1934-
Gooden, Dwight
Goodyear family

Goofy (Cartoon character)
    USE   Goofy (Fictitious character) *[AC only]*
Goofy (Fictitious character) *[AC only]*
    UF   Goofy (Cartoon character)
    BT   Cartoons and comics *[AC only]*
Goodall, Jane, 1934-
Gooden, Dwight
Goodman, Benny, 1909-
Goodwin, Jan
Gophers *[AC, S]*
    UF   Pocket gophers
Goras, Domingo Leal
Gorbachev, Mikhail Sergeevich, 1931-
Gordon, Barbara, 1935-
Gordon, Bruce
Gordy, Berry
Gorham Manufacturing Company
Gorilla *(May add geog subd)*
Goring, Hermann, 1893-1946
Gorman, R.C. (Rudolph Carl), 1932-
Goshawk *(May add geog subd)*
    BT   Hawks
Goshen-Gottstein, Moshe H. (Moshe Henry), 1925-
Gossip *[S]*
Gospel musicians
Gothic revival (Architechture) *(May add geog subd)*
Gothic revival (Literature) *(May add geog subd)*
    UF   Fiction, Gothic
Goths
    UF   Teutonic peoples
Gould, Glenn
Gould, Stephen Jay
Gout *[S]*
Gouzenko, Igor, 1915-
Government
    USE   Civics
              Political science
Government, Resistance to *[S] (May add geog subd)*
Government agencies
    USE   Administrative agencies
Government and the press *(May add geog subd)*
    RT   Press and politics
Government contracts
    USE   Public contracts
Government executives
Government investments
    USE   Public investments
Government publicity *(May add geog subd)*
Government purchasing *[S] (May add geog subd)*
Government records
    USE   Public records
Government spending policy *(May add geog subd)*
Governmental investigations *[S] (May add geog subd)*
Governors *[S]*
    —**Dwellings** *(May add geog subd)*
Goya, Francisco, 1746-1828
Gracchus, Gaius Sempronius, 154-121 B.C.
Grace (Theology) *[S]*
Grace, Princess of Monaco, 1929-1982
Grace at meals
Grade, Chaim, 1910-
Grading and marking (Students) *(May add geog subd)*
Graduate education
    USE   Universities and colleges—Graduate work
Graduate Management Admission Test

Graduate Record Examination *[S]*
   UF GRE
Graf, Stephanie, 1969-
Graf Zeppelin (Airship)
Graffiti *(May add geog subd)*
Grafting *[S] (May add geog subd)*
Graham, Billy, 1918-
Graham, Martha
Grail *[S]*
   UF Holy grail
Grain *[S] (May add geog subd)*
Gram (unit)
Grammar, Comparative and general
   UF Comparative and general grammar
   SA the subdivision —Grammar
Grand Canyon (Ariz.)
Grand Island (Neb.) Tornado, 1980
Grand Prix racing
Grand Teton National Park (Wyo.)
Grand unified theories (Nuclear physics)
Grandfathers
Grandmothers
Grandparent and child *(May add geog subd)*
Grandparents
Granger, Red, 1903-
Granger (Tex.)
Granivores *(May add geog subd)*
Grant, Cary, 1904-
Grant, Ulysses S. (Ulysses Simpson), 1822-1885
Grants-in-aid *[S] (May add geog subd)*
Graph theory *[S]*
Graphic arts *[S] (May add geog subd)*
Graphic methods *[S]*
Graphology *[S] (May add geog subd)*
Grasses *[S] (May add geog subd)*
Grasshoppers *[S] (May add geog subd)*
Grassland animals *[AC only] (May add geog subd)*
   UF Grassland fauna
Grassland ecology *(May add geog subd)*
Grassland fauna
   USE Grassland animals *[AC only]*
Grasslands *[S] (May add geog subd)*
Gratitude *(May add geog subd)*
   UF Thankfulness
Graves, John, 1920-
Graves, Robert, 1895-
Gravitation
   USE Gravity *[AC only]*
Gravity *[AC only]*
   UF Gravitation
Gray, Ted, 1923-
Gray, William R., 1946-
Gray squirrel *[S]*
Gray whale *[S] (May add geog subd)*
   UF Pacific gray whale
GRE
   USE Graduate Record Examination
Great auk
Great-aunts
Great Barrier Reef (Qld.)
   BT Coral reefs and islands—Australia
Great Basin
Great Basin National Park (Nev.)
Great blue heron *[S]*
   BT Herons

Great Britain *[S]*
   SA the names of specific countries, cities, etc. in Great Britain
  —Civilization
  — —To 1066
  — —Medieval period, 1066-1485
  — —19th century
  —Economic conditions
  — —19th century
  —History *[S]*
  — —To 1066
  — —Norman period, 1066-1154
  — —1066-1485
  — —Plantagenets, 1154-1399
  — —Richard I, 1189-1199
  — —Lancaster and York, 1399-1485
  — —War of the Roses, 1455-1485
  — —To 1485
  — —Tudors, 1485-1603
  — —Henry VIII, 1509-1547
  — —Elizabeth, 1558-1603
  — —Stuarts, 1603-1714
  — —Commonwealth and protectorate, 1649-1660
  — —1714-1837 *[S]*
  — —18th century
  — —George III, 1760-1820
  — —19th century
  — —Victoria, 1837-1901
  — —20th century
  —Politics and government
  — —1558-1603
  — —1714-1837
  — —19th century
  — —20th century
  —Social life and customs
  — —19th century
  — —20th century
Great Danes *[S] (May add geog subd)*
Great-grandmothers
Great horned owl *[S] (May add geog subd)*
Great International Paper Airplane Contest
Great Lakes
Great Lakes Region
Great Plains
Great Pyramid (Egypt)
Great Pyrenees *(May add geog subd)*
Great Smoky Mountains (N.C. and Tenn.)
Great Wall of China (China)
Great Western (Steamship)
Greco-Turkish War, 1921-1922
Greco, 1541-1614
Greece *[S]*
  —Civilization
  — —To 146 B.C.
  —Description and travel and travel
  — —To 323
  —History *[S]*
  — —To 146 B.C.
  — —Civil war, 1944-1949
Greed *[AC only]*
   UF Avarice
       Covetousness
Greek Americans
Greek drama *(May add geog subd)*
Greek language *[S] (May add geog subd)*

Greek letter societies *(May add geog subd)*
   UF   Fraternities
          Sororities
Greek literature *[S] (May add geog subd)*
Greek mythology
   USE   Mythology, Greek
Greeks *[S]*
Greeley, Horace, 1811-1872
Green Bay Packers (Football team)
Green
Green, Hetty Howland Robinson, 1835-1916
Green marketing
   UF   Environmental advertising claims
   BT   Marketing
Green turtle *(May add geog subd)*
Greenaway, Kate, 1846-1901
Greenbaum, Dorothy
Greenbelts *(May add geog subd)*
Greenberg, Richard
Greenberger, Laney
Greene, Bob
Greene, Catherine Littlefield
Greene, Graham, 1904-
Greene, Joe
Greene, Nathanael, 1742-1786
Greenfield, Eloise
Greenhouse effect, Atmospheric *(May add geog subd)*
Greenhouse gardening *(May add geog subd)*
Greenhouse plants *(May add geog subd)*
Greenhouses *[S] (May add geog subd)*
Greenhow, Rose O'Neal, 1814-1864
Greenland
Greenleaf, James, 1765-1843
Greenpeace Foundation
Greens, Edible *(May add geog subd)*
Greenstein, Joseph L.
Greenwich Village (New York, N.Y.)
Greeting cards *(May add geog subd)*
Gregory, Dick, 1932-
Gregory, Karen
Grenada
Grettir Asmundarson, 996-1031
Gretzky, Wayne, 1961-
Grey, Jane, Lady, 1537-1554
Grey, Zane, 1872-1939
Grey kangaroo
   USE   Eastern grey kangaroo *(May add geog subd)*
Grey seal *[S] (May add geog subd)*
Greylag goose *[S] (May add geog subd)*
Grief
Grieg, Edvard, 1843-1907
Grieg, Nina Hagerup, 1845-1935
Griese, Bob
Griffin, John Howard, 1920-
Griffins *[S]*
Griffith, D.W. (David Wark), 1875-1948
Grimaldi family
Grimm brothers
   USE   Grimm, Jacob, 1785-1863
          Grimm, Wilhelm, 1786-1859
Grimm, Jacob, 1785-1863
Grimm, Wilhelm, 1786-1859
Grizzly bear *[S] (May add geog subd)*
Grocery trade *(May add geog subd)*
Grooming *[AC only] (May add geog subd)*
   UF   Grooming for men

   RT   Cleanliness
Grooming behavior in animals
   USE   Animals—Grooming behavior *[AC only]*
Grooming for men
   USE   Grooming *[AC only]*
Grooms, Red
Grossman, Amy
Grosz, George, 1893-1959
Grotesque *(May add geog subd)*
Ground cover plants *(May add geog subd)*
Ground-effect machines
Ground Forces of the Soviet Union
   USE   Soviet Union. Ground Forces *[AC only]*
Groundhog
   USE   Woodchuck *[AC only]*
Groundhog Day
Group psychotherapy *(May add geog subd)*
Group reading *(May add geog subd)*
Group theory *[S]*
Group work in education
Grouse *[S]*
Growth *[S]*
   RT   Human growth
   SA   *the subdivision* —Growth
Growth (Plants) *(May add geog subd)*
Gruber, Franz Xavier, 1787-1863
Grunewald, Matthias, 16th century
GSX-140 Plus dot matrix printer (Computer printer)
Guadalcanal Island (Solomon Islands)
Guadalcanal Island (Solomon Islands), Battle of, 1942-1943
Guadalupe, Our Lady of
Guadalupe Mountains National Park (Tex.)
Guadeloupe
Guam
Guardian angels
Guatemala
Guerrillas *[S]*
Guevara, Ernesto, 1928-1967
Guiana
Guide dog schools *(May add geog subd)*
Guide dogs *[S]*
Guide Dogs for the Blind, Inc.
Guidebooks
   USE   —Guides
         Use the subdivision Description and travel—Guides under countries, regions, cities, etc., e.g., United States—Description and travel—Guides; Pittsburgh—Description and travel—Guides.
Guided missiles *[S]*
Guidry, Ron, 1950-
Guilds *(May add geog subd)*
Guillemin, Roger
Guilt
Guinea
Guinea pigs *[S]*
Guinea pigs as pets
Guinness, Alec, 1914-
Guion, Connie, 1882-
Guitar *[S]*
Guitar music *[S]*
Gulf Coast (Ala.)
Gulf Coast (Fla.)
Gulf Coast (U.S.)
Gulf Region (La.)
Gulf Region (Tex.)
Gulf States
Gulf Stream

Gulls *[S] (May add geog subd)*
Gums
    RT Dental care
Gun control *(May add geog subd)*
    RT Pistols
Guns
    USE Firearms
Gunpowder Plot, 1605
Gunter, Helen Clifford
Gunther, John, 1929-1947
Guppies *[S]*
Gurney, A.R. (Albert Ramsdell), 1930-
Gurus
Gutenberg, Johann, 1397?-1468
Guthrie, A. B., Jr., 1901-
Guthrie, Janet, 1938-
Guthrie, Woody, 1912-1967
Gutierrez-Magee Expedition, 1812-1813
Guy, Rosa
Guyana
Gymnastics *[S] (May add geog subd)*
Gymnastics for women *(May add geog subd)*
Gymnasts
Gymnosperms *(May add geog subd)*
Gynecology *(May add geog subd)*
Gypsies *[S]*
    —Folklore
        USE Folklore, Gypsy *[AC only]*
Gyroscopes *[S] (May add geog subd)*
Haast, William E., 1910-
Habit *[S]*
Habitat (Ecology) *(May add geog subd)*
    SA *the subdivision* —Habitat
Habitat for Humanity, Inc.
Habitat selection
Habsburg, House of
    UF Hapsburg, House of
Hadassah, the Women's Zionist Organization of America
Hadassah-University Medical Center (Jerusalem)
    USE Bet ha-halim "Hadasah" (Jerusalem)
Haddock, Sally
Hadrian I, Emperor of Rome, 76-138
Haganah (Organization)
Hagler, Marvin, 1954-
Haida Indians
Haig, Douglas, Sir, 1861-1928
Haiku *[S]*
Hail *[S] (May add geog subd)*
Hail Columbia (Song)
Hail Mary
    UF Ave Maria
Haile Selassie I, Emperor of Ethiopia, 1892-1975
Hailey, Kendall, 1966-
Hair *[S]*
Haircutting
Hairdressing *(May add geog subd)*
Hairstyles *(May add geog subd)*
Haiti
Haldeman, Harry R., 1926-
Hale, Nathan, 1755-1776
Hale, Sarah Josepha Buell, 1788-1879
Haleakala National Park (Hawaii)
Haley, Alex
Haley, Bill

Haley family
Hall, Dave
Hall, Lynn
Hall, Robert, 1814-1899
Halley, Edmond, 1656-1742
Halley, Sid (Fictitious character)
Halley's comet *[S]*
Hallmark Cards, Inc.
Hallmarks *[S] (May add geog subd)*
Halloween *[S] (May add geog subd)*
Halloween decorations
Hallowell (Me.)
Hallucinations and illusions *[S]*
Hallucinogenic drugs *(May add geog subd)*
    NT Phencyclidine
Hallucinogenic drugs and religious experience
Hallucinogenic mushrooms
    USE Mushrooms, Hallucinogenic
Hals, Frans, 1584-1666
Halsey, David, 1956-1983
Halsey, William Frederick, 1882-1959
Hambletonian 10 (Horse)
Hamer, Fannie Lou
Hamill, Dorothy
Hamilton, Alexander, 1757-1804
Hamilton, Emma, Lady, 1761?-1815
Hamilton, Virginia
Hamilton, William, Sir, 1730-1803
Hamlet
    RT Shakespeare, William, 1564-1616—Characters
Hammarskjold, Dag, 1905-1961
Hammer, Armand, 1897-
Hammer, Mike (Fictitious character)
Hammerhead shark *[S]*
Hammerstein, Oscar, 1895-1960
Hammett, Dashiell, 1894-1961
Hammons, Larry, 1937-
Hampton, Wade, 1752-1835
Hampton Roads (Va.), Battle of, 1862
Hamsters *[S] (May add geog subd)*
Hamsters as pets
Hancock, John, 1737-1793
Hancock, Lyn
Hand *[S]*
Hand games
Hand spinning *(May add geog subd)*
Hand-to-hand fighting *(May add geog subd)*
Hand-to-hand fighting, Oriental *(May add geog subd)*
    NT Kung fu
Hand weaving *(May add geog subd)*
Handball *[S] (May add geog subd)*
Handbooks, manuals, etc.
    UF Handbooks, vade-mecums, etc. *[AC only]*
    SA *the subdivision* —Handbooks, manuals, etc.
Handbooks, vade-mecums, etc.
    USE Handbooks, manuals, etc. *[AC only]*
Handel, George Frideric, 1685-1759
Handicapped *[S]*
    NT Physically handicapped
            Discrimination against the handicapped
Handicapped children *[S]*
Handicapped parents
Handicapped teachers

Handicraft *[AC, S] (May add geog subd)*
    UF Arts and crafts
          Creative activities and seat work
    RT Felt work
          Fiber work
          Leather work
          Miniature craft
          Paper work
          Woodwork
    SA *names of specific types of handicraft*
Handicrafts
    USE Handicraft
Handwriting
    USE Calligraphy
           Penmanship
    RT Writing
Hang gliding *[S] (May add geog subd)*
Hang-chou shih (China)
Hanks, Arly (Fictitious character)
Hanna, Jack, 1947-
Hannah, Page
Hannam, Charles
Hannay, Richard (Fictitious character)
Hannibal, 247-182 B.C.
Hanoi (Vietnam)
Hansberry, Lorraine, 1930-1965
Hanson, Brian
Hanukkah *[S]*
Hanukkah cookery
Happiness
Hapsburg, House of
    USE Habsburg, House of
Harbert, Virgil
Harbor seal *[S] (May add geog subd)*
Harbors *[S]*
Hard disks (Computer science)
Harding, Warren G. (Warren Gamaliel), 1865-1923
Hardware *(May add geog subd)*
Hardwoods *(May add geog subd)*
Hardy, Oliver, 1892-1957
Hardy, Thomas, 1840-1928
Hardy, Thomas, 1840-1928.   Tess of the d'Urbervilles
Hardyment, Christina
Hares *[S] (May add geog subd)*
Harlan, John Marshall, 1833-1911
Harlem (New York, N.Y.)
Harlem Globetrotters (Basketball team)
Harlem Renaissance *[S]*
Harley-Davidson Motor Company
Harley-Davidson motorcycle
Harlin County (Tex.)
Harlow, Jean, 1911-1937
Harmonica *[S]*
    RT Mouth organs
Harmony
    BT Music
Harmony (Aesthetics)
Harmsen, Dorothy
Harmsen, William
Harness racing *[S] (May add geog subd)*
Harold, King of England, 1022?-1066
Harp *[S]*
Harp seal *(May add geog subd)*
Harper, Valerie
Harpers Ferry (W. Va.)
Harrier (Jet fighter plane)

Harriman, W. Averell (William Averell), 1891-1986
Harris, Franco, 1950-
Harris, Harwell Hamilton, 1903-
Harris, Neil Patrick, 1973-
Harris, Rose Dilue, 1825-1914
Harrison, George, 1943-
Harrison, William Henry, 1773-1841
Hart, Emily, 1782-1877?
Hart, Moss, 1904-1961
Harte, Bret, 1836-1902
Harthoorn, Antonie Marinus
Harthoorn, Susanne
Hartnell, Norman
Harvard Divinity School
Harvard Law School
Harvest festivals *(May add geog subd)*
Harvest mouse, European *[AC only]*
    UF Micromys minutus
Harvestmen *[AC only]*
    USE Daddy longlegs
Harvey, William, 1578-1657
Hasekura, Tsunaga, 1571-1622
Hashish
Hassan II, King of Morocco, 1929-
Hastings, Battle of, 1066
Hate *(May add geog subd)*
Hatfield, Mark O., 1922-
Hatfield-McCoy Feud
Hatha yoga
    USE Yoga, Hatha
Hats *[S] (May add geog subd)*
Hatshepsut, Queen of Egypt
Hatteras, Cape (N.C.)
Haunted houses *(May add geog subd)*
Havel, Vaclav
Havelock the Dane (Legendary character)
Hawaii
Hawaii Volcanoes National Park (Hawaii)
Hawaiian language
Hawking, S. W. (Stephen W.)
Hawks *[S] (May add geog subd)*
    NT Goshawk
           Osprey
Hawks, Howard, 1896-
Hawthorne, Nathaniel, 1804-1864
Hawthorne, Nathaniel, 1804-1864.   Scarlet letter
Hawthorne, Sophia Amelia Peabody, 1811-1871
Hay *[S] (May add geog subd)*
Hay fever *[S] (May add geog subd)*
Hayden, Melissa
Haydn, Joseph, 1732-1809
Hayes, Billy
Hayes, Elvin, 1945-
Hayes, Rutherford Birchard, 1822-1893
Hay-fever plants *(May add geog subd)*
Haymarket Square Riot, Chicago (Ill.), 1886
Hays, John Coffee, 1817-1883
Hays County (Tex.)
Hayslip, Le Ly
Haywood, Big Bill, 1869-1928
Hayworth, Rita, 1918-1987
Hazardous occupations
    UF Occupations, Dangerous
Hazardous substances *[S] (May add geog subd)*
Hazardous wastes *[S] (May add geog subd)*
Hazing *(May add geog subd)*

Head *[S]*
Head in art
Head of the class (Television program)
Headache *[S]*
Heads of state *[S] (May add geog subd)*
> *NT* Kings, queens, rulers, etc.
> Women heads of state
> **—Dwellings** *(May add geog subd)*
Heal, David
Healing *(May add geog subd)*
Health *[AC, S] (May add geog subd)*
> *UF* Hygiene
> *NT* Cleanliness
> *SA* the subdivision —Health and hygiene
Health and race *(May add geog subd)*
Health attitudes *(May add geog subd)*
Health behavior *(May add geog subd)*
Health education *[S] (May add geog subd)*
Health facilities *(May add geog subd)*
Health insurance
> *USE* Insurance, Health
Health maintenance organizations *[S] (May add geog subd)*
Health occupations *(May add geog subd)*
Health occupations schools *(May add geog subd)*
Health officers
Health policy
> *USE* Medical policy
Health promotion *(May add geog subd)*
Health risk assessment *(May add geog subd)*
Health services
> *USE* Medical care
Healy, J.J. (John J.)
Healy, Johnny, 1840-1908
Healy, Katherine
Hearing *[S]*
Hearing aids *[S] (May add geog subd)*
Hearing disorders *(May add geog subd)*
> *NT* Tinnitus
Hearing ear dogs *[S] (May add geog subd)*
Hearing impaired *[S]*
> *BT* Physically handicapped
> *NT* Deaf
> Video recordings for the hearing impaired
Hearst, Patricia, 1954-
Hearst, William Randolph, 1863-1951
Heart *[S]*
Heart, Artificial
Heart arrest
> *USE* Cardiac arrest
Heart attack
> *USE* Myocardial infarction
Heat *[S]*
Heat Moon, William Least
Heath, Ralph
Heathcliff (Fictitious character)
Heating *[S]*
Heaven *[S]*
Heaven in art
> *UF* Heaven—Art
Heavy metal (Music)
Hebrew language *[S] (May add geog subd)*
> **—Readers** *[AC only]*
> > Use for reading texts in Hebrew containing materials for instruction and practice in reading that language.
> > *RT* Hebrew language materials *[AC only]*

Hebrew language materials *[AC only]*
> Use for works written in Hebrew intended primarily for general information or recreational reading. Such works with text also given in English are further subdivided by the subdivision —Bilingual.
> *RT* Hebrew language—Readers *[AC only]*
> **—Bilingual** *[AC only]*
Hebrides (Scotland)
Hecate (Greek deity)
Hedgehogs *[S]*
Hegel, Georg William Friedrich, 1770-1831
Heiden, Eric
Height, Body
> *USE* Stature
Hein, Piet, 1578-1629
Heinlein, Robert A. (Robert Anson), 1907-
Heisman Trophy
Heisman, John W. (John William), 1869-1936
Heldensage
> *UF* Heroic saga
Helen of Troy (Greek mythology)
Helfer, Tana
Helicopter ambulances *(May add geog subd)*
Helicopter pilots
Helicopters *[S]*
> **—Piloting** *[S]*
Hellcat (Fighter planes)
Hellenism *[S]*
Heller, Joseph. Catch 22
Hellman, Lillian, 1906-
Helmholtz, Hermann Ludwig Ferdinand von, 1821-1894
Helpfulness *[AC only]*
> *UF* Helping behavior
Helping behavior
> *USE* Helpfulness *[AC only]*
Hematology *(May add geog subd)*
Hemingway, Ernest, 1899-1961
Hemingway, Ernest, 1899-1961.   Farewell to arms
Hemingway, Ernest, 1899-1961.   Old man and the sea
Hemingway, Gregory H., 1931-
Hemiptera *(May add geog subd)*
> *BT* Insects
Henderson, James Pinckney, 1808-1858
Henderson, Rickey, 1958-
Henrich, Tommy
Hendrix, Jimi
Henrique, o Navegador, Infante of Portugal, 1394-1460
> *USE* Henry the Navigator, 1394-1460 *[AC only]*
Henry, Clifton
Henry, Infante of Portugal, 1394-1460
> *USE* Henry the Navigator, 1394-1460 *[AC only]*
Henry, Marguerite, 1902-
Henry, O., 1862-1910
> *UF* O'Henry, 1862-1910
> Porter, William Sidney, 1823-1910
Henry, Patrick, 1736-1799
Henry Ford Peace Expedition, 1915-1916
Henry Francis du Pont Winterthur Museum (Del.)
Henry I, King of England, 1068-1135
Henry II, King of England, 1133-1189
Henry III, King of England, 1207-1272
Henry IV, King of England, 1267-1413
Henry VII, King of England, 1457-1509
Henry the Navigator, 1394-1460 *[AC only]*
> *UF* Henrique, o Navegador, Infante of Portugal, 1394-1460
> Henry, Infante of Portugal, 1394-1460
Henry V, King of England, 1387-1422

Henry VIII, King of England, 1491-1547
Hens
    USE   Chickens
              Poultry
Henson, Anaukaq, 1906-
Henson, Jim
Henson, Matthew Alexander, 1866-1955
Hepatitis, Viral *(May add geog subd)*
Hepburn, Audrey, 1929-
Hepburn, Katharine, 1909-
Heracles (Greek mythology)
Heraldry *[S] (May add geog subd)*
    NT   Crests
Herb gardening *(May add geog subd)*
Herbalists
Herbals
    BT   Botanical literature
Herbert, Frank
Herbivores *(May add geog subd)*
Herbs *[S] (May add geog subd)*
Hercegovina
    USE   Bosnia and Hercegovina
Herculaneum (Extinct city)
Hercules (Roman mythology)
Heredity *[S]*
Hermes (Greek deity)
Hermit crabs *[S] (May add geog subd)*
Herodotus
Heroes
Heroes in literature
Heroin *[S] (May add geog subd)*
Heroin habit *(May add geog subd)*
Heroines
Herons *[S] (May add geog subd)*
    NT   Cattle egret
              Great blue heron
Herpesvirus diseases *(May add geog subd)*
Herr family
Herr, Hugh
Herring *(May add geog subd)*
Herriot, James
Herrmann, Alexander, 1843-1896
Herrmann, Carl, 1816-1887
Herschel, Caroline Lucretia, 1750-1848
Herschel, William, Sir, 1738-1822
Hersey, John, 1914-
Hersh, Gizelle, 1922-
Hershey, Milton Snavely, 1857-1945
Hershiser, Orel
Herzl, Theodor, 1860-1904
Hess, Markus
Hess, Rudolf, 1894-1987
Hesse, Hermann, 1877-1962
Hessians
Hewitt, Don, 1922-
Heydrich, Reinhard, 1904-1942
Heyerdahl, Thor
Hiawatha, 15th cent.
Hibernation
    SA   *the subdivision* —Hibernation
Hickok, Lorena A.
Hickok, Richard Eugene, 1931-1965
Hickok, Wild Bill, 1837-1876
Hicks, David, 1929-
Hicks, Edward, 1780-1849. Peaceable Kingdom
Hidalgo y Costilla, Miguel, 1753-1811

Hidden treasure (Parable)
Hide-and-go-seek
    USE   Hide-and-seek *[AC only]*
Hide-and-seek *[AC only]*
    UF   Hide-and-go-seek
    BT   Games
              Play
Hieroglyphics *[S]*
    RT   Picture-writing
High blood pressure
    USE   Hypertension
Higginbotham, Bill
High-carbohydrate diet *(May add geog subd)*
    BT   Diet
High-fiber diet
    BT   Diet
High-fidelity sound systems *[S]*
High interest-low vocabulary books
High-potassium diet *(May add geog subd)*
High school equivalency examinations *(May add geog subd)*
    BT   General educational development tests
High school attendance *(May add geog subd)*
High school dropouts
High school graduates
High school libraries *[S] (May add geog subd)*
   —Book lists
High school principals
High school students *[S]*
   —Library orientation
High school teachers
   —Salaries, etc.
High school teaching *(May add geog subd)*
High schools *[S] (May add geog subd)*
High-speed aeronautics *[S]*
High technology *(May add geog subd)*
    RT   Technology
High technology industries *(May add geog subd)*
Higher education
    USE   Education, Higher
Highlander Research and Education Center (Knoxville, Tenn.)
Highway engineering *[S] (May add geog subd)*
Hijacking of aircraft *(May add geog subd)*
Hiking *[S] (May add geog subd)*
Hilfiker, David
Hill, Anita
Hill, Jean
Hillary, Edmund, Sir
Hilliard, David
Himalaya Mountains
Himes, Chester B., 1909-
Himmler, Heinrich, 1900-1945
Hindenburg, Paul von, 1847-1934
Hindenburg (Airship)
Hindi language *[S] (May add geog subd)*
   —Readers *[AC only]*
      Use for reading texts in Hindi containing materials for instruction and practice in reading that language.
    RT   Hindi language materials *[AC only]*
Hindi language materials *[AC only]*
      Use for works written in Hindi intended primarily for general information or recreational reading. Such works with text also given in English are further subdivided by the subdivision —Bilingual.
    RT   Hindi language—Readers *[AC only]*
   —Bilingual *[AC only]*
Hinduism *[S] (May add geog subd)*

Hinduism *[S] (May add geog subd)*
   BT Religions
Hindus *[S]*
Hingle, Patricia
Hinton, S.E.
Hippeastrum
   USE Amaryllis (Hippeastrum) *[AC only]*
Hippies *[S]*
Hippocrates
Hippopotamus *[S]*
Hirohito, Emperor of Japan, 1901-
Hiroshima (Japan)
Hispanic American families
Hispanic American literature (Spanish) *(May add geog subd)*
Hispanic Americans *[S]*
   UF Latinos
   NT Cuban Americans
        Mexican Americans
        Puerto Ricans
Hispanic politicians
   USE Politicians, Hispanic
Hiss, Alger
Historians *[S]*
Historic buildings *[S] (May add geog subd)*
   RT Literary landmarks
Historic sites *[S] (May add geog subd)*
  —Interpretive programs
Historical fiction *[S]*
Historical geography
   SA the subdivision —Historical geography
Historical markers *(May add geog subd)*
Historical libraries
   USE History—Societies, etc.
Historical sociology
Historiography *[S] (May add geog subd)*
   SA the subdivision —Historiography
History *[S]*
   SA the subdivisions —History *and* —History—16th [17th, etc,] century, —History, Local, etc.
  —Errors, inventions, etc.
History, Ancient *[S]*
History, Modern *[S]*
  —17th century
  —18th century
  —19th century
  —19th century
  —20th century
  —1945- *[S]*
History in art
Hit-and-run drivers
Hitchcock, Alfred, 1899-
Hitler, Adolf, 1889-1945
  —Assassination attempt, 1944
Hitler-Jugend
   USE Hitler Youth *[AC only]*
Hitler Youth *[AC only]*
   UF Hitler-Jugend
       Nazi Youth Movement
   BT National Socialism *[AC only]*
       Youth movement—Germany *[AC only]*
Hittites *[S]*
HIV (Viruses) *(May add geog subd)*
   RT AIDS (Disease)
HIV infections *(May add geog subd)*

Hiva Oa (Marquesas Islands)
Hmong (Asian people) *(May add geog subd)*
  —Folklore *[AC, S]*
   UF Folklore, Hmong
Hmong language
  —Readers *[AC only]*
     Use for reading texts in Hmong containing materials for instruction and practice in reading the language.
   RT Hmong language materials *[AC only]*
Hmong language materials *[AC only]*
     Use for works written in Hmong intended primarily for general information or recreational reading. Such works with text also given in English are further subdivided by the subdivision —Bilingual.
   RT Hmong language—Readers *[AC only]*
  —Bilingual *[AC only]*
Ho, Chi Minh, 1890-1969
Ho Chi Minh City (Vietnam)
Hoarding of money
Hoban, James, ca. 1762-1831
Hobbies *[S]*
Hobbit (Motion picture)
Hobbs, Anne
Hocken, Sheila
Hockey *[S] (May add geog subd)*
Hockey players
Hodgkin's disease *[S] (May add geog subd)*
Hoffman, William, 1937-
Hofmann, Hans, 1880-1966
Hogan, Ben, 1912-
Hogarth, William, 1697-1764
Hogg, Ima
Hogrogian, Nonny
Holbein, Hans, 1497-1543
Holden, Edith, 1871-1920
Holding companies *(May add geog subd)*
Hole-in-the-Day, Chief, 1828-1868
Holes
Holiday, Billie, 1915-1959
Holiday cookery *(May add geog subd)*
Holiday decorations *[S]*
Holidays *[S] (May add geog subd)*
Holidays in art *[S]*
Holistic medicine *[S] (May add geog subd)*
Holland
Holley, Mary Austin, 1784-1846
Holly, Buddy, 1936-1959
Hollywood (Los Angeles, Calif.)
Holmes, Oliver Wendell, 1841-1935
Holmes, Sherlock (Fictitious character)
Holocaust, Jewish (1933-1945) *[S] (May add geog subd)*
   RT Righteous Gentiles in the Holocaust
Holocaust, Jewish (1933-1945), in art *[S]*
Holocaust, Jewish (1933-1945), in literature
Holocaust, Jewish (1933-1945), in motion pictures
Holocaust survivors
Holographic wills *(May add geog subd)*
   BT Wills
Holography *[S] (May add geog subd)*
   BT Three-dimensional display systems
Holy grail
   USE Grail
Holy Roman Empire *[S]*
Home *[S] (May add geog subd)*
   RT Dwellings
   SA the subdivision —Homes and haunts
Home, D.D. (Daniel Dunglas), 1833-1886

Home accidents *[S] (May add geog subd)*
Home and school *[S] (May add geog subd)*
Home banking services *(May add geog subd)*
Home-based businesses *(May add geog subd)*
    UF Home business
Home care services *[S] (May add geog subd)*
Home computers
    USE Microcomputers
Home economics *[S] (May add geog subd)*
    UF Housekeeping
Home labor *(May add geog subd)*
    RT Home businesses
Home nursing *[S] (May add geog subd)*
Home runs (Baseball)
Home schooling *(May add geog subd)*
Home video systems *[S]*
Homeless persons
Homeless youth
Homelessness *[S]*
Homeopathy *[S] (May add geog subd)*
    BT Alternative medicine
Homeostasis
Homer
Homer. Iliad
Homer. Odyssey
    UF Odyssey
Homer, Winslow, 1836-1910
Homer, Winslow, 1836-1910. Gulf stream
Homesickness *(May add geog subd)*
Homestead law *(May add geog subd)*
Homework
Homing pigeons *(May add geog subd)*
Homonyms
    SA *the subdivision* —Homonyms
Homoptera
    BT Insects
Homosexuality *[S] (May add geog subd)*
Homosexuality and education *(May add geog subd)*
Honduras
Honesty *[AC, S]*
    UF Truthfulness and falsehood
Honey *[S] (May add geog subd)*
Honey-eating animals
    USE Nectarivores
Honeybee *(May add geog subd)*
Honeymoon *(May add geog subd)*
Hong Kong
Honolulu
Hood (Battleship)
Hoodlums
Hoodoo (Cult) *(May add geog subd)*
Hoover, Herbert, 1874-1964
Hoover, J. Edgar (John Edgar), 1895-1972
Hope *[AC only]*
    NT Disappointment *[AC only]*
Hope, Anthony, 1863-1933. Prisoner of Zenda
Hope, Bob, 1903-
Hopi Indians
Hopi language *[S] (May add geog subd)*
    —Readers *[AC only]*
        Use for reading texts in Hopi containing materials for instruction and practice in reading that language.
        RT Hopi language materials *[AC only]*
Hopi language materials *[AC only]*

        Use for works written in Hopi intended primarily for general information or recreational reading. Such works with text also given in English are further subdivided by the subdivision —Bilingual.
    RT Hopi language—Readers *[AC only]*
    —Bilingual *[AC only]*
Hopkins, Sarah Winnemucca, 1844?-1891
Hopkins, Stephen, 1581-1644
Hopper, Edward, 1882-1967
Hopscotch
    BT Games
Horary astrology *(May add geog subd)*
    BT Astrology
Hormones *[S]*
    NT Pheromones
Horn, Tom, 1860-1903
Horn (Musical instrument) *[S]*
Hornblower, Horatio (Fictitious character)
Horne, Lena
Horowitz, Vladimir, 1904-
Horns *[S]*
Horror *[S]*
    —Fiction
        USE Horror stories *[AC only]*
Horror films *(May add geog subd)*
Horror stories *[AC only]*
    UF Horror—Fiction
           Horror tales
Horror tales
    USE Horror stories *[AC only]*
Horse breeding
    USE Horses—Breeding *[AC only]*
Horse breeds *(May add geog subd)*
Horse industry *(May add geog subd)*
Horse race betting
    USE Horse racing—Betting
Horse racing *[S] (May add geog subd)*
    UF Horse-racing
    RT Jockeys
    —Betting
Horse shows *[AC only] (May add geog subd)*
    UF Horse-shows
Horse sports *(May add geog subd)*
Horse trainers
Horsemanship *[S] (May add geog subd)*
    NT Steeplechasing
Horsemen and horsewomen
Horses *[S] (May add geog subd)*
    —Breeding *[AC, S]*
    UF Horse breeding
    NT Ponies
    SA *the names of specific breeds and types of horses*
Horses in art *[S]*
Horseshoe crabs *[AC, S]*
Horsewomen
    USE Horsemen and horsewomen
Hortense, consort of Louis Bonaparte, King of Holland, 1783-1837
Horticulture *[S] (May add geog subd)*
Horwitz, Tony, 1958-
Hospice care *(May add geog subd)*
Hospices (Terminal care) *(May add geog subd)*
Hospitals *[S] (May add geog subd)*
    SA *the subdivisions* —Hospital care *and* —Hospitals
    —Emergency service
Höss, Rudolf, 1900-1947
Hostages *[S]*

Hot air balloons
Hot peppers *(May add geog subd)*
Hot rods
    BT   Automobiles, Racing
Hot Springs (Ark.)
Hotcakes
    USE   Pancakes, waffles, etc.
Hotel management
Hotels, motels, etc. *[AC, S]*
    UF   Hotels, taverns, etc.
            Motels
Hotels, taverns, etc.
    USE   Hotels, motels, etc. *[AC only]*
Hotlines (Counseling) *(May add geog subd)*
Houdini, Harry, 1874-1926
Hours of labor *[S] (May add geog subd)*
House buying *(May add geog subd)*
House cleaning *[S]*
House construction *[S] (May add geog subd)*
House furnishings *(May add geog subd)*
House of Representatives
    USE   United States. Congress. House
House painting *[S]*
House plant industry *(May add geog subd)*
House plants
    USE   Indoor gardening *[AC only]*
House selling *(May add geog subd)*
Houseboats *[S] (May add geog subd)*
Household appliances, Electric *[S] (May add geog subd)*
Household ecology *(May add geog subd)*
Household employees *[AC, S]*
    UF   Domestic employees
            Domestics
            Servants
    RT   Labor
Household pests *(May add geog subd)*
Household supplies *(May add geog subd)*
Houseman, John
Housekeeping
    USE   Home economics
Houses
    USE   Architecture, Domestic
            Dwellings
    RT   Home
Housewives
Housing *[S] (May add geog subd)*
    SA   *the subdivision* —Housing
Housing and health *(May add geog subd)*
Housing policy *(May add geog subd)*
Houston Astros (Baseball team)
Houston, Sam, 1793-1863
Houston (Tex.)
Houston, Jeanne Wakatsuki
Houston, Margaret Lea, 1819-1867
Houston, Sam, 1793-1863
Houston, Temple Lea, 1860-1905
Houston Astros (Baseball team)
Houston Livestock Show And Rodeo
Houston Oilers (Football team)
Houston Rockets (Basketball team)
Hoving, Thomas, 1931-
Howarth, William L., 1940-
Howe, Elias, 1820-1895
Hoxic, Vinnie (Ream), 1847-1914
    USE   Ream, Vinnie, 1847-1914.
Hoyle, Edmond, 1672-1769

Hrubieszow (Poland)
Hubbel, James
Hubble, Edwin Powell, 1889-1953
Hubble Space Telescope
Hudson, Henry, d. 1611
Hudson River (N.Y. and N.J.)
Hudson, Rock, 1925-1985
Hudson's Bay Company
Huerta, Dolores, 1930-
Hugging *[S] (May add geog subd)*
Hughes, Arizona Houston, 1876-1969
Hughes, John R. (John Reynolds), 1855-1947
Hughes, Langston, 1902-1967
Hughes family
Hughes Flying-boat (Seaplane)
Hui-shen, 5th cent.
Hull House (Chicago, Ill.)
Human anatomy *(May add geog subd)*
    UF   Anatomy, Human
Human behavior *[S]*
Human biology
Human body
    USE   Body, Human
Human capital *(May add geog subd)*
Human ecology *[S] (May add geog subd)*
  —Moral and ethical aspects
      USE   Environmental ethics
Human engineering *[S] (May add geog subd)*
Human evolution
    USE   Evolution *[AC only]*
Human experimentation in medicine *[S] (May add geog subd)*
Human figure in art
    RT   Figure drawing
Human gene mapping *(May add geog subd)*
Human genetics
Human Genome Project
Human geography *(May add geog subd)*
Human growth *(May add geog subd)*
    RT   Growth
Human information processing
Human life cycle
    USE   Life cycle, Human
Human locomotion *[S] (May add geog subd)*
Human mechanics
Human physiology
    BT   Physiology
Human powered aircraft
Human relations
    USE   Interpersonal relations
Human reproduction *(May add geog subd)*
Human rights *[S] (May add geog subd)*
Human services *(May add geog subd)*
Human skeleton
Human-animal communication
Humanism *[S] (May add geog subd)*
Humanistic education
    USE   Education, Humanistic
Humanistic ethics
Humanists
Humanitarianism
Humanities *[S] (May add geog subd)*
    RT   Science and the humanities
Hume, George Basil
Humes, Arthur Grover, 1916-

Humidity [S] (May add geog subd)
Hummel art (May add geog subd)
Hummel figurines
Hummingbirds [S] (May add geog subd)
Humor
    USE   Anecdotes
             Wit and Humor [AC, S]
    SA   *the subdivisions* —Humor *and* —Wit and humor
Humorists [S]
Humorous poetry [S]
    NT   Limericks
             Nonsense verses
Humorous songs
Humorous stories [S]
Humpback whale [S] (May add geog subd)
Humphrey, Hubert H. (Hubert Horatio), 1911-1978
Humphrey, William
Humphrey (Whale)
Humphreys, George, 1899-
Humphry, Ann, d. 1991
Hundred Years' War, 1339-1453 [S]
Hungarian Americans
Hungary
    —History [S]
    — —Revolution, 1956
Hunger [S]
Huns
Hunt, Annie Mae, 1909-
Hunt family
Hunt, Leigh, 1784-1859
Hunt, W. Holman (William Holman), 1827-1910
Hunter, Jim, 1946-
Hunter, John, 1728-1793
Hunting [S] (May add geog subd)
    —Fiction [AC only]
        UF   Hunting stories
        BT   Sports—Fiction [AC only]
        NT   Decoys (Hunting)
               Muzzleloader hunting
        SA   *the subdivision* —Hunting
Hunting dogs
    BT   Dogs
Hunting guns
    BT   Firearms
Hunting stories
    USE   Hunting—Fiction [AC only]
Huntington's chorea (May add geog subd)
Huntley, Chet, 1911-1974
Huron Indians
    USE   Wyandot Indians
Hurricane Hugo, 1989
Hurricanes [S]
Hurston, Zora Neale
Husband and wife (May add geog subd)
Husbandry, Animal
    USE   Domestic animals
Husbands [S]
Hussein, King of Jordan, 1935-
Hussein, Saddam, 1937-
Hutchinson, Anne Marbury, 1591-1643
Hutton, James, 1726-1797
Huxley, Aldous, 1894-1963
Huxley, Elspeth Joscelin Grant, 1907-
Huynh, Quang Nhuong
Hydra (Greek mythology)

Hydrocephalus (May add geog subd)
Hydroelectric power plants [S] (May add geog subd)
Hydrologic cycle
Hydrology (May add geog subd)
Hydroponics [S] (May add geog subd)
Hydrostatics [S]
Hydrotherapy [S] (May add geog subd)
Hyenas [S]
Hygiene
    USE   Cleanliness [AC only]
Hyla crucifer
    USE   Spring peeper [AC only]
Hylidae
    USE   Tree frogs [AC only]
Hyman, Dick, 1927-
Hyman, Trina Schart
Hymenoptera
    BT   Insects
Hymn tunes
Hymn writers
Hymns [S] (May add geog subd)
Hyperactive child syndrome
    USE   Attention-deficit hyperactivity disorder
Hyperactive children [S]
    RT   Attention-deficit hyperactivity disorder
Hyperbola
    BT   Conic sections
Hypercard (Computer program)
Hypercholesteremia (May add geog subd)
Hypermedia systems (May add geog subd)
Hypersensitivity
    USE   Allergy
Hyperspace
    BT   Geometry
    RT   Space and time
Hypertension [S] (May add geog subd)
    UF   High blood pressure
Hypnotism [S]
Hypoglycemia
Hypothalamic hormones
Hysteria (May add geog subd)
Iacocca, Lee A.
Iago (Fictitious character)
Ibex
    UF   Alpine mountain goat
IBM-compatible computers
IBM computers
IBM/PC
    USE   IBM Personal Computer
IBM Personal Computer
IBM Personal Computer PC 51550 (Computer)
IBM PS/2 Model 25 (Computer)
IBM PS/2 Model 5150
IBM PS/2 Model 56SX (Computer)
    UF   Clones of IBM computers
Ibsen, Henrik, 1828-1906
Ibsen, Henrik, 1828-1906. Doll's house [AC only]
    UF   Ibsen, Henrik, 1828-1906. Dukkehjem
Ibsen, Henrik, 1828-1906. Dukkehjem
    USE   Ibsen, Henrik, 1828-1906. Doll's house [AC only]
Icarus (Greek mythology)
Ice (May add geog subd)
Ice caps (May add geog subd)
Ice cream, ices, etc.
Ice cream industry (May add geog subd)
Ice fishing [S] (May add geog subd)

Ice sheets *(May add geog subd)*
Ice skaters *[AC only]*
    UF   Skaters
Ice skating *[AC only]*
    UF   Skating
Icebergs
Iceboating *[S] (May add geog subd)*
Iceland
Ichthyologists
    RT   Fishes
Icon painting *(May add geog subd)*
Icons *(May add geog subd)*
    BT   Christian art and symbolism
Idaho
Identity (Psychology)
    RT   Individuality
           Personality
Idioms
    SA   *the subdivision* —Idioms
Idlefonso
Iditarod Trail Sled Dog Race, Alaska
Ifugaos
    BT   Philippines—Languages
Igbo (African people)
   —Folklore
        USE   Folklore, Igbo *[AC only]*
Igloos
    BT   Dwellings
Iguana (Genus) *(May add geog subd)*
Illegal aliens *[S]*
    UF   Aliens, Illegal
Illinois
Illiteracy
    USE   Literacy
    RT   Reading
Illness
    USE   Diseases
Illumination of books and manuscripts *[S] (May add geog subd)*
Illustrated books, Children's *(May add geog subd)*
    RT   Picture books
           Toy and movable books
Illustration of books *[S] (May add geog subd)*
    RT   Animal painting and illustration
Illustrators *[S]*
   Use also the names of individual illustrators.
Illustrators, English
Image processing
    BT   Imaging systems
    RT   Scanning systems
   —Digital techniques
Imagery (Psychology)
Imagewriter II
Imaginary companions
    USE   Imaginary playmates *[AC, S]*
Imaginary playmates *[AC, S]*
    UF   Friends, Imaginary
           Imaginary companions
           Imaginary friends
           Invisible playmates
           Make-believe playmates
           Playmates, Imaginary
    BT   Friendship
           Imagination
           Play
Imaginary wars and battles

Imagination *[S]*
    NT   Imaginary playmates *[AC only]*
Imaging systems in astronomy
Imitation
Imitation (in literature)
Immigrants
    NT   Teenage immigrants
Immigration
    USE   Emigration and immigration
Immortality *[S]*
    RT   Death
Immune system
    RT   AIDS (Disease)
           Immunology
Immunity *[S]*
    RT   Allergy
           Medicine
           Pathology
           Vaccination
Immunization in children
Immunologic diseases *(May add geog subd)*
Immunology *(May add geog subd)*
    RT   AIDS (Disease)
           Immune system
    NT   Phagocytocis
    SA   *the subdivision* —Immunology
Immunotherapy *(May add geog subd)*
Impeachments *[S] (May add geog subd)*
    SA   *the subdivision* —Impeachment
Imperial Trans-Antarctic Expedition, 1914-1917
Imperialism *[S]*
Impersonation
Impetigo
Implements, utensils, etc *(May add geog subd)*
Imports *(May add geog subd)*
Impostors and imposture *[S]*
    RT   Counterfeits and counterfeiting
           Forgery
           Fraud
           Quacks and quackery
Impotence *(May add geog subd)*
Impressionism (Art) *[S] (May add geog subd)*
    BT   Art, Modern—19th century
    RT   Post-impressionism (Art)
Impressionist artists
Improvisation (Acting)
    USE   Plays—Improvisation *[AC only]*
In-line skating *(May add geog subd)*
    UF   Rollerblading
    BT   Roller skating
Inboard-outboard engines
Incas *[S]*
Incense *(May add geog subd)*
Incest *[S]*
    RT   Child molesting
Incest victims *[S]*
Incineration *(May add geog subd)*
    RT   Refuse and refuse disposal
Inclined planes
Income distribution *(May add geog subd)*
Income tax *[S]*
    RT   Taxation
Incorporation *(May add geog subd)*
Independent regulatory commissions *(May add geog subd)*
Indexes *[S]*
    SA   *the subdivision* —Indexes

Indexing *[S]*
India
   —History
    — —1000-1526
    — —1526-1765
Indian architecture *(May add geog subd)*
Indian art *(May add geog subd)*
Indian calendar *(May add geog subd)*
Indian craft
Indian leatherwork
Indian mythology *(May add geog subd)*
   —North America, [South America, etc.]
      USE   Indians of North America, [South America, etc.]
          —Folklore *[AC, S]*
Indian Ocean
Indian outlaws
Indian painting *(May add geog subd)*
Indian paintbrush
   USE   Castilleja
Indian poetry *(May add geog subd)*
Indian python *(May add geog subd)*
Indiana
Indiana Dunes National Lakeshore (Ind.)
Indiana Pacers (Basketball team)
Indianapolis (Cruiser)
Indianapolis Colts (Football team)
Indianapolis Speedway Race
Indians *[S]*
   —Treatment *[AC only] (May add geog subd)*
      UF   Indians, Treatment of
      SA   *the names of specific Indian nations and tribes*
Indians, Treatment of
   USE   Indians—Treatment *[AC only]*
Indians in literature *(May add geog subd)*
Indians of Central America *[S]*
Indians of Mexico *[S]*
Indians of North America, [South America, etc.] *[AC, S]*
   —Folklore *[AC, S]*
      Single myths or collections of mythology of a specific tribe are entered under the name of the tribe with the subdivision —Folklore.
      UF   Indian mythology—North America, [South America, etc.]
          Indians of North America, [South America, etc.]—Legends
   —Legends
      USE   Indians of North America, [South America, etc.]
          —Folklore *[AC, S]*
Indians of South America *[S]*
Indians of the West Indies *[S]*
Indiantown (Fla.)
Indic literature *[S] (May add geog subd)*
Indic poetry *(May add geog subd)*
Indigenous peoples
   UF   Native peoples
Individual differences *(May add geog subd)*
Individualism *[S] (May add geog subd)*
Individuality *[S]*
   RT   Identity (Psychology)
        Self
Individualized instruction *[S]*
Individualized reading instruction
Indochina *[S]*
Indochinese Americans
Indochinese War, 1946-1954
Indonesia
Indoor air pollution *(May add geog subd)*
Indoor games *[AC, S] (May add geog subd)*

   UF   Creative activities and seat work
Indoor gardening *[S]*
   UF   House plants *[AC only]*
Indoor gardens *(May add geog subd)*
Indus civilization
   BT   Pakistan—Antiquities
Industrial arts *[S]*
   RT   Carpentry
        Vocational education
        Woodwork
Industrial arts education
Industrial housekeeping
Industrial hygienists
Industrial management *[S] (May add geog subd)*
Industrial mobilization *[S] (May add geog subd)*
   RT   War—Economic aspects
Industrial museums *(May add geog subd)*
Industrial productivity *(May add geog subd)*
Industrial promotion *(May add geog subd)*
Industrial psychology
   USE   Psychology, Industrial
Industrial publicity *(May add geog subd)*
Industrial relations *[S] (May add geog subd)*
   UF   Employer-employee relations
Industrial revolution
   USE   Industry—History
      SA   *the subdivisions* —Economic conditions *and* —Industries *under names of countries*
Industrial robots
   USE   Robots, Industrial
Industrialists
Industry *[S]*
      SA   *the subdivision* —Industries
Industry and education *(May add geog subd)*
Industry and state *(May add geog subd)*
Inefficiency, Intellectual
   USE   Mental efficiency
        Stupidity
Inertia (Mechanics)
Infant care
   USE   Babies—Care
Infantry
   BT   Armed forces
Infantry drill and tactics
Infants
   USE   Babies *[AC only]*
      SA   *the subdivision* —Infancy
Infants (Newborn)
   USE   Babies *[AC only]*
Infection
   RT   Viruses
Infertility *[S] (May add geog subd)*
Inflation (Finance) *[S] (May add geog subd)*
Influence (Psychology)
Influence (Literary, artistic, etc.)
Influenza *[S] (May add geog subd)*
Information networks *[S] (May add geog subd)*
Information retrieval
Information science *[S] (May add geog subd)*
Information services *[S] (May add geog subd)*
   RT   Libraries
        Reference services (Libraries)
Information society *(May add geog subd)*
Information storage and retrieval systems
   RT   Information retrieval
Information technology *(May add geog subd)*

Information theory
Informed consent (Medical law) *(May add geog subd)*
Infrared radiation *[S] (May add geog subd)*
    BT   Radiation
Infrared technology *(May add geog subd)*
    BT   Radiation
Ingredient substitutions (Cookery)
Ingenuity
    USE   Problem solving
Ingres, Jean-Auguste-Dominique, 1780-1867
Inheritance and succession *[S] (May add geog subd)*
    UF   Succession
Inheritance and transfer tax *[S] (May add geog subd)*
Injuries
    USE   Accidents
    USE   Wounds and injuries
Initials *[S]*
Initiations (into trades, societies, etc.)
Inland navigation *[S] (May add geog subd)*
Inner child
Inner cities *[S] (May add geog subd)*
Inner planets
Inquisition *[S] (May add geog subd)*
    RT   Catholic Church
Insane, Criminal and dangerous
Insect pests *[S] (May add geog subd)*
    UF   Insects, Injurious and beneficial
    RT   Insects
          Pests
Insect-plant relationships *(May add geog subd)*
Insect rearing *(May add geog subd)*
Insect societies *(May add geog subd)*
Insect sounds *(May add geog subd)*
Insecticides *[S] (May add geog subd)*
Insectivora
    USE   Insectivores *[AC only]*
Insectivores *[AC only] (May add geog subd)*
    UF   Insectivora
Insects *[S] (May add geog subd)*
    RT   Entomology
          Insect pests
    NT   Diptera
          Homoptera
          Hymenoptera
          Orthoptera
    SA   *the names of specific insects and types of insects*
    —Metamorphosis
Insects, Aquatic
    USE   Aquatic insects
Insects, Injurious and beneficial
    USE   Beneficial insects
          Insect pests
Insects as carriers of disease *[S] (May add geog subd)*
Insects as food *(May add geog subd)*
Insects as pets
Insects in art
Insignia *[S] (May add geog subd)*
    RT   Emblems
Insomnia *[S]*
    RT   Sleep
Installment plan *[S] (May add geog subd)*
Instinct *[S]*
Instructional materials
Instructional materials centers *[S] (May add geog subd)*
    —Acquisitions

    —Collection development
    —User education
Instructions to juries *(May add geog subd)*
Instrument flying *[S]*
Instrumental music *[S] (May add geog subd)*
Instrumentation and orchestration *[S]*
    UF   Orchestration
Instruments
Instruments, Musical
    USE   Musical instruments
Insulation (Heat) *[S]*
Insulin
    RT   Diabetes
Insurance, Automobile *(May add geog subd)*
Insurance, Casualty *(May add geog subd)*
Insurance, Disability *(May add geog subd)*
Insurance, Health *(May add geog subd)*
    NT   Medicaid
          Medicare
Insurance, Homeowners *(May add geog subd)*
Insurance, Life *(May add geog subd)*
Insurance, Long-term care *(May add geog subd)*
Insurance, Property *(May add geog subd)*
Insurance companies *(May add geog subd)*
Integrated software
    UF   Software, Integrated
    BT   Computer software
Intel 80486 (Microprocessor)
Intellect *[S]*
    RT   Cognition
          Personality and cognition
    NT   Cognitive styles
    SA   *the subdivision* —Intellectual life
Intellectual life *[S]*
Intellectual property *(May add geog subd)*
    NT   Copyright
          Inventions
          Patents
Intellectuals *[S]*
Intelligence levels *(May add geog subd)*
Intelligence officers
Intelligence service *[S] (May add geog subd)*
    Use for works on the organization, function, and activities of particular intelligence services. *[AC only]*
    RT   Espionage
          Spies
    —Fiction *[AC only]*
        Use for fictional works on the activities of an intelligence service.
        RT   Spies—Fiction *[AC only]*
Intelligence tests *[S] (May add geog subd)*
Interaction analysis in education
Interactive multimedia *(May add geog subd)*
    UF   Interactive media
Intercollegiate Conference of Faculty Representatives
Intercultural communication *(May add geog subd)*
Intercultural education *[S] (May add geog subd)*
Interdisciplinary approach in education *(May add geog subd)*
Interest *(May add geog subd)*
    NT   Interest rates
Interest rates *(May add geog subd)*
    BT   Interest
Interethnic dating *(May add geog subd)*
    BT   Dating
    RT   Interracial dating

Interferon
Intergenerational relations *(May add geog subd)*
Interior decoration *(May add geog subd)*
    UF Interior design
Interior decorators
Interior design
    USE Interior decoration
Internal combustion engines
    BT Engines
Internal medicine *(May add geog subd)*
Internal security *[S] (May add geog subd)*
International agencies *[S] (May add geog subd)*
International business enterprises *(May add geog subd)*
International competition
    UF Competition, International
International cooperation *[S]*
    RT League of Nations
          United Nations
International Criminal Police Organization
International economic relations *[S]*
International finance
International Geophysical Year, 1957-1958
International organization *[S]*
International Reading Association
International relations *[S]*
International trade *[S] (May add geog subd)*
Internet (Computer network) *[S]*
Interns (Education)
Interns (Medicine)
Internship programs
Interpersonal communication *(May add geog subd)*
Interpersonal conflict *(May add geog subd)*
Interpersonal confrontation *(May add geog subd)*
Interpersonal relations
    UF Human relations
          Social behavior
Interplanetary visitors
    USE Extraterrestrial beings *[AC only]*
Interplanetary voyages
Interpreting and translating
    USE Translating and interpreting
Interracial adoption *[S] (May add geog subd)*
Interracial dating *(May add geog subd)*
    BT Dating
    RT Interethnic dating
Interracial marriage *[S] (May add geog subd)*
    BT Marriage
Interstellar communication *[S]*
Interstellar travel
Intervention (International law) *[S]*
Interviewing *[S]*
Interviewing in radio
Interviewing in television
Interviews *(May add geog subd)*
    SA *the subdivision* —Interviews
Intifada, 1987
    BT Israel-Arab conflicts
Intimacy (Psychology)
Intimidation
Intracoastal waterways *(May add geog subd)*
Intractible pain *(May add geog subd)*
Inuit *[S]*
    BT Eskimos
Inuktitut poetry *(May add geog subd)*
Inventions *[S] (May add geog subd)*

    BT Intellectual property
Inventors *[S]*
    NT Women inventors
Invertebrates *[S] (May add geog subd)*
    BT Animals
Investment analysis
Investment banking *(May add geog subd)*
Investment trusts
    USE Mutual funds
Investments *[S] (May add geog subd)*
    NT Futures
          Mutual funds
          Securities
          Stocks
    RT Saving and investment
          Saving and thrift
          Stock exchange
Investments, Foreign *(May add geog subd)*
    UF Foreign investments
Invisible Man (Motion picture)
Invisible playmates
    USE Imaginary playmates
Ionesco, Eugene
Ionizing radiation
Iowa
Iran *[S]*
Iran-Contra Affair, 1985-1990
Iran Hostage Crisis, 1979-1981
Iran-Iraq War, 1980-1988
Iranians
    NT Scythians
Iraq
    —Civilization
    — —To 634
Iraq-Kuwait Crisis, 1990-1991
Ireland
    —History
    — —20th century
Irene, Empress of the East, 752?-803
Iridium
Iris (Plant)
Irish
Irish Americans
Irish fiction *(May add geog subd)*
Irish literature *(May add geog subd)*
Irish poetry *(May add geog subd)*
Irish question
Iron *[S]*
Iron Age *[S] (May add geog subd)*
Iron and steel workers
Iron industry and trade *(May add geog subd)*
Iron mines and mining *(May add geog subd)*
    BT Mines and mineral resources
Ironstone china
Ironworks *[AC only] (May add geog subd)*
    UF Iron-works
Irony in literature
Iroquois Indians
Irrational numbers
    UF Numbers, Irrational
Irreversible processes
Irvine, Sarah Agnes Estelle, 1887-1970
Irving, John, 1942-

Irving, Washington, 1783-1859
Isaac (Biblical patriarch)
Isaacman, Clara
Isabella, d'Aragona, Duchess of Milan, consort of Gian
    Galeazzo Sforza, Duke of Milan, 1470-1524
Isabella, Queen, consort of Edward II, King of England,
    1292-1358
Isabella I, Queen of Spain, 1451-1504
Ishi, d. 1916
Islam [S] (May add geog subd)
    BT   Religions
    RT   Sufism
Islam and literature
Islam and politics (May add geog subd)
    BT   Religion and politics
Islamic Empire
Islamic law [S] (May add geog subd)
Island animals [AC only]
    UF   Animal fauna
Island fauna
    USE   Island animals [AC only]
Island ecology (May add geog subd)
Islands [S] (May add geog subd)
Islands of the Pacific [S]
Isles of Shoals (Me. and N.H.)
Isometric exercises
    BT   Exercise
Isopoda
    USE   Isopods [AC only]
Isopods [AC only]
    UF   Isopoda
    NT   Wood lice (Crustaceans) [AC only]
Isopods as pets
    NT   Wood lice (Crustaceans) as pets [AC only]
Isozaki, Arata
Israel [S]
Israel-Arab conflicts (May add geog subd)
    NT   Intifada, 1987
Israel-Arab War, 1948-1949 [S] (May add geog subd)
Israel-Arab War, 1967 [S] (May add geog subd)
Israel-Arab War, 1973 [S]
Israel Museum (Jerusalem)
    UF   Muze'on Yisfa'el (Jerusalem)
Israel Philharmonic Orchestra
    UF   Tizmoret ha-filharmonit ha-Yisre'elit
Israelis [S] (May add geog subd)
Issus, Battle of, 333 B.C.
Istanbul (Turkey)
Isurus
    USE   Mako sharks [AC only]
Italia (Airship)
Italian Americans
Italian language (May add geog subd)
    —Readers [AC only]
        Use for reading texts in Italian containing materials for instruc-
        tion and practice in reading that language.
        RT   Italian language materials [AC only]
Italian language materials [AC only]
    Use for works written in Italian intended primarily for general
    information or recreational reading. Such works with text also given
    in English are further subdivided by the subdivision —Bilingual.
        RT   Italian language—Readers [AC only]
    —Bilingual [AC only]

Italian poetry (May add geog subd)
Italians
Italy [S]
    —History [S]
    — —19th century
    — —20th century
    — —German occupation, 1943-1945
    — —Allied occupation, 1943-1947
    —Politics and government [S]
    — —1914-1945
    — —20th century
Ivan IV, Czar of Russia, 1530-1584
Ivory (May add geog subd)
Ivory Coast
    USE   Côte d'Ivoire
Iwo Jima, Battle of, 1945
Iyengar, B.K.S., 1918-
Jack Frost [AC only]
    UF   Frost, Jack
    BT   Winter [AC only]
Jack-o-lanterns
Jack the Ripper Murders, London, England, 1888
Jackals [S]
Jacksboro (Tex.)
Jackson, Andrew, 1767-1845
Jackson, Anne, 1926-
Jackson, Bo, 1962-
Jackson, Jesse, 1941-
Jackson, Laura (Riding), 1901-
Jackson, Livia Bitton
Jackson, Mahalia, 1911-1972
Jackson, Michael, 1958-
Jackson, Rachel, 1767-1828
Jackson, Reggie
Jackson, Shirley, 1919-1965
Jackson, Stonewall, 1824-1863
Jacob (Biblical patriarch)
Jacobi, Carl Gustav, 1804-1851
Jacobite Rebellion, 1745-1746
Jacobites
    BT   Religions
Jacobs, Harriet A. (Harriet Ann), 1813-1897
Jade (May add geog subd)
Jaeger, Andrea
Jaguar (May add geog subd)
Jaguar automobile
Jails (May add geog subd)
Jam [S]
Jamaica
James, Alice, 1848-1892
James, Daniel, 1920-1978
James, Frank, 1844-1915
James, Henry. Washington Square
James, Jesse, 1847-1882
James, Will, 1892-1942
James, William, 1842-1910
James family
James I, King of England, 1566-1625
Jamestown (Va.)

Japan *[S]*
  —Foreign relations
  — —1945-
  —History *[S]*
  — —To 1868
  — —Tokugawa period, 1600-1868
  — —1868-
  — —20th century
  — —1912-1945
  — —Showa period, 1926-1989
  — —Allied occupation, 1945-1952
  — —1952- *[S]*
  —Social conditions
  — —1945-
Japanese
Japanese Americans
  —Evacuation and relocation, 1942-1945
Japanese crane *(May add geog subd)*
Japanese language *[S] (May add geog subd)*
  —**Readers** *[AC only]*
      Use for reading texts in Japanese containing materials for instruction and practice in reading that language.
      RT   Japanese language materials *[AC only]*
Japanese language materials *[AC only]*
    Use for works written in Japanese intended primarily for general information or recreational reading. Such works with text also given in English are further subdivided by the subdivision —Bilingual.
    RT   Japanese language—Readers *[AC only]*
  —**Bilingual** *[AC only]*
Japanese literature *(May add geog subd)*
Japanese macaque *(May add geog subd)*
Japanese poetry *(May add geog subd)*
Japanese Red Army
Japanese wrestling
    USE Sumo
Jason (Greek mythology)
Java (Indonesia)
Javelinas
    USE Peccaries
Javelin throwing
    BT   Track and field
    RT   Weight throwing
Jaworski, Leon
Jay, John, 1745-1829
Jazz *(May add geog subd)*
    BT   Music
Jazz musicians
Jea, John, b. 1773
Jealousy *(May add geog subd)*
Jefferson, Thomas, 1743-1826
Jehovah's Witnesses
Jellyfishes
    BT   Fishes
    NT Portuguese man-of-war
Jemison, Mary, 1743-1833
Jencken, Catherine Fox, 1836-1892
Jenkins, Barbara
Jenkins, Peter, 1951-
Jenner, Bruce, 1949-
Jenner, Edward, 1749-1823
Jennings, Waylon
Jensen, Smoke (Fictitious character)
Jerusalem
  —**History**
  — —**Siege, 1948**

Jesuits *[S]*
Jesus Christ *[S]*
  —**Crucifixion** *[S]*
  —**Nativity** *[S]*
  —**Parables** *[S]*
  —**Prayers**
    NT   Lord's prayer
  —**Resurrection** *[S]*
Jet lag *[S]*
Jet planes *[S]*
Jet propulsion *[S]*
Jet skiing *(May add geog subd)*
Jet transports
Jewell, Geri
Jewelry *[S] (May add geog subd)*
    NT   Paste jewelry
Jewelry as an investment
Jewish-Arab relations *[S]*
Jewish crafts
Jewish folk literature *(May add geog subd)*
Jewish law
Jewish New Year
    USE Rosh ha-Shanah
Jewish literature *[S] (May add geog subd)*
Jewish scribes
    USE Scribes, Jewish
Jewish way of life
Jewish wit and humor
Jewish women
    UF   Women, Jewish
Jews *[S]*
    SA   *the subdivisions* —Jews and —Jews—Rescue
  —**History**
  — —**1945-**
  —**Persecutions** *[S] (May add geog subd)*
Jews in art
Jig saws
Jin, Sarunna
Joachim, Harold, 1909-1983
Joan, of Arc, Saint, 1412-1431
Job (Biblical figure)
Job analysis *[S]*
Job descriptions *(May add geog subd)*
Job evaluation *(May add geog subd)*
Job hunting *[S] (May add geog subd)*
    RT   Applications for positions
           Interviewing
           Resumes (Employment)
           Unemployment
           Work
Job satisfaction *[S] (May add geog subd)*
Job security *(May add geog subd)*
Job stress *[S] (May add geog subd)*
Jockeys
    RT   Horse racing
Joffrey Ballet
Jogging
    USE Running *[AC only]*
Johannesburg (South Africa)
Johanson, Donald C.
John, Elton
John, King of England, 1167-1216
John, of Gaunt, Duke of Lancaster, 1340-1399
John F. Kennedy Space Center
John Henry (Legendary character)

John Newbery medal books
  USE Newbery medal books
John Paul II, Pope, 1920-
John XXIII, Pope, 1881-1963
Johnson, Adam Rankin, 1834-
Johnson, Amy
Johnson, Andrew, 1808-1875
Johnson, Bobby H., 1935-
Johnson, Earvin, 1959-
Johnson, E. Pauline, 1861-1913
Johnson, James Weldon, 1871-1938
Johnson, Jimmy, 1943-
Johnson, John H. (John Harold), 1918-
Johnson, Lady Bird, 1912-
Johnson, Lyndon B. (Lyndon Baines), 1908-1973
Johnson, Martin, 1884-1937
Johnson, Oliver, 1821-1907
Johnson, Osa, 1894-1953
Johnson, Samuel, 1709-1784
Johnston, Annie Bronn
Johnston, Carol, 1958-
Johnston, Harry Hamilton, Sir, 1858-1927
Johnstown (Pa.)—Flood, 1889
Joinery (May add geog subd)
Joint ventures (May add geog subd)
Joints (Engineering)
Joke books
  USE Jokes [AC only]
Jokes [AC, S]
  UF Joke books
  BT Wit and humor [AC, S]
  NT Practical jokes
  SA the subdivision —Wit and humor
Joking relationships
Joliet, Louis, 1645-1700
Jolson, Al, d. 1950
Jonah (Biblical prophet)
Jones, Jesse H. (Jesse Holman), 1874-1956
Jones, John Luther, 1863-1900
Jones, John Paul, 1747-1792
Jones, Pattie Ridley
Jones, Ruth Leggitt, 1892-1978
Jones family
Jonson, Ben, 1573?-1637
Joplin, Janis
Joplin, Scott, 1868-1917
Jordan
Jordan, Barbara, 1936-
Jordan, Gilbert John, 1902-
Jordan, Hamilton
Jordan, Michael, 1963-
Joseph, Nez Perce, Chief, 1840-1904
Joseph (Son of Jacob)
Joseph, Saint
**Josephine, Empress, consort of Napoleon I, Emperor of
  the French, 1763-1814**
Joshua (Biblical figure)
Josiah Wedgewood & Sons
Jouett, John, 1754-1822
Journalism [S] (May add geog subd)
  UF Journalism, School [AC only]
  RT Broadcasting
      Freedom of the press
      Press
      Publishers and publishing

  NT Newspapers
      Photojournalism
      Reporters and reporting
Journalism, College (May add geog subd)
Journalism, School
  USE Journalism [AC only]
Journalism, Pictorial
Journalistic ethics (May add geog subd)
Journalists [S]
  NT Women journalists
Joy
  BT Emotions
Joyce, James, 1882-1941
Juana Ines de la Cruz, Sister, 1651-1695
Juarez, Benito, 1806-1872
Judaism [S] (May add geog subd)
  BT Religions
  RT Fasts and feasts—Judaism
Judas, Maccabeus, d. 161 B.C.
Judd, Walter Henry, 1898-
Judd, Wynonna, 1964-
Judges [S]
Judicial error (May add geog subd)
Judicial opinions (May add geog subd)
Judicial power (May add geog subd)
Judicial power and politics
  USE Political questions and judicial power
Judo [S] (May add geog subd)
  RT Karate
Jugglers
Juggling [S] (May add geog subd)
Juilliard School
Jumayyil, Amin
Jumayyil, Bashir, 1947-1982
Jumbo (Elephant)
Jump rope rhymes (May add geog subd)
Jumping
  BT Track and field [AC only]
Jumping bean [AC only]
  UF Mexican jumping bean
Jung, C.G. (Carl Gustav), 1875-1961
Jungle animals [AC, S] (May add geog subd)
  UF Jungle fauna
Jungle ecology (May add geog subd)
Jungle fauna
  USE Jungle animals [AC only]
Jungle stories
  USE Jungles—Fiction [AC only]
Jungles [S] (May add geog subd)
  —Fiction [AC only]
  UF Jungle stories
Junior high school libraries (May add geog subd)
Junior high school students
Junior high schools [S] (May add geog subd)
Junior colleges [S] (May add geog subd)
  RT Community colleges
Junk bonds [S] (May add geog subd)
Junk food (May add geog subd)
Jupiter (Planet)
Jupiter probes
Jurassic Period
  USE Paleontology—Jurassic
Jurisprudence (May add geog subd)
  RT Law
Jury [S] (May add geog subd)
Jury, Richard (Fictitious character)

Justice *[S]*
> *RT* Courts
>> Jurisprudence
>> Law
>> Trials

Justice, Administration of *[S] (May add geog subd)*
Justices
> *USE* Judges

Justin Morgan (Horse)
Juvenile courts *[S] (May add geog subd)*
> *BT* Courts
> *RT* Criminal courts

Juvenile delinquency *[S] (May add geog subd)*
Juvenile delinquents *(May add geog subd)*
Juvenile homicide *(May add geog subd)*
Juvenile justice, Administration of *(May add geog subd)*
Juvenile prostitution
> *USE* Child prostitution

K.G.B.
> *USE* KGB *[AC only]*

Kachina dolls *(May add geog subd)*
Kachinas *(May add geog subd)*
Kafka, Franz, 1883-1924
Kafka, Franz, 1883-1924.   Metamorphosis *[AC only]*
> *UF* Kafka, Franz, 1883-1924.   Verwandlung

Kafka, Franz, 1883-1924.   Prozess
> *USE* Kafka, Franz, 1883-1924.   Trial *[AC only]*

Kafka, Franz, 1883-1924.   Trial *[AC only]*
> *UF* Kafka, Franz, 1883-1924.   Prozess

Kafka, Franz, 1883-1924.   Verwandlung
> *USE* Kafka, Franz, 1883-1924.   Metamorphosis *[AC only]*

Kahlo, Frida
Kainah Indians
> *BT* Indians of North America

Kaiulani, Princess of Hawaii, 1875-1899
Kalahari Desert
Kaleidoscope
Kamba (African people)
> —Folklore
>> *USE* Folklore, Kamba *[AC only]*

Kamchatskaia ekspeditsiia
> *USE* Bering's Expedition, 1st, 1725-1730 *[AC only]*

Kamehameha I, the Great, King of the Hawaiian Islands
Kamikaze airplanes
Kandinsky, Wassily, 1866-1944
Kangaroo rats
Kangaroos *[S] (May add geog subd)*
Kanjobal Indians
Kansas
Kansas City (Kan.)
Kansas City Chiefs (Football team)
Kansas City Royals (Baseball team)
Kapok
> *UF* Silk-cotton tree

Karan, Donna, 1948-
Karankawa Indians
Karate *[S] (May add geog subd)*
> *BT* Hand-to-hand fighting, Oriental
>> Kung fu
> *RT* Judo

Karcher, Carl Nicholas
Karloff, Boris, 1887-1969
Karnow, Stanley
Karolyi, Bela
Karting
Karts
> *USE* Karting

Katahdin, Mount (Me.)
Katsup
> *USE* Ketchup *[AC only]*

Katsushika, Hokusai, 1760-1849
Kaufmann family
Kayaking
> *USE* Kayaks and kayaking *[AC only]*

Kayaks and kayaking *[AC only]*
> *UF* Kayaking
> *RT* Canoes and canoeing *[AC only]*

Kaye, Marilyn
Kaysen, Susanna, 1948-
Kazakhs
> —Folklore
>> *USE* Folklore, Kazakh *[AC only]*

Kazan, Elia
Keaton, Buster, 1895-1966
Keaton, Diane
Keats, Ezra Jack
Keats, John, 1795-1821
Keewatin (N.W.T.)
Keita, Soundiata, d. 1255
Keller, Helen, 1880-1968
Kelly, Joann
Kelp bed ecology *(May add geog subd)*
Kelps *(May add geog subd)*
> *BT* Marine plants

Kemble, Frances Anne, 1809-1893
Kempe, Margery, b. ca. 1373
Kemp's loggerhead turtle
> *USE* Atlantic ridley turtle *[AC only]*

Kemp's turtle
> *USE* Atlantic ridley turtle *[AC only]*

Kendrick family
Kennebec River (Me.)
Kennedy family
Kennedy, Edward Moore, 1932-
Kennedy, John F. (John Fitzgerald), 1917-1963
Kennedy, Joseph P. (Joseph Patrick), 1888-1969
Kennedy, Robert F., 1925-1968
Kennedy, Rose Fitzgerald, 1890-
Kent (Conn.)
Kent State University Riot, May 4, 1970
Kenton, Simon, 1755-1836
Kentucky
Kentucky Derby, Louisville, Ky.
Kenya
Kenyatta, Jomo
Kepler, Johannes, 1571-1630
Keratotomy, Radial *(May add geog subd)*
Kerensky, Aleksandr Fyodorovich, 1881-1970
Kerouac, Jack, 1922-1969
Kerr, M.E.
Kerr-McGee Nuclear Corporation
Kerrey, Robert, 1943-
Kesey, Ken
Kesselring, Albert, 1885-1960
Kestrels *[AC only] (May add geog subd)*
> *BT* Falcons

Ketchup *[AC only]*
> *UF* Catchup
>> Catsup
>> Katsup
>> Tomato catchup
>> Tomato catsup

Tomato katsup
Tomato ketchup
Key West (Fla.)
Key, Francis Scott, 1779-1843
Keyboards (Electronics) *[S]*
Keys
   USE   Locks and keys
KGB
   UF   K.G.B.
            Soviet Union. Komitet gosudarstvennoi bezopasnosti
Kherdian, Veron, 1907-
Khmer language *[S] (May add geog subd)*
  —**Readers** *[AC only]*
        Use for reading texts in Khmer containing materials for instruction and practice in reading that language.
     RT   Khmer language materials *[AC only]*
Khmer language materials *[AC only]*
       Use for works written in Khmer intended primarily for general information or recreational reading. Such works with text also given in English are further subdivided by the subdivision —Bilingual.
     RT   Khmer language—Readers *[AC only]*
  —**Bilingual** *[AC only]*
Khmers *(May add geog subd)*
   BT   Cambodia
Khoikhoi (African people)
  —**Folklore**
     USE   Folklore, Khoikhoi *[AC only]*
Khomeini, Ruhollah
Khrushchev, Nikita Sergeevich, 1894-1971
Kibbutz
   USE   Kibbutzim
Kibbutzim
   UF   Kibbutz
   RT   Collective settlements
Kidd, William, d. 1701
Kidnapping *[S] (May add geog subd)*
   SA   the subdivision —Kidnapping [date]
Kidnapping, Parental *(May add geog subd)*
Kidneys *[S]*
  —**Diseases**
     NT   Nephritis, Interstitial
Kiep, O.C. (Otto Carl), 1886-1944
Kilimanjaro, Mount (Tanzania)
Killdeer *[S]*
Killer whale *(May add geog subd)*
Killing of police
   USE   Police murders
Killy, Jean Claude
Kilns *(May add geog subd)*
Kilroy, Mark James, d. 1989
Kim B'ai
Kimbell Art Museum
Kimbrough, Emily, 1899-
Kindergarten *[S] (May add geog subd)*
   RT   Education, Preschool
Kindness
Kinesiology *(May add geog subd)*
Kinetic art *[S] (May add geog subd)*
   NT   Optical art
King, Andy
King, Billie Jean
King, Carole
King, Coretta Scott, 1927-
King, Larry, 1933-
King, Martin Luther, Jr, 1929-1968
King, Stephen, 1947-

King Arthur
King County (Tex.)
King Kong (Motion picture)
King Philip's War, 1675-1676 *[S]*
King Ranch (Tex.)
King Ranch Corporation, Kingsville (Tex.)
King snakes *[AC only]*
   UF   Lampropeltis
Kingdom of God
Kings, queens, rulers, etc. *[AC, S]*
   UF   Caliphs
           Emperors
           Monarchs
           Pharaohs
           Queens
           Roman emperors
           Royalty
           Rulers
           Russian empresses
           Shahs
           Sovereigns
           Sultans
   BT   Heads of state
   RT   Dictators
           Presidents
           Prime ministers
           Statesmen
   SA   the subdivision —Kings and rulers
Kings, queens, rulers, etc. in art *[AC only]*
Kings Canyon National Park (Calif.)
Kings Mountain, Battle of, 1780
Kingsley, Mary Henrietta, 1862-1900
Kingston, Maxine Hong
Kingsville (Tex.)
Kinkajou *[S]*
   BT   Mammals
Kinmont, Jill
Kinte family
Kiowa Indians
Kipling, Rudyard, 1865-1936
Kirkland, Gelsey
Kirov Ballet Academy *[AC only]*
   UF   Kirov Ballet School
           Leningradiskoe akademicheskoe khoreograficheskoe
              uchilishche im. A. IA. Vaganovoi
           Vaganova Choreographic Institute
Kirov Ballet Company *[AC only]*
   UF   Leningradskii gosudarstvennyi akademicheskii teatr
              opery i baleta imeni S.M. Kirova
Kirov Ballet School
   USE   Kirov Ballet Academy *[AC only]*
Kisor, Henry
Kissing
Kissinger, Henry, 1923-
Kit fox
   UF   Swift fox
   BT   Foxes
Kitchen cabinets *(May add geog subd)*
Kitchen utensils *[S] (May add geog subd)*
Kitchens *[S] (May add geog subd)*
Kites *[S] (May add geog subd)*
Kitsch *(May add geog subd)*
   BT   Aesthetics
Kittens
   USE   Cats *[AC, S]*
Klamath Mountains (Calif. and Or.)

Klee, Paul, 1879-1940
Klein, Herbert G.
Klein, Kenneth
Klein, Norma, 1938-
Klimt, Gustav, 1862-1918
Klondike River Valley (Yukon)
Kluger, Ruth, 1914-
    USE   Aliav, Ruth, 1914-
Knee
Knievel, Evel, 1938-
Knifesmiths
Knight, Philip H., 1938-
Knights and knighthood *[AC, S] (May add geog subd)*
   —Fiction
        UF   Chivalry—Fiction *[AC only]*
Knit goods
Knitting *[S] (May add geog subd)*
   —Patterns
Knitting, Machine
Knitting-machines *(May add geog subd)*
Knives *(May add geog subd)*
Knock-knock jokes
Knollys, Lettice
Knossos (Extinct city)
Knots and splices *[S]*
Knotts Berry Farm
Knowledge, Theory of *[S]*
Knowles, John.   Separate peace
Knox, Henry, 1750-1806
Knysna (South Africa)
Koala *[S] (May add geog subd)*
Koasati Indians
        UF   Alabama-Coushatta Indians
               Coushatta Indians
Koch, Robert, 1843-1910
Koegler, Kurt
Koehn, Ilse
Koestler, Arthur, 1905-
Kohlberg Kravis Roberts & Co.
Koi
        UF   Ornamental carp
Koko (Gorilla)
Komodo dragon *(May add geog subd)*
Kon-Tiki ekspedisjonen (1947)
    USE   Kon-Tiki Expedition, 1947 *[AC only]*
Kon-Tiki Expedition, 1947 *[AC only]*
        UF   Kon-Tiki ekspedisjonen (1947)
Konigsberg (Cruiser)
Koran *[S]*
Korbut, Olga, 1955-
Korczak, Janusz, 1878-1942
Korda, Alexander, Sir, 1893-1956
Korea *[S]*
Korea (North) *[S]*
Korea (South) *[S]*
Korean Air Lines Incident, 1983
Korean American children
Korean Americans
Korean language *[S] (May add geog subd)*
   —Readers *[AC only]*
        Use for reading texts in Korean containing materials for in-
    struction and practice in reading that language.
        RT   Korean language materials *[AC only]*

Korean language materials *[AC only]*
        Use for works written in Korean intended primarily for general
information or recreational reading. Such works with text also given
in English are further subdivided by the subdivision —Bilingual.
    RT   Korean language—Readers *[AC only]*
   —Bilingual *[AC only]*
Korean poetry *(May add geog subd)*
Korean reunification question (1945-)
Korean War, 1950-1953 *[S]*
Korematsu, Fred, 1919-
Kornilov, Lavr Georgievich, 1870-1918
Kosterina, Nina Alekseevna, 1921-1941
Koufax, Sandy, 1935-
Kovacs, Ernie, 1919-1962
Kozol, Jonathan
Kraft, Randy Steven, 1945-
Krakatoa (Indonesia)
Kraus, Amanda
Kremlin (Moscow, Russia)
Krents, Harold
Krick, Irving
Krishna (Hindu deity)
Kruger, Herbie (Fictitious character)
Kruger, Horst, 1919-
Ku Klux Klan
Kublai Khan, 1216-1294
Kubler-Ross, Elisabeth
Kunetka, James W. 1944-
Kung fu
        BT   Hand-to-hand fighting, Oriental
        NT   Karate
Kuralt, Charles, 1934-
Kurds
Kushner, Harold S.
Kusu (African people)
        UF   Bukusu (African people)
   —Folklore
        USE   Folklore, Kusu *[AC only]*
Kusz, Natalie
Kuvasz
        BT   Dog breeds
Kuwait
Kwakiutl Indians
Kwanzaa
        UF   Kwanza
        BT   Harvest festivals
La Brea Pits (Calif.)
La Fontaine, Jean de, 1621-1695
La Guardia, Fiorello H. (Fiorello Henry), 1882-1947
La Salle, Robert Cavelier, Sieur de, 1643-1687
Laban, Rudolf von, 1879-1958
Labels *(May add geog subd)*
Labor *[S] (May add geog subd)*
        RT   Occupations
               Slavery
               Work
        NT   Household employees
               Migrant labor
Labor and laboring classes
    USE   Labor
            Working class
Labor camps *(May add geog subd)*
Labor Day *(May add geog subd)*
Labor disputes *[S] (May add geog subd)*
Labor laws and legislation *(May add geog subd)*
Labor market *(May add geog subd)*

Labor productivity *[S] (May add geog subd)*
Labor supply *[S] (May add geog subd)*
Labor unions *[AC, S] (May add geog subd)*
    UF   Trade unions
    —Poland
        NT   Solidarity (Polish labor organization) *[AC only]*
Laboratory animals *(May add geog subd)*
    RT   Animals—Treatment
Labrador retriever *[S] (May add geog subd)*
Labroides dimidiatus
    USE   Cleaner fish *[AC only]*
Lace and lace making *[S] (May add geog subd)*
Lacquer and lacquering *[S] (May add geog subd)*
Lacrosse *(May add geog subd)*
Lactation *(May add geog subd)*
Lactose intolerance *(May add geog subd)*
Ladner, Thomas
Ladybugs *[S] (May add geog subd)*
Lafayette, Marie Joseph
Laffite, J.-B.-P. (Jean-Baptiste-Pierre), 1796-1879
Lahr, Bert, 1895-1967
Lake animals
    UF   Lake fauna
Lake fauna
    USE   Lake animals *[AC only]*
Lake Malawi
    USE   Nyasa, Lake
Lake States
Lake Tanganyika
    USE   Tanganyika, Lake
Lake Nakuru National Park (Kenya)
Lake Wobegon (Imaginary place)
Lakes *[S] (May add geog subd)*
    RT   Shorelines
Lama (Genus) *(May add geog subd)*
Lamb family
Lamborghini automobile
Lambs *(May add geog subd)*
L'Amour, Louis, 1908-
Lampropeltis
    USE   King snakes *[AC only]*
Lamps *[S] (May add geog subd)*
Lancaster (Bombers)
Lancaster County (Pa.)
Lance, Bert, 1931-
Lancelot (Legendary character)
Land, Reclamation of
    USE   Reclamation of land
Land grants *(May add geog subd)*
Land settlement *[S] (May add geog subd)*
Land tenure *[S] (May add geog subd)*
Land titles *(May add geog subd)*
Land use *[S] (May add geog subd)*
    RT   Reclamation of land
Landforms *(May add geog subd)*
Landlord and tenant *[S] (May add geog subd)*
Landon, Michael, 1936-1991
Landry, Tom
Landscape *(May add geog subd)*
Landscape architects
Landscape architecture *[S] (May add geog subd)*
Landscape architecture and energy conservation *(May add geog subd)*
Landscape assessment *(May add geog subd)*
Landscape changes *(May add geog subd)*
Landscape drawing *[S] (May add geog subd)*

Landscape gardening *[S] (May add geog subd)*
    NT   Topiary work
Landscape in art
Landscape painting *[S] (May add geog subd)*
Landscape photography *(May add geog subd)*
Landscape protection *[S] (May add geog subd)*
Lange, Dorothea
Language acquisition
Language and languages *[S] (May add geog subd)*
    RT   Native language
           Philologists
    SA   *the names of individual languages and the subdivisions* —Language, —Language (New words, slang, etc.), *and* —Slang
    —Psychology
        USE   Psycholinguistics
Language arts *[S] (May add geog subd)*
Language arts (Elementary) *(May add geog subd)*
Language arts (Secondary) *(May add geog subd)*
Language experience approach in education *(May add geog subd)*
Language policy *(May add geog subd)*
Languages
    USE   Language and languages
    SA   *names of individual languages*
Languages, Modern *[S]*
    SA   *the names of individual modern languages*
Lansky, Meyer, 1902-
Laos
Lap books
    USE   Oversize books
Lapland
Laptop computers *(May add geog subd)*
    UF   Portable computers
Lapps
    USE   Sami (European people)
Larcom, Lucy, 1824-1893
Lardner, Ring, 1885-1933
Large type books
    RT   Visually handicapped
Larsson, Carl, 1853-1919
Lascaux Cave (France)
Laser industry *(May add geog subd)*
Laserjet III
Lasers *[S] (May add geog subd)*
LaserWriter (Printer)
Latchkey children *[S]*
    BT   Children of working parents
Lateness
    USE   Tardiness *[AC only]*
Lathom House, Ormskirk (England)
    —Siege, 1644
Latin America *[S]*
    —History
    — —1948-
Latin American fiction
Latin American literature *[S]*
Latin American poetry
Latin Americans
Latin epic poetry
    USE   Epic poetry, Latin
Latin language *[AC, S] (May add geog subd)*
    —Readers *[AC only]*
        Use for reading texts in Latin containing materials for instruction and practice in reading that language.
        RT   Latin language materials *[AC only]*

Latin language materials *[AC only]*
Use for works written in Latin intended primarily for general information or recreational reading. Such works with text also given in English are further subdivided by the subdivision —Bilingual.
> RT   Latin language—Readers *[AC only]*

—Bilingual *[AC only]*
Latin literature *[S] (May add geog subd)*
Latin poetry *(May add geog subd)*
Latinos
> USE   Hispanic Americans

Latrobe, Benjamin Henry, 1764-1820
Lattimore, Owen, 1900-
Laundry *[S] (May add geog subd)*
Laurel, Stan
Lauren, Ralph
Lavoisier, Antoine Laurent, 1743-1794
Law *[S] (May add geog subd)*
> RT   Courts
>   Judges
>   Jurisprudence
>   Justice
>   Lawyers
> NT   Press law
> SA   *the subdivisions* —Law and legislation *and* —Legal status, laws, etc.

Law enforcement *[S] (May add geog subd)*
> RT   Police shootings

Law students
Lawn care industry *(May add geog subd)*
Lawns *[S] (May add geog subd)*
Lawrence, D.H. (David Herbert), 1885-1930
Lawrence, Ernest Orlando, 1901-1958
Lawrence, Jacob, 1917-
Lawrence Livermore Laboratory
Lawrence, R.D., 1921-
Lawrence, T.E. (Thomas Edward), 1888-1935
Lawson family
Lawyers *[S]*
> RT   Jurisprudence
>   Judges
> NT   Women lawyers

Layard, Austen Henry, Sir, 1817-1894
Layout, Advertising
> USE   Advertising layout and typography

Laysan albatross *(May add geog subd)*
Lazarus, Charles P., 1926-
Lazarus, Emma, 1849-1887
Laziness
Le Guin, Ursula K., 1929-
Le Mans Endurance Race, France
Le Moyne family
Lea, Tom, 1907-
Lead
—Toxicology
> UF   Lead-poisoning

Leaders
> SA   *the names of individuals*

Leadership *[S]*
> RT   Ability

Leaflets
> USE   Pamphlets

League of Nations *[S]*
> RT   International cooperation
>   United Nations

Leakey, L.S.B. (Louis Seymour Bazett), 1903-1972
Lear, Edward, 1812-1888

Lear, King (Legendary character)
Lear, William Powell, 1902-
Learned institutions and societies *(May add geog subd)*
> RT   Learning and scholarship

Learning
This heading is used only with subdivisions in AC usage.
—Psychology
Learning, Psychology of *[S]*
> UF   Psychology of learning
> RT   Learning disabilities
> NT   Praise

Learning ability
Learning and scholarship *[S] (May add geog subd)*
> RT   Education

Learning disabled
Learning disabled teenagers
Learning disabled youth
Learning disabilities *[S] (May add geog subd)*
> RT   Learning, Psychology of
>   Slow learning children

Learning disabled children
> RT   Slow learning children

Learning disorders
> USE   Learning disabilities

Learning styles
> USE   Cognitive styles

Lease, Mary Elizabeth, 1853-1933
Leather *[S]*
> RT   Tanning

Leatherwork *(May add geog subd)*
> RT   Handicraft

Leaves *[S] (May add geog subd)*
> BT   Trees
>   Plants

Lebanese Americans
Lebanon
Led Zeppelin (Musical group)
Lee, Ann, 1736-1784
Lee, Arthur Stanley Gould
Lee, Laurie
Lee, Robert E. (Robert Edward), 1807-1870
Lee family
Leeches *[S] (May add geog subd)*
Leeuwenhoek, Antoni van, 1632-1723
LeFlore, Ron
Left and right *[AC, S]*
Use for works on left and right as location or direction. For works on Left and Right in politics, use Right and Left (Political Science). Works on the physical characteristics of favoring one hand or the other are entered under Left- and right-handedness.
Left and right (Psychology)
Left- and right-handedness *[AC, S] (May add geog subd)*
> UF   Left-handedness
>   Right-handedness

Leg
> UF   Extremities, Lower
>   Lower extremities

Legal assistants
Legal composition
Legal psychology
> USE   Psychology, Forensic

Legal research *(May add geog subd)*
Legal stories
> USE   Law—Fiction

Legends
> USE   Folklore

SA   subdivision —Folklore *under specific ethnic groups e.g., Eskimos, Indians of North America, Austrailian aboriginies, etc.*
Legends, Australian aboriginal
    USE   Australian aborigines—Folklore *[AC only]*
Legends, Jewish
    USE   Folklore, Jewish *[AC only]*
Legends (Maori)
    USE   Folklore, Maori *[AC only]*
Leif Ericson, d. ca. 1020
    USE   Ericson, Leif, d. ca. 1020 *[AC only]*
Leiv Eiriksson, d. ca. 1020
    USE   Ericson, Leif, d. ca. 1020 *[AC only]*
Legett, Kirvin Kade, 1857-1926
Legett, Lora Bryan, 1867-1923
Legionnaires' disease *(May add geog subd)*
    RT   Food contamination
Legislation *[S] (May add geog subd)*
    UF   Legislative process
    RT   Law
Legislative bodies *[S] (May add geog subd)*
Legislators
Leicester, Robert Dudley, Earl of, 1532?-1588
Leigh, Augusta, 1784-1851
Leigh, Richard, d. 1899
Leigh, Vivien, 1913-1967
Leigh, William Robinson, 1866-1955
Leigh-Mallory, George Herbert, 1886-1924
Leisure *[S] (May add geog subd)*
Leitner, Isabella
Lelyveld, Joseph
Lemmings *[S] (May add geog subd)*
Lemonade *(May add geog subd)*
Lemprière, John, 1765?-1824
Lemur *[S]*
    RT   Monkeys
Lending
    USE   Borrowing and lending *[AC only]*
    RT   Loans
            Mortgages
Lendl, Ivan, 1960-
Lenehan, Leslie
Lenin, Vladimir Il'ich, 1870-1924
Leningrad (Russia)
    USE   Saint Petersburg (Russia)
Leningradskii gosudarstvennyi akademicheskii teatr opery i baleta imeni S.M. Korpva
    USE   Kirov Ballet Company *[AC only]*
Leningradiskoe akademicheskoe khoreograficheskoe uchilishche im. A. IA. Vaganovoi
    USE   Kirov Ballet Academy *[AC only]*
Lennon, John, 1940-
Lennon, Julian, 1963-
Lenses *[S]*
Lenses, Photographic
    USE   Photographic lenses
Leo (Astrology) *(May add geog subd)*
    BT   Astrology
Leo, Richard
Leon County (Tex.)
Leonard, Sugar Ray, 1956-
Leonardo, da Vinci, 1452-1519
Leonowens, Anna Harriette, 1834-1914
Leopard *[S] (May add geog subd)*
Lepidochelys kempii
    USE   Atlantic ridley turtle *[AC only]*

Lepidoptera
    USE   Lepidopterans *[AC only]*
Lepidopterans *[AC only]*
    UF   Lepidoptera
Leprechauns
Leprosy *(May add geog subd)*
Lesbianism *[S] (May add geog subd)*
Lesbians *[S]*
Leslie-Melville, Betty
Lesseps, Ferdinand de, 1805-1894
Lesser panda *[AC only]*
    UF   Ailurus fulgens
            Red panda
            Wah
Lessing, Doris May, 1919-
Lesson planning *(May add geog subd)*
Lester, Julius
Letter writing *[S] (May add geog subd)*
Lettering *[S] (May add geog subd)*
    RT   Calligraphy
Letterman, David
Letters *[S]*
    RT   Written communication
Leucocytes
    BT   Blood
Leukemia *[S] (May add geog subd)*
    BT   Cancer
Leutze, Emanuel, 1816-1868
Levenson, Sam, 1911-
Leveraged buyouts *[S] (May add geog subd)*
Levers
Levi Strauss and Company
Levi-Montalcini, Rita
Lewes (Del.)
Lewis and Clark Expedition (1804-1806)
Lewis, C.S. (Clive Staples), 1898-1963
Lewis, C.S. (Clive Staples), 1898-1963. Chronicles of Narnia
Lewis, Carl, 1961-
Lewis, Jerry, 1926-
Lewis, John Llewellyn, 1880-1969
Lewis, Meriweather, 1774-1809
Lewis, Peter
Lewis, Sinclair, 1885-1951
Lewis family
Lexicographers
    RT   Encyclopedias and dictionaries
    SA   *the subdivision* —Lexicography
Lexington, Battle of, 1775
Liability (Law) *[S] (May add geog subd)*
Liability, Professional
    USE   Malpractice
Lhasa apsos *(May add geog subd)*
    BT   Dog breeds
Libel and slander *[S] (May add geog subd)*
Libel trials
    USE   Trials (Libel)
Liberalism *[S] (May add geog subd)*
Liberation theology
Liberia
Liberty
    USE   Freedom *[AC only]*
Liberty & Co.
Liberty Bell
Libra (Astrology) *(May add geog subd)*
    BT   Astrology

Librarians *[S]*
Libraries *[S] (May add geog subd)*
   RT   Education
          Information services
          Reading
   SA *specific types or audiences of libraries, e.g.,* Public libraries,
          and the subdivisions —Library *and* —Libraries
  —Law and legislation
    USE   Library legislation
  —Special collections
Libraries, Children's
   USE   Children's libraries
Libraries, Public
   USE   Public libraries
Libraries, Special
   USE   Special libraries
Libraries, Traveling *(May add geog subd)*
Libraries, University and college
   USE   Academic libraries
Libraries, Young people's
   USE   Young adults' libraries
Libraries and community *[S] (May add geog subd)*
Libraries and education *(May add geog subd)*
Libraries and publishing *(May add geog subd)*
Libraries and puppets *(May add geog subd)*
Libraries and readers *(May add geog subd)*
Libraries and schools *[S] (May add geog subd)*
Libraries and students *[S] (May add geog subd)*
Libraries and the aged *(May add geog subd)*
   UF   Libraries and the elderly
Libraries and the elderly
   USE   Libraries and the aged
Libraries and the handicapped *(May add geog subd)*
Library administration *(May add geog subd)*
Library associations
   USE   Library science—Societies
Library catalogs *[S] (May add geog subd)*
   RT   Online bibliographic searching
Library education *[S] (May add geog subd)*
Library exhibits *(May add geog subd)*
Library finance *[S] (May add geog subd)*
Library fund raising *(May add geog subd)*
Library legislation *(May add geog subd)*
   UF   Libraries—Law and legislation
Library materials *(May add geog subd)*
   RT   Library resources
Library orientation *(May add geog subd)*
Library publications *(May add geog subd)*
Library resources *[S] (May add geog subd)*
   RT   Library materials
Library planning *(May add geog subd)*
Library science *[S] (May add geog subd)*
Library signs *(May add geog subd)*
Library statistics *(May add geog subd)*
Library surveys
   RT   Library use studies
Library technical processes
   USE   Processing (Libraries)
Library use studies *(May add geog subd)*
   RT   Library surveys
Libya
Lice *[S] (May add geog subd)*
Lice as carriers of disease
License agreements
Lichens *(May add geog subd)*
   BT   Plants

Lichtenstein, Roy, 1923-
Liddell, Eric, 1902-1945
Lie detectors and detection *[S]*
Lieberman, Nancy
Life *[S]*
Life and death, Power over
Life expectancy *(May add geog subd)*
   RT   Longevity
Life, Quality of
   USE   Quality of life
Life (Biology) *[S]*
   SA *the subdivision* —Life cycles
Life (Periodical)
Life change events *(May add geog subd)*
Life cycle, Human
Life on other planets *[S]*
Life-saving
   USE   Lifesaving *[AC, S]*
Life sciences *[S] (May add geog subd)*
Life skills *[S] (May add geog subd)*
   SA *the subdivision* —Life skills guides
Life style *(May add geog subd)*
   UF   Counter culture
          Social environment
Lifeline For Wildlife (Veterinary Hospital)
Lifesaving *[AC, S]*
   UF   Life-saving
Ligachev, E.K. (Egor Kuz'mich)
Light *[AC, S]*
   UF   Lights *[AC usage]*
   RT   Photobiology
   SA *the subdivision* —Lighting
Lightfoot, Hannah, b. 1730
Lighthouse keepers
Lighthouses *[S] (May add geog subd)*
Lightner, Candy
Lightning *[S] (May add geog subd)*
Lightning bugs
   USE   Fireflies
Lightships *[AC, S]*
   UF   Light-ships
Liliuokalani, Queen of Hawaii, 1838-1917
Lilly, Ben, 1856-1936
Limbaugh, Rush H.
Limbourg, Jean-Philippe de, 1726-1811
Limbourg, Pol de, ca. 1385-ca. 1416
Limericks *[S]*
   BT   Humorous poetry
   RT   Nonsense verses
Limón, José.
Lincoln, Abraham, 1809-1865 *[S]*
Lincoln, Mary Todd, 1818-1882
Lincoln, Sarah Bush Johnston, 1788-1869
Lincoln, Thomas, 1853-1871
   UF   Lincoln, Tad, 1853-1871
Lincoln (England)
Lincoln Brigade
   USE   Abraham Lincoln Brigade *[AC only]*
Lincoln Day
Lincoln-Douglas debates, 1858
Lincoln Memorial (Washington, D.C.)
Lincoln Park Zoo
Lind, Jenny, 1820-1887
Lindbergh, Anne Morrow, 1906-
Lindbergh, Charles A. (Augustus), 1902-1974
Lindgren, Astrid, 1907-

Lindow Man
    BT   England—Antiquities
Lindsay, Howard, 1889-1968
Lindstrand, Per
Line (Art)
Linen *[S] (May add geog subd)*
Linguistics *[S] (May add geog subd)*
Linguists
Link, Frances R.
Linnscott, Robert Newton, 1886-
Lionel Corporation
Lions *[S] (May add geog subd)*
Lipids
Lipizzaner horse *(May add geog subd)*
Liquids *[S]*
Liquor laws *(May add geog subd)*
Liquors *[S]*
Lisbon (Portugal)
List, Julie Autumn
Listening *[S]*
Liszt, Franz, 1811-1886
Literacy *[S] (May add geog subd)*
    UF   Illiteracy
    RT   Reading
Literary agents
Literary appreciation
Literary awards
    USE Literary prizes
Literary calendars
Literary cookbooks *(May add geog subd)*
Literary criticism
    USE Criticism
           Literature—Criticism and interpretation
Literary curiosa
Literary ethics
Literary forgeries and mystifications
Literary form
    UF   Genre (Literature)
    NT   Biography as a literary form
           Drama
           Essay
           Fiction
           Poetry
           Short story
Literary landmarks *[S] (May add geog subd)*
    RT   Historic buildings
Literary prizes *[S] (May add geog subd)*
    UF   Literary awards
    BT   Awards
Literary recreations *[S]*
    BT   Amusements
    NT   Palindromes
Literature *[S]*
    RT   Authorship
           Biography as a literary form
           Books
           Music and literature
           Plots (Drama, novel, etc.)
           Romanticism
           Satire *[S]*
           Speeches, addresses, etc.
           Style, Literary
           Wit and Humor *[AC, S]*
           Women and literature
    NT   Children's literature
           Classical literature

           Drama
           Essay
           Fables
           Fairy tales
           Fiction
           Parody *[S]*
           Poetry
           Religious literature
           Short story
    SA   *names of literatures, e.g.,* Canadian literature, Latin
           American literature, etc., *and themes and topics*
           in literature, e.g., Adolescents in literature, My-
           thology in literature, etc.
           the subdivisions —Literary collections *and* —Collections
  —Criticism and interpretation
    UF   Literary criticism
Literature, Comparative *[S]*
Literature, Medieval *[S]*
Literature, Modern
Literature and music
    USE Music and literature
Literature and society *(May add geog subd)*
Lithography *[S] (May add geog subd)*
    BT   Printing
    RT   Prints
Lithuania
Lithuanians
Litter (Trash) *(May add geog subd)*
Little Big Horn, Battle of the, 1876
Little brown bat *(May add geog subd)*
Little League baseball *[S] (May add geog subd)*
Little Turtle, Miami chief, d. 1812
Little, Lessie Jones
Liturgies *[S]*
Liturgy and architecture *(May add geog subd)*
Live Aid (Fund raising enterprise)
Livebearers (Fish)
    UF   Poeciliidae
Liver *[S]*
Livestock *(May add geog subd)*
    BT   Domestic animals
Livestock brands *(May add geog subd)*
Livestock breeds *(May add geog subd)*
Living fossils
Living rooms
Livingston, Myra Cohn
Livingstone, David, 1813-1873
Lizards *[S] (May add geog subd)*
    BT   Reptiles
    NT   Monitor lizards
Llamas *[S] (May add geog subd)*
Llano Estacado
    BT   Plateaus *(May add geog subd)*
Lloyd George, David, 1863-1945
Lloyd, Chris
Loans *[S] (May add geog subd)*
    RT   Mortgages
           Borrowing and lending *[AC only]*
Loans, Foreign *(May add geog subd)*
Lobbying *(May add geog subd)*
    RT   Political corruption
           Politics, Practical
Lobbyists
Lobel, Arnold
Lobster fisheries *(May add geog subd)*
Lobsters *[S] (May add geog subd)*

Local area networks (Computer networks)
Local government *[S]* *(May add geog subd)*
    BT   Political science
    RT   Cities and towns
           Villages
    NT   Municipal government
Local officials and employees
Loch Ness monster
Locks and keys *[S]* *(May add geog subd)*
    UF   Keys
Locksmithing *(May add geog subd)*
Lockwood, Belva Ann, 1830-1917
Locomotive engineers
Locomotives *[S]* *(May add geog subd)*
Locusts *[S]* *(May add geog subd)*
Lodging houses *[AC only]* *(May add geog subd)*
    UF   Lodging-houses
Lodz (Poland)
Leowy, Raymond, 1893-1986
Log cabins *(May add geog subd)*
Log chopping (Sports) *[AC only]*
    UF   Log-chopping (Sports)
Logan, Johnny, 1774-1812
Loggerhead turtle *(May add geog subd)*
Logic *[S]* *(May add geog subd)*
Logic, Symbolic and mathematical *[S]*
LOGO (Computer program language)
Loki (Norse deity)
Loman, Willy (Fictitious character)
Lombard, Carole, 1908-1942
Lombardi, Vince
London, Jack, 1876-1916
London (England)
    SA   *names of specific buildings and activities in London*
Loneliness *(May add geog subd)*
Long, Huey Pierce, 1898-1935
Long, Jane Herbert Wilkinson, 1798-1880
Long-eared bat *[AC only]*
    UF   Plecotus auritus
Long-term care facilities *[S]* *(May add geog subd)*
Long Island (N.Y.)
Long March, 1934-1935
Longevity *[S]* *(May add geog subd)*
Longfellow, Henry Wadsworth, 1807-1882
Longhorn cattle
Longevity *[S]* *(May add geog subd)*
Longitude *[S]* *(May add geog subd)*
Loons *[S]* *(May add geog subd)*
    BT   Birds
Loos, Adolf, 1870-1933
Lopez, Nancy, 1957-
Lord's prayer *[S]*
    UF   Bible—Prayers
    BT   Jesus Christ—Prayers
Lorenz, Konrad, 1903-
Lorrain, Claude, 1600-1682
Los Alamos (N.M.)
Los Angeles (Calif.)
Los Angeles Clippers (Basketball team)
Los Angeles Dodgers (Baseball team)
Los Angeles Lakers (Basketball team)
Los Angeles Raiders (Football team)
Los Angeles Rams (Football team)
Lose, M. Phyllis
Losing and winning
    USE   Winning and losing *[AC only]*

Losing things
    USE   Lost and found possessions *[AC only]*
Loss (Psychology)
Lost and found possessions *[AC, S]* *(May add geog subd)*
    UF   Finding things
           Losing things
           Lost animals
           Lost articles
           Lost pets
           Possessions, Lost and found
    RT   Lost children *[AC only]*
Lost animals
    USE   Lost and found possessions *[AC only]*
Lost articles
    USE   Lost and found possessions *[AC only]*
Lost children *[AC only]*
    RT   Lost and found possessions
Lost pets
    USE   Lost and found possessions *[AC only]*
Lotteries *[S]* *(May add geog subd)*
Lottery winners
Lotus 1-2-3 (Computer program)
Lou Gehrig's disease
    USE   Amyotrophic lateral sclerosis
Loudspeakers *(May add geog subd)*
Louganis, Greg, 1960-
Louis XIV, King of France, 1638-1715
Louis XV, King of France, 1710-1774
Louis XVI, King of France, 1754-1793
Louis XVII, King of France, 1785-1795
Louis, Joe, 1914-
Louisiana
Louisiana irises *(May add geog subd)*
Louisiana Purchase
Louvre (Paris, France)
Love *[S]*
    RT   Courtship
           Dating
  —Fiction *[AC only]*
    UF   Love stories
  —Poetry *[AC only]*
    UF   Love poetry
Love, Maternal
    BT   Mothers
Love, Nat, 1854-1921
Love-hate relationships *(May add geog subd)*
Love in art
Love in motion pictures
Love-letters *(May add geog subd)*
Love poetry
    USE   Love—Poetry *[AC only]*
Love stories
    USE   Love—Fiction *[AC only]*
Lovebirds
Low, Juliette Gordon, 1860-1927
Low temperatures *[S]*
Low-calorie diet
    BT   Diet
  —Recipes
Low-cholesterol diet
Low-fat diet *(May add geog subd)*
    BT   Diet
Low-protein diet
Lowell (Mass.)
Lowell, James Russell, 1819-1891

Lowell, Robert, 1917-1977
Lower extremities
    USE   Leg
Lower Rio Grande Valley (Tex.)
Loyalty *[S]*
LSD (Drug)
Lubitsch, Ernst, 1892-1947
Lucas, George
Luce, Claire Boothe, 1903-1987
Luce, Henry Robinson, 1898-1967
Lucette (Schooner)
Luck *[AC only]*
    UF   Fortune
Luckenbach (Tex.)
Luckner, Felix, Graf von, 1881-
Ludington, Sybil, b. 1761
Ludwig, Ken
Luggage
    SA   *specific types of luggage*
Luke, Saint
Lullabies *[S]*
Lumber and lumbering *[AC, S]*
  —Terminology
        Use for works on technical terms of the industry. *[AC only]*
    RT   Lumbermen—Language
Lumbermen
  —Language
        Use for works on slang used by men in lumber camps, etc.
        [AC only]
    RT   Lumber and lumbering—Terminology *[AC only]*
Luna County (N.M.)
Lunar bases *[S]*
Lunar eclipses *[S]*
    UF   Eclipses, Lunar
Lunar petrology
    USE   Moon rocks *[AC only] (May add geog subd)*
Lunar probes
Lunch rooms
    USE   Restaurants, lunch rooms, etc.
Luncheons *[S]*
Lund, Eric
Lunden, Joan
Lundgren, Jeffrey
Lungs *[S]*
Lupus *(May add geog subd)*
Lusitania (Steamship)
Luther, Martin, 1483-1546
Lutz, George Lee
Lutz, Kathleen
Luxembourg
Lycaon pictus *(May add geog subd)*
Lycheva, Katerina
Lyell, Charles, Sir, 1797-1875
Lying
    USE   Honesty *[AC only]*
Lyme disease *[S] (May add geog subd)*
Lymph nodes
Lynn, Loretta
Lynx *(May add geog subd)*
Lyon, Danny
Lyricists *[S]*
Macao
Macaques *[S]*
Macaws *(May add geog subd)*
MacArthur, Douglas, 1880-1964
Macaulay, David

MacBeth, Hamish (Fictitious character)
MacCool, Finn (Legendary character)
    USE   Finn MacCool
MacDonald, Flora, 1722-1790
Machen, J. Gresham (John Gresham), 1881-1937
Machiavelli, Niccolo, 1469-1527
Machine learning
Machine quilting
Machine sewing
    NT   Serging
Machine-shop practice
Machine shops
Machine tools *[AC only]*
    UF   Machine-tools
Machinery *[S]*
Machu Picchu Site (Peru)
Macintosh (Computer)
Macintosh Basics (Computer program)
Macintosh Classic (Computer)
Macintosh-compatible computers
    UF   Clones of Macintosh computers
Macintosh LC (Computer)
Macintosh LC II (Computer)
Macintosh SE (Computer)
Mackenzie, Alexander, Sir, 1763-1820
Mackinac Island (Mich.)
MacLaine, Shirley, 1934-
Maclean, Donald Duart, 1913-
    UF   Maclean, Donal Duart, 1913-
MacLeish, Archibald, 1892-
Macondo (Imaginary place)
Macrame
Macrobiotic diet
Macroeconomics
Madagascar
Madison County (Iowa)
Madison, Dolly, 1768-1849
Madison, James, 1751-1836
Madog ab Owain Gwynedd, 1150-1180?
Madonna, 1959-
Mafia *(May add geog subd)*
Magalhaes, Fernao de, d. 1521
    USE   Magellan, Ferdinand, d. 1521
Magazine covers *(May add geog subd)*
Magellan, Ferdinand, d. 1521
    UF   Magalhaes, Fernao de, d. 1521
Magellanic penguin *(May add geog subd)*
    BT   Penguins
Magi
Magic *[AC, S] (May add geog subd)*
    RT   Magic tricks
           Tricks
Magic tricks *[AC only] (May add geog subd)*
        Use for books of simple tricks.
    UF   Conjuring
    RT   Magic *[AC only]*
           Tricks
Magicians
Magill, Frank Northen, 1907-
Magna Carta *[S]*
Magnetic recorders and recording
    USE   Tape recorders and recording *[AC only]*
Magnetism *[S]*
Magnets *[S]*
Mahanes, Mike
Maheu, Robert

Mahfuz, Najib, 1912-
Mahler, Gustav, 1860-1911
Maigret, Jules (Fictitious character)
Mailboxes *(May add geog subd)*
Mail-order business *[S] (May add geog subd)*
Mailing lists *(May add geog subd)*
Maine
Maine (Battleship)
Mainstreaming in education *[S] (May add geog subd)*
Majors, Alexander, 1814-1900
Majors, Lee
Makah Indians
Make-believe playmates
    USE   Imaginary playmates
Makeig-Jones, Daisy, 1881-1945
Makeup, Theatrical *[AC, S]*
    UF   Theatrical makeup
Mako sharks *[AC only]*
    UF   Isurus
    BT   Sharks
Malaria *[S] (May add geog subd)*
Malawi
Malay Peninsula
Malays (Asian people)
  —Folklore
    USE   Folklore, Malay *[AC only]*
Malaysia
Malaysia, East
Malcolm X
    USE   X, Malcolm, 1925-1965
Male reproductive system
    USE   Reproductive system, Male
Malevich, Kazimir Severinovich, 1878-1935
Mali
Mallard *(May add geog subd)*
Malnutrition *(May add geog subd)*
Malone, Moses, 1955-
Malory, Thomas, Sir, 15th cent.
Malpractice
    UF   Liability, Professional
          Tort liability of professions
Malraux, Andre, 1901-1976. Condition humaine
    USE   Malraux, Andre, 1901-1976. Man's fate *[AC only]*
Malraux, Andre, 1901-1976. Man's estate
    USE   Malraux, Andre, 1901-1976. Man's fate *[AC only]*
Malraux, Andre, 1901-1976. Man's fate *[AC only]*
    UF   Malraux, Andre, 1901-1976. Condition humaine
          Malraux, Andre, 1901-1976. Man's estate
Malta
Malva (Ireland)
Mälzel, Johann Nepomuk, 1772-1838
Mambas *(May add geog subd)*
Mambo (Dance)
Mammals *[S] (May add geog subd)*
    SA   *the names of specific mammals and types of animals*
Mammals, Fossil *[S] (May add geog subd)*
    UF   Fossil mammals
Mammary glands
Mammoth Cave National Park (Ky.)
Mammoths
Man *[S]*
  —Influence of environment
  —Influence on nature
Man, Prehistoric *(May add geog subd)*
    UF   Prehistoric man

Man o' War (Horse)
Man-woman relationships *(May add geog subd)*
Management *[S] (May add geog subd)*
    SA   *the subdivision* —Management
Management information systems *[S]*
Managerial economics *(May add geog subd)*
Manatees *[S]*
Manchester, William Raymond, 1922-
Mandan Indians
Mandela, Nelson, 1918-
Mandela, Winnie
Mandingo (African people) *(May add geog subd)*
Manet, Edouard, 1832-1883
Mangrove swamps *(May add geog subd)*
Manhattan (New York, N.Y.)
Manhattan Project
Manic-depressive psychoses *[S] (May add geog subd)*
Mankiller, Wilma Pearl, 1945-
Mann, Anthony, 1906-1967
Mann, Horace, 1796-1859
Mann, Mary Tyler Peabody, 1806-1887
Mann, Thomas, 1875-1955. Magic mountain *[AC only]*
    UF   Mann, Thomas, 1875-1955. Zauberberg
Mann, Thomas, 1875-1955. Zauberberg
    USE   Mann, Thomas, 1875-1955. Magic mountain *[AC only]*
Manned space flight
Manned undersea research stations
    UF   Undersea research stations
          Underwater research stations
Manners and customs *[AC, S]*
    UF   Customs, Social
          Social Customs
    RT   Etiquette
    SA   *the subdivisions* —Social life and customs *and* —Customs
          and practices
Manors *(May add geog subd)*
Mansions *(May add geog subd)*
Manson, Charles, 1934-
Mantle, Mickey, 1931-
Manufactures *[S]*
Manufacturing engineering
    USE   Production engineering
Manufacturing processes *(May add geog subd)*
Manus (Papua New Guinea people)
Manuscript preparation (Authorship)
Manuscripts *[S] (May add geog subd)*
Manville Corporation
Manzanar War Relocation Center
Mao Tse-tung, 1893-1976
Maori (New Zealand people)
  —Folklore
    USE   Folklore, Maori *[AC only]*
  —Legends
    USE   Folklore, Maori *[AC only]*
Map drawing *[S]*
Maple *(May add geog subd)*
Maple sugar *[S] (May add geog subd)*
Maple syrup *(May add geog subd)*
Maps *[S]*
    SA   *specific types of maps and the subdivision* —Maps
Maps, World
    USE   World maps
Marathon running *[S] (May add geog subd)*
Maravich, Pete, 1948-
Marblehead (Mass.)

Marbles (Game)
Marbling
MARC formats
Marcello, Carlos
March of Time (Motion picture)
Marches (Music) [S]
Marching drills
    UF   Drill (not military)
Marconi, Guglielmo, Marchese, 1874-1937
Marcos, Ferdinand E. (Ferdinand Edralin), 1917-
Marcos, Imelda Romualdez, 1929-
Marcus, Stanley, 1905-
Mardi Gras [AC only] (May add geog subd)
    UF   Carnival
Margaret, of Anjou, consort of Henry VI, King of
    England, 1430-1482
Margaret, Princess, Countess of Snowdon, 1930-
Marie Antoinette, Queen, consort of Louis XVI, King of
    France, 1755-1793
Marihuana
    USE   Marijuana
Marijuana [S] (May add geog subd)
    UF   Marihuana
Marine animals [AC, S] (May add geog subd)
    UF   Marine fauna
    BT   Animals
Marine animals in art (May add geog subd)
    UF   Marine fauna in art
Marine aquarium fishes (May add geog subd)
Marine aquariums [S]
Marine biologists
Marine biology [S] (May add geog subd)
Marine Corps
    USE   United States. Marine Corps
Marine ecology [S] (May add geog subd)
Marine engineering [S] (May add geog subd)
Marine engineers
Marine engines [S]
    BT   Engines
Marine fauna
    USE   Marine animals [AC only]
Marine fauna in art
    USE   Marine animals in art
Marine fishes (May add geog subd)
Marine flora
    USE   Marine plants [AC only]
Marine mammals [S] (May add geog subd)
Marine mineral resources [S] (May add geog subd)
Marine plants [AC, S] (May add geog subd)
    UF   Marine flora
    BT   Plants
    NT   Kelps
Marine pollution [S] (May add geog subd)
Marine resources [S] (May add geog subd)
Marine resources conservation (May add geog subd)
Marineland
Mariner Project
Marines
Marino, Dan, 1961-
Marion, Francis, 1732-1795
Marital property (May add geog subd)
Marital psychotherapy (May add geog subd)
Maritime anthropology
Maritime Provinces
Marius, Gaius, ca. 157-86 B.C.
Marjoribanks, Archibald John

Market research
    USE   Marketing research
Market share (May add geog subd)
Market surveys [S] (May add geog subd)
Marketing [S] (May add geog subd)
    NT   Direct marketing
          Green marketing
          Multilevel marketing
    SA   the subdivision —Marketing
Marketing research
    UF   Market research
    NT   Motivation research (Marketing)
Markets [S] (May add geog subd)
Markham, Beryl
Marking and grading
    USE   Grading and marking (Students)
Marlborough, John Churchill, Duke of, 1650-1722
Marlborough, Sarah Jennings Churchill, Duchess of, 1660-1744
Marlow (Fictitious character)
Marlowe, Christopher, 1564-1593
Marlowe, Philip (Fictitious character)
Marmots [AC, S] (May add geog subd)
    Use for works on several species of marmot.
    NT   Woodchuck [AC only]
Marple, Jane (Fictitious character)
Marquesas Island
Marquetry (May add geog subd)
    BT   Woodwork
Marquette, Jacques, 1637-1675
Marrakesh (Morocco)
Marriage [S] (May add geog subd)
    UF   Teenage marriage [AC only]
    RT   Weddings
    NT   Interracial marriage
          Remarriage
Marriage brokerage (May add geog subd)
Marriage customs and rites [S] (May add geog subd)
Marriage law (May add geog subd)
Marriage licenses (May add geog subd)
Marriage service (May add geog subd)
    BT   Weddings
Married people [S]
Mars (Planet) [S]
Mars probes [S]
Marsh, Othniel Charles, 1831-1899
Marsh animals [AC only]
    UF   Marsh fauna
    BT   Animals
Marsh ecology (May add geog subd)
    RT   Marshes
Marsh fauna
    USE   Marsh animals [AC only]
Marsh flora
    USE   Marsh plants [AC only]
Marsh plants [AC only]
    UF   Marsh flora
Marshall, Catherine, 1914-
Marshall, George C. (George Catlett), 1880-1959
Marshall, John, 1755-1835
Marshall, Peter, 1902-1949
Marshall Plan
Marshall, Thurgood, 1908-
Marshes [S] (May add geog subd)
    RT   Marsh ecology
          Swamps
          Wetlands

Marsupialia
  USE Marsupials *[AC only]*
Marsupials *[AC only]*
  UF Marsupialia
Martens *[S]*
  BT Mammals
Martha's Vineyard (Mass.)
Marti, Jose, 1853-1895
Martial arts *[S] (May add geog subd)*
Martin, Harvey
Martin, Melody
Martin Luther King, Jr., Day *(May add geog subd)*
Martin's Hundred Site (Va.)
Martinez, Antonio Jose, 1793-1867
Martinez, Maria Montoya
Martinez, Vilma
Martinique
Martyrs *[S] (May add geog subd)*
Marvell, Andrew, 1621-1678
Marx, Karl, 1818-1883
Mary, Blessed Virgin, Saint
Mary Kay Cosmetics
Mary I, Queen of England, 1516-1558
Mary II, Queen of England, 1662-1694
Mary, Queen, consort of Louis XII, King of France, 1496-1533
Mary, Queen of Scots, 1542-1587
Maryland
Masada Site (Israel)
Masai (African people)
  —Folklore
    USE Folklore, Masai *[AC only]*
Masai Mara Game Reserve (Kenya)
Masatoshi
Masculinity (Psychology) *(May add geog subd)*
Masefield, John, 1878-1967
Mask making *(May add geog subd)*
Masks *[S] (May add geog subd)*
Masks (Sculpture) *(May add geog subd)*
Masochism
  RT Suffering
Mason, Joseph
Mason, Robert, 1942-
Mason-Dixon Line
Masonry *[S] (May add geog subd)*
Mass media *[S] (May add geog subd)*
Mass media and minorities *(May add geog subd)*
Mass murder *(May add geog subd)*
Massachuset Indians
Massachusetts
  —History
  — —To 1775
  — —New Plymouth, 1620-1691
  —Social life and customs
  — —To 1775
Massage *[S] (May add geog subd)*
Massasoit (Indian chief), 1580-1661
Mastectomy *(May add geog subd)*
Mastodon *[S]*
Matchbox labels *(May add geog subd)*
Matches *(May add geog subd)*
Mate selection *(May add geog subd)*
Materia medica *[S] (May add geog subd)*
Materialism *[S] (May add geog subd)*
Materials *[S] (May add geog subd)*

  SA the subdivision —Materials
Materials handling *[S]*
Maternity leave *(May add geog subd)*
Mathabane, Gail, 1962-
Mathabane, Mark
Mathematical analysis *[S]*
Mathematical instruments *(May add geog subd)*
Mathematical logic
  USE Logic, Symbolic and mathematical
Mathematical models *[S]*
  SA the subdivision —Mathematical models
Mathematical recreations *[S]*
  UF Creative activities and seat work
  NT Counting games *[AC only]*
    Number games *[AC only]*
Mathematical statistics *(May add geog subd)*
Mathematicians *[S]*
  NT Women mathematicians
Mathematics *[S] (May add geog subd)*
  SA specific branches of mathematics, e.g., Geometry *and the subdivision* —Mathematics
  —**Remedial teaching**
Mather, Cotton, 1663-1728
Mathias, Bob, 1930-
Mathias, Robert Bruce, 1930-
Matilda, Empress, consort of Henry V, Holy Roman Emperor, 1102-1167
Matisse, Henri, 1869-1954
Matrices
Matrimonial actions *(May add geog subd)*
Mattachine Society
Matter *[S]*
Matterhorn, Mount
Maturation (Psychology)
Maturin, Stephen (Fictitious character)
Matzos
Maugham, W. Somerset (William Somerset), 1874-1965
Mauna Ulu (Hawaii)
Maury, Matthew Fontaine, 1806-1873
Maverick, Samuel Augustus, 1803-1870
Maverick automobile
Maximilian, Emperor of Mexico, 1832-1867
Maxims
  RT Proverbs
Maxwell, Gavin
May Day
Maya architecture *(May add geog subd)*
Maya art *(May add geog subd)*
Maya mythology *(May add geog subd)*
Mayas *[S]*
Mayborn, Frank Willis, 1903-1987
Mayer, Louis B. (Louis Burt), 1885-1957
Mayer, Maria Goeppert, 1906-1972
Mayflower (Ship)
Mayflower Compact, 1620
Maynard, Joyce, 1953-
Mayo, Charles Horace, 1865-1939
Mayo, William James, 1861-1939
Mayo, William Worrall, 1819-1911
Mayors *(May add geog subd)*
  —**Dwellings** *(May add geog subd)*
Mays, Willie, 1931-
Maze puzzles
  UF Mazes
Mazer, Norma Fox, 1931-

Mazes
    USE   Maze puzzles
McAuliffe, Christa, 1948-1986
McCaffrey, Anne
McCaffrey, Anne.   Dragonriders of Pern
McCall family
McCallum, Jane Y.
McCambridge, Mercedes
McCarthy, Joseph, 1908-1957
McCarthy-Army Controversy, 1954
McCay, Winsor
McClellan, George Brinton, 1826-1885
McClintock, Barbara, 1902-
McConkey, Phil
McCullers, Carson, 1917-1967
McCutchan, Joseph D, 1823-1853
McDaniel, Hattie, 1895-1952
McDermott, Gerald
McDonald family
McDonald Observatory
McDuck, Scrooge (Fictitious character) *[AC only]*
    UF   Scrooge (Cartoon character)
            Scrooge (Fictitious character)
            Scrooge McDuck (Fictitious character)
            Uncle Scrooge (Fictitious character)
    BT   Cartoons and comics *[AC only]*
McEntire, Reba
McGarr, Peter (Fictitious character)
McGee, Travis (Fictitious character)
McGinnis, Virginia
McGreal, William
McJunkin, George
McKay, Claude, 1890-1948
McKenna, Virginia, 1931-
McKinley, Mount (Alaska)
McKinley, William, 1843-1901
McMahon, Jim, 1959-
McMillen, Tom, 1952-
McMullen, Jeanine
McMurtry, Larry
McPartland, Marian
McQueen, Steve, 1930-1980
McRae family
Mead, Margaret, 1901-1978
Meadow animals *[AC only]*
    UF   Meadow fauna
    BT   Meadows
Meadow ecology *(May add geog subd)*
Meadow plants *(May add geog subd)*
Meadows *(May add geog subd)*
    NT   Meadow animals *[AC only]*
Meagher, Thomas Francis, 1823-1867
Meaning (Psychology)
Mear, Roger
Measles *[S]*
Measurement *[AC, S]*
    UF   Measuring
            Mensuration
            Physical measurements
Measuring
    USE   Measurement *[AC only]*
Measuring instruments *[S] (May add geog subd)*
Meat *[S] (May add geog subd)*
Meat industry and trade *(May add geog subd)*
Mech, L. David
Mechanical drawing *[S]*

Mechanical engineering *[S] (May add geog subd)*
Mechanical engineers
Mechanical movements *[S]*
Mechanics *[S]*
    BT   Physics
Mechanics, Applied
Mechanics (Persons) *[S]*
Medal of honor
Medals *[S] (May add geog subd)*
    RT   Decorations of honor
Medals, Military and naval
    USE   Military decorations
Medea (Greek mythology)
Medes
Media
    USE   Mass media
Media programs (Education) *(May add geog subd)*
    UF   School media programs
    RT   Audio-visual library service
            Audio-visual materials
Medicaid *[S]*
    BT   Insurance, Health
            Poor—Medical care
Medical anthropology
Medical botany
    RT   Medicinal plants
Medical care *[S] (May add geog subd)*
    UF   Delivery of health care
            Health services
    SA   *the subdivision* —Medical examinations
Medical care, Cost of *(May add geog subd)*
    UF   Medical care—Costs
Medical centers *[S] (May add geog subd)*
Medical colleges *(May add geog subd)*
    UF   Medicine—Study and teaching
Medical emergencies *(May add geog subd)*
Medical ethics *[S] (May add geog subd)*
    UF   Ethics, Medical
Medical examiners (Law) *(May add geog subd)*
Medical genetics *[S] (May add geog subd)*
Medical innovations *(May add geog subd)*
Medical instruments and apparatus *(May add geog subd)*
Medical jurisprudence *[S] (May add geog subd)*
Medical laws and legislation
    UF   Medicine—Law and legislation
Medical misconceptions *(May add geog subd)*
Medical missions
    USE   Missions, Medical
Medical novels
    USE   Medicine—Fiction
Medical personnel
Medical personnel and patient *(May add geog subd)*
Medical policy *(May add geog subd)*
    UF   Health policy
Medical prognosis
    USE   Prognosis
Medical research
    USE   Medicine—Research
Medical scientists
    NT   Women medical scientists
Medical students
Medical teaching personnel
Medical technology *[S] (May add geog subd)*
Medical terminology
    USE   Medicine—Terminology
Medical writing

Medically uninsured persons
Medicare *[S] (May add geog subd)*
    BT   Aged—Medical care
          Insurance, Health
Medication abuse *(May add geog subd)*
Medici, Lorenzo de, 1449-1492
Medicinal plants *(May add geog subd)*
    RT   Medical botany
Medicine *[S] (May add geog subd)*
    RT   Diagnosis
          Pathology
          Therapeutics
    NT   Sports medicine
    SA   *the subdivision* —Medicine
—Research
    UF   Medical research
—Terminology
    UF   Medical terminology
—Vocational guidance
    UF   Medicine as a profession
Medicine, Chinese *(May add geog subd)*
    UF   Chinese medicine
Medicine, Military *[S] (May add geog subd)*
    UF   Military medicine
Medicine, Oriental *(May add geog subd)*
Medicine, Physical *(May add geog subd)*
Medicine, Popular *[S] (May add geog subd)*
Medicine, Psychosomatic
Medicine, Preventive *(May add geog subd)*
    UF   Preventive medicine
Medicine, Rural *(May add geog subd)*
Medicine, State *[S] (May add geog subd)*
Medicine and psychology *(May add geog subd)*
Medicine as a profession
    USE   Medicine—Vocational guidance
Medicine man
    USE   Shamans
Medicine shows
Medieval literature
    USE   Literature, Medieval
Medina River (Tex.), Battle of, 1813
Meditation *[S] (May add geog subd)*
Meditations *[S]*
Mediterranean Region
Mediterranean Sea
Medusa (Greek mythology)
Meetings
Megalithic monuments *(May add geog subd)*
Mehta, Zubin, 1936-
Meir, Golda, 1898-1978
Meitner, Lise, 1878-1968
Mekong River
Melanesia
Melanoma *(May add geog subd)*
Melbourne, William Lamb, Viscount, 1779-1848
Mellon, Paul
Meltzer, Milton, 1915-
Melville, Herman, 1819-1891
Melville, Herman, 1819-1891. Billy Budd
Memorial Day *[S]*
Memory *[S]*
    RT   Mnemonics
Memory training
    USE   Mnemonics
Memphis (Tenn.)

Men *[S]*
Men-hating
    USE   Misandry
Men's clothing *[S] (May add geog subd)*
Mencken, H.L. (Henry Louis), 1880-1956
Mendel, Gregor, 1822-1884
Mendelssohn-Bartholdy, Felix, 1809-1847
Mendelssohn family
Mendes, Chico, d. 1988
Menehune *[AC only]*
    BT   Fairies
Menendez de Aviles, Pedro, 1519-1574
Mengele, Josef, 1911-
Meningitis *[S]*
Mennonites *[S]*
Menopause *[S] (May add geog subd)*
Menstrual cycle
    USE   Menstruation *[AC only]*
Menstruation *[AC, S]*
    UF   Menstrual cycle
Mensuration
    USE   Measurement *[AC only]*
Mental arithmetic *[S]*
    UF   Arithmetic, Mental
Mental discipline
Mental disorders
    USE   Mental illness
Mental efficiency
    UF   Inefficiency, Intellectual
    RT   Stupidity
Mental healing *[S] (May add geog subd)*
Mental health *[S] (May add geog subd)*
Mental health policy *(May add geog subd)*
Mental health services *(May add geog subd)*
Mental illness *[S] (May add geog subd)*
    Use for works on specific kinds of mental illness and on the special problems encountered by those dealing with mentally ill persons.
    UF   Mental disorders
    RT   Mentally ill
          Neuroses
          Psychiatry
          Psychotropic drugs
Mental patients
    USE   Psychotherapy patients
Mental retardation *[S] (May add geog subd)*
Mental tests
    USE   Psychological tests
Mentally handicapped *[S]*
Mentally handicapped children *[S]*
Mentally ill *[S]*
    Use for works on mentally ill persons and their relationship to their environment.
    RT   Mental illness
Mentally ill children *[S]*
Menten, Pieter Nicolaas, 1899-1987
Mentors in education
Menudo (Musical group)
Menus *[S]*
Mer (Indic people)
Mercedes automobile
Mercedes-Benz (Firm)
Mercedes-Benz of North America
Mercer, A.S. (Asa Shinn), 1839-1917
Merchant ships
Merchants *[S]*
Mercury (Planet)

Mercury probes
Meredith, James
Merlin (Legendary character)
Mermaids
    BT   Animals, Mythical
          Ocean—Folklore
          Ocean—Mythology
    RT   Mermen
Mermen
    BT   Animals, Mythical
          Ocean—Folklore
          Ocean—Mythology
    RT   Mermaids
Merriam, Eve, 1916-
Merrick, Joseph Carey, 1862 or 3-1890
Merrimack (Frigate)
Merry-go-round
Mesa Petroleum Co.
Mesa Verde National Park (Colo.)
Messerschmitt 109 (Fighter planes)
Messiah (Musical work)
Messiness
    USE Cleanliness
          Orderliness
Messing, Shep
Metabolic diseases
    USE Metabolism—Disorders
Metabolism *[S]*
  —Disorders
      UF   Metabolic diseases
Metacognition
Metal detectors
Metal work
    USE Metalwork *[AC only]*
Metals *[S]*
    SA   the names of specific metals and the subdivision
          —Metallurgy
Metals, Precious
    USE Precious metals
Metals as an investment *(May add geog subd)*
Metalwork *[AC, S]*
    UF   Metal work
    NT   Silverwork
Metamorphosis
Metaphor
    BT   Figures of speech
Metaphysics *[S] (May add geog subd)*
Metazoa
    USE Metazoans *[AC only]*
Metazoans *[AC only]*
    UF   Metazoa
Metchnikoff, Elie, 1845-1916
Meteorites *[S] (May add geog subd)*
Meteoroids
Meteorological optics *(May add geog subd)*
Meteorological stations *(May add geog subd)*
Meteorologists
Meteorology *[S] (May add geog subd)*
Meteorology in aeronautics *[S] (May add geog subd)*
Meteors *[S]*
Methadone maintenance *(May add geog subd)*
Methamphetamine *(May add geog subd)*
Methaqualone
Methodism *(May add geog subd)*
Methodist Church *(May add geog subd)*

Methodists
Metric system *[S] (May add geog subd)*
Metropolitan areas *[S] (May add geog subd)*
Metropolitan Museum of Art (N.Y.)
Metternich, Clemens Wenzel Lothar, Furst von, 1773-1859
Mexican American art *(May add geog subd)*
Mexican American artists
Mexican American authors
Mexican-American Border Region
Mexican American folk art *(May add geog subd)*
Mexican American literature
    USE American literature—Mexican American authors
Mexican American literature (Spanish)
Mexican American poets
Mexican Americans *[S]*
    BT   Hispanic Americans
Mexican jumping bean
    USE Jumping bean *[AC only]*
Mexican literature *[S] (May add geog subd)*
Mexican War, 1845-1848
Mexicans *[S]*
Mexico
  —History
  — **—Conquest, 1519-1540**
Mexico, Gulf of
Mexico City (Mexico)
Meyer, Carolyn
Muller, Jorg
Miami (Fla.)
Miami Dolphins (Football team)
Miami Indians
Mice *[S]*
Mice as pets
Michelangelo Buonarroti, 1475-1564
Michener, James A. (James Albert), 1907-
Michigan
Michiko, Empress, consort of Akihito, Emperor of Japan, 1934-
Mickey Mouse (Cartoon character)
Microbiologists
Microbiology *[S] (May add geog subd)*
Microcomputers *[S] (May add geog subd)*
    UF   Home computers
Microeconomics
Microelectronics *[S] (May add geog subd)*
Micromys minutus
    USE Harvest mouse, European *[AC only]*
Micronesia (Federated States)
Microorganisms *[S] (May add geog subd)*
Microphone
Microprocessors *[S] (May add geog subd)*
Microscopes *[S] (May add geog subd)*
Microsoft Corporation
Microsoft Word (Computer program)
Microwave cookery *[S]*
Microwaves *[S]*
Micrurus
    USE Coral snakes *[AC only]*
Midas
Middle age *[S] (May add geog subd)*
Middle aged persons *[S]*
Middle Ages *[S]*
    NT   Twelfth century
Middle Atlantic States
Middle class *(May add geog subd)*

Middle East *[S]*
    UF   Near East
  —Civilization
  — —To 622
  —Politics and government
  — —1945-
  — —1979-
Middle eastern literature
Middle managers
Middle school libraries *(May add geog subd)*
Middle schools *(May add geog subd)*
Middle West *[S]*
    UF   Midwest
MIDI (Standard)
    UF   Musical Instrument Digital Interface
Midlands (England)
Midler, Bette
Midway, Battle of, 1942
Midway Islands
Midwest
    USE Middle West
Midwives *[S]*
Mier Expedition, 1842
Miers, Earl Schenck, 1910-1972
Mies van der Rohe, Ludwig, 1886-1969
Mifepristone
    BT   Oral contraceptives
MIG (Fighter planes)
    BT   Fighter planes
          Jet planes
Migraine
Migrant agricultural laborers
Migrant labor *[S] (May add geog subd)*
    BT   Labor
Migration
    Use as the subdivision —Migration.
Migration, Internal *[S] (May add geog subd)*
Migrations of nations
Mikasuki Indians
Milan (Italy)
Miles, Nelson Appleton, 1839-1925
Military art and science *[S] (May add geog subd)*
Military bases *(May add geog subd)*
Military biography
    BT   Biography
Military decorations
    UF   Medals, Military and naval
Military dependents
Military engineering *[S] (May add geog subd)*
Military ethics *(May add geog subd)*
Military history *[S]*
    SA   *the subdivision* —History, Military *under geographic*
          names, names of battles, etc.
          the subdivision —History *under names of individual*
          armies, e.g., United States. Army—History
Military history, Ancient
Military history, Medieval
Military history, Modern
  —20th century
Military-industrial complex *(May add geog subd)*
Military intelligence *(May add geog subd)*
Military museums *(May add geog subd)*
Military offenses *[S] (May add geog subd)*
Military pensions
    UF   Pensions, Military
Military personnel

    USE Soldiers
Military policy *[S]*
    SA   *the subdivision* —Military policy
Military service, Draft
    USE Draft
Military service, Voluntary *[S] (May add geog subd)*
    RT   Armed forces
Military surveillance *(May add geog subd)*
Military training camps *[S] (May add geog subd)*
Military transportation
    USE Transportation, Military
Military uniforms
    UF   Uniforms, Military
Military weapons *(May add geog subd)*
    UF   Armaments
Milk *[S]*
Milk, Human
    USE Breast milk
Milkweed butterflies *(May add geog subd)*
Milky Way
Millais, John Everett, Sir, 1829-1896
Millard, Bill
Millay, Edna St. Vincent, 1892-1950
Miller, Arthur, 1915-
Miller, Arthur, 1915- . Death of a salesman
Miller, Arthur, 1915- . Crucible
Miller, Henry, 1891-1980
Miller, Johnny, 1947-
Miller, Kathy
Miller, Richard W.
Millhone, Kinsey (Fictitious character)
Millie (Dog)
Million (The number)
Millionaires *[S]*
Millipedes *[S] (May add geog subd)*
Mills and millwork *(May add geog subd)*
Millwork (Woodwork)
Milne, A.A. (Alan Alexander), 1882-1956
Milne, Christopher, 1920-
Milton, John, 1608-1674
Milwaukee (Wis.)
Milwaukee Brewers (Baseball team)
Milwaukee Bucks (Basketball team)
Mime
    USE Pantomime *[AC only]*
Mimicry (Biology)
    USE Camouflage (Biology) *[AC only]*
Mimosas *[AC, S] (May add geog subd)*
    UF   Sensitive plants
Minamoto, Yoshitsune, 1159-1189
Mind and body *(May add geog subd)*
Mineralogy *[S] (May add geog subd)*
Mineral resources, Marine
    USE Marine mineral resources
Mineral resources in submerged lands *(May add geog subd)*
    RT   Mines and mineral resources
Minerals *(May add geog subd)*
Minerals in human nutrition
    BT   Nutrition
Miners *[S]*
Mines and mineral resources *[S] (May add geog subd)*
    RT   Minerals in submerged lands
    NT   Gold mines and mining
          Iron mines and mining
          Silver mines and mining
Ming porcelain *(May add geog subd)*

Miniature cameras *(May add geog subd)*
Miniature craft
   RT   Handicraft
Miniature flower arrangement *(May add geog subd)*
   BT   Flower arrangement
Miniature furniture *(May add geog subd)*
Miniature horses
Miniature objects *(May add geog subd)*
Minibike racing *(May add geog subd)*
Minibikes
Minicomputers *[S] (May add geog subd)*
Mining
   USE   Gold mines and mining
Mining engineering *[S] (May add geog subd)*
Minkow, Barry
Minks *[S] (May add geog subd)*
Minneapolis Metropolitan Area (Minn.)
   UF   Twin Cities Metropolitan Area (Minn.)
   RT   Saint Paul Metropolitan Area (Minn.)
Minnesota
Minnesota Twins (Baseball team)
Minnesota Vikings (Football team)
Minoans
Minor league baseball *(May add geog subd)*
Minority artists
Minority women
Minorities *[S]*
Minority literature (American)
   USE   American literature—Minority authors
          American literature—Afro-American authors
          American literature—Indian authors
          American literature—Mexican American authors
Minotaur (Greek mythology)
Minstrel shows
Minstrels *[S]*
Mints
   RT   Money
Minuet
Miracle plays
   USE   Mysteries and miracle plays
Miracles *[S]*
Miriam (Biblical figure)
Miro, Joan, 1893-
Mirrors *[S] (May add geog subd)*
Misandry
   UF   Men-hating
Miscarriage *[S] (May add geog subd)*
Misericordia Sisters
Misers
Miss America Pageant, Atlantic City (N.J.)
Missing children *[S]*
Missing in action *[S]*
Missing mass (Astronomy)
Missing persons *[S]*
Missionaries
   RT   Christian biography
Missionaries, Medical *[S]*
Missions *(May add geog subd)*
   SA   *the subdivision* —Missions
Missions, Medical *(May add geog subd)*
   UF   Medical missions
Missions, Spanish *(May add geog subd)*
   UF   Spanish missions
Mississippi
Mississippi River
Mississippi River Valley *[S]*

Missouri
Mistletoes
   UF   Mistletoe
Misty (Horse)
Mitchell, Arthur, 1934-
Mitchell, Clarence M. (Clarence Maurice), 1911-1984
Mitchell, Margaret, 1900-1949
Mitchell, Maria, 1818-1889
Mitchell, Napoleon Bonaparte
Mitosis
   BT   Cells
Mittens *(May add geog subd)*
Miwok Indians
Mix, Tom, 1880-1940
Mnemonics
   UF   Memory training
   RT   Memory
Mobile (Ala.)
Mobile home industry *(May add geog subd)*
Mobile home living *[S] (May add geog subd)*
Mobile homes *[S] (May add geog subd)*
Mobiles (Sculpture) *[S] (May add geog subd)*
Mock trials
   BT   Trials
Mockingbirds *[S]*
Model car racing
Modeling *[S]*
   RT   Models and modelmaking
   NT   Clay modeling *[AC only]*
   SA   *the subdivision* —Models
Models (Clay, plaster, etc.)
Models (Persons)
   UF   Fashion models
          Models, Fashion
Models, Artists'
   USE   Artists' models
Models, Fashion
   USE   Models (Persons)
Models and modelmaking *[S] (May add geog subd)*
   RT   Modeling
   SA   *the subdivision* —Models
Modems
Modern art
   USE   Art, Modern
          Modernism (Art)
Modern dance *[S] (May add geog subd)*
Modern literature
   USE   Literature, Modern
Modernism (Art) *(May add geog subd)*
   RT   Art, Modern
Modigliani, Amedeo, 1884-1920
Modisane, Bloke, d. 1986
Modular arithmetic
Mogul Empire
Mohammed Reza Pahlavi, Shah of Iran, 1919-
Mohawk Indians
Mohawk River (N.Y.)
Mohegan Indians
   UF   Mohican Indians
Mohegan Lake (N.Y.)
Mohr, Joseph, 1792-1848
Mojave Desert (Calif.)
Molasses
Molds (Fungi)
Mole crickets *(May add geog subd)*
   BT   Crickets

Molecular biology *[S]*
    UF   Biology, Molecular
Molecular genetics *(May add geog subd)*
Molecular structure
Molecules *[S]*
Moles (Animals) *(May add geog subd)*
Moliere, Jean Baptiste Poquelin, 1622-1673
Molina, Gloria
Mollusks *[S] (May add geog subd)*
Molly Maguires
    BT   Coal miners—Pennsylvania
Molting
Momentum (Mechanics)
Monaco
Monaco Grand Prix Race
Monarch butterfly *[S]*
    BT   Butterflies
Monarchs
    USE   Kings, queens, rulers, etc. *[AC only]*
Monarchy *[S] (May add geog subd)*
Monasteries *[S] (May add geog subd)*
Monastic and religious life
    USE   Religious life *[AC only]*
Monasticism and religious orders
    USE   Religious life *[AC only]*
Monet, Claude, 1840-1926
Monetary policy *[S] (May add geog subd)*
Monette, Paul
Money *[S] (May add geog subd)*
    RT   Mints
Money laundering *(May add geog subd)*
Money market *(May add geog subd)*
Money-making projects for children
    USE   Moneymaking projects *[AC only]*
Moneymaking projects *[AC only]*
    UF   Money-making projects for children
Mongolia
Mongols
Mongooses *[S]*
Monitor lizards
    BT   Lizards
Monkeys *[S] (May add geog subd)*
    RT   Lemur
Monkeys as aids for the handicapped *(May add geog subd)*
Monkeys as laboratory animals
Monmouth, Battle of, 1778
Monmouth's Rebellion, 1685
Monograms *[S]*
Monographic series
Monologues
Mononucleosis *(May add geog subd)*
Monorail railroads
    USE   Monorails *[AC only]*
Monorails *[AC only]*
    UF   Monorail railroads
Monosodium glutamate
Monotremata
    USE   Monotremes *[AC only]*
Monotremes *[AC only]*
    UF   Egg-laying mammals
             Monotremata
    NT   Echidnas
Monroe, James, 1758-1831
Monroe, Marilyn, 1926-1962
Monroe, Robert A.
Monroe doctrine

Monster trucks *(May add geog subd)*
Monsters *[S]*
Monsters in art *[S]*
Monsters in mass media
Montague County (Tex.)
Mont-Saint-Michel (France)
Montana
Montana, Joe, 1956-
Montcalm de Saint-Veran, Louis-Joseph, Marquis de, 1712-1759
Montessori method of education *[S]*
Montezuma, Carlos, 1866-1923
Montfort, Simon de, Earl of Leicester, 1208?-1265
Montgomery (Ala.)
Months *[S]*
Monticello (Va.)
Montreal Expos (Baseball team)
Montreal Island (Quebec)
Monuments *(May add geog subd)*
    NT   National monuments
             Natural monuments
Mooar, J. Wright, 1851-1940
Moody, Anne, 1940-
Moody, Ralph, 1898-
Moon *[S]*
   —Exploration
      RT   Space flight to the moon
   —Phases
Moon, Sun Myung
Moon cars *[S]*
Moon rocks *[AC only]*
    UF   Lunar petrology
Moore, Clement Clarke, 1779-1863
Moore, Henry Spencer, 1898-
Moore, Marianne, 1887-1972
Moore, Mary Carr, 1873-1957
Moore, Mary Tyler, 1937-
Moore County (Tex.)
Moose *[S] (May add geog subd)*
    BT   Mammals
Mopeds *(May add geog subd)*
Moral development *(May add geog subd)*
Moral education *[S] (May add geog subd)*
    SA   *the subdivision* —Moral conditions
Morar, Loch (Scotland)
Moravia (Czech Republic)
Moravians *[S]*
    BT   Sects *[AC only]*
Mordred (Legendary character)
More, Thomas, Sir, Saint, 1478-1535
Morgan, Elizabeth, 1947-
Morgan, Gib, 1842-1909
Morgan, Henry, Sir, 1635?-1688
Morgan, Julia, 1872-1957
Morgan, Sally, 1951-
Morgan Grenfell & Co.
Morgan Guaranty Trust Company of New York
Morgan horse
Morgan le Fay (Legendary character)
Morgan Stanley & Co.
Morimoto, Junko
Morita psychotherapy *(May add geog subd)*
Mormon Church *(May add geog subd)*
    NT   Church of Jesus Christ of Latter-day Saints
Mormons *[S]*

Morning *[AC only]*
    BT   Chronology
           Day
           Time
Morning glories *[S] (May add geog subd)*
    BT   Flowers
Morocco
Morphology (Animals)
Morrill, George P., 1920-
Morris, Desmond
Morris, Willie
Morrison, George, 1919-
Morrison, Jim, 1943-1971
Morrison, Toni
Morse, Samuel Finley Breese, 1791-1872
Morse, Thomas S.
Mortality *[S] (May add geog subd)*
Mortgage loans *(May add geog subd)*
Mortgages *[S] (May add geog subd)*
    RT   Loans
           Borrowing and lending *[AC only]*
Mosaics *[S] (May add geog subd)*
Moscow (Russia)
Moses, Grandma, 1860-1961
Moses (Biblical leader)
Mosley, Diana, Lady, 1910-
Mosley, Oswald, Sir, 1896-
Mosques *(May add geog subd)*
Mosquito (Bombers)
Mosquito Indians
Mosquitoes *[S] (May add geog subd)*
    BT   Insect pests
           Insects
Mosquitoes as carriers of disease *(May add geog subd)*
Moss, Claude Scott, 1924-
Mosses *[S] (May add geog subd)*
Mote Marine Laboratory
Motels
    USE   Hotels, motels, etc. *[AC only]*
Mother and child *[S]*
Mother Goose
Mother Teresa
Motherhood *(May add geog subd)*
Mothers *[S]*
    RT   Fathers
    NT   Love, Maternal
           Surrogate mothers
           Teenage mothers
           Unmarried mothers
           Working mothers
Mothers and daughters *[S]*
    RT   Daughters
           Fathers and daughters
           Mothers and sons
Mothers and sons *[S]*
    RT   Fathers and sons
           Mothers and daughters
           Sons
Mother's Day
Moths *[S] (May add geog subd)*
Motion *[S]*
    UF   Movement
Motion perception (Vision)
Motion picture acting
Motion picture actors and actresses
    USE   Actors and actresses *[AC only]*

Motion picture authorship
Motion picture industry *[S] (May add geog subd)*
Motion picture music *(May add geog subd)*
Motion picture plays *[S]*
Motion picture producers and directors *[S]*
Motion picture sequels
Motion picture serials *[S]*
Motion picture theaters *(May add geog subd)*
Motion pictures *[AC, S] (May add geog subd)*
    UF   Films
           Movies
           Moving pictures
    RT   Film criticism
           Video tapes
    SA   *specific types, e.g.,* Vampire films *and the subdivision*
                —Films and video adaptations
    —Biography
        USE   Actors and actresses *[AC only]*
    —Plots, themes, etc.
    —Production and direction
    —Science fiction
        USE   Science fiction films
Motivation (Psychology) *[S]*
    NT   Achievement motivation
Motivation in education
Motivation research (Marketing)
    BT   Advertising—Psychological aspects
           Marketing research
Motor ability
Motor learning
Motor vehicle driving
    NT   Driving, Automobile
Motor vehicles *(May add geog subd)*
Motor vehicles in art
Motorboat racing *(May add geog subd)*
Motorboats *[S] (May add geog subd)*
Motorcycle industry *(May add geog subd)*
Motorcycle racing *(May add geog subd)*
Motorcycles *[S] (May add geog subd)*
    SA   *the names of specific makes of motorcycle*
Motorcycling *(May add geog subd)*
Motown Record Corporation
Mottoes *[S] (May add geog subd)*
Mound builders *[AC only]*
    UF   Mound-builders
Mount Rushmore National Memorial (S.D.)
Mount Vernon (Va. : Estate)
Mountain animals *[AC, S]*
    UF   Alpine animals
           Alpine fauna
           Mountain fauna
Mountain fauna
    USE   Mountain animals *[AC, S]*
Mountain bikes
    USE   All terrain bicycles
Mountain ecology *(May add geog subd)*
Mountain life *[S] (May add geog subd)*
Mountain railroads
    BT   Railroads
    NT   Rack railroads
Mountain sheep
Mountain whites (Southern States)
    UF   Appalachian people (Southern States)
Mountaineering *[S] (May add geog subd)*
    NT   Snow and ice climbing

Mountaineers
  NT Women mountaineers
Mountains *[S] (May add geog subd)*
Mountbatten of Burma, Louis, Earl, 1900-1979
Mourning etiquette *(May add geog subd)*
  RT Funeral rites and ceremonies
Mouth *[S]*
  —Cancer
Mouth organs *[S]*
  RT Harmonica
Movement
  USE Motion
Movement, Psychology of
Movement disorders
  NT Paralysis
Movement education *[S] (May add geog subd)*
  RT Dancing
      Physical education and training
Movement songs
  USE Political ballads and songs
Movie stars
  USE Actors and actresses *[AC only]*
Movies
  USE Motion pictures
Moving, Household *[S] (May add geog subd)*
Moving of buildings, bridges, etc.
Moving pictures
  USE Motion pictures
Mowat, Farley
Moyers, Rich
Mozambique
Mozart, Wolfgang Amadeus, 1756-1791
Mozart, Wolfgang Amadeus, 1756-1791. Magic flute
Mpongwe (African people)
  —Folklore
      USE Folklore, Mpongwe *[AC only]*
MS-DOS (Computer operating system)
Mud *(May add geog subd)*
Mugs *(May add geog subd)*
Muhammad, d. 632
Muhammad Ali, 1942-
Muir, John, 1838-1914
Mulching *(May add geog subd)*
Mule deer *[S] (May add geog subd)*
Mules *[S] (May add geog subd)*
Multilevel marketing *(May add geog subd)*
  BT Marketing
Multiple birth *[S]*
  UF Birth, multiple
Multiple personality *[S] (May add geog subd)*
Multiple sclerosis *(May add geog subd)*
Multiplication *[S]*
Mummies *[S] (May add geog subd)*
Mumps *[S] (May add geog subd)*
Munch, Edvard, 1863-1944
Mundy, John Hine, 1917-
Munich Four-power Agreement (1938)
Municipal engineering *[S] (May add geog subd)*
  BT Engineering
Municipal government *[S] (May add geog subd)*
  BT Local government
      Political science
Municipal services
  UF Community services
      Public services
  BT County services

Munitions *[S]*
Muñoz Marín, Luis, 1898-
Munro, Roxie
Muppet Show (Television program)
Mural painting and decoration *[S] (May add geog subd)*
Murchison, Clinton Williams, 1895-1969
Murchison family
Murder *(May add geog subd)*
  RT Trials (Murder)
  NT Parricide
  —Investigation *(May add geog subd)*
Murder victims
Murderers
Murphy, Dale, 1956-
Murphy, Gerald, 1888-1964
Murphy, Sara
Murphy family
Murrow, Edward R.
Muscle strength
  UF Strength of muscles
Muscles *[AC, S]*
  NT Muscular system *[AC only]*
Muscular dystrophy
Muscular system *[AC only]*
  UF Musculoskeletal system
  BT Muscles *[AC only]*
Musée d'Orsay
Musée du Louvre
Museo del Prado
Museo Nacional de Antropología (Mexico)
Museology
  USE Museum techniques
Museum conservation methods
  SA *the subdivision* —Conservation and restoration
Museum directors
Museum methods
  USE Museum techniques
Museum of Fine Arts (Boston, Mass.)
Museum of Modern Art (New York, N.Y.)
Museum of New Mexico
Museum of Science and Industry (Chicago, Ill.)
Museum techniques
  UF Museology
      Museum methods
Museum voor Volkenkunde (Rotterdam, Netherlands)
Museums *[S] (May add geog subd)*
  NT Natural history museums
  SA *the subdivision* —Museums
Mushrooms *[S] (May add geog subd)*
Mushrooms, Edible *(May add geog subd)*
Mushrooms, Hallucinogenic *(May add geog subd)*
  UF Hallucinogenic mushrooms
Mushrooms, Poisonous *(May add geog subd)*
Musial, Stanley Frank, 1920-
Music *[S] (May add geog subd)*
  SA *the names of specific forms of music, and the subdivisions*
      —Music *and* —Songs and music
  —Acoustics and physics
  —Analysis
      USE Musical analysis
  —Games
      UF Music games
          Musical games
      BT Games
      NT Harmony

RT   Singing games
—**Theory**
    UF   Music theory
Music, African
    USE   Music—Africa
Music, Broadway
    USE   Musical theater
Music, Japanese
    USE   Music—Japan
Music, Mexican
    USE   Music—Mexico
Music, Norwegian
    USE   Music—Norway
Music, Origin of
Music, Patriotic
    USE   Patriotic music
Music, Popular
    USE   Popular music
Music and literature *[S]*
    RT   Literature
Music and society
Music appreciation
Music camps *[AC only]*
    UF   Camps, Music
Music festivals *[S] (May add geog subd)*
Music games
    USE   Music—Games
    BT   Games
    NT   Singing games
Music theory
    USE   Music—Theory
Music therapy *(May add geog subd)*
Music trade *(May add geog subd)*
Music videos *[S] (May add geog subd)*
   —**Production and direction**
Musical analysis
    UF   Music—Analysis
Musical films *[S] (May add geog subd)*
Musical form *[S]*
Musical Instrument Digital Interface
    USE   MIDI (Standard)
Musical instruments *[S] (May add geog subd)*
    UF   Instruments, Musical
    SA   *the names of specific instruments and types of instruments*
Musical instruments, Electronic *[S]*
Musical instruments in art
Musical landmarks *(May add geog subd)*
Musical meter and rhythm *[S]*
Musical notation *[S]*
Musical revues, comedies, etc.
    USE   Musicals
Musical theater *(May add geog subd)*
Musicals *[S] (May add geog subd)*
    UF   Musical revues, comedies, etc.
Musicians *[S]*
    NT   Women musicians
    SA   *the names of specific musicians, instruments, and types of music*
Musicians, Austrian
Musicians, English
Musicians, French
Musicians, Irish
Musicians, Polish
Musicians, Spanish
    USE   Musicians
Musk ox

    USE   Muskox
Muskogean Indians
Muskox *[S]*
    UF   Musk ox
Muskrat *(May add geog subd)*
Muslims *[S]*
Mussolini, Benito, 1883-1945
Mussorgsky, Modest Petrovich, 1839-1881.   Night on Bald Mountain
    UF   Mussorgsky, Modest Petrovich, 1839-1881.   Noch'na Lysoi gore (1880)
Mussorgsky, Modest Petrovich, 1839-1881.   Noch'na Lysoi gore (1880)
    USE   Mussorgsky, Modest Petrovich, 1839-1881.   Night on Bald Mountain
Mustang *[S] (May add geog subd)*
Mustang automobile
Mustelidae
    BT   Carnivores *[AC, S]*
Mutism *(May add geog subd)*
Mutual funds *(May add geog subd)*
    UF   Investment trusts
    BT   Investments
Muze'on Yisfa'el (Jerusalem)
    USE   Israel Museum (Jerusalem)
Muzzle-loading firearms
    NT   Firearms
Muzzleloader hunting
    BT   Hunting
Myers, Ariel
Myers, Janet Cannon
Myers, Walter Dean, 1937-
Myers-Briggs Type Indicator
    BT   Personality tests
Myerson, Bess
Myocardial infarction *(May add geog subd)*
    UF   Heart attack
Mysteries
    USE   Mystery and detective stories
Mysteries and miracle plays *[AC, S]*
    UF   Mysteries and miracle-plays
Mystery and detective plays *[AC, S]*
    UF   Detective and mystery plays
Mystery and detective stories *[AC, S]*
    UF   Detective and mystery stories
    NT   Ciphers—Fiction *[AC only]*
Mystery and detective television programs *[AC only]*
    UF   Detective and mystery television programs
Mysticism *[S] (May add geog subd)*
Myth
Myth in literature
Mythology *[S] (May add geog subd)*
    SA   *the subdivision* —Religion *and headings of the type:* Indian mythology
Mythology, African *[S]*
Mythology, Asian *[S] (May add geog subd)*
Mythology, Celtic *[S]*
Mythology, Chinese *[S]*
Mythology, Classical *[S]*
Mythology, Egyptian *[S]*
Mythology, Greek *[S]*
Mythology, Hindu
Mythology, Indian
    USE   Indian mythology
Mythology, Indic
Mythology, Japanese *[S]*

Mythology, Norse *[S]*
Mythology, Peruvian *[S] (May add geog subd)*
Mythology, Roman
Mythology and art
    USE Art and mythology
Mythology in literature
Naaman, the Syrian
Nabokov, Vladimir Vladimirovich, 1899-1977
Nacogdoches County (Tex.)
Nader, Ralph
Nagasaki (Japan)—Bombardment, 1945
Nagurski, Bronko, 1908-
Nahuas
Nahuatl language *(May add geog subd)*
    UF Aztec language
Naikan psychotherapy
    BT Psychotherapy
Nail-biting *(May add geog subd)*
Nail craft
    BT Handicraft
Nails (Anatomy)
Nairobi National Park (Kenya)
Namath, Joe Willie, 1943-
Nameless Detective (Fictitious character)
Names *[S] (May add geog subd)*
    UF Nomenclature
    SA the subdivision —Names
Names, Geographical *(May add geog subd)*
    RT Geography
Names, Personal *(May add geog subd)*
    UF Personal names
    —Jewish
Namibia
Nansen, Fridtjof, 1861-1930
Nanticoke Indians
Nantucket Island (Mass.)
Naples (Kingdom)
Napkin folding
Naples (Italy)
Napoleon I, Emperor of the French, 1769-1821
Napoleon Solo (Yacht)
Napoleonic Wars, 1800-1815
Naps (Sleep) *(May add geog subd)*
Narcissism *(May add geog subd)*
Narcotic addiction
    USE Narcotic habit
Narcotic addicts
Narcotic enforcement agents
Narcotic habit
    UF Narcotic addiction
Narcotics *[S] (May add geog subd)*
Narcotics, Control of *(May add geog subd)*
Narcotics and crime *(May add geog subd)*
    UF Crime and narcotics
Narcotics dealers
    UF Drug dealers
        Narcotics traffic
Narcotics traffic
    USE Narcotics dealers
Narraganset Indians
Narration (Rhetoric)
Narration in the Bible
Narrative poetry
    BT Poetry
Narvaez, Panfilo de, d. 1528
Narwhal *(May add geog subd)*

    BT Whales
NASA
    USE United States. National Aeronautics and Space Administration
Nascapee Indians
    USE Naskapi Indians
Nascimento, Edson Arantes do, 1940-
    USE Pele, 1940-
Nash, Ogden, 1902-1971
Nashua River (Mass. and N.H.)
Naskapi Indians
    UF Nascapee Indians
Nason, Susan
Nassau (Bahamas)
Nasser, Gamal Abdel, 1918-1970
Nast, Thomas, 1840-1902
Natick High School (Natick, Mass.)
Nation-state
    USE National state
National Association for the Advancement of Colored People
National bank notes *(May add geog subd)*
National Baseball Hall of Fame and Museum
National Basketball Association
National Broadcasting Company, Inc.
National characteristics
    BT Anthropology
        Social psychology
National characteristics, American, [Argentine, British, English, etc.]
National Collegiate Athletic Association
National Council of Teachers of English
National emblems
    USE Emblems, National
National Fire Protection Association
National Football League
National Foundation on the Arts and the Humanities
National Gallery of Art (U.S.)
National Geographic (Periodical)
National Geographic Society (U.S.)
National Hockey League
National League of Professional Baseball Clubs
National liberation movements *[S] (May add geog subd)*
    RT Freedom
National Merit Scholarship Qualifying Test
National monuments *(May add geog subd)*
    BT Monuments
National Museum of American Art (U.S.)
National Museum of American History
National Museum of Natural History
National Museum of Women in the Arts (U.S.)
National parks and reserves *[S] (May add geog subd)*
    BT Parks
National Rifle Association of America
National Scenic Trail
National Security Council (U.S.)
National service *(May add geog subd)*
National socialism *[S] (May add geog subd)*
    NT Hitler Youth *[AC only]*
National socialism and art
National Socialist German Workers Party
National socialists
National songs *[S] (May add geog subd)*
National state
    UF Nation-state
    BT State, The
National Storytelling Festival

National Weather Service
    RT   Weather forecasting
National Zoological Park (U.S.)
    RT   Zoos
Nationalism *[S] (May add geog subd)*
Nationalists
Native language
    RT   Language and languages
Native peoples
    USE   Indigenous peoples
Native plant gardening *(May add geog subd)*
    BT   Gardening
Native plants for cultivation *(May add geog subd)*
NATO
    USE   North Atlantic Treaty Organization
Natt, James, 1736-1819
Natural childbirth *[S] (May add geog subd)*
Natural disasters *[S] (May add geog subd)*
Natural family planning *(May add geog subd)*
Natural foods *[S] (May add geog subd)*
Natural gas *[S] (May add geog subd)*
Natural history *[S] (May add geog subd)*
Natural history museums *(May add geog subd)*
    BT   Museums
Natural monuments *[S] (May add geog subd)*
    BT   Monuments
Natural numbers
    USE   Numbers, Natural
Natural pesticides *[S] (May add geog subd)*
Natural resources *[S] (May add geog subd)*
    NT   Nonrenewable natural resources
    SA   *the subdivision* —Environmental aspects
Natural selection *[S]*
Naturalists *[S]*
Naturalization *(May add geog subd)*
Nature
Nature (Aesthetics)
    UF   Art and nature
             Nature in art
Nature, Healing power of
Nature and nurture
Nature conservation
    USE   Conservation of natural resources *[AC only]*
Nature craft *[S]*
    BT   Handicraft
Nature in art
    USE   Nature (Aesthetics)
Nature in literature *[S]*
Nature in the Bible
    RT   Bible
Nature photography *[S]*
    BT   Photography
Nature printing and nature prints *[AC only]*
    UF   Nature-printing and nature-prints
Nature sounds *(May add geog subd)*
Nature study *[S] (May add geog subd)*
    NT   Wildlife watching
Nature worship *(May add geog subd)*
Naturopathy *[S] (May add geog subd)*
Nautical almanacs *[S]*
Nautical charts *(May add geog subd)*
Nautilus (Submarine)
Navajo Indians *[S]*
Navajo language *[S] (May add geog subd)*
    —Readers *[AC only]*

    Use for reading texts in Navajo containing materials for instruction and practice in reading that language.
    RT   Navajo language materials *[AC only]*
Navajo language materials *[AC only]*
    Use for works written in Navajo intended primarily for general information or recreational reading. Such works with text also given in English are further subdivided by the subdivision —Bilingual.
    RT   Navajo language—Readers *[AC only]*
    —Bilingual *[AC only]*
Naval art and science *(May add geog subd)*
    SA   *the subdivision* —Naval operations
Naval battle groups *(May add geog subd)*
Naval battles *[S] (May add geog subd)*
Naval convoys
Naval history *[S]*
Navarro, José Antonio, 1795-1871
Navel
    USE   Belly button *[AC only]*
Navies *[S] (May add geog subd)*
Navigation *[S] (May add geog subd)*
    RT   Seamanship
    SA   *the subdivision* —Navigation
Navigation (Aeronautics) *[S] (May add geog subd)*
Navratilova, Martina, 1956-
Navy
    USE   Naval art and science
             United States. Navy
Navy Fighter Weapons School (U.S.)
Naylor, Phyllis Reynolds
Nazca Site (Peru)
Nazi criminals
    USE   War criminals
Nazi Youth Movement
    USE   Hitler Youth
Nazis
    USE   National socialists
Nazism
    USE   National socialism
NBC News
Neanderthals
Near-death experiences
    USE   Apparent death
Near East
    USE   Middle East
Neatness
    USE   Cleanliness *[AC only]*
             Orderliness *[AC only]*
Nebraska
Nebulae
Nectarivores *(May add geog subd)*
    UF   Honey-eating animals
Needham, Ann
Needlepoint
    USE   Canvas embroidery
Needlework *[S]*
    NT   Canvas embroidery
Neelley, Judith
Nefertiti, Queen of Egypt, 14th century B.C.
Negativism *(May add geog subd)*
Negotiation *[S] (May add geog subd)*
    UF   Bargaining
    BT   Psychology, Applied
    NT   Conflict management
Negotiation in business *(May add geog subd)*

Negroes
   USE Blacks *(see scope note)*
       Afro-Americans
Negroes in art
   USE Blacks in art
Negroes in literature
   USE Blacks in literature
Nehru, Jawaharlal, 1889-1964
Nehru, Motilal, 1861-1931
Neighborhood *(May add geog subd)*
Neighborhood watch programs *(May add geog subd)*
Neighborliness
Neihardt, John Gneisenau, 1881-1973
Neill, Alexander Sutherland, 1883-1973.   Summerhill
Nelson, Gaylord, 1916-
Nelson, Horatio Nelson, Viscount, 1758-1805
Nelson, Rachel West
Nelson, Willie, 1933-
Nemean lion (Greek mythology)
Neo-nazism
   USE Fascism
Neoclassicism (Art) *(May add geog subd)*
Neoplasms
   USE Tumors
Nepal
Nephritis, Interstitial *(May add geog subd)*
   BT Kidneys—Diseases
Neptune (Planet)
Nero, Emperor of Rome, 37-68 *[S]*
Neruda, Pablo, 1904-1973
Nerves *[S]*
Nervous system *[S]*
Nesbit, E. (Edith), 1858-1924
Neshoba County (Miss.)
Ness, Loch (Scotland)
Nest building
Netherlands *[S]*
   —History
   — —Wars of independence, 1556-1648
   — —German occupation, 1940-1945
   — —1945-
Neuhaus, Bo, 1973-1985
Neuralgia
Neuroimmunology *(May add geog subd)*
Neurofibromatosis *[S]*
Neurolinguistic programming *(May add geog subd)*
Neurologists
Neurology *(May add geog subd)*
Neurophysiology *(May add geog subd)*
   BT Brain
Neuropsychology *(May add geog subd)*
   BT Psychology
Neuroses *[S]* *(May add geog subd)*
   RT Mental illness
Neurosurgeons
Neutron bomb
Nevada
Nevelson, Louise, 1899-1988
New Age movement *[S]*
   UF Aquarian Age movement
   BT Social movements
New Brunswick
New business enterprises *[S]* *(May add geog subd)*
New Deal, 1933-1939
New England *[S]*
   —Social life and customs

   — —To 1775
   — —1783-1865 *[AC only]*
New England Aquarium Corporation
New England Patriots (Football team)
New Guinea
New Hampshire
   —History
   — —To 1775
New Jersey
New Jersey Nets (Basketball team)
New Kids on the Block (Musical group)
New London (Tex.)
New Mexico
New Orleans (La.)
   —History
   — —Capture, 1862
New Orleans, Battle of, 1815
   USE New Orleans (La.), Battle of, 1815
New Orleans, Battle of, 1862
   USE New Orleans (La.)—History—Capture, 1862
New Orleans (La.), Battle of, 1815
   UF New Orleans, Battle of, 1815
New Orleans (La.). Vieux Carre
   USE French Quarter (New Orleans, La.)
New Orleans (Steamboat)
New Orleans Saints (Football team)
New Plymouth Colony
   UF Plymouth Colony
New products *(May add geog subd)*
New Year *(May add geog subd)*
New York (N.Y.)
   As a geographic subdivision, this heading is used directly.
New York (N.Y.). Police Dept.
New York (N.Y.) in art
New York (N.Y.) Plaza Hotel
   —History
   — —To 1775
   — —1775-1865
   — —1865-1898
New York (State)
   —History
   — —To 1775
   — —Revolution, 1775-1783
   —Social life and customs
   — —1918-1945 *[AC only]*
New York Giants (Baseball team)
New York Jets (Football team)
New York Knickerbockers (Basketball team)
New York Mets (Baseball team)
New York Public Library
New York school of art
   BT Art, Modern—20th century
New York Stock Exchange
New York Times
New York to Paris Race, 1908
New York Yankees (Baseball team)
New York Zoological Park
New Yorker (Magazine)
New Zealand
Newbery medal books
   UF John Newbery medal books
       Newbery prize books
   RT Caldecott Medal
Newbery prize books
   USE Newbery medal books

Newcomb College
Newcomb pottery
Newfoundland
Newman, Arnold, 1918-
Newman, Paul, 1925-
News photographers
News reporting
    USE   Reporters and reporting
Newsletters *(May add geog subd)*
Newspaper carriers
Newspaper editorials
    USE   Newspapers—Sections, columns, etc.—Editorials
Newspaper publishing *(May add geog subd)*
Newspapers *[S]*
    —Sections, columns, etc.
      ——Editorials
        UF   Newspaper editorials
        RT   Journalism
Newspapers, School
    USE   Student newspapers and periodicals
Newton, Isaac, Sir, 1642-1727
Newton-John, Olivia
Newts *[S]*
    BT   Amphibians
Ney, Elisabet, 1833-1907
Nez Perce Indians
Ngo Dinh Diem, 1901-1963
Niagara Falls (N.Y.)
Nibelungenlied (Musical work)
    RT   Wagner, Richard, 1813-1883
Nicaragua
    —Social conditions
      ——1979-
Nicholas, Saint, Bp. of Myra
Nicholas II, Emperor of Russia, 1860-1918
Nicklaus, Jack
Nicknames *[S] (May add geog subd)*
Nicotine *[S]*
    RT   Tobacco
            Smoking
Nigeria
Night *[AC only]*
    RT   Bedtime
Night people
Night work *(May add geog subd)*
Nightingale
    BT   Birds
Nightingale, Florence, 1820-1910
    RT   Nursing
Nightmares
Nike (Firm)
Nile River
Nile River Valley
Nili (Palestine organization)
Nimitz, Chester William, 1885-1966
Nimoy, Leonard
Nineteenth century *[S]*
    SA   *the subdivisions* —19th century *and* —History—19th
          century
Nineveh (Extinct city)
Nintendo video games
    BT   Video games
Niska Indians
    BT   Indians of North America—British Columbia
Nitrogen *[S]*

Nitze, Paul H.
Niven, David, 1910-
Nixon, Joan Lowery
Nixon, Richard M. (Richard Milhous), 1913-
Njeri, Itabari
Njeri family
No-fault divorce *(May add geog subd)*
Noah (Biblical figure)
Noah's ark
Nobel, Alfred Bernhard, 1833-1896
Nobel Prizes
    BT   Awards
Nobility *[S]*
Nocturnal animals *(May add geog subd)*
Noel Hume, Ivor
Noguchi, Thomas T., 1927-
Noise *[S] (May add geog subd)*
Noise pollution *[S] (May add geog subd)*
    BT   Pollution
Nolen, William A., 1928-
Nomads *[S] (May add geog subd)*
Nomberg-Przytyk, Sara, 1915-
Nome (Alaska)
Nomenclature
    USE   Names
Non-formal education *(May add geog subd)*
Non-governmental organizations *(May add geog subd)*
Non-insulin-dependent diabetes *(May add geog subd)*
Nonrenewable natural resources *(May add geog subd)*
    BT   Natural resources
Nonsense verses *[S]*
    BT   Humorous poetry
    RT   Limericks
Nonsense verses, English *(May add geog subd)*
Nonverbal communication (Psychology) *(May add geog subd)*
    BT   Communication
Nonviolence *[S]*
Noonan, Peggy, 1950-
Nootka Indians
Nore Mutiny, 1797
Norfolk terrier *[S] (May add geog subd)*
Noriega, Manuel Antonio, 1934-
Normandy (France) *[S]*
Normandy (France), Attack on, 1944
Normans *[S]*
North, John Ringling, 1903-
North, Oliver
North, Sterling, 1906-
North America *[S]*
    —History
      ——Colonial period, ca. 1600-1775
North American porcupine
North American Soccer League
North Atlantic Ocean
North Atlantic Treaty Organization *[S]*
    UF   NATO
North Carolina
    —History
      ——To 1775
North Dakota
North Pole *[S]*
Northeastern States
Northern elephant seal *(May add geog subd)*
    BT   Seals
Northern Ireland

Northern Pacific Railway Company
Northmen
    USE   Vikings *[AC only]*
Northwest, Canadian
Northwest, Old
Northwest, Pacific
    UF   Pacific Northwest
Northwest Coast of North America
Northwest Frontier Province (Pakistan)
Northwest Passage *[S]*
    BT   Arctic regions
Northwestern States
Norway
Norwegian Americans
Norwegian literature *[S]*
Norwegians
Nose *[S]*
Nostalgia
Nostradamus, 1503-1566
Notaries
Notre-Dame de Reims (Cathedral)
Nova (Television program)
Nova Scotia
Novak, William
Novelists *[S]*
Novelists, American, [English, French, etc.]
Novelists, Victorian
Novels
    USE   Fiction
NSZZ "Solidarnosc" (Labor organization)
    USE   Solidarity (Polish labor organization) *[AC only]*
Nubia
Nuclear aircraft carriers *(May add geog subd)*
Nuclear arms control *(May add geog subd)*
Nuclear astrophysics
Nuclear disarmament
Nuclear energy *[S] (May add geog subd)*
Nuclear engineering *[S] (May add geog subd)*
Nuclear fusion
Nuclear industry *[S] (May add geog subd)*
Nuclear physics *[S]*
Nuclear power
    USE   Nuclear energy
Nuclear power plants *[S] (May add geog subd)*
Nuclear propulsion *[S]*
Nuclear reactors *[S] (May add geog subd)*
Nuclear submarines *[S] (May add geog subd)*
Nuclear warfare *[S]*
Nuclear weapons *[S] (May add geog subd)*
Nuclear winter *(May add geog subd)*
Nuestra Señora de Atocha (Ship)
Nudibranchia
    USE   Sea slugs *[AC only]*
Nulisch family
Number concept
    SA   *the subdivision* —Number
Number games *[AC, S]*
    BT   Mathematical recreations
    NT   Counting games *[AC only]*
Number systems *[AC only]*
    UF   Numeration
            Numbers
    NT   Roman numerals
Number theory *[S]*
Numbers
    USE   Number systems

Numbers, Natural
    UF   Natural numbers
Numbers, Irrational
    USE   Irrational numbers
Numbers, Prime
    UF   Prime numbers
Numbers in art
Numerals *[S]*
    NT   Roman numerals
    SA   *the subdivision* —Numerals.
Numeration
    USE   Number systems *[AC only]*
Numerology
    UF   Symbolism of numbers *[AC only]*
Numismatics
    USE   Coins *[AC only]*
Núñez Cabeza de Vaca, Alvar, 16th cent.
    USE   Cabeza de Vaca, Alvar Núñez, 16th cent. *[AC only]*
Nuns *[S]*
Nuremberg (Germany)
Nuremberg Trials of Major German War Criminals, 1945-1946
Nurse-patient relations
    USE   Nurse and patient
Nurse and patient
    UF   Nurse-patient relations
Nurse sharks *[AC only]*
    UF   Ginglymostoma
    BT   Sharks
Nurseries (Horticulture) *[S] (May add geog subd)*
Nursery rhymes *[S]*
Nursery rhymes, Chinese *(May add geog subd)*
Nursery rhymes, English
Nursery rhymes, Spanish American
Nursery rhymes, Spanish *(May add geog subd)*
Nursery schools *[S] (May add geog subd)*
Nurses *[S]*
Nursing *[S] (May add geog subd)*
    RT   Nightingale, Florence, 1820-1910
Nursing home care *(May add geog subd)*
Nursing homes *[S] (May add geog subd)*
Nursing schools *(May add geog subd)*
Nursing services *(May add geog subd)*
Nutcracker (Choreographic work)
Nutrition *[S] (May add geog subd)*
    NT   Minerals in human nutrition
            Vitamins in human nutrition
    SA   *the subdivision* —Nutrition
Nutrition disorders *(May add geog subd)*
Nutritionally induced diseases *(May add geog subd)*
    RT   Fool allergy
Nuts *[S] (May add geog subd)*
NX-1001 multifont dot matrix printer
Nyasa, Lake
    UF   Lake Malawi
Oak *[S] (May add geog subd)*
Oakie, Jack, 1903-
Oakland Athletics (Baseball team)
Oakland Raiders (Football team)
Oakley, Annie, 1860-1926
Obedience *[S]*
Oberlin (Ohio)
Oberski, Jona, 1938-
Obert J., 1952-
Obese persons
    USE   Overweight persons

Obesity *[S] (May add geog subd)*
Obituaries *[S] (May add geog subd)*
Oboe *[S]*
Observation (Psychology)
Obsessive behavior
    USE Obsessive-compulsive disorder
Obsessive-compulsive disorder
    UF Obsessive behavior
Obstetrics *(May add geog subd)*
Obstinacy
O'Casey, Sean, 1880-1964
Occult, The
    USE Occultism
Occult sciences
    USE Occultism
Occultism *[S]*
    UF Occult sciences
        Occult, The
    BT Supernatural
    RT Parapsychology
    NT Alchemy
        Magic
        Satanism
        Spiritualism
        Witchcraft
Occultism and science *(May add geog subd)*
Occultists
Occupational aptitude tests
    UF Vocational aptitude tests
Occupational diseases *[S] (May add geog subd)*
Occupational forecasting
    USE Employment forecasting
Occupational therapy *[S] (May add geog subd)*
Occupational training *(May add geog subd)*
Occupations *[S] (May add geog subd)*
    RT Labor
    NT Household employees
    SA the subdivision —Occupations
Occupations, dangerous
    USE Hazardous occupations
Occupations in art
Ocean *[S]*
   —**Folklore**
      NT Mermaids
         Mermen
   —**Mythology**
      NT Mermaids
         Mermen
Ocean bottom *[S] (May add geog subd)*
Ocean currents *[S] (May add geog subd)*
Ocean farming
    USE Aquaculture
Ocean liners *(May add geog subd)*
Ocean travel *[S]*
Ocean waves *[S] (May add geog subd)*
Oceanographers
Oceanography *[S] (May add geog subd)*
    RT Submarine geology
Ocean engineering *[S] (May add geog subd)*
Ocean mining *[S] (May add geog subd)*
Oceania *[S]*
Oceanographic research
    USE Oceanography—Research
Oceanographic submersibles *(May add geog subd)*
    RT Submersibles
Ocelots *[S]*

O'Connor, Sandra Day, 1930-
Octopus *(May add geog subd)*
O'Dell, Scott, 1903-
O'Donell, Hugh Rowe, 1571?-1602
Odysseus (Greek mythology)
Odyssey
    USE Homer. Odyssey
Oedipus (Greek mythology)
Office practice *[S]*
Oglala Indians
Oglethorpe, James Edward, 1696-1785
Ogorodnikova, Svetlana
O'Henry awards
O'Henry, 1862-1910
    USE Henry, O., 1862-1910
Ohio *[S]*
Ohio River
Oil
    USE Oils and fats
        Petroleum
Oil field equipment and supplies industry *(May add geog subd)*
Oil pollution of rivers, harbors, etc. *(May add geog subd)*
Oil spills *[S] (May add geog subd)*
Oil well drilling *[S] (May add geog subd)*
Oil wells *[S] (May add geog subd)*
Oils and fats *[S]*
    UF Fats and oils
Ojibwa Indians
    UF Chippewa Indians
Oka (Airplane)
Okapi
O'Keeffe, Georgia, 1887-1986
Okefenokee Swamp (Ga. and Fla.)
O'Kelley, Mattie Lou
Okinawa Island (Japan)
Oklahoma
    UF Oklahoma Territory
Old age *[S] (May add geog subd)*
    RT Aged
        Aging
Old age assistance *(May add geog subd)*
Old age in literature
Old age pensions *[S] (May add geog subd)*
Old French Quarter (New Orleans, La.)
    USE French Quarter (New Orleans, La.) *[AC only]*
Old Sturbridge Village (Sturbridge, Mass.)
Oliver, Susan
Olivier, Laurence, 1907-
Olmecs
Olmsted, Frederick Law, 1822-1903
Olympic games
    USE Olympics
Olympic games (Ancient)
Olympic National Park (Wash.)
Olympic Peninsula (Wash.)
Olympics
    UF Olympic games
    RT Special Olympics
    NT Winter Olympics
    SA the names of specific athletic events, e.g., Track and field
Omaha (Neb.)
O'Malley, Grace
Oman
Onassis, Jacqueline Kennedy, 1929-
Oñate, Juan de, 1549?-1624

Oncogenes
  UF Cancer genes
Oncologists
  UF Cancer specialists
One (The number)
One-act plays
  USE Plays *[AC only]*
O'Neal, Shaquille
Oneida Indians
O'Neill, Cherry Boone, 1954-
O'Neill, Eugene, 1888-1953
O'Neill, Terry, 1944-
Online bibliographic searching
  RT Library catalogs
Online data processing *[S]*
Only child *[S]*
Ono, Yoko
Onondaga Indians
Op art
  USE Optical art
Open adoption *(May add geog subd)*
Open-air zoos *(May add geog subd)*
Open plan schools *[S] (May add geog subd)*
Opera *[S] (May add geog subd)*
    Use for works about opera.
Operas
    Use for musical works composed in this form.
  —Performances
Operating systems (Computers)
Operation Cerberus, 1942
Operation Desert Shield, 1990-1991
Operation Mincemeat
Operation Overlord
  UF Normandy Invasion, 1944 (Planning)
Ophthalmology *(May add geog subd)*
Opiliones *(May add geog subd)*
  NT Daddy longlegs *[AC only]*
Opium *[S]*
Opossums *(May add geog subd)*
Oppenheimer, J. Robert, 1904-1967
Opposites
  USE Polarity
Optical art *(May add geog subd)*
  UF Op art
  BT Kinetic art
Optical disks *(May add geog subd)*
Optical illusions *[S] (May add geog subd)*
Optical instruments *[S] (May add geog subd)*
Optical pattern recognition
Optical publishing *(May add geog subd)*
Optical scanners
Optical storage devices *[S] (May add geog subd)*
Optics *[S] (May add geog subd)*
  NT Photonics
        Physiological optics
Optics, Physiological
  USE Physiological optics
Optimism
Optometry *[S] (May add geog subd)*
  RT Vision disorders
Oracles *[S]*
Oral biography
  BT Biography
Oral communication *(May add geog subd)*
  BT Communication
Oral contraceptives *(May add geog subd)*

  NT Mifepristone
Oral history *[S] (May add geog subd)*
  RT Oral tradition
Oral interpretation of poetry
Oral reading
Oral tradition *(May add geog subd)*
  RT Folklore
        Oral history
Orange *[S] (May add geog subd)*
Orange County (Calif.)
Orange industry *(May add geog subd)*
Orangutan *(May add geog subd)*
Orations
  USE Speeches, addresses, etc.
Oratorio *(May add geog subd)*
Orbison, Roy
Orchards *(May add geog subd)*
Orchestra *[S]*
Orchestral music *[S]*
Orchestration
  USE Instrumentation and orchestration
Orchids *[S] (May add geog subd)*
Orderliness *[AC only]*
  UF Messiness
        Neatness
        Tidiness
        Untidiness
  RT Cleanliness *[AC only]*
Ordnance *[S]*
Oregon
Oregon Trail *[S]*
Orellana, Francisco de, d. ca. 1546
Orenstein, Henry, 1923-
Organ *[S]*
Organ donors
Organ transplantation
  USE Transplantation of organs, tissues, etc.
Organic architecture *(May add geog subd)*
  NT Usonian houses
Organic farming
  UF Organiculture
  RT Organic foods
Organic gardening *[S] (May add geog subd)*
Organiculture
  USE Organic farming
Organization
Organization charts
Organizational behavior *(May add geog subd)*
Organizational change *[S] (May add geog subd)*
Organizational effectiveness
Organized crime *[S] (May add geog subd)*
  BT Crime
  RT Criminals
Organized crime investigation *(May add geog subd)*
Oriard, Michael, 1948-
Oriental literature
Orientation *(May add geog subd)*
Origami *[S]*
Orlando Magic (Basketball team)
Orlando (Fla.)
Ornamental carp
  USE Koi
Ornamental plants
  USE Plants, Ornamental
Ornithologists

Ornithology *(May add geog subd)*
    RT   Birds
Orozco, Jose Clemente, 1883-1949
Orphanages
    USE   Orphans *[AC only]*
Orphans *[AC, S]*
      Use for works on orphans and orphan homes.
    UF   Orphanages
Orr, Lisa, 1966-
Orres, John Albert
Orsini, Mary Lee
Orthodontics *(May add geog subd)*
Orthomolecular therapy *(May add geog subd)*
Orthopedic surgery *(May add geog subd)*
Orthopedics *[S] (May add geog subd)*
Orthoptera *[S] (May add geog subd)*
    BT   Insects
    NT   Crickets
Orwell, George, 1903-1950
Orwell, George, 1903-1950.   Nineteen eighty-four
Oryctolagus cuniculus
    USE   European rabbits *[AC only]*
Osage Indians
Osborn, Jaime
Oscar II (Ship)
Osceola, Seminole chief, 1804-1838
Osprey *[S] (May add geog subd)*
    BT   Hawks
Osteoarthritis *[S] (May add geog subd)*
Osteogenesis imperfecta *(May add geog subd)*
    UF   Brittle bones
    BT   Bones—Diseases
            Osteoporosis
Osteoporosis *[S] (May add geog subd)*
    RT   Bones—Diseases
Ostriches *[S] (May add geog subd)*
Oswald, Lee Harvey
Otolaryngology *(May add geog subd)*
Ottawa (Can.)
Ottawa Indians
Otters *[S] (May add geog subd)*
Ouija board
    BT   Games
Our Gang films
    BT   Motion pictures
Out-of-print books
Outboard motors
Outdoor life *[S] (May add geog subd)*
Outdoor life in art
Outdoor cookery
Outdoor recreation *(May add geog subd)*
Outer Banks (N.C.)
Outer planets
Outer space *[S]*
    UF   Space
    —Exploration *[S] (May add geog subd)*
Outlaws
    USE   Robbers and outlaws *[AC only]*
Outline maps
    BT   Maps
Outlines
    SA   *the subdivision* —Outlines, syllabi, etc.
Outward bound schools *(May add geog subd)*
    BT   Schools

Ovaries
    BT   Reproductive system, Female
Ovenbird *[S] (May add geog subd)*
Overhead projection
    RT   Audio-visual equipment
Overland journeys to the Pacific (U.S.)
Oversize books
      Here are entered actual specimens of books having at least one dimension (height or width) 40 cm. (16 in.) and intended to be read aloud in a group setting.
    UF   Big books
            Giant books
            Lap books
            Oversized books
    —Specimens *(Do not use: AC only)*
Oversized books
    USE   Oversize books
Overweight persons
    UF   Fat persons
            Obese persons
Owen, Robert, 1771-1858
Owens, Jesse, 1913-
Owens, William A., 1905-
Owls *[S] (May add geog subd)*
Oxford (England)
Oxygen *[S]*
Oyster Bay (N.Y.)
Oysters *[S]*
Ozark Mountains
Ozark Mountains Region
Ozone *[S]* (May add geog subd)
Ozone layer
Pacific Area
    UF   Asian and Pacific Council countries
Pacific Coast (Calif.)
Pacific Crest Trail
Pacific gray whale
    USE   Gray whale
Pacific Northwest
    USE   Northwest, Pacific
Pacific Ocean
Pacific States *[S]*
Pacifism *[S]*
Pacifists
Pack, Amy Thorpe
Paddle steamers *(May add geog subd)*
Paderewski, Ignace Jan, 1860-1941
Padre Island (Tex.)
Paganism *[S] (May add geog subd)*
Pageants *[S] (May add geog subd)*
Paige, Leroy, 1906-
Pain *[S]*
    NT   Toothache
Pain clinics *(May add geog subd)*
Paine, Thomas, 1737-1809
Paint *[S]*
Painters
    USE   Artists *[AC only]*
Painting *[S] (May add geog subd)*
Painting, Acrylic
    USE   Acrylic painting
Painting, American, [Belgian, Chinese, etc.] *(May add geog subd)*
Painting, Indian
    USE   Indian painting
Painting, Medieval *(May add geog subd)*

Painting, Modern *(May add geog subd)*
  —17th-18th centuries
  —19th century
  —20th century
Painting, Renaissance *(May add geog subd)*
Painting, Victorian *(May add geog subd)*
Paisley, Melvyn R., 1924-
Paiute Indians
Pakistan
Pakistani Americans
Pakistanis
Palaces *[S] (May add geog subd)*
Palenque Site (Ecuador)
Palenque Site (Mexico)
Paleolithic period *(May add geog subd)*
Paleontologists
Paleontology *(May add geog subd)*
  RT Fossils
  —Jurassic
    UF Jurassic Period
    BT   Paleontology—Mezozoic
  —Mezozoic
    NT   Paleontology—Jurassic
Palestine
Palestinian Arabs *[S]*
  BT Arabs
Palindromes
  NT Literary recreations
      Puzzles
      Word games
Palmer, Arnold, 1929-
Palmer, Jim, 1945-
Palmer Drug Abuse Program
Palmistry *[S]*
Palo Pinto County (Tex.)
Palomar Observatory
Pampas (Argentina)
Pamphlets *[S]*
  UF Leaflets
Pan (Greek deity)
Panama
Panama Canal (Panama)
Panama Pacific International Exposition (San Francisco, Ca.)
Pancakes, waffles, etc. *(May add geog subd)*
  UF Hotcakes
      Pancakes
      Waffles
Pandas *[S]*
Pandora (Greek mythology)
Panic
Pankhurst, Emmeline, 1858-1928
Panthers *[S] (May add geog subd)*
Pantomime *(May add geog subd)*
  UF Mime *[AC only]*
Pantomimes *[S]*
Pap test
Papacy *[S]*
Papago Indians
  USE Tohono O'Odham Indians
Paper *[S]*
Paper, Handmade *(May add geog subd)*
Paper airplanes
Paper crafts
  USE Paper work
Paper dolls *(May add geog subd)*

Paper flowers
Paper industry *[S] (May add geog subd)*
Paper-mache
  USE Papier-mâché
Paper money *[S] (May add geog subd)*
Paper sculpture
Paper toy making
Paper work
  UF Paper crafts
  BT Handicraft
Paperbacks *(May add geog subd)*
  BT Books
Paperhanging *(May add geog subd)*
Papermaking *(May add geog subd)*
Paperweights *(May add geog subd)*
Papier-mâché
  UF Paper-mache
Papilionidae
  USE Swallowtail butterflies *[AC only]*
Parables *[S]*
  RT Allegories
      Fables
Parabola
  RT Conic sections
Paracelsus, 1493-1541
Parachute troops
  SA *the subdivision* —Parachute troops
Parachutes *[S]*
Parades *[S] (May add geog subd)*
Paradise fish *(May add geog subd)*
Paraguay
Parakeets *[AC, S]*
  UF Budgerigar
Paralysis
  BT Movement disorders
Paramedical education *(May add geog subd)*
  RT Allied health personnel
Paraplegia *(May add geog subd)*
Parapsychology *[S] (May add geog subd)*
  UF Psychical research
  RT Occultism
      Spiritualism
Parapsychology and business *(May add geog subd)*
Parapsychology and geography *(May add geog subd)*
Parapsychology and science *(May add geog subd)*
Parapsychology in criminal investigation *(May add geog subd)*
Parasols
  USE Umbrellas and parasols
Pare, Ambroise, 1510?-1590
Pareja, Juan de, 1606-1670
Parent and adult child *(May add geog subd)*
Parent and child *[S] (May add geog subd)*
  RT Parricide
Parent and teenager *(May add geog subd)*
Parent-teacher relationships *[S] (May add geog subd)*
  UF Teacher-parent relationships
Parental behavior in animals
  BT Animals—Habits and behavior
Parenthood
Parenting *[S] (May add geog subd)*
Parents
  NT Teenage parents
Parents-in-law
Parfleches *(May add geog subd)*
  BT Containers
      Indian leatherwork

Paricutin (Volcano)
Paris (France)
Parish, Peggy
Park rangers
Parker, Bonnie, 1910-1934
Parker, Cynthia Ann, 1827?-1864
Parker, Dave, 1951-
Parker, Ely Samuel, 1828-1895
Parker, George Leroy, b. 1866
   USE Cassidy, Butch, b. 1866
Parker, Quanah, 1845?-1911
Parker, Robert B., 1932-
Parker family
Parkinson's disease
   USE Parkinsonism
Parkinsonism *[S] (May add geog subd)*
Parkinsonism, Postencephalitic *(May add geog subd)*
Parks *[S] (May add geog subd)*
   NT National parks and reserves
Parks, Gordon, 1912-
Parks, Lillian Rogers
Parks, Rosa, 1913-
Parliamentary practice *[S] (May add geog subd)*
   UF Parliamentary procedure
Parliamentary procedure
   USE Parliamentary practice
Parmenter, Frederick Albert, 1874-1920
Parnell, Charles Stewart, 1846-1891
Parnell, Katharine Wood
Parodies *[S]*
   SA *the subdivision* —Parodies, imitations, etc.
Parody *[S]*
   BT Literature *[S]*
   RT Satire *[S]*
       Wit and humor *[AC, S]*
Parr, George B.
Parricide *(May add geog subd)*
   BT Murder
   RT Parent and child
Parrish, Maxfield, 1870-1966
Parrots *[S] (May add geog subd)*
   BT Birds
   NT Cockatoos
Parsons, Johnnie, 1918-
Part-time employment *[S] (May add geog subd)*
Parthenon (Athens, Greece)
Particle accelerators *(May add geog subd)*
Particles (Nuclear physics)
Parties *[AC, S]*
   UF Children's parties
   RT Entertaining
       Piñatas
Partnership *(May add geog subd)*
Parton, Dolly
Parturition
   USE Birth *[AC only]*
Party decorations
Pascal (Computer program language)
Paso fino horse
Passenger pigeon *(May add geog subd)*
Passeriformes
   USE Passerines *[AC only]*
Passerines *[AC only]*
   UF Passeriformes
       Perching birds
Passover *[S]*

   BT Judaism
   RT Fasts and feasts—Judaism
   NT Seder
Passover cookery
   BT Cookery, Jewish
   RT Judaism
Pasta products *[AC only]*
   RT Cookery—Pasta
   NT Spaghetti
Paste jewelry
Pastel drawing *[S] (May add geog subd)*
   BT Drawing
Pasteur, Louis, 1822-1895
Pastoral fiction *[S]*
Pastoral theology *(May add geog subd)*
Pastry *[S] (May add geog subd)*
   NT Pies *[AC only]*
Patchwork *(May add geog subd)*
  —Patterns
     RT Handicraft
Patchwork quilts *(May add geog subd)*
Patent lawyers
Patent offices *(May add geog subd)*
Patents *[S] (May add geog subd)*
   BT Intellectual property
Paterson, Andrew Barton, 1864-1941
Paterson, Katherine
Pathological psychology
   USE Psychology, Pathological
Pathology *[S]*
   RT Diagnosis
       Diseases
       Immunity
       Medicine
       Therapeutics
Patience *[S]*
Patient education *(May add geog subd)*
Patio gardening *(May add geog subd)*
Patios *[S]*
   RT Decks (Domestic architecture)
Patriarchy
Patrick, Frank, 1885-1960
Patrick, Lester, 1883-1960
Patrick, Saint, ca. 373-463
Patriotic songs
   USE Patriotic music
Patriotic music *(May add geog subd)*
   UF Music, Patriotic
       Patriotic songs
       Songs, Patriotic
Patriotic poetry
   BT Poetry
Patriotism *[S] (May add geog subd)*
Pattern glass *(May add geog subd)*
   BT Glass
Patton, George S. (George Smith), 1885-1945
Patton, Ray Vernon
Paul, the Apostle, Saint
Paul, Wesley
Pauling, Linus, 1901-
Paulsen, Gary
Pavarotti, Luciano
Pavlova, Anna, 1881-1931
Pawnee Indians
Pawtucket (R.I.) Old Slater Mill
Payne, Lewis, 1845-1865

Payton, Walter, 1954-
PCP (Drug)
  USE Phencyclidine
  BT Hallucinogenic drugs
Peabody, Elizabeth Palmer, 1804-1894
Peace, Charles Frederick, 1832-1879
Peace *[S]*
  SA *the subdivision* —Peace
Peace Corps (U.S.)
Peace in literature
Peace Mission Movement
Peace movements *(May add geog subd)*
Peace of mind
Peace officers
  NT Police
Peacocks *[S] (May add geog subd)*
  UF Peafowl *[AC only]*
Peale, Charles Willson, 1741-1827
Peale family
Peale's Museum (Philadelphia, Pa.)
Peanut butter
Peanuts *(May add geog subd)*
Peanuts (Comic strip)
Pear *(May add geog subd)*
Pearl diving *[AC only]*
  Use for works on old methods of diving with rocks, baskets, etc.
  RT Pearl industry and trade *[AC only]*
Pearl-fisheries *(May add geog subd)*
Pearl Harbor (Hawaii), Attack on, 1941
Pearl industry and trade *[AC only]*
  Use for works on the modern industry and modern diving methods.
  RT Pearl diving *[AC only]*
Pearls *(May add geog subd)*
Peary, Kali, 1906-
Peary, Robert E. (Robert Edwin), 1856-1920
Peas *[S] (May add geog subd)*
Peccaries
  UF Javelinas
Peck, Richard, 1934-
Peckinpah, Sam, 1925-1984
Pecos Bill (Legendary character)
Pecos River (N.M. and Tex.)
Peddlers and peddling *[S]*
Pediatricians
  BT Physicians
Pediatrics *(May add geog subd)*
Pedodontics *(May add geog subd)*
  UF Pediatric dentistry
Peer-group tutoring of students *(May add geog subd)*
Peer pressure *[S]*
Peet, Bill
Pegasus (Greek mythology)
Peggy Guggenheim Collection
Peking (China)
Pele, 1940-
Pelew Islands
Pelicans *(May add geog subd)*
Pen drawing *[S]*
Pen pals
Penal colonies *[S] (May add geog subd)*
  RT Prisons
Penarth (Wales)
Pencil drawing *[S]*
  BT Drawing
Pencils
Penguins *[S]*

  NT Magellanic penguin
Penicillin *[S]*
  BT Antibiotics
Peninsular Campaign, 1862
Penmanship
  UF Handwriting
Penmanship, Left-handed
Penn, William, 1644-1718
Pennington family
Pennsylvania
  —History
  — —To 1775
  — —Revolution, 1775-1783
Pennsylvania Dutch
Penobscot Expedition, 1779
Pension trusts *(May add geog subd)*
Pensions, Military
  USE Military pensions
Pentecostal churches *(May add geog subd)*
Pentecostalism *(May add geog subd)*
People's Party of the United States
Pepys, Samuel, 1633-1703
Peramelidae
  USE Bandicoots *[AC only]*
  BT Marsupials *[AC only]*
Percentage *[S]*
Perception *[S]*
Perception in animals *(May add geog subd)*
Perceval (Legendary character)
Perching birds
  USE Passerines *[AC only]*
Percussion instruments *[S]*
  BT Musical instruments
Percussion music
Peregrine falcon *(May add geog subd)*
Perennials *[S] (May add geog subd)*
  BT Flowers
Perfectionism (Personality trait) *[S] (May add geog subd)*
Performance standards *[S]*
Performing arts *[S] (May add geog subd)*
Pericles, 499-429 B.C.
Periodic law
Periodical editors
Periodicals *[S]*
  SA *the subdivision* —Periodicals
Periodicity
  USE Cycles
Perkins, Frances, 1882-1965
Pern (Imaginary place)
Peromyscus
  USE White-footed mouse *[AC only]*
Peron, Eva, 1919-1952
Peron, Juan Domingo, 1895-1974
Perot, H. Ross, 1930-
Perry, Edmund, d. 1985
Perry, Matthew Calbraith, 1794-1858
Perry, Oliver Hazard, 1785-1819
Perry, William, 1962-
Perry, Willie Clayborne, 1910-
Persecution *[S]*
Persephone (Greek deity)
Perseus (Greek mythology)
Pershing, John J. (John Joseph), 1860-1948
Persian Gulf
Persian Gulf Region
Persian Gulf War, 1991 *[S]*

Persian language (*May add geog subd*)
—**Readers** [*AC only*]
Use for reading texts in Persian containing materials for instruction and practice in reading that language.
RT   Persian language materials [*AC only*]
Persian language materials [*AC only*]
Use for works written in Persian intended primarily for general information or recreational reading. Such works with text also given in English are further subdivided by the subdivision —Bilingual.
RT   Persian language—Readers [*AC only*]
—**Bilingual** [*AC only*]
Persistence
Personal development
USE   Self-actualization (Psychology)
Success
Personal names
USE   Names, Personal
Personality [*S*]
Personality (Law) (*May add geog subd*)
Personality and cognition
RT   Cognition
Intellect
NT   Cognitive styles
Personality and occupation
Personality change
Personality disorders [*S*] (*May add geog subd*)
Personality tests
NT   Myers-Briggs Type Indicator
Personnel management [*S*] (*May add geog subd*)
RT   Supervision of employees
Perspective [*S*]
Persuasion (Psychology)
Peru
Pesticides (*May add geog subd*)
Pesticides and wildlife [*S*] (*May add geog subd*)
UF   Wildlife and pesticides
Pesticides industry (*May add geog subd*)
Pests
RT   Insect pests
Pet owners
Peter, the Apostle, Saint
Peter I, Emperor of Russia, 1672-1725
Petersburg (Va.)
Petrarca, Francesco, 1304-1374
USE   Petrarch, 1304-1374 [*AC only*]
Petrified forests (*May add geog subd*)
UF   Forests, Petrified
Petrofsky, Jerrold Scott
Petroleum [*S*] (*May add geog subd*)
—**Refining**
Petroleum as fuel [*S*] (*May add geog subd*)
RT   Fuel
Petroleum engineering (*May add geog subd*)
Petroleum industry and trade (*May add geog subd*)
Petroleum law and legislation (*May add geog subd*)
UF   Petroleum—Law and legislation
Petroleum workers
Petrology [*S*] (*May add geog subd*)
NT   Rocks
Pets [*S*] (*May add geog subd*)
SA   *the names of specific animals, e.g.,* Birds as pets [*AC only*]
Pets and travel (*May add geog subd*)
Petting zoos [*S*] (*May add geog subd*)
BT   Zoos
Petty, Elijah P. (Elijah Parsons), 1828-1864
Pewter [*S*] (*May add geog subd*)

BT   Metals
Phaedrus
Phagocytosis
BT   Immunology
Phantom II (Jet fighter plane)
Pharaohs
USE   Kings, queens, rulers, etc. [*AC only*]
Pharmaceutical industry (*May add geog subd*)
Pharmaceutical policy (*May add geog subd*)
Pharmacology [*S*] (*May add geog subd*)
RT   Drugs
Pharmacy [*S*] (*May add geog subd*)
RT   Drugs
Pharmacology
Pheasants
Phencyclidine [*S*]
UF   Angel dust
PCP (Drug)
BT   Hallucinogenic drugs
Pheromones (*May add geog subd*)
BT   Hormones
Philadelphia (Pa.)
Philadelphia 76ers (Basketball team)
Philadelphia Eagles (Football team)
Philadelphia Flyers (Hockey team)
Philadelphia Phillies (Baseball team)
Philadelphia Zoological Garden
Philanthropists [*S*]
RT   Fund raising
Philby, Kim, 1912-
Philemon (Greek mythology)
Philip II, King of Macedonia, 382-336 B.C.
Philip II, King of Spain, 1527-1598
Philippine Sea, Battles of the, 1944
Philippines
—**Politics and government**
— —**1946-**
SA   Filipinos
Philologists
RT   Language and languages
Philosophers [*S*]
Philosophical literature (*May add geog subd*)
Philosophy [*S*] (*May add geog subd*)
SA   *the subdivision* —Philosophy
Philosophy, American, [English, European, etc.] [*S*]
Philosophy, Ancient [*S*]
Philosophy, Medieval [*S*]
Philosophy, Modern [*S*]
Philosophy and religion [*S*]
Phobias [*S*]
RT   Fear
Phobic disorders
USE   Phobias
Phoenicians
BT   Ethnology—Syria
RT   Carthage (Extinct city)
Phoenix (Ariz.)
Phoenix, River
Phoenix Cardinals (Football team)
Phoenix Suns (Basketball team)
Phonetics [*S*]
RT   Reading
Sound
Speech
Phonics
USE   Reading (Elementary)—Phonetic method

Photo-realism *(May add geog subd)*
Photobiology
    BT Biology
           Light
    NT Bioluminescence
Photograms
    BT Photography
Photograph collections *(May add geog subd)*
Photographers
Photographic chemicals *(May add geog subd)*
Photographic industry *(May add geog subd)*
Photographic lenses
    UF Lenses, Photographic
Photographs
    RT Pictures
    SA *the subdivision* —Photographs
Photography *[S] (May add geog subd)*
    NT Nature photography
           Photograms
           Space photography
           Underwater photography
  —**Collections** *[AC only]*
      Use for collections of photographs by one or more photographers intended as examples of the art of photography.
  —**Developing and developers**
  —**Enlarging**
  —**Films**
  —**Printing processes**
  —**Processing**
Photography, Abstract
Photography, Artistic
Photography, Commercial
    USE Commercial photography
Photography, Humorous
Photography, Stereoscopic
Photography of animals *[S] (May add geog subd)*
Photography of birds *[S] (May add geog subd)*
Photography of children
Photography of fishes
Photography of gardens *(May add geog subd)*
Photography of plants *[S] (May add geog subd)*
Photography of railroads *(May add geog subd)*
Photography of sports *(May add geog subd)*
Photojournalism *[S] (May add geog subd)*
    BT Journalism
    RT Photography
Photomicrography *(May add geog subd)*
Photonics
    BT Optics
Photosynthesis *[S]*
    BT Plants
Physical chemistry
    USE Chemistry, Physical and theoretical
Physical distribution of goods *(May add geog subd)*
Physical education and training *(May add geog subd)*
    UF Physical education
    RT Movement education
           Physical fitness
Physical endurance
    USE Physical fitness
Physical fitness *[S] (May add geog subd)*
    UF Fitness
           Physical endurance
    RT Physical education and training
           Weight training

Physical fitness centers *(May add geog subd)*
Physical geography *[S] (May add geog subd)*
    BT Geography
Physical geology
    BT Geology
Physical measurements
    USE Measurement *[AC only]*
Physical sciences *(May add geog subd)*
Physical therapists
Physical therapy *[S] (May add geog subd)*
Physically handicapped *[S]*
    BT Handicapped
Physically handicapped, Teachers of the
    USE Teachers of the physically handicapped *[AC only]*
Physician and patient
    UF Doctor-patient relationship
Physicians *[S]*
    NT Pediatricians
           Plastic surgeons
           Women physicians
Physicians' assistants
Physicists *[S]*
Physics *[S] (May add geog subd)*
    NT Mechanics
Physics projects
    BT Science projects
Physiognomy *[S] (May add geog subd)*
    RT Face
Physiological optics *(May add geog subd)*
    UF Optics, Physiological
    BT Optics
Physiologists
    BT Biologists
Physiology *[S] (May add geog subd)*
    RT Anatomy
    NT Human physiology
    SA *the subdivisions* —Physiological effect *and* —Physiology
Physiology, Comparative
Phytogeography
    USE Plant distribution *[AC only]*
Piaget, Jean, 1896-
Pianists *[S]*
Piano *[S]*
Piano music *[S]*
Picardy (France)
Picasso, Pablo, 1881-1973
Piccard, Auguste, 1884-1962
Piccolo, Brian, 1943-1970
Pickens, T. Boone (Thomas Boone)
Pickford, Mary, 1893-
Pickett, Bill, 1860-1932
Pickle, J.J.
Pickles
Picnicking
Picture books *[AC only]*
    UF Stories without words
    RT Illustrated books, Children's
Picture dictionaries *[S]*
    BT Encyclopedias and dictionaries
Picture dictionaries, English
Picture dictionaries, French
Picture dictionaries, Spanish
Picture frames and framing *[S] (May add geog subd)*
Picture interpretation *(May add geog subd)*
Picture puzzles
    BT Puzzles

Picture-writing *(May add geog subd)*
   RT   Cave drawings
          Hieroglyphics
          Rock paintings
Pictures *[S] (May add geog subd)*
   RT   Photographs
   SA   *the subdivision* —Pictorial works
Pictorial works
   USE   Pictures
   SA   *the subdivision* —Pictorial works
Pied Piper of Hamelin (Legendary character)
Pierce, Franklin, 1804-1869
Piercy, Marge
Piersall, Jimmy
Pies *[AC only]*
   BT   Pastry
Pigeon racing
Pigeons *[S] (May add geog subd)*
   BT   Birds
Pigs *[AC, S]*
   UF   Swine
Pike, Zebulon Montgomery, 1779-1813
Pikul, Diane Whitmore, 1943-1987
Pikul, Joseph, 1934-1989
Pilgrimages
   USE   Pilgrims and pilgrimages
Pilgrim fathers
   USE   Pilgrims (New Plymouth Colony)
Pilgrims (New Plymouth Colony)
Pilgrims and pilgrimages *[S]*
Pill bugs
   USE   Wood lice (Crustaceans) *[AC only]*
Pillows
Piloting of airplanes
   USE   Airplanes—Piloting
Pilots (Aeronautics)
   USE   Air pilots
Pima Indians
Piñatas
   RT   Handicraft
          Parties
Pinckney, Eliza Lucas, 1723-1793
Pinkerton, Allan, 1819-1884
Pinkerton's National Detective Agency
   BT   Detectives
Pinnipedia
   USE   Pinnipeds *[AC only]*
Pinnipeds *[AC only]*
   BT   Mammals
   NT   Seals
Pins and needles
Pinter, Harold, 1930-
Pioneer (Space probes)
Pioneers
Pipe fitting *[S]*
   RT   Plumbing
Pirates *[S]*
   BT   Criminals
          Privateering
Pirsig, Robert M.
Pisces (Astrology) *(May add geog subd)*
Pistols *[S] (May add geog subd)*
   BT   Weapons
   RT   Gun control

Pit vipers
   BT   Snakes
Pitcairn Island
Pitcher plants *(May add geog subd)*
Pitcher, Molly, 1754-1832
Pitchers
   BT   Containers
Pitchers (Baseball)
Pitching (Baseball)
Pitt, William, Earl of Chatham, 1708-1778
Pittsburgh (Pa.)
Pittsburgh Pirates (Baseball team)
Pittsburgh Steelers (Football team)
Pittsylvania County (Va.)
Pizarro, Francisco, 1475-1541
Pizarro, Gonzalo, d. 1548
Pizza
Plagiarism *(May add geog subd)*
Plague *[S] (May add geog subd)*
Plains *(May add geog subd)*
Plains prairie dog
   USE   Black-tailed prairie dog *[AC only]*
Plaisted, Elenore
Plane geometry
   USE   Geometry, Plane
Plane trigonometry
   UF   Trigonometry, Plane
Planetaria
   USE   Planetariums *[AC only]*
Planetariums *[AC, S]*
   UF   Planetaria
Planets *[S]*
   BT   Astronomy
  —Exploration
Plankton *(May add geog subd)*
   BT   Aquatic biology
Plant breeding *[S] (May add geog subd)*
Plant collectors
Plant conservation *[S] (May add geog subd)*
Plant containers
   UF   Planters (Containers)
Plant diseases *[S] (May add geog subd)*
Plant distribution *[AC only]*
   UF   Biogeography
          Geographical distribution of animals and plants
          Phytogeography
Plant life cycles *(May add geog subd)*
Plant names, Popular *[S] (May add geog subd)*
   UF   Popular plant names
   RT   Botany—Terminology
Plant physiology *[S]*
Plant prints
   BT   Plants in art
Plant propagation *[S]*
   UF   Propagation
Plant shutdowns *(May add geog subd)*
   UF   Closing of factories
Plantagenet, House of
Plantation life *[S] (May add geog subd)*
Plantations *(May add geog subd)*
Planters (Containers)
   USE   Plant containers

Plants *[S] (May add geog subd)*
   RT   Photosynthesis
   BT   Botany
   NT   Leaves
          Lichens
          Trees
   SA   *names of specific plants and environments, e.g.,* Marsh plants
Plants, Cultivated *[S] (May add geog subd)*
   UF   Cultivated plants
Plants, Edible *(May add geog subd)*
   UF   Edible plants
Plants, Effect of fires on *(May add geog subd)*
Plants, Fossil *[S] (May add geog subd)*
   UF   Fossil plants
Plants, Medicinal
   USE   Medicinal plants
Plants, Ornamental *(May add geog subd)*
   UF   Ornamental plants
Plants, Poisonous
   USE   Poisonous plants
Plants, Rare
   USE   Rare plants *[AC only]*
Plants, Potted
   UF   Potted plants
Plants, Protection of *(May add geog subd)*
Plants, Sex in
   BT   Sex (Biology)
Plants, Useful
   UF   Useful plants
Plants and history *(May add geog subd)*
Plants in art *[S]*
   NT   Plant prints
Plaster casts *[S]*
   UF   Casting
Plastic craft
   USE   Plastics craft
   BT   Handicraft
Plastic scrap *(May add geog subd)*
Plastic surgeons
   BT   Physicians
          Surgeons
Plastic surgery
   USE   Surgery, Plastic
Plastics *[S]*
Plastics craft
   UF   Plastic craft
Plastics industry and trade *(May add geog subd)*
Plate
   BT   Goldwork
          Silverwork
Plate tectonics *[S] (May add geog subd)*
   BT   Submarine geology
   NT   Continental drift
Plateaus *(May add geog subd)*
   NT   Llano Estacado
Plates (Tableware) *(May add geog subd)*
Plath, Sylvia
Plathelminthes
   USE   Flatworms *[AC only]*
Plato
Platyhelminthes
   USE   Flatworms *[AC only]*
Platypus *[S]*
   BT   Mammals
Play *[S] (May add geog subd)*

   NT   Games
          Imaginary playmates *[AC only]*
Play behavior in animals
   USE   Animals—Play behavior *[AC only]*
Play on words
   BT   Word games
Playgrounds *[S] (May add geog subd)*
Playmates, Imaginary
   USE   Imaginary playmates *[AC only]*
Plays *[AC only]*
   Use for single or collected works by one author or joint authors. Collections of plays by several authors are entered under Plays—Collections.
   UF   Children's plays
          One-act plays
   SA   *the subdivision* —Drama
  —Collections *[AC only]*
   UF   Drama—Collections
  —Improvisation *[AC only]*
   UF   Improvisation (Acting)
  —Presentation, etc.
   USE   Plays—Production and direction *[AC only]*
  —Production and direction *[AC only]*
   UF   Plays—Presentation, etc.
Playwriting
   RT   Poets
Pleasant Bay (Mass.)
Plecotus auritus
   USE   Long-eared bat *[AC only]*
Pledge of Allegiance *[AC only]*
   UF   Bellamy, Francis.   Pledge of allegiance to the flag
   RT   Flags—United States *[AC only]*
Plenty Coups, Chief of the Crows, 1848-1932
Plot-your-own stories *[S]*
Plots (Drama, novel, etc.) *[S]*
   RT   Literature
Plovers *[S]*
   BT   Shore birds
Plumbing *[S]*
   RT   Pipe fitting
Plunkett, Jim, 1947-
Pluralism (Social sciences)
Pluto (Planet)
Plutonium
Plymouth (Mass.)
Plymouth Colony
   USE   New Plymouth Colony
Plymouth Rock
PMS
   USE   Premenstrual syndrome
Pneumonia *[S] (May add geog subd)*
Poaching *(May add geog subd)*
Pocahontas, d. 1617
Pocket calculators
   USE   Calculators *[AC only]*
Pocket gophers
   USE   Gophers *[AC only]*
Pockets
Podgorodtsy (Ukraine)
Podiatry *[S] (May add geog subd)*
Poe, Edgar Allan, 1809-1849
Poeciliidae
   USE   Livebearers (Fish) *[AC only]*
Poetics *[S]*

Poetry *[S] (Not subd geog)*
    BT Literary form
           Literature
    SA *specific forms of poetry, e.g.,* Sea poetry, *and the subdivision* —Poetry
Poetry, American, [Danish, English, etc.]
    USE American, [Danish, English, etc.] poetry (based on geographic names)
Poetry, Ancient
Poetry, Medieval
Poetry, Modern
Poets *[S]*
    RT Playwriting
    NT Women poets
Poets, Canadian, [Danish, English, etc.] *[S]*
    UF Canadian, [English, Danish, etc.] poets
Poikilotherms
    USE Cold-blooded animals *[AC only]*
Point Reyes National Seashore (Calif.)
Poison ivy *[S] (May add geog subd)*
Poisoning of insects
    USE Insecticides
Poisonous animals *[S] (May add geog subd)*
    UF Animals, Poisonous
Poisonous plants *[S] (May add geog subd)*
    UF Plants, Poisonous
Poisonous snakes *(May add geog subd)*
    UF Snakes, Poisonous
Poisons
Poitier, Sidney
Poland
Polar bear *[S] (May add geog subd)*
Polar regions *[S]*
Polarity
    UF Opposites
Poles
    RT Polish Americans
Police *[S]*
    BT Peace officers
Police, State
    UF State police
Police administration
    UF Police management
Police chiefs
Police corruption *[S] (May add geog subd)*
Police dogs *(May add geog subd)*
    BT Dogs
Police murders *(May add geog subd)*
    UF Killing of police
Police shootings *(May add geog subd)*
    RT Law enforcement
           Violence
Police stations *(May add geog subd)*
Police training *(May add geog subd)*
Policewomen *[S]*
Policy analysts
    USE Policy scientists
Policy scientists
    UF Policy analysts
Poliomyelitis *[S] (May add geog subd)*
Polish Americans
    RT Poles
Polish drama *(May add geog subd)*
    BT Plays
Polish language *(May add geog subd)*
Political Action Committees

    RT Politics, Practical
    SA *the subdivision* —Political activity
Political ballads and songs
    UF Movement songs
           Political songs
Political cartoons
Political collectibles *(May add geog subd)*
Political conventions *[S] (May add geog subd)*
Political culture *(May add geog subd)*
Political corruption *(May add geog subd)*
    UF Corruption (in politics)
    RT Lobbying
Political crimes and offenses *[S] (May add geog subd)*
    BT Crime
    RT Trials (Political crimes and offenses)
Political ethics *[S] (May add geog subd)*
    UF Ethics, Political
    BT Ethics
Political fiction, English
Political geography *(May add geog subd)*
    RT Geopolitics
Political leadership *(May add geog subd)*
Political oratory *(May add geog subd)*
Political participation *(May add geog subd)*
Political parties *[S] (May add geog subd)*
Political persecution *(May add geog subd)*
Political prisoners *[S]*
    UF Prisoners, Political
    BT Prisoners
Political questions and judicial power *(May add geog subd)*
    UF Judicial power and politics
Political science *[S] (May add geog subd)*
    UF Government
    RT Civics
    NT Political sociology
    SA *the subdivisions* —Political aspects *and* —Politics and government
Political scientists
Political sociology
    BT Political science
           Sociology
Political songs
    USE Political ballads and songs
Politicians *[S]*
Politicians, Hispanic
    UF Hispanic politicians
Politics
    USE Electioneering
           Political science
Politics, Practical *[S] (May add geog subd)*
    UF Practical politics
    RT Lobbying
           Political Action Committees
    SA *the subdivision* —Political activity
Politics and culture *(May add geog subd)*
Politics and education *(May add geog subd)*
Politics and the press
    USE Press and politics
Polk, James K. (Knox), 1795-1849
Pollination *(May add geog subd)*
Pollination by insects *(May add geog subd)*
Pollutants *(May add geog subd)*
Pollution *[S] (May add geog subd)*
    SA *specific forms of pollution, e.g.,* Noise pollution
Pollution control industry *[S] (May add geog subd)*
Polo, Marco, 1254-1323

Polovchak, Walter
Poltergeists *(May add geog subd)*
Poltoratsky, Ellen Sarah (Southee), 1819-1908
Poltoratsky, Frances Hermione de, 1850-1916
Polyglot materials *[AC only]*
  UF   Polyglot texts, selections, quotations, etc.
Polyglot texts, selections, quotations, etc.
  USE   Polyglot materials *[AC only]*
Polymer painting
  USE   Acrylic painting
Polymerization
  UF   Polymers and polymerization
  BT   Chemical reactions
Polymers
  UF   Polymers and polymerization
Polymers and polymerization
  USE   Polymers
Polynesians
Polyphemus (Greek mythology)
Pomo Indians
Pompeii (Extinct city)
Ponca Indians
Ponce de León, Juan, ca. 1460?-1521
Pond animals *(May add geog subd)*
  UF   Pond fauna
Pond ecology *(May add geog subd)*
Pond fauna
  USE   Pond animals *[AC only]*
Pond flora
  USE   Pond plants *[AC only]*
Pond plants *[AC only] (May add geog subd)*
  UF   Plant flora
Ponds *[S] (May add geog subd)*
Ponies *[S] (May add geog subd)*
  BT   Horses
Pontiac, Ottawa chief, d. 1769
Pontiac's Conspiracy, 1763-1765
Pony express *[S]*
Poodles *[S] (May add geog subd)*
Pool (Game) *(May add geog subd)*
Poor *[S]*
  —Medical care
    NT   Medicaid
Poor children
  UF   Children, Poor
Pop art *(May add geog subd)*
Popcorn *(May add geog subd)*
Pope, Alexander, 1688-1744
Popes *[S]*
Poppies *[S] (May add geog subd)*
Popular culture *[S] (Not subd geog)*
  UF   Culture, Popular
  SA   *the subdivision* —Popular culture
Popular literature *(May add geog subd)*
Popular medicine
  USE   Folk medicine
Popular music *[S] (May add geog subd)*
  UF   Music, Popular
  —Writing and publishing
Popular plant names
  USE   Plant names, Popular
Popularity *[S]*
Population *[S]*
  SA   *the subdivision* —Population
Population density
Population forecasting *(May add geog subd)*

  UF   Forecasting, Population
Population genetics *(May add geog subd)*
  BT   Genetics
Populism *(May add geog subd)*
Populist Party (U.S.)
Porcelain *[S] (May add geog subd)*
Porcupines *[S]*
Pornography *[S] (May add geog subd)*
Porpoises *[S]*
Porsche automobile
Portable computers
  USE   Laptop computers
Portable databases *(May add geog subd)*
Porter, David, 1780-1843
Porter, Frank W., 1947-
Porter, Katherine Anne, 1890-1980
Porter, William Sidney, 1862-1910
  USE   Henry, O., 1862-1910
Porter family
Porters
Portfolios in education *(May add geog subd)*
Portland Trail Blazers (Basketball team)
Portrait drawing *(May add geog subd)*
  BT   Drawing
  RT   Portraits
Portrait painters
  USE   Artists *[AC only]*
Portrait painting *[S] (May add geog subd)*
Portrait photography *[S] (May add geog subd)*
Portraits *[S] (May add geog subd)*
  RT   Portrait drawing
          Portrait painting
  SA   *the subdivision* —Portraits
Portraits, American *(May add geog subd)*
Portugal
Portuguese language *(May add geog subd)*
Portuguese man-of-war *(May add geog subd)*
  BT   Jellyfishes
Possessions, Lost and found
  USE   Lost and found possessions *[AC only]*
Post-impressionism (Art) *(May add geog subd)*
  BT   Art, Modern—19th century
  RT   Impressionism (Art)
Post-traumatic stress disorder *(May add geog subd)*
  UF   PTSD
Postage stamps *[S] (May add geog subd)*
  UF   Stamps
Postal service *(May add geog subd)*
  —Letter carriers
Postcards *[S] (May add geog subd)*
Posters *[S] (May add geog subd)*
Posters in education *(May add geog subd)*
Postman, Neil
Postmodernism
  BT   Arts, Modern—20th century
Posture *[S] (May add geog subd)*
Potassium *[S]*
Potato famine
  USE   Famines
  BT   Food supply
Potato printing
Potatoes *[S] (May add geog subd)*
Potawatomi Indians
  BT   Algonquian Indians
Potok, Chaim

Potpourris (Scented floral mixtures)
Potsdam Conference (1945)
Potted plants
    USE Plants, Potted
Potter, Beatrix, 1866-1943
Potter, Beatrix, 1866-1943.   Tale of Peter Rabbit
Pottery *[S] (May add geog subd)*
    RT Stoneware
    SA *names of specific types and brands of pottery*
Pottery craft *(May add geog subd)*
    BT Handicraft
Potts, L.J. (Leonard James), 1897-
Poultry *[S] (May add geog subd)*
    RT Chickens
Pound, Ezra, 1885-1972
Poussin, Nicolas, 1594?-1665
Poverty *[S]*
Powell, A. Clayton (Adam Clayton), 1908-1972
Powell, John Wesley, 1834-1902
Power (Christian theology)
Power (Mechanics) *[S]*
    UF Energy
Power (Social sciences) *[S]*
Power lawn mowers *(May add geog subd)*
Power of attorney *(May add geog subd)*
Power resources *(May add geog subd)*
    UF Energy resources
Power tools *(May add geog subd)*
    BT Tools
Power transmission
    UF Transmission
Powers, Francis Gary, 1929-
POWs
    USE Prisoners of war
Powhatan, ca. 1550-1618
Powhatan Indians
Practical jokes *[S]*
    BT Jokes
Practical politics
    USE Politics, Practical
Prague (Czech Republic)
Prairie animals *[AC only] (May add geog subd)*
    UF Prairie fauna
Prairie dogs *(May add geog subd)*
Prairie ecology *(May add geog subd)*
Prairie fauna *(May add geog subd)*
Prairie flora
    USE Prairie plants *[AC only]*
Prairie plants *[AC only]*
    UF Prairie flora
Prairies *(May add geog subd)*
Praise
    BT Learning, Psychology of
Prayer books and devotions *[AC only]*
    UF Devotional exercises
           Family—Prayer-books and devotions
           Prayer-books
Prayers *[S]*
Praying mantis *[S]*
Pre-Lenten festivities
    USE Mardi gras *[AC only]*
Preble, Edward, 1761-1807
Precious metals *[S] (May add geog subd)*
    UF Metals, Precious
    BT Metals
Precious stones *[S] (May add geog subd)*

    RT Gems
Predation (Biology)
Predatory animals *(May add geog subd)*
    UF Animals, Predatory
Prefabricated houses *[S] (May add geog subd)*
    BT Dwellings
Pregnancy *[S] (May add geog subd)*
    NT Teenage pregnancy
Pregnancy, Adolescent
    USE Teenage pregnancy
Pregnancy, Termination of
    USE Abortion
Prehistoric animals *[AC, S]*
    UF Animals, Prehistoric
    RT Fossils
Prehistoric man
    USE Man, Prehistoric
Prehistoric roads
    USE Roads, Prehistoric
Prejudices *[S] (May add geog subd)*
Premenstrual syndrome *[S] (May add geog subd)*
    UF PMS
Pre-Raphaelitism *(May add geog subd)*
    RT Raphael, 1483-1520
Presbyterians
Preschool education
    USE Education, Preschool
Preschool teachers
    UF Teachers, Preschool
Preservation of organs, tissues, etc. *[S] (May add geog subd)*
    RT Anatomy
    SA *the subdivision* —Preservation
Presidential candidates
Presidential elections
    USE Presidents—Election
Presidents *[S]*
    RT Kings, queens, rulers, etc. *[AC only]*
    —Children
    —Dwellings *(May add geog subd)*
    —Election *[subdivided by date, if appropriate]*
    —Messages
    —Nomination
    —Staff
    —Wives
        USE First ladies *[AC only]*
Presidents' wives
    USE First ladies *[AC only]*
Presidio la Bahia
Presley, Elvis, 1935-1977
Presley, Priscilla Beaulieu
Press *[S] (May add geog subd)*
    RT Journalism
Press and politics *(May add geog subd)*
    UF Politics and the press
    RT Government and the press
Press and propaganda
    UF Propaganda and the press
Press law *(May add geog subd)*
    BT Law
Press releases
    BT Public relations
        Publicity
Pressed flower pictures
    UF Flowers, Pressed
    BT Handicraft

Pressed glass
  BT Glass
Pressure
  BT Mechanics
        Physics
Pressure cookery
Pressure groups *(May add geog subd)*
Preteens
Preventive medicine
  USE Medicine, Preventive
Pretzels
Price, Leontyne
Price, Vincent, 1911-
Prices *[S] (May add geog subd)*
  SA *the subdivision* —Prices
Pride, Charley
Pride and vanity
Priestley, Joseph, 1733-1804
Priests *[S]*
Primal therapy
  BT Therapy
Primaries *[S] (May add geog subd)*
  BT Elections
Primary education
  USE Education, Primary
Primates *[S]*
  NT Bush babies
        Cercopithecus
Primatologists
  NT Women primatologists
Prime ministers *[S]*
  RT Kings, queens, rulers, etc. *[AC only]*
Prime numbers
  USE Numbers, Prime
Primers *[AC only]*
    This heading is not subdivided by date or subject.
  UF Readers (Kindergarten)
        Readers (Preschool)
        Readers (Primary)
Primitive religions
  USE Religion, Primitive
Primitivism in art *(May add geog subd)*
Primroses *(May add geog subd)*
Prince Edward Island (Prince Edward Islands)
Prince William Sound Region (Alaska)
Princes
Princesses
Printers
Printers (Data processing systems)
Printing *[S] (May add geog subd)*
  RT Blind—Printing and writing systems
        Books
        Publishers and publishing
        Rubber stamp printing
  NT Lithography
        Screen process printing
        Type and type-founding
Printing, Practical
  —Style manuals
Printing industry *(May add geog subd)*
Printmakers
Prints *[S] (May add geog subd)*
  RT Lithography
Prints, Dutch *(May add geog subd)*

Prints, Renaissance
  BT Prints—16th century
Prison reformers
  USE Reformers *[AC only]*
Prisoners *[S]*
  NT Political prisoners
  SA *the subdivision* —Prisoners and prisons
Prisoners, Political
  USE Political prisoners
Prisoners' families
Prisoners of war *[S]*
  UF POWs
Prisons *[S] (May add geog subd)*
  RT Penal colonies
  SA *the names of specific prisons, e.g.,* Tower of London
        (London, England) *and the subdivision* —Prisoners
        and prisons
Privacy, Right of *(May add geog subd)*
  UF Right to privacy
Private flying *(May add geog subd)*
  UF Airplanes—Private flying
Private schools *[S] (May add geog subd)*
Private secretaries
  USE Secretaries *[AC only]*
Privateering *[S] (May add geog subd)*
  RT Pirates
Pro-choice movement *[S] (May add geog subd)*
  RT Abortion
Pro Football Hall of Fame (U.S.)
  RT Football
Probabilities *[S]*
Problem children
  UF Children, Problematic
Problem solving *[S]*
  UF Cleverness
        Ingenuity
  SA *the subdivision* —Problems, exercises, etc.
Pro-choice movement *[S] (May add geog subd)*
Processing (Libraries)
  UF Technical services (Libraries)
Procrustes (Greek mythology)
Prodigal son (Parable)
Prodigy (Videotex system)
Produce trade *(May add geog subd)*
  BT Agriculture
        Food industry and trade
Product coding *(May add geog subd)*
  UF Bar coding of products
        Coding, Product
  —Computer programs
Product safety *[S] (May add geog subd)*
Production engineering
  UF Manufacturing engineering
Professional education *[S] (May add geog subd)*
  UF Education, Professional
Professional employees
  UF Employees, Professional
Professions *[S] (May add geog subd)*
Prognosis
  UF Medical prognosis
Programmable calculators
Programmed instruction *[S] (May add geog subd)*
  RT Teaching machines
  SA *the subdivision* —Programmed instruction

Programming (Computers) *[AC, S]*
  UF Computers—Programming
       Programming (Electronic computers)
  BT Data processing *[AC only]*
  RT Programming languages (Computers) *[AC only]*
  SA *the subdivision* —Programming
Programming (Electronic computers)
  USE Programming (Computers) *[AC only]*
Programming languages (Computers) *[AC, S]*
  UF Programming languages (Electronic computers)
  RT Data processing *[AC only]*
       Programming (Computers) *[AC only]*
  SA *the subdivision* —Programming
Programming languages (Electronic computers)
  USE Programming languages (Computers) *[AC only]*
Progress *[S]*
Progressivism (United States politics)
Prohibited books *(May add geog subd)*
  UF Banned books
  RT Censorship
Prohibition *[S] (May add geog subd)*
  RT Alcohol—Law and legislation
Prohibition Party
Project Apollo (U.S.)
Project Head Start (U.S.)
Project Mariner
  BT Astronautics
Project method in teaching *[S]*
  BT Teaching
Project Sealab
Project Voyager *[S]*
Projectile points *(May add geog subd)*
Projectiles *[S]*
Prokof'ev, Sergei Sergeevich, 1891-1953
Prometheus (Greek mythology)
Promotion of special events
  UF Special events, Promotion of
Promptness *[AC only]*
  RT Tardiness *[AC only]*
Pronghorn antelope *(May add geog subd)*
Proofreading *[S]*
Propaganda *[S]*
Propaganda and the press
  USE Press and propaganda
Propagation
  USE Plant propagation
Prophecies *[AC only]*
  UF Prophecies (Occultism)
  BT Occultism
  SA *the subdivision* —Prophecies
Prophecies (Occultism)
  USE Prophecies *[AC only]*
Prophets *[S]*
Proposal writing for grants *(May add geog subd)*
Proposal writing in business
Prose literature
Prospecting *(May add geog subd)*
Prosser, Gabriel, ca. 1775-1800
Prostate
Prosthesis *(May add geog subd)*
  RT Artificial limbs
       Artificial organs
       Prosthetics
Prosthetic make-up, Theatrical
  USE Theatrical prosthetic makeup
Prosthetics
  USE Prosthesis

Prostitutes
Prostitution *[S] (May add geog subd)*
Prostitution, Juvenile
  USE Child prostitution *(May add geog subd)*
Protectionism *(May add geog subd)*
Proteins *[S]*
Protestant reformation
  USE Reformation
Protista
  USE Protists *[AC only]*
  NT Protozoans *[AC only]*
Protists *[AC only]*
  UF Protista
Protozoa
  USE Protozoans *[AC only]*
Protozoans *[AC only]*
  UF Protozoa
Proust, Marcel, 1871-1922.   A la recherche du temps perdu
  USE Proust, Marcel, 1871-1922.   Remembrance of things past
Proust, Marcel, 1871-1922.   Remembrance of things past
  UF Proust, Marcel, 1871-1922.   A la recherche du temps perdu
Provence (France)
Proverbs *[S]*
  UF Sayings
  RT Aphorisms and apothegms
       Maxims
  SA *the subdivision* —Quotations, maxims, etc. *under topical headings*
Proverbs, American, [African, English, etc.]
Providence and government of God *[S]*
  —Judaism
Pruning *[S]*
Prussia (Germany)
Prynne, Hester (Fictitious character)
Przewalski's horse
  UF Asian wild horse
Przheval'skii, Nikolai Mikhailovich, 1839-1888
Psoriasis *(May add geog subd)*
Psyche (Greek deity)
Psychiatric hospital patients
Psychiatric hospitals *(May add geog subd)*
Psychiatric patients
  USE Psychotherapy patients
Psychiatrists *[S]*
Psychiatry *[S] (May add geog subd)*
  RT Mental illness
Psychical research
  USE Parapsychology
Psychics
Psychoanalysis *(May add geog subd)*
Psychoanalysis and literature
Psychoanalysis and religion
Psychoanalysts
Psychokinesis *[S] (May add geog subd)*
Psycholinguistics
  UF Language and languages—Psychology
Psychological literature *(May add geog subd)*
Psychological tests *[S] (May add geog subd)*
  UF Mental tests
       Tests, Psychological
Psychologists *[S]*
Psychology *[S] (May add geog subd)*
  NT Neuropsychology
  SA *the subdivisions* —Psychological aspects *and* —Psychology
  —Early works to 1850

Psychology, Applied *[S]*
 UF Applied psychology
 NT Negotiation
  Conflict management
Psychology, Comparative *[S]*
 UF Comparative psychology
Psychology, Forensic
 UF Forensic psychology
  Legal psychology
Psychology, Industrial
 UF Business psychology
  Industrial psychology
Psychology, Pathological *[S]*
 UF Pathological psychology
Psychology of learning
 USE Learning, Psychology of
Psychology of movement
 USE Movement, Psychology of
Psychology, Religious
 UF Religion—Psychological aspects
Psychometrics
Psychophysiology *[S] (May add geog subd)*
Psychoses *(May add geog subd)*
Psychotherapist and patient
Psychotherapists
Psychotherapy *[S] (May add geog subd)*
 BT Therapy
 SA *the names of specific forms of therapy*
Psychotherapy patients
 UF Mental patients
  Psychiatric patients
Psychotropic drugs *[S] (May add geog subd)*
 BT Drugs
 RT Mental illness
Psychotropic plants *(May add geog subd)*
Pterodactyls *[AC only]*
 BT Pterosaurs *[AC only]*
Pterosauria
 USE Pterosaurs *[AC only]*
Pterosaurs *[AC only]*
 UF Pterosauria
 NT Pterodactyls *[AC only]*
PTSD
 USE Post-traumatic stress disorder
Puberty *(May add geog subd)*
Public administration *[S] (May add geog subd)*
Public buildings *[S] (May add geog subd)*
Public contracts
 UF Government contracts
Public health *[S] (May add geog subd)*
Public health laws *(May add geog subd)*
Public investments
 UF Government investments
Public lands *(May add geog subd)*
Public libraries *[S] (May add geog subd)*
 BT Libraries
Public meetings *[S] (May add geog subd)*
Public opinion *[S] (May add geog subd)*
 SA *the subdivision* —Public opinion
Public opinion polls *[S]*
Public policy *(May add geog subd)*
 SA *the subdivision* —Government policy
Public prosecutors
 UF District attorneys
Public records
 UF Government records

Public relations *[S] (May add geog subd)*
 NT Press releases
—**Police**
Public schools *[S] (May add geog subd)*
 BT Schools
Public sculpture *(May add geog subd)*
 BT Sculpture
Public services
 USE County services
  Municipal services
Public speaking *[S]*
 RT Speeches, addresses, etc.
Public utilities *(May add geog subd)*
 NT Underground utility lines
Public welfare *[S] (May add geog subd)*
 UF Welfare
Public works *(May add geog subd)*
Publicity *[S]*
 NT Press releases
Publishers and publishing *[S]*
 RT Editing
  Editors
  Journalism
Publishers' catalogs
 USE Catalogs, Publishers'
Publishing
 USE Publishers and publishing
 RT Books
  Booksellers and bookselling
  Printing
 SA *the subdivision* —Publishing
Puccini, Giacomo, 1858-1924. Madam Butterfly
Puckett, Kirby
Pueblo (Ship)
Pueblo Indians
Pueblo Revolt, 1680
Pueblos
 BT Indians of North America—Dwellings
Puente, Dorothea
Puerto Rican fiction *(May add geog subd)*
Puerto Rican literature *(May add geog subd)*
Puerto Ricans
 BT Hispanic Americans
Puerto Rico
Puffins *[S]*
Pulaski, Kazimierz, 1748-1779
Pulitzer, Joseph, 1847-1911
Pulitzer Prizes
Pulleys
Pullman Company
Pulsars *[S]*
Pumas *(May add geog subd)*
 UF Cougars
Pumping machinery *[S]*
Pumpkin *[S]*
Punctuation *[S]*
Punic War, 2nd, 218-201 B.C.
Punishment *[S] (May add geog subd)*
 RT Discipline
  Discipline of children
Punk culture *(May add geog subd)*
Puns and punning *[S]*
 RT Word games
Puppet making *(May add geog subd)*
Puppet plays
Puppet theater *(May add geog subd)*

Puppet theater in education *(May add geog subd)*
Puppet theaters *(May add geog subd)*
Puppeteers
Puppets *(May add geog subd)*
Puppies
    USE Dogs *[AC only]*
Purchasers
    USE Vendors and purchasing
    RT Purchasing
Purchasing
    UF Buying
    RT Vendors and purchasers
Purim (Feast of Easter)
Puritans *[S]*
Putnam family
Putter, Shira, 1974-1983
Putting (Golf)
    BT Golf
Puzzles *[AC, S]*
    UF Creative activities and seat work
    NT Palindromes
        Picture puzzles
Pygmalion (Greek mythology)
Pygmies
    RT Dwarfs
Pyle, Ernie, 1900-1945
Pym, Barbara
Pyramids *(May add geog subd)*
Pyrography
    UF Fire etching
        Woodburning
Pyromania
Pythons
Quacks and quackery *[S]*
    RT Fraud
        Impostors and imposture
Quadrilaterals
    BT Geometry
Quadriplegics
Quail shooting *(May add geog subd)*
Quails *(May add geog subd)*
Quakers
    BT Society of Friends
Quality assurance *(May add geog subd)*
Quality control *[S] (May add geog subd)*
Quality of life *[S] (May add geog subd)*
    UF Life, Quality of
Quality of products *(May add geog subd)*
Quality of work life *(May add geog subd)*
Quant, Mary
Quantity cookery *[S]*
    BT Cookery
Quantril, William Clarke, 1837-1865
Quantum theory *[S]*
Quapaw Indians
Quarks *[S]*
Quarries and quarrying *[S] (May add geog subd)*
Quarter horse
    BT Horses
Quarterback (Football)
Quartz *[S] (May add geog subd)*
Quasars *[S]*
Québec (Québec)—Siege, 1775-1776
Québec Campaign, 1759
Queen Charlotte Islands
Queen Elizabeth I

    USE Elizabeth, Queen of England, 1533-1603
Queens
    USE Kings, queens, rulers, etc. *[AC only]*
Queensland
Questioning
Questions and answers *[S]*
    UF Answers
    RT Examinations
Quick and easy cookery *[S]*
    BT Cookery
Quicksand *(May add geog subd)*
Quietude
Quileute Indians
Quilting *[S] (May add geog subd)*
    NT Trapunto
—Patterns
Quiltmakers
Quilts *[S] (May add geog subd)*
Quinary system
Quinceañera (Social custom) *(May add geog subd)*
    BT Manners and customs
Quintuplets
Quotations *[S]*
    SA *the subdivisions* —Quotations *and* —Quotations,
        maxims, etc.
Quotations, English *(May add geog subd)*
Qwilleran, Jim (Fictitious character)
Ra (Boat)
Rabbis *[S]*
Rabbit breeds *(May add geog subd)*
Rabbits *[S] (May add geog subd)*
Rabies *[S] (May add geog subd)*
Rabies in animals *(May add geog subd)*
Rabun Gap (Ga.)
Raccoons *[S] (May add geog subd)*
Race *[S]*
Race awareness *[S] (May add geog subd)*
Race discrimination *[S] (May add geog subd)*
    RT Apartheid
        Discrimination
        Racism
        Segregation
Race horses *(May add geog subd)*
    BT Horses
Race relations *[S]*
    SA *the subdivision* —Race relations
Racing
    NT Automobile racing
        Running races
        Speed skating
Racism *[S] (May add geog subd)*
    RT Apartheid
        Race discrimination
        Segregation
Rack railroads *[AC only]*
    BT Mountain railroads
        Railroads
Racket games *(May add geog subd)*
    BT Games
Racketeering *[S] (May add geog subd)*
    BT Crime
Rackham, Arthur, 1867-1939
Racquetball *[S] (May add geog subd)*
    BT Sports
Radar *[S] (May add geog subd)*
Radial saws

Radiation *[S]*
    NT Infrared radiation
          Infrared technology
Radicalism *(May add geog subd)*
Radio *[S] (May add geog subd)*
Radio, Shortwave *[AC only]*
    UF Shortwave radio
Radio astronomy *[S] (May add geog subd)*
    BT Astronomy
Radio broadcasting *[S] (May add geog subd)*
    BT Broadcasting
Radio plays *[S]*
Radio programs *[S] (May add geog subd)*
Radio scripts *[S]*
Radio serials *[S]*
Radio stations *[S] (May add geog subd)*
Radioactive pollution *[S] (May add geog subd)*
Radioactive waste disposal *[S] (May add geog subd)*
Radioactive wastes
Radioactivity *[S]*
Radiography *(May add geog subd)*
    RT X rays
Radiography, Medical *(May add geog subd)*
Radisson, Pierre Esprit, ca. 1636-1710
Radium *[S]*
Radon *[S]*
Raffaello Sanzio Santi
    USE Raphael, 1483-1520
Raffia
    BT Handicraft
    RT Basket making
Rafting (Sports) *[S] (May add geog subd)*
Railroad travel *(May add geog subd)*
Railroads *[S] (May add geog subd)*
    NT Mountain railroads
          Rack railroads
  —Signaling
  —Trains
Railroads, Cable
    RT Mountain railroads
    NT Cable cars *[AC only]*
Railroads, Mountain
    USE Mountain railroads
    NT Rack railroads
          Street-railroads
Railroads in art *[S]*
Rails (Birds)
Rain, acid
    USE Acid rain
Rain and rainfall *(May add geog subd)*
Rain forest animals *[AC only]*
    UF Rain forest fauna
Rain forest conservation *(May add geog subd)*
Rain forest ecology *(May add geog subd)*
Rain forest fauna
    USE Rain forest animals *[AC only]*
Rain forests *[S] (May add geog subd)*
Rain-making *(May add geog subd)*
Rainbow *[S]*
Raku pottery
Raleigh, Sir Walter
    USE Raleigh, Walter, Sir, 1552?-1618
Raleigh, Walter, Sir, 1552?-1618
    UF Raleigh, Sir Walter

Raleigh's Roanoke Colonies, 1584-1590
Rama (Hindu deity)
Rameses II, King of Egypt
Ramona (Television program)
Ramusi, Molapatene Collins
Ranch life *[S] (May add geog subd)*
Ranchers
Ranches *(May add geog subd)*
Rand, Ayn
Randolph, A. Philip (Asa Philip), 1889-
Randolph, Martha Jefferson, 1772-1836
Range management *(May add geog subd)*
Rangelands *(May add geog subd)*
Rap (Music) *(May add geog subd)*
Rap musicians
Rape *[S] (May add geog subd)*
Rape victims
Raphael, 1483-1520
    UF Raffaello Sanzio Santi, 1483-1520
          Raphael Santi, 1483-1520
    RT Preraphaelitism
Raphael Santi, 1483-1520
    USE Raphael, 1483-1520
Rapid reading *[S]*
Rapists
Rare amphibians
    USE Rare animals *[AC, S]*
Rare animals *[AC, S] (May add geog subd)*
    UF Animals, Rare
          Endangered species
          Rare amphibians
          Rare birds
          Rare fishes
          Rare insects
          Rare invertebrates
          Rare mammals
          Rare reptiles
Rare birds
    USE Rare animals
    UF Birds, Rare
Rare books *[S] (May add geog subd)*
Rare breeds *(May add geog subd)*
Rare fishes
    USE Rare animals
Rare insects
    USE Rare animals
Rare invertebrates
    USE Rare animals
Rare mammals
    USE Rare animals
Rare plants *[AC, S] (May add geog subd)*
    UF Plants, Rare
          Endangered species
Rare reptiles
    USE Rare animals
Rascal (Raccoon)
Rasputin, Grigori Efimovich, ca. 1870-1916
Rat snakes *[AC, S] (May add geog subd)*
    BT Snakes
Ratio analysis
Rationalism *[S]*
Rats *[S] (May add geog subd)*

Rats as pets
Rattan furniture
Rattlesnakes *[S] (May add geog subd)*
    NT   Timber rattlesnake
Ravens *[S]*
Ravensbruck (Germany : Concentration camp)
Raw foods *(May add geog subd)*
Raw materials *(May add geog subd)*
Rawalt, Marguerite, 1895-
Rawlings, Marjorie Kinnan, 1896-1953
Rawlison, Henry Creswicke, Sir, 1810-1895
Ray, James Earl, 1928-
Rayburn, Sam, 1882-1961
Rays (Fishes) *[S] (May add geog subd)*
Razin, Stepan Timofeevich, d. 1671
rDNA
    UF   Recombinant DNA
    BT   DNA
Rea, Daniel J., 1948-
Readers
    This heading is not subdivided by date or subject. Use for works containing material for reading and practice in reading in English. Readers in other languages are entered under the name of the language with subdivision —Readers. Works containing reading material in a particular subject field or literary genre are entered under headings such as the following illustrations: *For English:* Readers— Agriculture [Art, Drama, Fairy tales, Geography, etc.] *For other languages:* French language—Readers—Science [Art, Drama, Fairy tales, Geography, etc.].
  —Agriculture [Art, Drama, Fairy tales, Geography, etc.]
    NT   Primers
Readers (Elementary)
    Use for works in English containing reading material limited to this age level.
  —Phonetic method
    UF   Phonics
Readers (Kindergarten)
    USE   Primers *[AC only]*
Readers (Preschool)
    USE   Primers *[AC only]*
Readers (Primary)
    USE   Primers *[AC only]*
Readers' theater *[S]*
Reading *[S] (May add geog subd)*
    Use for works on the art of reading. Works on the significance of books in people's lives, including their attitudes toward and interest in reading are entered under Books and reading.
    UF   Reading—Study and teaching
    BT   Language arts
    RT   Books and reading
          Education
          Libraries
          Phonetics
  —Remedial teaching
Reading (Early childhood) *(May add geog subd)*
Reading (Elementary) *(May add geog subd)*
Reading (Kindergarten) *(May add geog subd)*
Reading (Preschool) *(May add geog subd)*
Reading (Primary) *(May add geog subd)*
Reading (Secondary) *(May add geog subd)*
    Use for works in English containing reading material limited to this age level.
Reading aloud
    USE   Group reading
Reading comprehension *[S]*
Reading disability *[S] (May add geog subd)*
Reading games

Reading interests *(May add geog subd)*
Reagan, Nancy, 1923-
Reagan, Ronald
Real estate agents
Real estate business *[S] (May add geog subd)*
Real estate developers
Real estate investment *[S] (May add geog subd)*
Real property *(May add geog subd)*
Real property, Exchange of *(May add geog subd)*
Realism *[S]*
Realism in art *(May add geog subd)*
Reality *[S]*
Ream, Vinnie, 1847-1914
Reasoner, Harry, 1923-
Reasoning *[S]*
Rebellion
    USE   Alienation (Social psychology)
Rebuses *[S]*
Recessions *(May add geog subd)*
    UF   Economic recessions
Recipes *(May add geog subd)*
Recitations
Reclamation of land *[S] (May add geog subd)*
    UF   Land, Reclamation of
    RT   Land use
Recombinant DNA
    USE   rDNA
    BT   DNA
    RT   Genetics
Reconnaissance aircraft *(May add geog subd)*
Reconstruction *(May be subd geog by State names)*
Recorded books
    USE   Talking books
Recorder (Musical instrument) *[S]*
Recreation *[S] (May add geog subd)*
    SA   *the subdivisions* —Recreations *and* —Recreational use
Recreation areas *(May add geog subd)*
Recreation centers *(May add geog subd)*
Recreation rooms *(May add geog subd)*
Rectangle
Recycling (Waste) *[AC only] (May add geog subd)*
    UF   Salvage (Waste, etc.)
    SA   *the subdivision* —Recycling
Red *[S]*
    BT   Color
Red Cloud, 1822-1909
Red Cross *(May add geog subd)*
Red fox *(May add geog subd)*
Red Horse, Chief
Red panda
    USE   Lesser panda *[AC only]*
Red River War, 1874-1875
Red Sea
Red squirrels *[AC, S] (May add geog subd)*
    UF   Tamiasciurus
Red-tailed hawk *(May add geog subd)*
Redford, Robert
Redon, Odilon, 1840-1916
Reducing
    USE   Weight control *[AC only]*
Reducing exercises
Redwood *[S]*
Redwood National Park (Calif.)
Reed, Don C.
Reed, John, 1887-1920
Reed, Walter, 1851-1902

Reefs *(May add geog subd)*
Reese, Pee Wee, 1919-
Reese family
Reeves, Richard Stone
Reference books *[S]*
Reference services (Libraries) *[S] (May add geog subd)*
   RT Information services
Reflection (Optics)
Reflections
Reflexes
Reflexotherapy *(May add geog subd)*
Reforestation *[S] (May add geog subd)*
Reformation *[S] (May add geog subd)*
   RT Christianity—History *[AC only]*
Reformed Church *(May add geog subd)*
Reformers *[S]*
   UF Prison reformers *[AC only]*
        Social reformers *[AC only]*
Refugees *[S]*
   SA *the subdivision* —Refugees
Refugees, Asian
Refugees, Chinese
Refugees, Cuban
Refugees, Estonian
Refugees, German
Refugees, Hungarian
Refugees, Jewish
Refugees, Political
Refugees, Thai
Refugees, Vietnamese *[S]*
Refugio County (Tex.)
Refuse and refuse disposal *[S] (May add geog subd)*
Refuseniks
Regalia (Insignia) *(May add geog subd)*
Regency *(May add geog subd)*
Registers of births, etc. *[S] (May add geog subd)*
Regulatory agencies
   USE Administrative agencies
Rehabilitation *(May add geog subd)*
Reichel, Sabine, 1946-
Reilly, Sidney George, 1874-1925
Reincarnation *[S]*
Reindeer *[S] (May add geog subd)*
Reiss, Johanna
Rejuvenation
Relationship addiction *(May add geog subd)*
Relationships, Interpersonal
   USE Interpersonal relations
Relativity (Physics) *[S]*
Relaxation
Relief printing
Religion *[S]*
   NT Worship
   SA *the subdivisions* —Religion *and* —Religious aspects
  —Psychological aspects
     USE Psychology, Religious
Religion, Primitive
   USE Religion
Religion and art
   USE Art and religion
Religion and astronautics
   UF Astronautics and religion
Religion and literature
Religion and politics *[S] (May add geog subd)*
   NT Islam and politics

Religion and science *[S] (May add geog subd)*
   UF Science and religion
Religion historians
Religion in the public schools *[S] (May add geog subd)*
   RT Church and education
Religions *[S]*
   RT Cults
        Sects
   NT Jacobites
        Shinto
   SA *names of specific religions*
Religious camps
Religious biography
   USE Religious leaders
Religious calendars *(May add geog subd)*
Religious ethics
   UF Ethics, Religious
   BT Ethics
Religious experience and hallucinogenic drugs
   USE Hallucinogenic drugs and religious experience
Religious leaders
   UF Religious biography
Religious life *[S]*
   UF Monasticism and religious orders
   Use for works on the religious and monastic life of monks, priests, saints, nuns, etc. *[AC only]*
   SA *the subdivision* —Religious life *under classes of persons,*
      e.g., Children—Religious life
   UF Monastic and religious life
   RT Christian life
Religious literature *[S]*
   BT Literature
Religious orders
   USE Religious life
Religious poetry *[S]*
   BT Poetry
Religious thought *(May add geog subd)*
Religious tolerance *(May add geog subd)*
Remarriage *[S] (May add geog subd)*
   BT Marriage
Remarried people
Rembrandt, Harmenszoon Van Rijn, 1606-1669
Remedial teaching *(May add geog subd)*
   UF Teaching, Remedial
Remedies (Law) *(May add geog subd)*
Remington, Frederic, 1861-1909
Remote sensing *[S] (May add geog subd)*
Renaissance *[S] (May add geog subd)*
Rendezvous Mountain (Wyo.)
Renewable energy resources *[S] (May add geog subd)*
   RT Energy consumption
Renoir, Auguste, 1841-1919
   UF Renoir, Pierre Auguste, 1841-1919
Rental housing *(May add geog subd)*
Repairing *[S] (May add geog subd)*
   SA *the subdivision* —Repairing
Repatriation *(May add geog subd)*
Repetitive patterns (Decorative arts) *(May add geog subd)*
Report writing *[S]*
   BT Composition (Language arts)
        Written composition
Reporters and reporting *[S]*
   RT Journalism
   NT War correspondents

Representative government and representation *[S] (May add geog subd)*
    RT Republics
Reproduction *[S]*
    NT Birth
          Childbirth
    SA *the subdivision* —Reproduction
Reproductive system, Female *[AC only]*
    UF Generative organs, Female
    NT Ovaries
Reproductive system, Male *[AC only]*
    UF Generative organs, Male
Reptiles *[S] (May add geog subd)*
    NT Lizards
Reptiles, Fossil *[S] (May add geog subd)*
    UF Fossil reptiles
Reptiles in art
Republican Party (U.S.) *[S]*
Republics *[S]*
    RT Representative government and representation
Rescue dogs
    BT Dogs
Rescue work *[AC, S]*
    UF Search and rescue operations
Research *[S] (May add geog subd)*
    SA *the subdivisions* —Longitudinal studies *and* —Research
Research aircraft *(May add geog subd)*
    UF Experimental aircraft
          Airplanes, Experimental
Research grants *(May add geog subd)*
Research institutes *(May add geog subd)*
Reserva Biosferica en los Galápagos (Galapagos Islands)
    USE Galapagos Islands Biosphere Reserve (Galapagos Islands)
          [AC only]
Reserve Mining Company
Residents (Medicine)
Resilience (Personality trait) *(May add geog subd)*
Resnick, Judith, 1949-1986
Resnick, Rose
Resorts *(May add geog subd)*
Resource programs (Education)
Respect
Respiration *[S]*
Respiratory allergy *(May add geog subd)*
Respiratory organs
    USE Respiratory system *[AC, S]*
Respiratory system *[AC, S]*
    UF Respiratory organs
    SA *the names of specific respiratory organs*
Responsibility
Rest *[S]*
Restaurant management *(May add geog subd)*
Restaurants, lunch rooms, etc. *(May add geog subd)*
Restaurateurs
Résumés (Employment) *[S]*
    RT Applications for positions
          Job hunting
Resuscitation
Retail trade *[S] (May add geog subd)*
    RT Selling
Reticulated python
Retired teachers
Retirees
Retirement *[S] (May add geog subd)*
Retirement age *(May add geog subd)*
Retirement income *[S] (May add geog subd)*

Retrievers
    BT Dogs
Retton, Mary Lou, 1968-
Reusable space vehicles
    BT Space vehicles
Revenge
    RT Vendetta
Revere, Paul, 1735-1818
Reverse culture shock *(May add geog subd)*
Revis, Alesia
Revivals *[S] (May add geog subd)*
Revolutionaries
Revolutions *[S] (May add geog subd)*
Revolvers *(May add geog subd)*
Rewards (Prizes, etc.)
    USE Awards
Rexroth, Kenneth, 1905-
Rey, Margret
Reye's Syndrome *[S] (May add geog subd)*
Reynolds, Joshua, 1723-1792
Reynolds family
Rhetoric *[S] (May add geog subd)*
    SA *the subdivision* —Rhetoric
Rheumatic fever *[S] (May add geog subd)*
Rheumatism *[S] (May add geog subd)*
Rheumatoid arthritis *[S] (May add geog subd)*
    BT Arthritis
Rheumatology *(May add geog subd)*
Rhine River
Rhine River Valley
Rhinoceros *[S]*
Rhode Island
    —History
    — —To 1775
    — —Revolution, 1775-1783
Rhodes, Cecil, 1853-1902
Rhodesia
Rhododendron *(May add geog subd)*
    BT Flowers
Rhyme *[S]*
    SA *the subdivision* —Rhyme
Rhyming games *(May add geog subd)*
    NT Word games
Rhys, Jean
Rhythm *[S]*
Rhythm and blues music *(May add geog subd)*
    RT Blues (Music)
Ribbon flowers
Ribbon work *(May add geog subd)*
Ribonucleic acid
    USE RNA
Rice *(May add geog subd)*
Rice, Anne, 1941-
Richard I, King of England, 1157-1199
Richard II, King of England, 1367-1400
Richard III, King of England, 1452-1485
Richard, Maurice, 1921-
Richards, Ann, 1933-
Richards, Linda, 1841-1930
Richmond, C. Adam (Carl Adam), 1958-
Richtofen, Manfred, Freiherr von, 1892-1918
Rickenbacker, Eddie, 1890-1973
Rickey, Branch, 1881-1965
Riddles *[S]*
    SA *the subdivision* —Wit and humor
Ride, Sally

Ridge, Major, ca. 1771-1839
Riding lawn mowers *(May add geog subd)*
Rifles *[S]*
Right
    USE   Left and right *[AC only]*
Right and left (Political science) *[AC, S]*
    UF   Left (Political science)
          Right (Political science)
    BT   Political science
Right-handedness
    USE   Left- and right-handedness *[AC only]*
Right to die *[S] (May add geog subd)*
Right to privacy
    USE   Privacy, Right of
Righteous Gentiles in the Holocaust
    RT   Holocaust, Jewish (1933-1945)
Riis, Jacob A. (Jacob August), 1849-1914
Riley, Bridget, 1931-
Ring-necked pheasant *(May add geog subd)*
Ringling Brothers
Ringworm *(May add geog subd)*
Rings *(May add geog subd)*
Rio de Janeiro (Brazil)
Rio Grande
Rio Grande Valley
Riots *[S] (May add geog subd)*
Ripken, Cal, 1960-
Risk assessment *(May add geog subd)*
Rites and ceremonies *[S] (May add geog subd)*
    UF   Ceremonies
    SA   *the subdivision* —Rites and ceremonies
River animals
    USE   Stream animals *[AC only]*
Rittenberg, Sidney
River life *(May add geog subd)*
River otters *[AC only] (May add geog subd)*
Rivera, Diego, 1886-1957
Rivers *[S] (May add geog subd)*
Rizzuto, Phil, 1918-
RNA *[S]*
    UF   Ribonucleic acid
Roadrunner
    UF   Road runner (Bird)
Roads *[S] (May add geog subd)*
Roads, Norman *[AC only]*
    UF   Roads, Prehistoric—England
Roads, Prehistoric *(May add geog subd)*
    UF   Prehistoric roads
Roadside ecology *(May add geog subd)*
Roadside improvement *[S] (May add geog subd)*
Roanoke Colony (N.C.)
Roanoke Island (N.C.)
Robbery *(May add geog subd)*
Robbers and outlaws *[AC only]*
    UF   Brigands and robbers
          Outlaws
          Thieves
Robbins family
Robert-Houdin, Jean Eugene, 1805-1871
Robert I, King of Scotland, 1274-1329
Roberts, Churchill
Roberts, Julia, 1967-
Roberts, Willo Davis
Robeson, Paul, 1898-1976
Robespierre, Maximilien, 1758-1794
Robie House (Chicago, Ill.)

Robin Hood (Legendary character)
Robins *[S]*
Robinson, Brooks, 1937-
Robinson, Frank, 1935-
Robinson, Harriet Jane Hanson, 1825-1911
Robinson, Jackie, 1919-1972
Robot City (Series)
Robotics *[S] (May add geog subd)*
Robots *[S] (May add geog subd)*
    Use for automated devices or machines which take human form
  and perform human activities. *[AC only]*
    UF   Androids
    RT   Automata
Robots, Industrial
    UF   Industrial robots
Rock climbing *[S] (May add geog subd)*
Rock craft
Rock music *[S] (May add geog subd)*
Rock musicians
Rock paintings *(May add geog subd)*
    RT   Picture-writing
Rockefeller family
Rockefeller, John D. (John Davison), 1839-1937
Rockefeller, Nelson A. (Nelson Aldrich), 1908-1979
Rocket planes *[S] (May add geog subd)*
    RT   Airplanes
Rocketry *[S] (May add geog subd)*
Rockets (Aeronautics) *[S]*
Rockets (Ordnance)
Rocking chairs *(May add geog subd)*
Rockne, Knute, 1888-1931
Rocks *[S] (May add geog subd)*
    BT   Petrology
    NT   Shale
Rockwell, Norman, 1894-1978
Rocky Mountain goat *(May add geog subd)*
Rocky Mountain National Park (Colo.)
Rocky Mountain spotted fever *[S]*
Rocky Mountains
Rodents *(May add geog subd)*
Rodeos *[S] (May add geog subd)*
Rodgers, Richard, 1902-
Rodin, August, 1840-1917
    UF   Rodin, Francois
Rodin, Francois
    USE   Rodin, August, 1840-1917
Rodriguez, Richard
Roe, Jane
Roe deer *[S] (May add geog subd)*
    UF   Capreolus
Roethke, Theodore, 1908-1963
Rogers, Kenny, 1937-
Rogers, Lynn L.
Rogers, Maggie
Rogers, Robert, 1731-1795
Rogers, Robin Elizabeth, 1950-1952
Rogers, Will, 1879-1935
Rogers, Woodes, d. 1732
Rogues and vagabonds
    UF   Vagabonds
Rohr, Janelle, 1963-
Roland (Legendary character)
Role conflict *[S]*
Role playing *[S]*
Roller coasters *(May add geog subd)*

Roller skaters *[AC only]*
    UF   Skaters
Roller skating *[AC, S]*
    UF   Skating
Rollerblading
    USE In-line skating
    BT   Roller skating
Rolling Stones (Musical group)
Rolls-Royce automobile
Roman emperors
    USE Kings, queens, rulers, etc. *[AC only]*
Roman numerals
    BT   Number systems
          Numerals
Romance languages *[S] (May add geog subd)*
    SA   *the names of specific Romance languages, e.g.,* French
          language
Romance novels
    USE Love—Fiction
Romances *[S] (May add geog subd)*
Romanesque architecture
    USE Architecture, Romanesque
Roman Empire
    USE Rome
Romania
Romanian Americans
Romans
Romanticism *[S] (May add geog subd)*
    RT   Literature
Rome *[S]*
    UF   Ancient Roman Empire
          Roman Empire
   —History
   — —Republic, 265-30 B.C.
   — —Empire, 30 B.C.-476 A.D.
Rome (Italy) *[S]*
    RT   Rome
Rommel, Erwin, 1891-1944
Ronne Antarctic Research Expedition, 1946-1948
Roofing *(May add geog subd)*
Roofs *[S] (May add geog subd)*
Room layout (Dwellings) *(May add geog subd)*
Roommates
Rooney, Mickey
Roos, Karen L.
Roosevelt, Anna, 1906-1975
Roosevelt, Eleanor, 1884-1962
Roosevelt, Franklin D. (Delano), 1882-1945
Roosevelt, Nicholas J., 1767-1854
Roosevelt, Theodore, 1858-1919
Roosevelt family
Roosters *[S]*
Root crops *[S] (May add geog subd)*
Rope *[S]*
Rope skipping *[S]*
Ropework
Rosalind (Fictitious character)
Rose, Mike
Rose, Pete, 1941-
Rose culture *(May add geog subd)*
Rosebud Indian Reservation (S.D.)
Rosen, Barbara
Rosen, Barry
Rosenberg, Ethel, 1915-1953
Rosenberg, Julius, 1918-1953
Rosenberg, Steven A.

Roses *[S] (May add geog subd)*
Rosetta Stone
Rosetti, Christina Georgina, 1830-1894
Rosh ha-Shanah
    UF   Jewish New Year
Ross, Betsy, 1752-1836
Ross, Diana, 1944-
Ross, John, 1790-1866
Rossi, John F.
Rostand, Edmond, 1868-1918.   Cyrano de Bergerac
Rotary tillers *(May add geog subd)*
    UF   Tillers, Rotary
Rote, Kyle, 1950-
Roth family
Roth-Hano, Renee, 1931-
Rottweiler dog
Rounds (Music) *[AC only]*
    UF   Glees, catches, rounds, etc.
Rousseau, Henri Julien Félix, 1844-1910
Rousseau, Jean Jacques, 1712-1778
Routers (Tools)
Roux, Emile, 1853-1933
Rowing *[S] (May add geog subd)*
Royal, Darrell
Royal Ballet School (London, England)
Royal Ballet
Royal Canadian Mounted Police
Royal Doulton figurines
Royal Opera House (London, England)
Royalty
    USE Kings, queens, rulers, etc. *[AC only]*
Rubber *[S] (May add geog subd)*
Rubber stamp printing
    RT   Printing
Rubber tires
    USE Tires, Rubber
Rubbing *(May add geog subd)*
Rubens, Peter Paul, Sir, 1577-1640
Rudolph, Wilma, 1940-
Ruede, Howard, 1854-1925
Ruffian (Race horse)
Rugs *[S] (May add geog subd)*
Rugs, Braided
Rugs, Hooked *(May add geog subd)*
Rugs, Oriental *(May add geog subd)*
Ruisdael, Jacob van, 1628 or 9-1682
    UF   Van Ruisdael, Jacob, 1628?-1682
Rulers
    USE Kings, queens, rulers, etc. *[AC only]*
Rumpole, Horace (Fictitious character)
Runaway children
Runaways *[AC only]*
    UF   Runaway children [slaves, teenagers, etc.]
Runners (Sports)
Running *[S] (May add geog subd)*
    UF   Jogging *[AC only]*
    BT   Track and field *[AC only]*
Running backs (Football)
Running races *(May add geog subd)*
    BT   Racing
Runyon, Damon, 1880-1946
Rupert, Prince, Count Palatine, 1619-1682
Rural families
Rural poor
Rural schools *[S] (May add geog subd)*
Rural-urban migration *(May add geog subd)*

Rushdie, Salman
Rush-work *(May add geog subd)*
 BT Handicraft
Rusk, Thomas J. (Thomas Jefferson), 1803-1857
Russell, Bill, 1934-
Russell, Charles M. (Charles Marion), 1864-1926
Russell, Willy
Russia
 —History
  — —1533-1613
  — —House of Romanov, 1613-1917
  — —Peter I, 1689-1725
  — —Catherine II, 1762-1796
  — —Revolution of 1905
  — —1917-
  — —Revolution, 1917-1921
  — —1925-1953
  — —German occupation, 1941-1944
  — —1953-1985
Russian Americans
Russian drama *(May add geog subd)*
Russian empresses
 USE Kings, queens, rulers, etc. *[AC only]*
Russian Far East (Russia)
 UF Far East (Russia)
Russian fiction *(May add geog subd)*
Russian language *[S] (May add geog subd)*
 —Readers *[AC only]*
  Use for reading texts in Russian containing materials for instruction and practice in reading that language.
  RT Russian language materials *[AC only]*
Russian language materials *[AC only]*
 Use for works written in Russian intended primarily for general information or recreational reading. Such works with text also given in English are further subdivided by the subdivision —Bilingual.
  RT Russian language—Readers *[AC only]*
 —Bilingual *[AC only]*
Russian literature *[S] (May add geog subd)*
Russian music
Russian thistle
 USE Tumbleweeds *[AC only]*
Russians *[S]*
Russo, Leslie
Russwurm, John Brown, 1799-1851
Rutan, Richard
Ruth (Biblical character)
Ruth, Babe, 1895-1948
Rutherford, Ernest, 1871-1937
Rwanda
Ryan, Kerry
Ryan, Nolan, 1947-
Rylant, Cynthia
Ryun, Jim, 1947-
S.A.T.
 USE Scholastic Aptitude Test
Sabbatarians
Sabbath *[S]*
Saber-toothed tigers *[AC, S]*
 UF Smilodon
Sabin, Florence Rena, 1871-1953
Sabine Pass, Battle of, 1863
Sable automobile
Sabotage *[S] (May add geog subd)*
Sacagawea, 1786-1884
Sacco-Vanzetti case
 USE Sacco-Vanzetti Trial, Dedham, Mass., 1921

Sacramento Kings (Basketball team)
Sacred books *[S]*
 RT Bible
Sacred space *(May add geog subd)*
Sadat, Anwar, 1918-
Saddle Club (Series)
Sadness
Safaris *(May add geog subd)*
Safe sex in AIDS prevention *[S] (May add geog subd)*
 BT AIDS (Disease)—Prevention
Safety *[AC only]*
 UF Accidents—Prevention
   Safety education
 SA *the subdivision* —Safety measures
Safety appliances *[S] (May add geog subd)*
Safety education *[S] (May add geog subd)*
Safety regulations *(May add geog subd)*
Safro, Millicent, 1934-
Sagan, Carl, 1934-
Sager family
Sagittarius (Astrology) *(May add geog subd)*
 BT Astrology
Saguaro *(May add geog subd)*
 UF Giant cactus
Sahara
Sailboat racing *[S] (May add geog subd)*
Sailboats *(May add geog subd)*
Sailing *[S] (May add geog subd)*
Sailing, Single-handed *(May add geog subd)*
Sailing ships *(May add geog subd)*
Sailors *[S]*
 UF Seamen
 RT Seafaring life
Saint Bernard dog
Saint Catherine (Mount Sinai Monastery)
Saint-Exupery, Antoine de, 1900-1944
Saint Helens, Mount (Wash.)
 —Eruption, 1980
Saint Kilda (Scotland)
Saint Lawrence River
Saint Lawrence River Valley
Saint Lawrence Seaway
Saint Louis (Mo.)
Saint Louis Cardinals (Baseball team)
Saint Lucia
Saint Patrick's Day
Saint Paul Metropolitan Area (Minn.)
 UF Twin Cities Metropolitan Area (Minn.)
 RT Minneapolis Metropolitan Area (Minn.)
Saint Paul's School (Concord, N.H.)
Saint Petersburg (Russia)
 UF Leningrad (Russia)
Saint-Saens, Camille, 1835-1921
Saint-Saens, Camille, 1835-1921. Carnaval del animaux
 USE Saint-Saens, Camille, 1835-1921. Carnival of the animals *[AC only]*
Saint-Saens, Camille, 1835-1921. Carnival of the animals *[AC only]*
 UF Saint-Saens, Camille, 1835-1921. Carnaval del animaux
Saint-Simon, Louis de Rouvroy, Duc de, 1675-1755
Saint Thomas Harbor (V.I.)
Saint Valentine's Day
 USE Valentine's Day
Saints *[S]*
 UF Buddhist saints *[AC only]*
   Christian saints *[AC only]*

Saki, 1870-1916
Salads [S]
Salamanca, Battle of, 1812
Salamanders [S] (May add geog subd)
Salamanders as pets
Salem (Mass.)
—History
— —Colonial period, ca. 1600-1775
Salerno, Battle of, 1943
Salerno-Sonnenberg, Nadja
Sales management [S] (May add geog subd)
Sales personnel [S]
    RT   Selling
Sales presentations (May add geog subd)
Salieri, Antonio, 1750-1825
Salinas River (Calif.)
Saline water conversion (May add geog subd)
    RT   Water supply
Salinger, J.D. (Jerome David), 1919-
Salinger, Pierre
Salk, Jonas, 1914-
Salm, Herbert
Salmon [S] (May add geog subd)
Salmon fishing
    UF   Atlantic salmon fishing
          Pacific salmon fishing
          Salmon fisheries [AC only]
    BT   Fishing
Salomon, Haym, 1740-1785
Salsa (May add geog subd)
Salt (May add geog subd)
Salt-free diet (May add geog subd)
    BT   Diet
Salt marshes (May add geog subd)
    UF   Tide marshes
Salter, Charlie (Fictitious character)
Salvadorans
Salvage (Waste, etc.)
    USE   Recycling (Waste) [AC only]
Salvant, J. U. (Joan Usner), 1932-
Salvation Army (May add geog subd)
Salvationists
Salzman, Mark
Sami (European people)
    UF   Lapps
Samoan Islands
Samplers [S] (May add geog subd)
Samurai
San (African people)
—Folklore
    USE   Folklore, San [AC only]
San Antonio (Tex.)
San Antonio Spurs (Basketball team)
San Carlos Indian Reservation (Ariz.)
San Diego (Calif.)
San Diego Chargers (Football team)
San Diego Padres (Baseball team)
San Diego Zoo (Calif.)
San Felipe (Tex.)
San Francisco (Calif.)
San Francisco Bay Area (Calif.)
San Francisco 49ers (Football team)
San Francisco Giants (Baseball team)
San Jacinto, Battle of, 1836

San Jose Earthquakes (Soccer team)
San Juan Hill, Battle of, 1898
San Nicolas Island (Calif.)
San Pasqual, Battle of, 1846
Sand (May add geog subd)
Sand, George, 1804-1876
Sand casting
    BT   Handicraft
    RT   Sand sculpture
Sand Creek Massacre, Colo., 1864
Sand dune animals
    UF   Sand dune fauna
Sand dune fauna
    USE   Sand dune animals [AC only]
Sand dunes [S] (May add geog subd)
Sand sculpture
    RT   Sand casting
Sand tiger shark [S]
    BT   Sharks
Sandburg, Carl, 1878-1967
Sanders, Barry, 1968-
Sandhill crane (May add geog subd)
Sandman [AC only]
    UF   Sandmen
Sandwiches [S]
Sanger, Margaret, 1879-1966
Sanitation [S]
    NT   Cleanliness [AC only]
Santa Anna, Antonio Lopez de, 1794?-1876
Santa Claus [S]
Santa Fe Trail
Santee Indians
Santos-Dumont, Alberto, 1873-1932
Sapelo Island (Ga.)
Saratoga Campaign, 1777
Sargasso Sea
Sargent, John Singer, 1856-1925
Sarto, Andrea del, 1486-1531
Sarton, May
Sartre, Jean Paul, 1905-
Sasaki, Sadako, 1943-1955
Sasquatch [S]
SAT
    USE   Scholastic Aptitude Test
Satanism (May add geog subd)
Satellites
Satire [S]
    RT   Literature
          Parody
          Wit and humor [AC, S]
Satire, French (May add geog subd)
Saturn (Planet) [S]
Saturn probes
Saudi Arabia
Sauk Indians
Saunders, Cicely M., Dame
Savage, Augusta
Savanna ecology (May add geog subd)
Saving and investment (May add geog subd)
    RT   Investments
Saving and thrift [S] (May add geog subd)
    RT   Investments
Savings and loan associations [S] (May add geog subd)
Savitch, Jessica
Sawyer, Diane, 1945-

Saxophone *[S]*
Sayers, Gale, 1943-
Sayings
    USE   Aphorisms and apothegms
             Proverbs
Scalds
    USE   Burns and scalds
Scandinavia
Scandinavian Americans
Scarecrows *[S] (May add geog subd)*
Scarfo, Nicodemo Domenic, 1929-
Scarlatina *[S] (May add geog subd)*
    UF   Scarlet fever
Scarlet fever
    USE   Scarlatina
Scavengers (Zoology) *(May add geog subd)*
Scene painting *[S] (May add geog subd)*
    RT   Theaters—Stage setting and scenery
Schally, Andrew V.
Schedules, School *(May add geog subd)*
    UF   School schedules
Scheffer, Victor B.
Schenk von Stauffenberg, Klaus Philipp, graf, 1907-1944
Schiwetz, Edward Muegge, 1898-
Schizophrenia *[S] (May add geog subd)*
Schizophrenics
Schliemann, Heinrich, 1822-1890
Schliemann, Sophie Kastromenos
Schloss Colditz (Colditz, Germany)
Schmidt, Mike, 1949-
Scholars
Scholarship
    USE   Learning and scholarship
    RT   Education
Scholarships *[S] (May add geog subd)*
Scholastic Aptitude Test
    BT   Examinations
    RT   Universities and colleges—Admission
Scholl family
School and home
    USE   Home and school
School administrators
School attendance *[S] (May add geog subd)*
School buses
School choice
School discipline *[S] (May add geog subd)*
    RT   Discipline
             Self-control
School districts *(May add geog subd)*
School excursions
    USE   School field trips
School field trips
    UF   Field trips
             School excursions
School improvement programs *(May add geog subd)*
School integration *[S] (May add geog subd)*
    RT   Segregation in education
             Busing for school integration
School libraries *[S] (May add geog subd)*
  —Acquisitions
  —Activity programs
  —Administration
  —Book lists
  —Book selection
School management and organization *(May add geog subd)*

School media programs
    USE   Media programs (Education)
School newspapers
    USE   Student newspapers and periodicals
School of American Ballet
School schedules
    USE   Schedules, School
School sports *[S] (May add geog subd)*
School stories
    USE   Schools—Fiction *[AC only]*
School supervision *[S] (May add geog subd)*
School violence *[S] (May add geog subd)*
    BT   Violence
Schools *[S] (May add geog subd)*
    RT   Volunteer workers in education
    NT   Outward bound schools
             Public schools
             Summer schools
  —Exercises and recreations
  —Fiction
      UF   School stories *[AC only]*
Schrodinger, Erwin, 1887-1961
Schubert, Franz, 1797-1828
Schulz, Charles M.
Schulz, Charles M.   Peanuts
Schumann, Clara, 1819-1896
Schumann, Robert, 1810-1856
Schwartzkopf, H. Norman, 1934-
Schweitzer, Albert, 1875-1965
Science *[S] (May add geog subd)*
    RT   Art and science
             Bible and science
    SA   *the subdivision* —Scientific applications
Science, Ancient
    UF   Ancient science
Science and civilization *[S]*
    RT   Civilization and science
Science and the humanities *[S] (May add geog subd)*
    RT   Bible and science
             Humanities
Science and religion
    USE   Religion and science
Science fiction *[S]*
Science fiction, English *(May add geog subd)*
Science fiction, French *(May add geog subd)*
Science fiction films *(May add geog subd)*
Science fiction television programs
Science news *(May add geog subd)*
Science projects *(May add geog subd)*
    SA   *specific types of projects, e.g.,* Physics projects
Scientific apparatus and instruments *[S] (May add geog subd)*
    UF   Scientific equipment
Scientific equipment
    USE   Scientific apparatus and instruments
Scientific expeditions *[S] (May add geog subd)*
    UF   Expeditions
Scientific recreations *[S]*
Scientists *[S]*
    NT   Women scientists
Scientology
    RT   Dianetics
Scissors bill
    USE   Black skimmer
Scoliosis *[S] (May add geog subd)*
Scopes, John Thomas

Scorpio (Astrology) *(May add geog subd)*
    BT Astrology
Scorpions *[S] (May add geog subd)*
Scotland
    —History
    — —To 1057
    — —1057-1603
Scots language *(May add geog subd)*
Scott, Peter Markham, Sir, 1909-
Scott, Robert Falcon, 1868-1912
Scott, Walter, Sir, 1771-1832
Scottish Americans
Scottish poetry *(May add geog subd)*
Scouting
    USE Scouts and scouting
Scouts and scouting *[S]*
    NT Boy Scouts
           Cub Scouts
           Girl Scouts
Scrap, Plastic
    USE Plastic scrap
Scrap metals *(May add geog subd)*
Screech owls *[S]*
Screen process printing
    BT Printing
Screenwriters
Scribes, Jewish
    UF Jewish scribes
Scrooge (Cartoon character)
    USE McDuck, Scrooge (Fictitious character) *[AC only]*
Scrooge (Fictitious character)
    USE McDuck, Scrooge (Fictitious character) *[AC only]*
Scrooge McDuck (Fictitious character)
    USE McDuck, Scrooge (Fictitious character) *[AC only]*
Scuba diving *[S] (May add geog subd)*
Sculley, John
Sculptors *[S]*
Sculpture *[S] (May add geog subd)*
    NT Public sculpture
    SA *the subdivision* —Sculpture
Sculpture, African, [American, etc.] *(May add geog subd)*
Sculpture, Modern *[S] (May add geog subd)*
    —20th century *(May add geog subd)*
Sculpture, Renaissance *(May add geog subd)*
Scylla and Charybdis (Greek mythology)
Scythians
    BT Iranians
Sea
    USE Ocean
    —Fiction
        USE Sea stories
Sea birds *(May add geog subd)*
    NT Bermuda petrels
           Cormorants
Sea farming
    USE Aquaculture
Sea horses *[S] (May add geog subd)*
Sea level *(May add geog subd)*
Sea life
Sea lions *[S]*
Sea monsters *(May add geog subd)*
Sea otter *[S] (May add geog subd)*
Sea poetry *[S]*
    BT Poetry
Sea-power *(May add geog subd)*

Sea shells
    USE Shells
Sea slugs *[AC only]*
    UF Nudibranchia
Sea songs *[S] (May add geog subd)*
Sea stories *[S]*
    UF Sea—Fiction
Sea turtles *[S] (May add geog subd)*
Sea-water
    USE Seawater
Seabiscuit (Race horse)
Seafaring life *[S] (May add geog subd)*
    RT Sailors
Seager, Stephen B.
Sealab
    USE Project Sealab
Sealing *(May add geog subd)*
Seals (Animals) *[S] (May add geog subd)*
    NT Northern elephant seals
Seals (Numismatics) *[S] (May add geog subd)*
Seamanship
    RT Navigation
Seamen
    USE Sailors
Search and rescue operations
    USE Rescue work *[AC only]*
Search dogs *(May add geog subd)*
    BT Dogs
Searches and seizures *(May add geog subd)*
    UF Seizures
Seashore *[S]*
Seashore biology *(May add geog subd)*
    BT Biology
Seashore ecology *(May add geog subd)*
    BT Ecology
Seashore fauna *(May add geog subd)*
Seasonal labor *(May add geog subd)*
Seasons *[S] (May add geog subd)*
    SA *the names of the seasons*
Seattle, Chief, 1790-1866
Seattle (Wash.)
Seattle Mariners (Baseball team)
Seattle Seahawks (Football team)
Seattle Supersonics (Basketball team)
Seaver, Tom, 1944-
Seawater
    UF Sea-water
Secondary education
    USE Education, Secondary
Secondhand trade *[S] (May add geog subd)*
    RT Selling
Secrecy
Secret service *(May add geog subd)*
    SA *the subdivision* —Secret service
Secret societies *[S] (May add geog subd)*
Secretariat (Race horse)
Secretaries
    UF Private secretaries *[AC only]*
Secrets *[AC only]*
    UF Children's, [Military, Trade, etc.] secrets
Sects *[S] (May add geog subd)*
    UF Christian sects *[AC only]*
    RT Cults
           Religions
    SA *the names of specific religious sects, e.g.,* Shakers
Secularism *[S] (May add geog subd)*

Securities *[S] (May add geog subd)*
    RT   Investments
Securities fraud *(May add geog subd)*
Securities industry *(May add geog subd)*
Security
    USE   Internal security
            Social security
    SA   *the subdivision* —Security measures
Security systems *(May add geog subd)*
Seder
    BT   Passover
Seeds *[S] (May add geog subd)*
Seeing
    USE   Vision
Seeing Eye, Inc. (Morristown, N.J.)
Segovia, Andres, 1893-
Segregation *[S] (May add geog subd)*
    RT   Apartheid
            Race discrimination
Segregation in education *[S] (May add geog subd)*
    RT   School integration
Seguin, Juan Nepomuceno, 1806-1890
Seidick, Michael, 1969-
Seine River (France)
Seine River Valley (France)
Seismology *(May add geog subd)*
Seizures
    USE   Searches and seizures
Selectivity (Psychology)
Self *[S]*
    RT   Identity (Psychology)
            Individuality
Self-acceptance
Self-actualization (Psychology)
    UF   Personal development
            Personal improvement
    RT   Success
Self-care, Health *(May add geog subd)*
Self-confidence *[S]*
Self-consciousness *[S]*
Self-control *[S]*
    UF   Self-discipline
    BT   Decision making
            Discipline
Self-culture *[S]*
Self-defeating behavior *(May add geog subd)*
Self-defense *[S]*
Self-defense for women *[S]*
Self-employed *[S]*
Self-esteem
    UF   Self-respect
Self-evaluation *(May add geog subd)*
Self-examination, Medical
Self-help devices for the disabled *(May add geog subd)*
Self-improvement
    USE   Self-actualization (Psychology)
Self-perception *[S] (May add geog subd)*
Self-pity
    USE   Sadness
Self-portraits *(May add geog subd)*
Self-realization *[S]*
Self-reliance *[S]*
Self-respect
    USE   Self-esteem
Selfishness *[AC only]*
    UF   Egoism

Self-interest
    BT   Conduct of life
Selkirk, Alexander, 1676-1721
Sellers, Peter, 1925-
Selling *[S]*
    RT   Retail trade
            Sales personnel
            Secondhand trade
            Wholesale trade
    NT   Booksellers and bookselling
Selma (Ala.)
Selma-Montgomery Rights March, 1965
Selmon, Lee Roy, 1954-
Selous Game Reserve (Tanzania)
Semantics *[S] (May add geog subd)*
Semantics (Philosophy)
Seminole Indians
Seminole War, 1st, 1817-1818
Seminole War, 2nd, 1835-1842
Semiotics *[S] (May add geog subd)*
Senate
    USE   Legislators
            United States. Congress. Senate
Senators
    USE   Legislators
            United States. Congress. Senate
Sendak, Maurice
Sender, Ruth Minsky
Seneca Indians
Senegal
Senesh, Hannah, 1921-1944
Sense organs
Senses and sensation *[S]*
Sensitive plants
    USE   Mimosas *[AC only]*
Sentimentalism in literature
Senufo (African people)
Separation (Psychology)
Separation anxiety *[AC only]*
    UF   Separation anxiety in children
Separation anxiety in children
    USE   Separation anxiety *[AC only]*
Sequels (Literature)
Sequist, David B.
Sequoia National Park (Calif.)
Sequoyah, 1770?-1843
Serendipity in science *(May add geog subd)*
Serengeti National Park (Tanzania)
Serengeti Plain (Tanzania)
Serging *(May add geog subd)*
    BT   Machine sewing
Serial murders *(May add geog subd)*
Series (Publications)
Sermon on the mount *[S]*
Serpents
    USE   Snakes *[AC only]*
Serpico, Frank
Serra, Junipero, 1713-1784
Servants
    USE   Household employees
Service dogs *(May add geog subd)*
Service industries *[S] (May add geog subd)*
Service stations *(May add geog subd)*
    UF   Automobiles—Service stations
Set theory *[S]*
Seton, Elizabeth Ann, Saint, 1774-1821

Setting (Literature)
Seurat, Georges, 1859-1891
Seuss, Dr.
Sevareid, Eric, 1912-
Sevela, Efraim
Seven (The number)
Seven Wonders of the World
Sevengill (Shark)
Seventeenth century *[S]*
    SA the subdivisions —17th century *and* —History—17th
        century
Seventh-Day Adventists *(May add geog subd)*
Severe storms *(May add geog subd)*
Sevres porcelain
Sewage
Seward, William Henry, 1801-1872
Seward Park High School
Sewing *[S]* *(May add geog subd)*
Sewing machines
Sex
    SA the subdivision —Sexual behavior
Sex (Biology) *[S]*
    NT Plants, Sex in
Sex (Psychology)
Sex addiction *(May add geog subd)*
Sex crimes *[S]* *(May add geog subd)*
    UF Sexual abuse
    RT Teenage sex offenders
Sex customs *(May add geog subd)*
    SA the subdivision —Sexual behavior
Sex differences (Psychology) *[S]*
Sex discrimination *[S]* *(May add geog subd)*
    BT Discrimination
        Sexism
Sex discrimination against women *(May add geog subd)*
Sex discrimination in employment *(May add geog subd)*
Sex in literature
Sex in mass media *(May add geog subd)*
Sex instruction *(May add geog subd)*
Sex instruction for girls *(May add geog subd)*
Sex instruction for teenagers *(May add geog subd)*
Sex instruction for youth *(May add geog subd)*
Sex offenders
    USE Sex crimes
Sex preselection
Sex role *[S]* *(May add geog subd)*
    UF Gender role
        Subordination of women
Sex role in literature
Sexism *[S]* *(May add geog subd)*
    RT Sex discrimination
Sexism in language *(May add geog subd)*
Sexton, Anne
Sexual abuse
    USE Sex crimes
Sexual deviance
    USE Sexual deviation
Sexual deviation *[S]* *(May add geog subd)*
    UF Sexual deviance
Sexual education
    USE Sex instruction
Sexual ethics *[S]* *(May add geog subd)*
Sexual harassment *[S]* *(May add geog subd)*
Sexual harassment of women *(May add geog subd)*
Sexual selection in animals
Sexually abused children

Sexually transmitted diseases *[S]* *(May add geog subd)*
    UF STDs
        Venereal diseases
    SA the names of specific sexually transmitted diseases
Shackleton, Ernest Henry, Sir, 1874-1922
Shades and shadows
    USE Shadows *[AC only]*
Shadow (Fictitious character)
Shadow pantomimes and plays
    USE Shadow shows
Shadow pictures *[AC, S]*
    UF Shadow-pictures
Shadow shows *(May add geog subd)*
    UF Shadow pantomimes and plays
Shadows *[AC only]*
    UF Shades and shadows
Shahs
    USE Kings, queens, rulers, etc.
Shaker furniture *(May add geog subd)*
Shakers *[S]*
    BT Sects
Shakespeare, William, 1564-1616 *[S]*
Shakespeare, William, 1564-1616. As you like it
Shakespeare, William, 1564-1616. Hamlet
Shakespeare, William, 1564-1616. Henry V
Shakespeare, William, 1564-1616. Julius Caesar
Shakespeare, William, 1564-1616. King Lear
Shakespeare, William, 1564-1616. Macbeth
Shakespeare, William, 1564-1616. Merchant of Venice
**Shakespeare, William, 1564-1616. Midsummer night's
dream**
Shakespeare, William, 1564-1616. Much ado about nothing
Shakespeare, William, 1564-1616. Romeo and Juliet
Shakespeare, William, 1564-1616. Midsummer night's dream
Shale *(May add geog subd)*
    BT Rocks
Shanghai (China)
Shannon River (Ireland)
Shape *[AC only]*
    UF Size and shape
Shapiro, Paul D.
Sharansky, Natan
Shareware (Computer software)
Sharing
Shark attacks *(May add geog subd)*
Sharks *[S]* *(May add geog subd)*
    NT Mako sharks
        Nurse sharks
        Sand tiger shark
Sharks in art
Sharpshooters *[AC only]*
    UF Shooters (of arms)
        Shooters of firearms
Shaving mugs *(May add geog subd)*
Shaw, Bernard, 1856-1950
Shaw, Nate
Shawnee Indians
Shays' Rebellion, 1786-1787
Sheep *[S]* *(May add geog subd)*
    RT Shepherds
Sheep dogs *(May add geog subd)*
Sheep herders
    USE Shepherds
Sheep ranches *(May add geog subd)*
Sheep shearing *(May add geog subd)*

Sheffield plate *[S]*
    BT   Plate
Shellcraft *(May add geog subd)*
Shelley, Harriet Westbrook, d. 1816
Shelley, Kate
Shelley, Mary Wollstonecraft, 1797-1851
Shelley, Mary Wollstonecraft, 1797-1851.   **Frankenstein**
Shelley, Percy Bysshe, 1792-1822
Shells *[S]* *(May add geog subd)*
    —Collection and preservation *[AC only]*
        UF   Sea shells
              Seashell collecting
              Shell collecting
Shenandoah National Park (Va.)
Shenandoah Valley Campaign, 1861
Shenandoah Valley Campaign, 1862
Shenandoah Valley Campaign, 1864 (May-August)
Shepard, Alan B. (Alan Bartlett), 1923-
Shepherds
    UF   Sheep herders
    RT   Sheep ranches
Sheppard Air Force Base (Tex.)
Sheridan, Philip Henry, 1831-1888
Sheridan, Richard Brinsley, 1751-1816
Sheriffs
Sherman, William T. (William Tecumseh), 1820-1891
Sherman's March through the Carolinas
Sherman's March to the Sea
Sherwood family
Shetland (Scotland)
Shetland sheepdog
Shiatsu
    USE   Acupressure
Shiloh, Battle of, 1862
Shingles (Disease)
    USE   Herpes zoster
Shinto *[S]* *(May add geog subd)*
    BT   Religions
Ship models
Ship models in bottles *(May add geog subd)*
Shipbuilding *[S]* *(May add geog subd)*
    RT   Ships
Shipbuilding industry *(May add geog subd)*
Shipler, David K., 1942-
Shipping *[S]* *(May add geog subd)*
Ships *[S]* *(May add geog subd)*
    RT   Shipbuilding
    SA   *specific types and uses of ships*
Ships in art *[S]*
Shipwrecks *[S]* *(May add geog subd)*
    RT   Accidents
              Disasters
Shirley, Dame, 1819-1906
Shivers, Allan, 1907-
Shoe industry *[S]* *(May add geog subd)*
Shoes *[S]* *(May add geog subd)*
    NT   Boots
Shoemaker, Willie
Shoji screens
Shona Island (Scotland)
Shooters (of arms)
    USE   Sharpshooters *[AC only]*
Shooters of firearms
    USE   Sharpshooters *[AC only]*
Shooting *[S]* *(May add geog subd)*
    RT   Violence

Shoplifting *(May add geog subd)*
Shopping *[S]* *(May add geog subd)*
Shopping centers *(May add geog subd)*
Shore birds *(May add geog subd)*
    NT   Plovers
Shore protection *(May add geog subd)*
    SA   *the subdivision* —Shorelines
Shore, Jane, d. 1527?
Shorelines *(May add geog subd)*
Short stories *[S]*
    UF   Short stories, American
    —Afro-American authors
    —Mexican American authors
    —Minority authors
    —Women authors
Short stories, Chinese, [English, Latin American, etc.]
    (May add geog subd)
Short story *[S]*
    BT   Literary form
              Literature
Shorter, Frank, 1947-
Shorthand *[S]*
Shoshoni Indians
Shotguns *[S]* *(May add geog subd)*
    BT   Weapons
Showers (Parties) *[S]*
Shreve, Henry Miller, 1785-1851
Shrews *[S]*
Shrimps *(May add geog subd)*
Shrubs *[S]* *(May add geog subd)*
Shuptrine, Hubert, 1936-
Shylock (Fictitious character)
Siamese fighting fish
Siberia (Russia)
Siberian huskies *[S]* *(May add geog subd)*
Sibling rivalry
    RT   Brothers and sisters
Siblings
    USE   Brothers and sisters
Sicily (Italy)
Sick *[S]*
Sick building syndrome *(May add geog subd)*
Sickles, Daniel Edgar, 1825-1914
Sidransky, Ruth
Siegal, Aranka
Siegel, Jessica
Siegfried (Legendary character)
Siena (Italy)
Sierra Leone
Sierra Madre (Mexico)
Sierra Nevada Mountains (Calif. and Nev.)
Sign language *[S]*
    SA   *the subdivision* —Sign language
Signboards
    USE   Signs and signboards
Signals and signaling *[S]*
    NT   Traffic signs and signals
Signs and signboards *[S]* *(May add geog subd)*
    UF   Signboards
Signs and symbols *[S]* *(May add geog subd)*
    UF   Symbols
    RT   Signals and signaling
Sikhism *(May add geog subd)*
Sikhs
Siksika Indians

Silent films *[S] (May add geog subd)*
Silent myocardial ischemia *(May add geog subd)*
    BT   Coronary heart disease
Silhouettes *(May add geog subd)*
Silesia, Upper (Poland and Czech Republic)
Silk *[S] (May add geog subd)*
Silk-cotton tree
Silk flowers
Silk painting *(May add geog subd)*
    USE   Kapok
Silkwood, Bill
Silkwood, Karen, 1946-1974
Silkworms *[S] (May add geog subd)*
Sills, Beverly
Silver *[S] (May add geog subd)*
Silver coins *(May add geog subd)*
Silver flatware *(May add geog subd)*
Silver jewelry *(May add geog subd)*
Silver mines and mining *[S] (May add geog subd)*
    BT   Mines and mineral resources
Silverman, Fred
Silversmiths
Silverware *[S] (May add geog subd)*
Silverwork *[S] (May add geog subd)*
    BT   Metalwork
Simenon, Georges, 1903-
Simile
Simmons, Jake, 1901-1981
Simms, Phil
Simon, Carly
Simon, Neil
Simon, Paul
Simon, Ted, 1931-
Simple machines
Simpson, Louis Aston Marantz, 1923-
Simpson, O.J., 1947-
Simulation games in education *[S]*
Simulation methods
Sin *[S]*
Sinclair, Upton Beall, 1878-1968
Singapore
Singer, Isaac Bashevis, 1904-
Singers *[S]*
Singing *[S]*
Singing games *[S] (May add geog subd)*
    BT   Games
Single fathers
Single mothers
Single-parent family *[S] (May add geog subd)*
    BT   Family
Single parents
Single people *[S]*
Siphons
Sirenia
Sirens (Mythology)
Siri (Elephant)
Siringo, Charles A., 1855-1928
Sirius *[S]*
    BT   Stars
Sisters
    RT   Brothers
          Brothers and sisters *[AC only]*
Sitting Bull, 1834?-1890
Sitting position
Sitwell, Edith, Dame, 1887-1964

Sitwell, Osbert, 1892-1969
Sitwell, Sacheverell, 1897-
Six Flags Great Adventure Safari Park (N.J.)
Sixteenth century *[S]*
    SA   *the subdivisions* —16th century *and* —History—16th century
Size *[AC only]*
    UF   Size and shape
Size and shape
    USE   Shape *[AC only]*
          Size *[AC only]*
Size judgment
Size perception
Skateboarding *[S] (May add geog subd)*
Skateboards *(May add geog subd)*
Skaters
    USE   Ice skaters *[AC only]*
          Roller skaters *[AC only]*
Skating
    USE   Ice skating *[AC only]*
          Roller skating *[AC only]*
          Speed skating
Skeleton *[S]*
Ski acrobatics
    BT   Skis and skiing
Skiers
Skiing
    USE   Skis and skiing
Skin *[S]*
—Cancer *(May add geog subd)*
Skin diving *[S] (May add geog subd)*
Skinner, Burrhus Frederic, 1904-
Skinner, Cornelia Otis, 1901-
Skinner, Maud Durbin, d. 1936
Skinner, Otis, 1858-1942
Skis and skiing *[S] (May add geog subd)*
    RT   Ski acrobatics
    SA   *specific types of skis and forms of skiing, e.g.,* Water skiing
Skunks *[S]*
Sky
Sky divers
    USE   Skydivers
Sky diving
    USE   Skydiving
Skydivers
    UF   Sky divers
Skydiving *[S] (May add geog subd)*
    UF   Sky diving
Skye, Island of (Scotland)
Skylab Program
Skylights
Skyscrapers *[S] (May add geog subd)*
Slander
Slate sculpture *(May add geog subd)*
Slater, Joy
Slater, Samuel, 1768-1835
Slave trade *[AC only]*
    UF   Slave-trade
Slave traders
Slavery *[S] (May add geog subd)*
    RT   Labor
          Underground railroad
    —Anti-slavery movements
        USE   *the heading:* Antislavery movements
Slavery and the church *(May add geog subd)*

Slaves *(May add geog subd)*
  —Emancipation *(May add geog subd)*
    UF   Emancipation of slaves
Slaves' writings
Slavic Americans
Slavs
  —Folklore *[AC, S]*
    UF   Folklore, Slavic
Sled dog racing *[S] (May add geog subd)*
Sled dogs *(May add geog subd)*
  BT   Dogs
Sleds *[AC only]*
  UF   Sleighs and sledges
Sleep *[S]*
  RT   Bedtime *[AC only]*
        Insomnia
        Sandman *[AC only]*
Sleep behavior in animals
  USE   Animals—Sleep behavior *[AC only]*
Sleep disorders
Sleeping Beauty (Choreographic work)
Sleeping customs *(May add geog subd)*
Sleepwear *(May add geog subd)*
Sleighs and sledges
  USE   Sleds *[AC only]*
Slessor, Mary Mitchell, 1848-1915
Slide rule *[AC, S]*
  UF   Slide-rule
Slides (Photography) *[S]*
Sloane, Eric
Slogans
Sloths
Slovak Americans
Slovaks
Slow learning children *[S]*
  RT   Learning disabilities
        Learning disabled children
Slugs (Mollusks) *[S] (May add geog subd)*
Slugs (Mollusks) as pets *(May add geog subd)*
Small animal culture *(May add geog subd)*
Small business *[S] (May add geog subd)*
Small churches *(May add geog subd)*
Small claims courts *(May add geog subd)*
Smallpox *[S] (May add geog subd)*
Smell *[S]*
Smile
Smilodon
  USE   Saber-toothed tiger *[AC only]*
Smith, Abigail Adams, 1765-1813
Smith, Erastus, 1787-1837
Smith, Jedediah Strong, 1799-1831
Smith, Jessie Wilcox, 1863-1935
Smith, Jill (Fictitious character)
Smith, John, 1580-1631
Smith, Joseph, 1805-1844
Smith, Peter, 1928-
Smith, Samantha
Smith, Theobald, 1859-1934
Smith, Xenia (Fictitious character)
Smith Island (Md. And Va.)
Smithsonian Institution Building (Washington, D.C.)
Smocking
  BT   Needlework
Smoke *(May add geog subd)*
Smokeless tobacco *(May add geog subd)*

Smoking *[S] (May add geog subd)*
  RT   Nicotine
        Tobacco habit
Smoking cessation programs *[S] (May add geog subd)*
Smuggling *[S] (May add geog subd)*
Snack foods *(May add geog subd)*
Snails *[S] (May add geog subd)*
Snails as pets
Snake culture *(May add geog subd)*
Snake River (Wyo.-Wash.)
Snakes *[AC, S] (May add geog subd)*
  UF   Serpents
  NT   Pit vipers
        Rat snakes
Snakes, Poisonous
  USE   Poisonous snakes
Snakes as pets
Sneakers
Snell, Tony, 1922-
Sniffing
  USE   Aerosol sniffing
Snidow, Gordon, 1936-
Snoopy (Fictitious character)
Snoring *(May add geog subd)*
Snow *[AC, S] (May add geog subd)*
  NT   Snowmen *[AC only]*
Snow, Clyde C.
Snow and ice climbing *(May add geog subd)*
  BT   Mountaineering
Snow goose *(May add geog subd)*
Snow leopard *(May add geog subd)*
Snowboarding
Snowmen *[AC only]*
  BT   Snow
Snowmobile racing *[S] (May add geog subd)*
Snowmobiles *[S] (May add geog subd)*
Snowshoes and snowshoeing *(May add geog subd)*
Soap *[S]*
Soap operas *[S] (May add geog subd)*
Soap box derbies
Soap bubbles *(May add geog subd)*
Soap sculpture
Soaring
  USE   Gliding and soaring *[AC only]*
Sobell, Morton
Sobibor (Poland : Concentration camp)
Sobol, Donald J., 1924-
Soccer *[S] (May add geog subd)*
Soccer players
Social action *(May add geog subd)*
Social adjustment *[S]*
Social behavior
  USE   Interpersonal relations
Social behavior in animals
Social change *[S]*
  RT   Social evolution
Social classes *[S] (May add geog subd)*
Social conflict *[S] (May add geog subd)*
Social customs
  USE   Manners and customs
Social environment
  USE   Life style
Social ethics *[S]*
Social evolution
  RT   Social change
Social groups *[S]*

Social history
    SA the subdivision —Social life and customs
—**Modern, 1500-**
—**1945-**
—**1945-1960**
Social indicators *(May add geog subd)*
    SA the subdivision —Social conditions
Social institutions *(May add geog subd)*
Social interaction *(May add geog subd)*
    SA the subdivision —Social life and customs
Social justice
Social medicine *[S] (May add geog subd)*
Social movements *[S] (May add geog subd)*
    SA the names of specific movements
Social networks *(May add geog subd)*
Social prediction
Social pressure
Social problems *[S]*
    SA the subdivision —Social conditions
Social problems in literature
Social reformers
    USE Reformers *[AC only]*
Social psychology *[S] (May add geog subd)*
Social responsibility of business *(May add geog subd)*
Social sciences *[S] (May add geog subd)*
    UF Social studies
    SA the subdivision —Social aspects
Social security *[S] (May add geog subd)*
Social service *(May add geog subd)*
Social skills *(May add geog subd)*
Social structure *(May add geog subd)*
Social studies
    USE Social sciences
Social values *[S]*
Social workers
Socialism *[S] (May add geog subd)*
    RT Communism
Socialization *[S]*
Socially handicapped *[S]*
Society, Primitive
Society and architecture
    USE Architecture and society
Society and art
    USE Art and society
Society and literature
    USE Literature and society
Society of Friends *[S] (May add geog subd)*
    RT Quakers
Society of Separatists of Zoar
Sociobiology *[S]*
Socioeconomics
    USE Economics—Sociological aspects
Sociology *[S] (May add geog subd)*
    NT Political sociology
Sociology, Military *(May add geog subd)*
Sociology, Urban *[S] (May add geog subd)*
    UF Urban sociology
Socrates
Sod houses *(May add geog subd)*
Soft drink industry *(May add geog subd)*
Soft sculpture *(May add geog subd)*
Soft toy making
Soft toys *(May add geog subd)*
Softball *[S]*
Software, Computer

    USE Computer software
Software, Integrated
    USE Integrated software
Soil animals *(May add geog subd)*
    UF Soil fauna
Soil biology *(May add geog subd)*
Soil conservation *[S] (May add geog subd)*
Soil ecology *(May add geog subd)*
Soil erosion *[S] (May add geog subd)*
Soil fauna
    USE Soil animals *[AC only]*
Soiling *[AC only]*
    UF Encopresis in children
    RT Fecal incontinence
Soils *[S] (May add geog subd)*
Solar eclipses *[S]*
    UF Eclipses, Solar
Solar energy *(May add geog subd)*
—**Passive systems**
Solar heating *[S] (May add geog subd)*
Solar houses *(May add geog subd)*
Solar radiation *[S] (May add geog subd)*
Solar system *[S]*
Soldiers *[S]*
    UF Military personnel
    NT Women soldiers
Soldiers in art
Soldiers' monuments *(May add geog subd)*
Solferino, Battle of, 1859
Solidarity (Polish Labor Organization) *[AC only]*
    UF NSZZ "Solidarnosc" (Labor organization)
    BT Labor unions—Poland
Solids *[S]*
Solitude
Solomon Islands
Solomon R. Guggenheim Foundation
Solvent abuse *[S] (May add geog subd)*
    NT Aerosol sniffing
Somatoform disorders
Somers, Suzanne, 1946-
Somme, 1st Battle of the, France, 1916
Somoza, Anatasio, 1925-1980
Sondheim, Stephen
Songbirds *(May add geog subd)*
    NT Corvidae
            Passerines *[AC only]*
Song-books
    USE Songs *[AC only]*
Songs *[S] (May add geog subd)*
    UF Song-books *[AC only]*
            Songs, American *[AC only]*
    SA the subdivision —Songs and music
Songs, French, [German, Hebrew, etc.] *(May add geog subd)*
Songs, Patriotic
    USE Patriotic music
Songs with piano
Sonnets
Sonnets, English *(May add geog subd)*
Sonoran Desert
Sons
    USE Fathers and sons
            Mothers and sons
Sons of the American Revolution
Sopranos (Singers)
Sorbian Americans

Sororities
    USE   Greek letter societies
Soto, Hernando de, ca. 1500-1542
    USE   De Soto, Hernando, ca. 1500-1542 *[AC only]*
Soul music *(May add geog subd)*
Soul musicians
Sound *[S] (May add geog subd)*
    UF   Sounds *[AC only]*
    RT   Phonetics
    —Recording and reproducing
Sound effects
    USE   Sound *[AC only]*
Sound engineering
    USE   Acoustical engineering
Sound production by animals
    USE   Animal sounds *[AC only]*
Sound production by insects
    USE   Animal sounds *[AC only]*
Sound recording executives
Sound recording industry *(May add geog subd)*
Sound recordings *[S]*
    —Album covers
Sound-waves *[S]*
Sounds
    USE   Sound *[AC only]*
Soups *[S] (May add geog subd)*
Sousa, John Philip, 1854-1932
South Africa
South African War, 1899-1902
South Africans
South America
South Carolina
    —History
    — —To 1775
South Dakota
South Pacific Ocean
South Pole *[S]*
Southampton Insurrection, 1831
Southeast Asia
    USE   Asia, Southeastern
Southeastern States
    USE   Southern States
Southern Baptist Convention
Southern Conference Educational Fund
Southern Conference for Human Welfare
Southern Pacific Railroad
Southern States
Southwest, New
    —History
    — —To 1848
    — —1848-
Southwest, Old
    —History
    — —Civil war, 1861-1865
Southwest States
    USE   Southwestern States
Southwestern States
    UF   Southwest States
Souvenirs (Keepsakes) *(May add geog subd)*
Sovereigns
    USE   Kings, queens, rulers, etc. *[AC only]*
Soviet Ground Forces
    USE   Soviet Union. Ground Forces *[AC only]*
Soviet Navy
    USE   Soviet Union. Navy

Soviet Union *[S]*
    —Foreign relations
    — —1985-1991
    —Politics and government
    — —1917-
    — —1925-1953
    — —1953-1985
    — —1985-1991
Soviet Union. Ground Forces *[AC only]*
    UF   Ground Forces of the Soviet Union
           Soviet Ground Forces
           Soviet Union. Ground Troops
           Soviet Union. Sukhoputnye voiska
Soviet Union. Ground Troops
    USE   Soviet Union. Ground Forces *[AC only]*
Soviet Union. Komitet gosudarstvennoi bezopasnosti
    USE   KGB *[AC only]*
Soviet Union. Navy *[AC only]*
    UF   Soviet Navy
           Soviet Union. Soviet Navy
           Soviet Union. Voenno-Morskoi Flot
Soviet Union. Soviet Navy
    USE   Soviet Union. Navy *[AC only]*
Soviet Union. Sukhoputnye voiska
    USE   Soviet Union. Ground Forces *[AC only]*
Soviet Union. Voenno-Morskoi Flot
    USE   Soviet Union. Navy *[AC only]*
Sovietologists
Soviets (People) *[S]*
Sow bugs
    USE   Wood lice (Crustaceans) *[AC only]*
Soybean industry *(May add geog subd)*
Soyuz Test Project
    USE   Apollo Soyuz Test Project
Space
    USE   Outer space
           Space and time *[AC only]*
Space (Architecture) *(May add geog subd)*
Space and time *[AC, S]*
    UF   Space
           Time and space
    BT   Time
Space biology *[S]*
    BT   Biology
Space colonies *[S]*
Space debris *[S]*
Space environment *[S]*
    UF   Extraterrestrial environment
Space flight *[S]*
    SA   *names of specific planets and flights into space*
Space flight to Jupiter
Space flight to Mars
Space flight to the moon *[S]*
    RT   Moon—Exploration
Space industrialization *[S] (May add geog subd)*
Space laboratories
    USE   Space stations
Space law *[S]*
Space medicine *[S] (May add geog subd)*
Space perception
Space photography *[S] (May add geog subd)*
    BT   Photography
    SA   *the subdivision* —Photographs from space
Space pollution
Space probes *[S]*

Space rescue operations *[S]*
Space sciences *[S]* *(May add geog subd)*
Space ships *[S]*
   BT Space vehicles
Space ships in art *[S]*
Space shuttles *[S]*
   BT Space vehicles
Space stations *[S]*
Space surveillance *(May add geog subd)*
Space vehicles *[S]*
   UF Spacecraft
   NT Reusable space vehicles
         Space ships
         Space shuttles
  —Recovery
Space vehicles in art *[S]*
Space warfare *[S]*
Space weapons *[S]*
Spacecraft
   USE Space vehicles
Spacelab Project
Spaghetti *[AC, S]*
   BT Pasta products
Spain *[S]*
  —History
  — —Civil war, 1936-1939
  — —1939-1975
  —History, Naval
Spain. Ejercito Popular de la Republica. 15th International
   Brigade
   USE Abraham Lincoln Brigade *[AC only]*
Spain. Ejercito Popular de la Republica. Brigada
   Internacional, XV
   USE Abraham Lincoln Brigade *[AC only]*
Spallanzani, Lazzaro, 1729-1799
Spaniards
Spaniels *[S]* *(May add geog subd)*
Spanische Reitschule (Vienna, Austria)
   USE Spanish Riding School (Vienna, Austria) *[AC only]*
Spanish American fiction
Spanish-American War, 1898 *[S]*
Spanish Americans
Spanish Americans (Latin America)
Spanish as a second language
   USE Spanish language—Study and teaching—Foreign speakers
Spanish drama *(May add geog subd)*
Spanish essays *(May add geog subd)*
Spanish fiction *(May add geog subd)*
Spanish language *[S]* *(May add geog subd)*
  —Readers *[AC only]*
     Use for reading texts in Spanish containing materials for in-
struction and practice in reading that language.
    RT Spanish language materials *[AC only]*
Spanish language materials *[AC only]*
     Use for works written in Spanish intended primarily for general
information or recreational reading. Such works with text also given
in English are further subdivided by the subdivision —Bilingual.
    RT Spanish language—Readers *[AC only]*
  —Bilingual *[AC only]*
Spanish literature *[S]* *(May add geog subd)*
  —20th century
Spanish Main
Spanish missions
   USE Missions, Spanish

Spanish poetry *(May add geog subd)*
Spanish prose literature
Spanish Riding School (Vienna, Austria) *[AC only]*
   UF Spanische Reitschule (Vienna, Austria)
Spark, Muriel
Sparrows *[S]*
Sparta (Extinct city)
Spassky, Boris, 1937-
Spaulding, Brian
Spawning *(May add geog subd)*
Spear fishing *[S]* *(May add geog subd)*
   BT Fishing
Special education *[S]* *(May add geog subd)*
Special events, Promotion of
   USE Promotion of special events
Special forces (Military science) *(May add geog subd)*
Special Olympics *[S]*
   RT Olympics
         Sports for the handicapped
   SA *the names of specific events*
Special operation (Military science)
Speculation *[S]*
Speech *[S]*
   RT Phonetics
  —Disorders *[AC only]* *(May add geog subd)*
   UF Speech disorders
Speech therapy *[S]* *(May add geog subd)*
   UF Therapy, Speech
Speeches, addresses, etc. *[S]*
   UF Addresses
   RT Literature
         Public speaking
Speechwriters
Speed *[S]*
Speed skating *[S]* *(May add geog subd)*
Speer, Albert, 1905-
Speleology
   RT Caves
Spellers *[S]*
   SA *the subdivision* —Spelling
Spelling
   USE English language—Spelling
         [other] language—Spelling
Spelunking
   USE Caving
Spencer, Edmund, 1552?-1599
Spenser (Fictitious character)
Sperm whale *[S]*
   BT Whales
Sphere
Sphinxes (Mythology)
Spices *[S]* *(May add geog subd)*
Spider webs
Spiders *[S]* *(May add geog subd)*
   NT Argyoneta
         Black widow spider
         Fisher spiders
         Funnel-web spiders
Spiegelman, Art
Spiegelman, Vladek
Spielberg, Steven, 1947-
Spier, Peter

Spies *[S]*
Use for nonfiction works on individuals involved in espionage. *[AC only]*
   RT   Espionage
             Intelligence service
 —Fiction
     Use for fictional works on individuals working independently to secure information for an organization or government. *[AC only]*
    UF   Espionage—Fiction
             Spy stories
    RT   Intelligence service—Fiction *[AC only]*

Spin fishing

Spine *[S]*

Spinning *[S]*

Spiny anteaters
   USE   Echidnas *[AC only]*

Spirit of St. Louis (Airplane)

Spiritual healing *[S] (May add geog subd)*

Spiritual life *[S]*

Spiritualism *[S] (May add geog subd)*
   RT   Parapsychology

Spirituality *(May add geog subd)*

Spirituals (Songs) *[S] (May add geog subd)*

Spit bug
   USE   Spittle insects *[AC only]*

Spitfire (Fighter planes)

Spithead Mutiny, 1797

Spittle insects *[AC, S]*
   UF   Frog hopper
             Spit bug
             Spittlebug

Spittlebug
   USE   Spittle insects *[AC only]*

Spitz, Mark

Splices
   USE   Knots and splices

Sponged ware *(May add geog subd)*
   BT   Pottery

Spoonbills

Spoons *(May add geog subd)*

Sporting goods industry *(May add geog subd)*

Sports *[S] (May add geog subd)*
   RT   Games
             Fishing
             Hunting
    SA   *the names of specific sports and activities*
 —Fiction *[AC only]*
    UF   Sports stories
    SA   *the names of specific sports and activities, followed by the subdivision —Fiction [AC only]*

Sports and state *(May add geog subd)*

Sports cars *[S] (May add geog subd)*
   BT   Automobiles
   RT   Automobiles, Racing

Sports facilities *[S] (May add geog subd)*

Sports for the handicapped *[S] (May add geog subd)*
   RT   Special Olympics

Sports illustrated (Periodical)

Sports in art *[S]*

Sports injuries
   UF   Athletic injuries

Sports medicine *[S] (May add geog subd)*
   BT   Medicine

Sports officiating *(May add geog subd)*

Sports stories
   USE   Sports—Fiction *[AC only]*

Sports team owners

Sports uniforms *(May add geog subd)*
   UF   Uniforms, Sports

Sportscasters *[S]*

Sportsmanship

Spot removal
   USE   Spotting (Cleaning)

Spotsylvania, Battle of, 1864

Spotted hyena *[S]*

Spotting (Cleaning)
   UF   Spot removal

Spreadsheets
   USE   Electronic spreadsheets

Sprinklers

Spring *(May add geog subd)*

Spring in art

Spring peeper *[AC, S]*
   UF   Hyla crucifer
   BT   Tree frogs

Springsteen, Bruce

Sprint cars *(May add geog subd)*

Spurs
   RT   Boots

Spy films *[S]*

Spy stories
   USE   Spies—Fiction *[AC only]*

Squabble Hollow School (Caledonia County, Vt.)

Squamata, Fossil *[S]*

Squanto

Square *[S]*

Square dancing *(May add geog subd)*
   BT   Dancing

Square foot gardening *(May add geog subd)*
   BT   Gardening

Square root *[S]*

Squashes *(May add geog subd)*

Squids *[S] (May add geog subd)*

Squirrels *[S] (May add geog subd)*

Squirt (Dolphin)

SR-71 (Jet reconnaisance plane)

Sri Lanka

SSL
   USE   Spanish language—Study and teaching—Foreign speakers

St. George, Judith

St. Martin, Alexis, 1797?-1880

St. Valentine's Day
   USE   Valentine's Day *[AC only]*

St. Mary's Episcopal Church (Mohegan Lake, N.Y.)

St. Nicholas (Church: Durham, England)

St. Petersburg Pelicans (Baseball team)

Stables *(May add geog subd)*

Staden, Wendelgard von

Stadiums *[S] (May add geog subd)*

Staffordshire pottery

Stage adaptations

Stage fright
   BT   Fear

Stage lighting *[S]*

Stage props *(May add geog subd)*

Stained glass
   USE   Glass painting and staining

Stalin, Joseph, 1879-1953

Stalingrad, Battle of, 1942-1943

Stamford (England)

Stampley, Leroy

Stamps
    USE   Postage stamps
Standard of living
    USE   Cost and standard of living
Starch
Standardbred horse
Standish, Myles, 1584?-1656
Stanhope, Hester Lucy, Lady, 1776-1839
Stanley, Francis Edgar, 1849-1918
Stanley, Freelan Oscar, 1849-1940
Stanley, Henry M. (Henry Morton), 1841-1904
Stanley Steamer automobile
Stansky, Peter
Stanton, Elizabeth Cady, 1815-1902
Star of Bethlehem
Star Trek (Television program)
Star Trek films
Star Wars (Motion picture)
Star-spangled banner (Song)
Starfishes *[S] (May add geog subd)*
Stargell, Willie, 1941-
Starr, Bart
Starr, Belle, 1848-1889
Stars *[S]*
    NT   Sirius
Starvation *[S]*
State and agriculture
    USE   Agriculture and state
State and industry
    USE   Industry and state
State birds *[S] (May add geog subd)*
State emblems
    USE   Emblems, State
State flowers *[S] (May add geog subd)*
State governments *[S] (May add geog subd)*
State police
    USE   Police, State
State rights *[S]*
State, The
    NT   National state
State songs *[S] (May add geog subd)*
State trees *(May add geog subd)*
Staten Island (New York, N.Y.)
Statesmen *[S]*
    RT   Kings, queens, rulers, etc. *[AC only]*
Stationery
Statistical services
Statisticians
Statistics *[S] (May add geog subd)*
    SA   *the subdivisions* —Statistical methods, —Statistics,
            —Statistics, Medical, *and* —Tables
Statue of Liberty (New York, N.Y.) *[AC only]*
    UF   Statue of Liberty National Monument (New York, N.Y.)
Statue of Liberty National Monument (New York, N.Y.)
    USE   Statue of Liberty (New York, N.Y.) *[AC only]*
Statues *(May add geog subd)*
Stature
    UF   Body height
Stature, Short *(May add geog subd)*
Stature, Tall *(May add geog subd)*
    UF   Tall stature
Status (Law) *(May add geog subd)*
Staubach, Roger, 1942-
STDs
    USE   Sexually transmitted diseases
Stead, Christina, 1902-

Stealing
Stealth aircraft *(May add geog subd)*
Steam
Steam-navigation *(May add geog subd)*
Steam engines *[AC, S] (May add geog subd)*
    UF   Steam-engines
Steam shovels *[AC only]*
    UF   Steam-shovels
Steamboats *[S] (May add geog subd)*
    UF   Steamships
Steamships
    USE   Steamboats
Steel *[S]*
Steeplechasing *[S] (May add geog subd)*
    BT   Horsemanship
Stefanidis, John
Steffens, Lincoln, 1866-1936
Stegosaurus *(May add geog subd)*
Stein, Gertrude, 1874-1946
Steinbeck, John, 1902-1968
Steinbeck, John, 1902-1968.   Grapes of wrath
Steinbeck, John, 1902-1968.   Pearl
Steinem, Gloria
Steinmetz, Charles Proteus, 1865-1923
Stelk, Lincoln Frank, 1934-
Stems (Botany)
    NT   Tubers
Stencil work *[S] (May add geog subd)*
    BT   Handicraft
Stendhal, 1783-1842.   Red and the black *[AC only]*
    UF   Stendhal, 1783-1842.   Rouge et le noir
Stendhal, 1783-1842.   Rouge et le noir
    USE   Stendhal, 1783-1842.   Red and the black *[AC only]*
Stengel, Casey
Stenographers
Step families
    USE   Stepfamilies
Stepchildren
Stepfamilies
Stepfathers
Stephen, King of England, 1097?-1154
Stephens, John Lloyd, 1805-1852
Stephenson, David Curtis, 1891-1966
Stephenson, George, 1781-1848
Stephenson, Robert, 1803-1859
Stephenson, William Samuel, Sir, 1896-
Stepmothers
Stepparents
Steptoe, Patrick Christopher
Stereophonic sound systems
Stereoscope
Stereotype (Psychology) *(May add geog subd)*
Sterling (Seal)
Stern, Melissa, 1986-
Stern, William, 1946-
Sterner, Jerry
Steroids *[S]*
    NT   Anabolic steroids
Stevens, Wallace, 1879-1955
Stevenson, Adlai E. (Adlai Ewing), 1900-1965
Stevenson, James, 1929-
Stevenson, Robert Louis, 1850-1894
Stews *(May add geog subd)*
Sticklebacks *[S]*
    BT   Insects
Stieglitz, Alfred, 1864-1946

Stigma (Social psychology)
Still-life painting
Stilts
Stilwell, Joseph Warren, 1883-1946
Stings
    USE   Bites and stings
Stinson, Katherine, 1891-1977
Stock car racing *(May add geog subd)*
Stock exchange *[AC, S]*
    UF   Stock market
    RT   Investments
          Stocks
Stock market
    USE   Stock exchange
Stock photography *(May add geog subd)*
Stock rooms
    USE   Stores or stock room keeping *[AC only]*
Stockbrokers
Stockdale, James B.
Stockholm (Ship)
Stocks *[S] (May add geog subd)*
    BT   Investments
    RT   Stock exchange
Stokowski, Leopold, 1882-1977
Stoll, Clifford
Stomach *[S]*
Stone *[S] (May add geog subd)*
Stone, Cast
Stone age *(May add geog subd)*
Stone carvers
Stone carving *(May add geog subd)*
Stone houses *(May add geog subd)*
Stone implements *[S] (May add geog subd)*
Stonecutters *[AC only]*
    UF   Stone-cutters
Stonehenge (England)
Stonemasonry *(May add geog subd)*
Stoner, Anna Louisa Wellington
Stoneware
    RT   Pottery
Stoppard, Tom
Storage batteries *[S] (May add geog subd)*
Store location *(May add geog subd)*
Stores, Retail *(May add geog subd)*
Stores or stock room keeping *[AC only]*
    UF   Stock rooms
Stories
    USE   Children's literature
          Fiction
          Short stories *[etc.]*
Stories in rhyme *[AC, S]*
Stories without words
    USE   Picture books *[AC only]*
Storks *[S] (May add geog subd)*
Storm King Art Center
Stormalong, Alfred Bulltop
Storms *[S] (May add geog subd)*
    NT   Winter storms
Storytelling *[S] (May add geog subd)*
    —Collections *[AC only]*
            Use for collections of stories compiled primarily for oral presentation.
Stout, Rex, 1886-1975
Stoves *(May add geog subd)*
Stowaways
Stowe, Harriet Beecher, 1811-1896

Strangers *[AC only]*
    UF   Children and strangers
Strategic Arms Limitation Talks
Strategic Defense Initiative
Strategic planning *(May add geog subd)*
Strategy *[S]*
    SA   *the subdivision* —Strategic aspects
Strauss, Johann, 1804-1849
Strauss, Johann, 1825-1899
Strauss, Levi, 1829-1902
Strauss, Richard, 1864-1949
Stravinsky, Igor, 1882-1971
Strawberries *[S] (May add geog subd)*
Strawberry, Darryl
Stream animals *[S]*
    UF   River animals
          Stream fauna
Stream conservation *(May add geog subd)*
Stream ecology *(May add geog subd)*
Stream fauna
    USE   Stream animals *[AC only]*
Streep, Meryl
Street art *(May add geog subd)*
Street-railroads *(May add geog subd)*
    UF   Streetcar lines
          Trolley car lines
    BT   Railroads
Street signs *(May add geog subd)*
Street theater *(May add geog subd)*
Streetcar lines
    USE   Street-railroads
Streets *[S] (May add geog subd)*
Streisand, Barbra
Strength of materials *[S]*
Strength of muscles
    USE   Muscle strength
Stress (Physiology) *[S]*
Stress (Psychology) *[S] (May add geog subd)*
Stress management *(May add geog subd)*
Strikes and lockouts *[S] (May add geog subd)*
String craft
    BT   Handicraft
String figures *(May add geog subd)*
String trimmers
    BT   Lawns—Equipment and supplies
Stringed instruments *[S]*
Striped skunk
Stripes *[AC only]*
Stroke
    USE   Cerebrovascular disease
Strong, Arturo Carrillo, 1930-
Structural analysis (Engineering)
    UF   Structures, Theory of
Structural drawing
Structural engineering *[S] (May add geog subd)*
    BT   Engineering
    RT   Buildings
Structural failures *[S] (May add geog subd)*
Structures, Theory of
    USE   Structural analysis
Stuart, Arabella, Lady, 1575-1615
Stuart, Gilbert, 1755-1828
Stuart, House of
Stuart, Jeb, 1833-1864
Stuart, Jesse, 1907-
Stuart, Mary, 1926-

Stubby (Dog)
Student aid *[S] (May add geog subd)*
   UF Financial aid, Student
        Student financial aid
Student counselors
Student financial aid
   USE Student aid
Student exchange programs *(May add geog subd)*
   UF Students, Interchange of
Student loan funds *[S] (May add geog subd)*
Student newspapers and periodicals *(May add geog subd)*
   UF Newspapers, School
        School newspapers
Student-teacher relationships
   USE Teacher-student relationships
Students *[S] (May add geog subd)*
   NT Students, Part-time
Students, Foreign *(May add geog subd)*
Students, Interchange of
   USE Student exchange programs
Students, Part-time *(May add geog subd)*
   BT Students
Students, Transfer of *(May add geog subd)*
Study, Method of
   SA *the subdivisions* —Study and teaching *and* —Study guides
Study skills
Stuffed animals (Toys) *(May add geog subd)*
Stuka (Bombers)
Stump work
   BT Embroidery
Stunt flying *[S] (May add geog subd)*
Stunt performers *[S] (May add geog subd)*
   NT Women stunt performers
Stupidity
   UF Inefficiency, Mental
   RT Mental efficiency
Sturbridge (Mass.)
Stuttering *(May add geog subd)*
   RT Speech—Disorders
Stuyvesant, Peter, 1592-1672
Style, Literary *[S]*
   RT Literature
Style manuals
   USE Authorship—Style manuals
Styles, Cognitive
   USE Cognitive styles
Styles, Learning
   USE Cognitive styles
Styron, William, 1925-
Subconsciousness *[S]*
Subject headings *[S]*
   RT Cataloging
        Classification—Books
Subliminal perception *(May add geog subd)*
Subliminal projection *(May add geog subd)*
Submachine guns
   BT Weapons
Submarine boats *(May add geog subd)*
   RT Submarines *[AC only]*
   NT Torpedo boats
Submarine diving
   USE Deep diving
Submarine geology *[S]*
   RT Oceanography
   NT Plate tectonics
Submarine topography *(May add geog subd)*

Submarine warfare *[S]*
Submarines *[AC, S] (May add geog subd)*
   Use for works on submarines only. Works on other underwater craft are entered under Submarine boats.
   RT Submarine boats
Submersibles *[S] (May add geog subd)*
   RT Oceanographic submersibles
Subordination of women
   USE Sex role
Substance abuse *[S] (May add geog subd)*
   NT Aerosol sniffing
        Solvent abuse
   SA *the names of specific substances of abuse*
Substitute teachers
   BT Teachers
Subtraction *[S]*
Suburban life *[S] (May add geog subd)*
Subversive activities *[S] (May add geog subd)*
Subways *[S] (May add geog subd)*
Success *[S] (May add geog subd)*
   RT Self-actualization (Psychology)
Success in business *(May add geog subd)*
   RT Business
Succession
   USE Inheritance and succession
Succulent plants *(May add geog subd)*
Sucking of thumbs
   USE Thumb sucking
Sudan
Sudden death *(May add geog subd)*
Sudden infant death syndrome *(May add geog subd)*
Suez Canal (Egypt)
Suffering
   RT Masochism
Suffrage *[S] (May add geog subd)*
   RT Voting
   SA *the subdivision* —Suffrage
Suffragists
Sufism *(May add geog subd)*
   RT Islam
Sugar *[S]*
Sugar maple
  —Tapping
Sugars
Suggestive therapeutics
   USE Therapeutics, Suggestive
Suicide *[S] (May add geog subd)*
Suicide victims
Sukkot
Sullivan, Annie, 1866-1936
Sullivan, Arthur, Sir, 1842-1900
Sullivan, Tom, 1947-
Sullivan, Louis H., 1856-1924
Sultana, 1956
Sultans
   USE Kings, queens, rulers, etc. *[AC only]*
Sumerians
Sumie
   BT Ink painting, Japanese
Summer *(May add geog subd)*
Summer, Donna
Summer employment *[S] (May add geog subd)*
   BT Work
Summer homes
   USE Vacation homes
Summer in art

Summer resorts *[S] (May add geog subd)*
Summer schools *[S] (May add geog subd)*
    BT Schools
Summerdog (Motion picture)
Summerhill School
Summers, Gerald
Sumo
    UF Japanese wrestling
Sun *[S]*
    —Rising and setting
Sun, Yat-sen, 1866-1925
Sun worship *[S] (May add geog subd)*
    —Rising and setting
Suncoast Seabird Sanctuary (Fla.)
Sunday schools *[S]*
    BT Church schools
Sundials *[S] (May add geog subd)*
Sunfishes *[S]*
Sunflowers *(May add geog subd)*
Sunken treasure
    USE Buried treasure *[AC only]*
Sunshine *(May add geog subd)*
Super Bowl (Football game)
Superconductivity
Superconductors *[S]*
Superior, Lake
Superior National Forest (Minn.)
Superman (Comic strip)
Supermarkets *[S] (May add geog subd)*
Supernatural *[S]*
Supernatural in literature *[S]*
Supernova 1987A
Supernovae
Supersonic planes *(May add geog subd)*
Superstition *[S] (May add geog subd)*
    SA specific superstitions, e.g., Vampires
Superstring theories
Supervision of employees
    RT Personnel management
Supply and demand
Support (Domestic relations)
Supreme Court Building (Washington, D.C.)
Suquamish Indians
Surface tension
Surfaces (Technology)
Surfing *[S] (May add geog subd)*
Surgeons *[S]*
    NT Plastic surgeons
        Women surgeons
Surgery *[S] (May add geog subd)*
    SA the subdivision —Surgery
Surgery, Plastic
    UF Plastic surgery
Surgery, Unnecessary *(May add geog subd)*
Surinam
Surrealism *[S] (May add geog subd)*
    BT Art
Surrealism (Literature) *(May add geog subd)*
Surrogate motherhood *(May add geog subd)*
Surrogate mothers *[S]*
    BT Mothers
Surveying *[S] (May add geog subd)*
    RT Geometry, Plane
    NT Area measurement
Surveyors
Surveys *(May add geog subd)*

Survival *[AC only]*
    UF Survival (after airplane accidents, shipwrecks, etc.)
Survival (after airplane accidents, shipwrecks, etc.)
    USE Survival *[AC only]*
Survival Game
Survival skills *[S] (May add geog subd)*
Sushi
    BT Cookery (Rice)
        Cookery, Japanese
Sustainable agriculture *(May add geog subd)*
Sutherland, Joan, 1926-
Sutlers
    BT Merchants
Suzuki motorcycle
Swahili language *(May add geog subd)*
    —Readers *[AC only]*
        Use for reading texts in Swahili containing materials for instruction and practice in reading that language.
        RT Swahili language materials *[AC only]*
Swahili language materials *[AC only]*
    Use for works written in Swahili intended primarily for general information or recreational reading. Such works with text also given in English are further subdivided by the subdivision —Bilingual.
    RT Swahili language—Readers *[AC only]*
    —Bilingual *[AC only]*
Swallow, Chimney
    USE Chimney swift
Swallows *[S] (May add geog subd)*
Swallowtail butterflies *[AC, S]*
    UF Papilionidae
Swamp animals *[AC, S]*
    UF Swamp fauna
Swamp ecology *(May add geog subd)*
Swamp fauna
    USE Swamp animals *[AC only]*
Swamps *(May add geog subd)*
    RT Marshes
        Wetlands
Swan, Robert O.
Swans *[S] (May add geog subd)*
Swansea (Wales)
Swanson, Gloria
Swartz, Larry, 1966-
Swearing *(May add geog subd)*
Swearingen (Tex.)
Sweaters *(May add geog subd)*
Sweden
Swedes
Swedish Americans
Swenson, Christine
Swift, Jonathan, 1667-1745
Swift, Jonathan, 1667-1745.   Gulliver's travels
Swift fox
    USE Kit fox
Swift River (Mass.)
Swifts
    NT Chimney swift
Swimmers
Swimming *[S] (May add geog subd)*
Swindlers and swindling *[S]*
Swine
    USE Pigs *[AC only]*
Swing (Golf)
Swing (Music) *(May add geog subd)*
Swisher, Karin, 1966-
Swiss

Swiss Americans
Switzerland
Switzerland in art
Swords *(May add geog subd)*
Sydney (N.S.W.)
Symbionese Liberation Army
Symbiosis
Symbolic logic
    USE Logic, Symbolic and mathematical
Symbolism *[S]*
    RT Christian art and symbolism
Symbolism (Psychology)
Symbolism in literature *[S]*
Symbolism of numbers
    USE Numerology *[AC only]*
Symbols
    USE Signs and symbols
              Signals and signaling
Symmetry
Symmetry (Art) *(May add geog subd)*
Symmetry (Physics)
Sympathy
Symphony *[S] (May add geog subd)*
Symptomatology *(May add geog subd)*
Synagogues *[S] (May add geog subd)*
Synanon Foundation
Synonyms
    SA *the subdivision* —Synonyms and antonyms
Synthetic training devices
Syphilis *[S] (May add geog subd)*
Syria
Syrian Americans
Syskind, Sara
System 7 (Computer operating system)
System failures (Engineering)
System theory *[S]*
Systemic lupus erythematosus *(May add geog subd)*
Systems (Computers)
Szpital im. Bersonow i Baumanow
Szold, Henrietta, 1860-1945
Szumski, Bonnie, 1958-
T-ball *[S] (May add geog subd)*
T-shirts *(May add geog subd)*
Table etiquette *[S]*
    BT Etiquette
    RT Eating customs *[AC only]*
Table tennis *[S] (May add geog subd)*
Tables
    BT Furniture
Tableware *[S] (May add geog subd)*
Tachyglossidae
    USE Echidnas *[AC only]*
Tadpoles *[S]*
Taft, William H. (William Howard), 1857-1930
Tail
Tailoring *[S]*
Tailors
Taino Indians
Tait, Norman
Taiwan *[S]*
Talbot, Elizabeth Hardwick, Countess of Shrewsbury
Talent shows *(May add geog subd)*
Tales
    USE Folklore *[AC, S] (May add geog subd)*
    SA subdivisions —Legends *and* —Fiction *under topical headings*
Taliesin West (Scottsdale, Ariz.)

Talk shows *[S] (May add geog subd)*
Talking books
    UF Recorded books
    BT Sound recordings
Tall buildings *(May add geog subd)*
Tall stature
    USE Stature, Tall
Tall tales *[S] (May add geog subd)*
Tallchief, Maria
Talleyrand, Dorothee, Duchess of
    USE Dino, Dorothee, duchesse de, 1793-1862
Tam Lin (Legendary character)
Tamba pottery
    USE Tanba pottery
Tamberlain, 1336-1405
    USE Tamerlane, 1336-1405 *[AC only]*
Tamburlaine, 1336-1405
    USE Tamerlane, 1336-1405 *[AC only]*
Tamerlane, 1336-1405 *[AC only]*
    UF Tamberlain, 1336-1405
              Tamburlaine, 1336-1405
              Timur, 1336-1405
Tampa Bay Buccaneers (Football team)
Tang, Charles
Tang, Yungmei
Tanganyika, Lake
    UF Lake Tanganyika
Tank warfare
Tankers
Tanks (Military science) *[S] (May add geog subd)*
Tanning *[S] (May add geog subd)*
    RT Leather
Tanzania
Taoism *[S] (May add geog subd)*
Taos Indians
Tap dancing *[S] (May add geog subd)*
Tape recorders and recording *[AC only]*
    —Cassette recorders
    UF Magnetic recorders and recording
Tapestry *(May add geog subd)*
Tarantulas *[S] (May add geog subd)*
Tarbell, Ida M. (Ida Minerva), 1857-1944
Tardiness *[AC only]*
    UF Lateness
    RT Promptness
Tarkenton, Fran
Tarot *[S] (May add geog subd)*
Tarrant County (Tex.)
Tartans *[S] (May add geog subd)*
Tarzan (Fictitious character)
Tasaday (Philippine people)
Tasmania
Tasmanian devil *(May add geog subd)*
TASP Test
    UF Texas Academic Skills Program Test
Taste *[S]*
Tatting
Tattooing *(May add geog subd)*
Taurus (Astrology) *(May add geog subd)*
    BT Astrology
Taurus automobile
Tax administration and procedure
Tax auditing *(May add geog subd)*
Tax collection *(May add geog subd)*
    RT Taxation
Tax planning *(May add geog subd)*

Tax protests and appeals *(May add geog subd)*
Taxation *(May add geog subd)*
   RT   Income tax
           Tax collection
Taxation, State
Taxicabs *(May add geog subd)*
Taxidermy *[S]*
Tay-Sachs disease *[S] (May add geog subd)*
Taylor, David, 1934-
Taylor, Elizabeth, 1932-
Taylor, Florence Starr, 1904-
Taylor, Joseph, 1860-1933
Taylor, Ken
Taylor, Teresa, 1959-
Taylor, Theodore B., 1925-
Taylor, Zachary, 1784-1850
Tchaikovsky, Peter Ilich, 1840-1893
Tchaikovsky, Peter Ilich, 1840-1893. Schelkunchik
Tea *[S] (May add geog subd)*
Tea trade *(May add geog subd)*
Teach, Edward, d. 1718
   USE   Blackbeard, d. 1718 *[AC only]*
Teacher participation in personnel service *(May add geog subd)*
Teacher-parent relationships
   USE   Parent-teacher relationships
Teacher-student relationships *[S] (May add geog subd)*
   UF   Student-teacher relationships
Teachers *[S]*
   NT   Preschool teachers
           Substitute teachers
           Tutors and tutoring
Teachers, Preschool
   USE   Preschool teachers
Teachers of gifted children
Teachers of the physically handicapped *[AC only]*
   UF   Physically handicapped, Teachers of the
Teachers of the deaf
Teaching *[S] (May add geog subd)*
   NT   College teaching
           Project method in teaching
           Remedial teaching
           Tutors and teaching
           Unit method of teaching
   SA   *the subdivision* —Study and teaching
 —**Aids and devices**
     NT   Flannelgraphs
Teaching English as a foreign language
   USE   English language—Study and teaching—Foreign speakers
Teaching English as a second language
   USE   English language—Study and teaching—Foreign speakers
Teaching English to speakers of other languages
   USE   English language—Study and teaching—Foreign speakers
Teaching machines *[S]*
   RT   Programmed instruction
Teaching teams *[S]*
Teaff, Grant, 1933-
Team learning approach in education
Teapot Dome Scandal, 1921-1924
Teatown Woods (N.Y.)
Technical education *[S] (May add geog subd)*
Technical institutes *(May add geog subd)*
Technical manuals
   USE   Processing (Libraries)
Technical writing
Technological innovations *(May add geog subd)*

Technologists
Technology *[S] (May add geog subd)*
   RT   High technology
Technology and civilization *[S]*
   UF   Civilization and technology
Technology transfer *[S] (May add geog subd)*
Tecumseh, Shawnee Chief, 1768-1813
Teddy bears
Teenage boys
   UF   Adolescent boys
Teenage fathers *[S]*
Teenage girls
   UF   Adolescent girls
 —**Growth**
Teenage immigrants *(May add geog subd)*
   BT   Immigrants
Teenage marriage
   USE   Marriage *[AC only]*
Teenage mothers *[S]*
   BT   Mothers
Teenage Mutant Ninja Turtles (Fictitious characters)
Teenage parents
   BT   Parents
Teenage pregnancy *[S] (May add geog subd)*
   UF   Pregnancy, Adolescent
   BT   Pregnancy
Teenage sex offenders
   RT   Sex crimes
Teenagers *[S]*
   BT   Youth
Teenagers and death
Teeth *[S]*
   RT   Toothache
TEFL
   USE   English language—Study and teaching—Foreign speakers
Tejas, Vernon
Telecommunication *[S] (May add geog subd)*
Teleconferencing *[S] (May add geog subd)*
Telegraph *[S] (May add geog subd)*
Telemarketing *[S] (May add geog subd)*
Telepathy *[S] (May add geog subd)*
Telephone *[S] (May add geog subd)*
Telephone etiquette
   BT   Etiquette
Telephone in business
Telescope makers
Telescopes *(May add geog subd)*
Television *[S] (May add geog subd)*
 —**Production and direction**
Television actors and actresses
   USE   Actors and actresses *[AC only]*
Television advertising *[S] (May add geog subd)*
Television and children *[S] (May add geog subd)*
Television and family *(May add geog subd)*
Television and youth *[S] (May add geog subd)*
Television authorship *[S]*
Television broadcasting *[S] (May add geog subd)*
Television cameras
Television graphics
Television in education *[S] (May add geog subd)*
Television in politics *[S] (May add geog subd)*
Television journalists
Television news anchors
Television personalities
Television plays *[S]*
Television producers and directors

Television programs *[S] (May add geog subd)*
Television scripts *[S]*
Television serials *(May add geog subd)*
Television specials *(May add geog subd)*
　—Production and direction
Television stations *[S] (May add geog subd)*
Television viewers
Tell, Wilhelm
　　USE Tell, William *[AC only]*
Tell, William *[AC only]*
　　UF Tell, Wilhelm
Temperament *[S]*
Temperance *[S] (May add geog subd)*
Temperature
Temperature measurements
　　UF Thermometry
　　RT Thermometer
Templars
Temple, Shirley, 1928-
Temple of Jerusalem (Jerusalem)
Temples *[S] (May add geog subd)*
Ten Boom, Corrie
Ten commandments *[S]*
Teng, Hsiao-p'ing, 1904-
Tennessee
Tennis *[S] (May add geog subd)*
Tennis elbow *(May add geog subd)*
Tennis players
　—Doubles
Tents *[S] (May add geog subd)*
Teresa, Mother, 1910-
Terezin (Czechoslovakia : Concentration camp)
Terminal care *[S] (May add geog subd)*
　　RT Death
Terminally ill *[S]*
Termination of pregnancy
　　USE Abortion
Termites *[S] (May add geog subd)*
Terni, Giorgio
　　USE Da Terni, Giorgio Maria
Terra cotta sculpture
Terrariums *[S]*
Terrorism *[S] (May add geog subd)*
Terrorists
Terry family
TESL
　　USE English language—Study and teaching—Foreign speakers
Tesla, Nikola, 1856-1943
TESOL
　　USE English language—Study and teaching—Foreign speakers
Test bias *(May add geog subd)*
Test-taking skills *(May add geog subd)*
Test tube babies *[AC only]*
　　UF Fertilization in vitro, Human
　　BT Babies
　　　Genetic engineering
Testing
　　SA *the subdivision* —Testing
Tests, Psychological
　　USE Psychological tests
Tet Offensive, 1968
Tetanus *[S] (May add geog subd)*
Teton Indians
Teutonic peoples
　　USE Goths
Tewa Indians

Texas
　—History
　— —To 1846
　— —1835-1836
　— —1836-1846
　—Politics and government
　— —1865-1950
　— —1951-
Texas, East
Texas A & M University
Texas Academic Skills Program Test
　　USE TASP Test
Texas Bluebonnet Award
Texas Committee for the Humanities
Texas Hazard Communication Act
Texas Hill Country (Tex.)
Texas in literature
Texas longhorn cattle *(May add geog subd)*
　　BT Cattle
Texas Rangers
Texas Rangers (Baseball team)
Texas State Capitol (Austin, Tex.)
Text processing (Computer science)
Textbooks *[S] (May add geog subd)*
　　SA *the subdivisions* —Textbooks for foreign speakers *and*
　　　—Texts
Textile crafts *(May add geog subd)*
Textile design *[S] (May add geog subd)*
Textile fabrics
　　USE Textiles *[AC only]*
　　SA *the subdivision* —Textile industry and fabrics
Textile factories *(May add geog subd)*
Textile fibers
　　USE Fibers *[AC only]*
Textile industry *[AC, S]*
　　RT Textiles *[AC only]*
　　SA *the subdivision* —Textile industry and fabrics
Textile printing *[S] (May add geog subd)*
Textile workers
　　NT Women textile workers
Textiles *[AC only]*
　　UF Fabrics
　　　Textile fabrics
　　RT Fibers *[AC only]*
　　　Textile industry *[AC only]*
Texture (Art)
Textures *[AC only]*
Thackeray, William Makepeace, 1811-1863
Thai, Paul
Thailand
　—History
　— —1945-
Thalberg, Irving G., 1899-1936
Thames River (England)
Thames River Valley (England)
Thank-you notes *(May add geog subd)*
Thankfulness
　　USE Gratitude
Thanksgiving cookery
Thanksgiving Day
Thanksgiving decorations *(May add geog subd)*
That's Incredible! (Television program)
Thatcher, Margaret
Theater *[S] (May add geog subd)*
　—Production and direction

Theater architecture (*May add geog subd*)
Theater of the absurd
Theaters *[S]* (*May add geog subd*)
—**Stage-setting and scenery** *[AC only]*
    UF   Stage-setting
    RT   Scene painting
Theatrical prosthetic makeup
    UF   Prosthetic make-up, Theatrical
Theismann, Joe
Themistocles, ca. 524-ca. 459 B.C.
Theodicy
    BT   Good and evil
Theodore II, Negus of Ethiopia, d. 1868
Theologians
Theological seminaries (*May add geog subd*)
Theology *[S]*
Theology, Doctrinal (*May add geog subd*)
    UF   Doctrinal theology
Theory of knowledge
    USE   Cognition
Theosophists
Thera Island (Greece)
Therapeutic communities (*May add geog subd*)
Therapeutics *[S]* (*May add geog subd*)
    RT   Diagnosis
            Medicine
            Pathology
    SA   *the subdivision* —Therapeutic use
Therapeutics, Physiological (*May add geog subd*)
Therapeutics, Suggestive *[S]* (*May add geog subd*)
    UF   Suggestive therapeutics
Therapy
    See specific forms of therapy.
Thermodynamics *[S]*
Thermometers *[S]* (*May add geog subd*)
Thermometry
    USE   Temperature measurements
Thermoplastics
Thesauri
    SA   *the subdivision* —Synonyms and antonyms *under names*
            of languages, e.g., English language—Synonyms
            and antonyms
Theseus (Greek mythology)
Thieves
    USE   Robbers and outlaws *[AC only]*
Thimble theater (Comic strip)
Thinking
    USE   Thought and thinking
Third grade (Education) (*May add geog subd*)
Third parties (United States politics) *[S]*
Third World
    USE   Developing countries
Thirty Years' War, 1618-1648 *[S]*
Thomas à Becket, Saint, 1118?-1170
Thomas, Aquinas, Saint, 1225?-1274
Thomas, Barbara, 1956-
Thomas, Bigger (Fictitious character)
Thomas, Clarence, 1948-
Thomas, Dylan, 1914-1953
Thomas, Ella Gertrude Clanton
Thomas, Isaiah, 1961-
Thomas, Kurt, 1957-
Thomas, Lowell, 1892-1981
Thomas, Piri, 1928-
Thomas, R. David, 1932-
Thomas Gilcrease Institute of American History and Art

Thomas Jefferson Building (Washington, D.C.)
Thompson, James Harrison Wilson, b. 1906
Thompson, John, 1941 Sept. 2-
Thompson, Snowshoe, 1827-1876
Thoreau, Henry David, 1817-1862
Thoreau, Henry David, 1817-1862.   Walden
Thornton, William, 1759-1828
Thoroughbred horse (*May add geog subd*)
Thorpe, Jim, 1887-1953
Thought and thinking *[S]*
    UF   Thinking
    RT   Critical thinking
Thousand Islands (N.Y. and Ont.)
Three-dimensional display systems
    NT   Holography
Three Mile Island Nuclear Power Plant (Pa.)
Three-spined stickleback
Thresher sharks *[AC, S]*
    UF   Alopiidae
Threshing machines (*May add geog subd*)
Thubten Jigme Norbu, 1922-
Thumb, Tom, 1838-1883
Thumb sucking (*May add geog subd*)
    UF   Sucking of thumbs
Thumbprints in art
    RT   Fingerprints
Thunderstorms *[S]* (*May add geog subd*)
Thurber, James, 1894-1961
TI-99 (Computer)
Ti, Jen-chieh, 629-700
Tiananmen (Beijing, China)
Tiber River (Italy)
Tiberius, Emperor of Rome, 42 B.C.-37 A.D.
Tibet (China)
Tibetan language (*May add geog subd*)
—**Readers** *[AC only]*
    Use for reading texts in Tibetan containing materials for instruction and practice in reading that language.
    RT   Tibetan language materials *[AC only]*
Tibetan language materials *[AC only]*
    Use for works written in Tibetan intended primarily for general information or recreational reading. Such works with text also given in English are further subdivided by the subdivision —Bilingual.
    RT   Tibetan language—Readers *[AC only]*
—**Bilingual** *[AC only]*
Tiburzi, Bonnie
Tic-tac-toe *[S]*
    BT   Games
Ticonderoga, Battle of, 1758
Tidal marshes
    USE   Salt marshes
Tide pool ecology (*May add geog subd*)
Tide pools (*May add geog subd*)
Tidal waves
    USE   Tsunamis
Tides *[S]* (*May add geog subd*)
Tidiness
    USE   Cleanliness *[AC only]*
            Orderliness *[AC only]*
Tie dying *[AC, S]*
    UF   Tie-dying
Tiepolo, Giambattista
    USE   Tiepolo, Giovanni Battista, 1696-1770
Tiepolo, Giovanni Battista, 1696-1770
    UF   Tiepolo, Giambattista
Tiffany and Company

Tiffany, Louis Comfort, 1848-1933
Tigers *[S] (May add geog subd)*
Tightrope walking *(May add geog subd)*
Tigris (Boat)
Tigua Indians
Tijerina, Reies
Tilden, Samuel J. (Samuel Jones), 1814-1886
Tiles *[S] (May add geog subd)*
Tiles, Victorian *(May add geog subd)*
Tiling (Mathematics)
Tillers, Rotary
   USE   Rotary tillers
Timber *(May add geog subd)*
   BT   Forest products
Timber rattlesnake *[S] (May add geog subd)*
   BT   Rattlesnakes
Time *[S]*
   NT   Morning *[AC only]*
       Space and time
Time management *[S] (May add geog subd)*
Time measurements
Time perception *(May add geog subd)*
Time travel
Timex Sinclair (Computer)
Timur, 1336-1405
   USE   Tamerlane, 1336-1405 *[AC only]*
Tinkers
Tinnitus *(May add geog subd)*
   BT   Hearing disorders
Tintin (Fictitious character)
Tinware *(May add geog subd)*
   NT   Tole painting
Tires, Rubber
   UF   Rubber tires
Titanic (Steamship)
Titans (Mythology)
Titian, ca. 1488-1576
Titles of honor and nobility *(May add geog subd)*
Tito, Josip Broz, 1892-1980
Tituba
Tizmoret ha-filharmonit ha-Yisre'elit
   USE   Israel Philharmonic Orchestra *[AC only]*
Tlingit Indians
Tlokwa (African people)
TM
   USE   Transcendental Meditation
Toads *[S] (May add geog subd)*
Toasts *[S]*
Tobacco *[S] (May add geog subd)*
   RT   Nicotine
Tobacco habit *[S] (May add geog subd)*
   RT   Smoking
Tobacco industry *(May add geog subd)*
Tobago
   USE   Trinidad and Tobago
Toby jugs
Toddlers
Toes
Tohono O'Odham Indians
   UF   Papago Indians
Tokens *(May add geog subd)*
Toklas, Alice B.
Tokyo (Japan)
Tole painting
   BT   Tinware
Toleration *[S]*

Tolkien, J.R.R. (John Ronald Reuel), 1892-1973
Toll-free telephone calls *(May add geog subd)*
Tolstoy, Alexandra, 1884-1979
Tolstoy, Leo, graf, 1828-1910
Tolstoy, Leo, graf, 1828-1910. Voina i mir
   USE   Tolstoy, Leo, graf, 1828-1910. War and peace *[AC only]*
Tolstoy, Leo, graf, 1828-1910. War and peace *[AC only]*
   UF   Tolstoy, Leo, graf, 1828-1910. Voina i mir
Toltecs
   BT   Indians
Tomato catchup
   USE   Ketchup *[AC only]*
Tomato catsup
   USE   Ketchup *[AC only]*
Tomato katsup
   USE   Ketchup *[AC only]*
Tomato ketchup
   USE   Ketchup *[AC only]*
Tombs *[S] (May add geog subd)*
   SA   *the subdivision* —Tomb
Tonga (Zambesi people)
  —Folklore
      USE   Folklore, Tonga *[AC only]*
Tongue
Tongue twisters *[S]*
   BT   Word games
Tonkawa Indians
Tool and die industry *(May add geog subd)*
Tool use in animals
Tools *(May add geog subd)*
   NT   Power tools
   SA   *the names of specific tools*
Tooth Fairy *[AC only]*
Toothache
   BT   Pain
   RT   Teeth
Topiary work
   BT   Landscape gardening
Topographical drawing *[S]*
   BT   Drawing
Topology *[S]*
   RT   Geometry
   BT   Mathematics
Toponymy
   BT   Lexicography
Tops *(May add geog subd)*
Torah scrolls
Tornado (Jet fighter plane)
Tornadoes *[S] (May add geog subd)*
Toronto (Ont.)
Toronto Blue Jays (Baseball team)
Torpedo boats *[AC only]*
   UF   Torpedo-boats
   BT   Submarine boars
Tort liability of professions
   USE   Malpractice
Torts *(May add geog subd)*
Toscanini, Arturo, 1867-1957
Tosi, Larry
Totalitarianism *[S]*
   RT   Dictators
       Fascism
Totem poles *(May add geog subd)*
Totems
Touch *[S]*
Toulouse-Lautrec, Henri de, 1864-1901

Tour Eiffel (Paris, France)
  USE   Eiffel Tower (Paris, France) [AC only]
Tour de France (Bicycle race) (May add geog subd)
Tourette syndrome (May add geog subd)
Tourist camps, hostels, etc. (May add geog subd)
Tourist trade (May add geog subd)
Toussaint L'Ouverture, 1743?-1803
Tower, John G. (John Goodwin), 1925-1991
Tower of Babel
  USE   Babel, Tower of
Tower of London (London, England)
  BT   London, England
         Prisons
Towns
  USE   Cities and towns
Toxic shock syndrome [S] (May add geog subd)
  UF   TSS
Toxicological emergencies (May add geog subd)
Toxicology (May add geog subd)
  SA   the subdivision —Toxicology
Toy and movable books [S]
  RT   Illustrated books, Children's
         Picture books
  —**Specimens** (Do not use: AC only)
Toy industry (May add geog subd)
Toy making
Toys [S] (May add geog subd)
  SA   the names of specific toys, e.g., Whirligigs
Trachtenberg, Jakow, 1888-
Track and field [AC only]
  UF   Track-athletics
  SA   the names of specific track and field events, e.g., Javelin
         throwing
Track and field athletes
  SA   the names of individual athletes
Track-athletics
  USE   Track and field [AC only]
  BT   Olympics
         Special Olympics
Tracklaying vehicles
Tracking and trailing [S] (May add geog subd)
Tractor trailer combinations
  USE   Tractor trailors [AC only]
Tractor trailors [AC only]
  UF   Eighteen wheelers
         Tractor trailor combinations
  BT   Trucks
Tractors (May add geog subd)
Tracy, Spencer, 1900-1967
Trade, Balance of
  USE   Balance of trade
Trade and professional associations [S] (May add geog subd)
Trade names
  USE   Business names
         Trademarks
Trade routes [S] (May add geog subd)
Trade schools (May add geog subd)
Trade unions
  USE   Labor unions [AC, S]
Trade winds
  UF   Trade-winds
Trademarks [S] (May add geog subd)
  UF   Trade names
Trading companies (May add geog subd)
Tradition (Philosophy)

Traditional medicine [S] (May add geog subd)
  UF   Folk medicine
         Popular medicine
Trafalgar (Cape), Battle of, 1805
Traffic accidents [S] (May add geog subd)
Traffic regulations [S] (May add geog subd)
Traffic safety (May add geog subd)
Traffic signs and signals (May add geog subd)
  RT   Signals and signaling
         Signs and symbols
Tragedy [S]
  RT   Death
  SA   the subdivision —Tragedies
Trail of Tears, 1838
  UF   Cherokee Removal, 1838
Trailer camps
  UF   Trailer parks
Trailer parks
  USE   Trailer camps
Trails (May add geog subd)
Train robberies (May add geog subd)
Trains, Railroad
  USE   Railroads—Trains
Trampolining [S] (May add geog subd)
Tramps [S]
Tranquilizing drugs (May add geog subd)
  BT   Drugs
Trans-Alaska Pipeline (Alaska)
Trans-Siberian Railway [AC only]
  UF   Velikaia Sibirskaia magistral
Transaction costs
Transactional analysis (May add geog subd)
Transatlantic flights
  BT   Air travel
Transcendental Meditation
  UF   TM
Transcendentalism
Transfer students
Transistor television receivers
Transistors [S]
Translating and interpreting [S] (May add geog subd)
  UF   Interpreting and translating
  SA   the subdivisions —Translations and —Translations into
         French, [German, etc.]
Translators
Transmission, Power
  USE   Power transmission
Transplantation of organs, tissues, etc. [S] (May add geog
  subd)
  SA   the subdivision —Transplantation
Transport planes (May add geog subd)
Transportation [S] (May add geog subd)
  SA   the subdivision —Transportation
Transportation, Automotive (May add geog subd)
Transportation, Military [S] (May add geog subd)
  UF   Military transportation
Transylvania (Romania)
Trap-door spiders
  BT   Spiders
Trapp, Maria Augusta
Trapp Family Singers
Trappers
Trapping [S] (May add geog subd)
Trappists
Trapunto
  BT   Quilting

Trash
  USE Refuse and refuse disposal
       Waste products
Trauma centers (May add geog subd)
Travel [S] (Not subd geog)
  UF Voyages and travels
  SA the subdivisions —Journeys, —Description and travel,
       and —Travel
Travel agents
Travel photography (May add geog subd)
Travelers [S]
Traveller (Horse)
Travis, William Barret, 1809-1836
Travis County (Tex.)
Treason (May add geog subd)
Treasure hunts [AC, S]
  BT Amusements
Treasure trove
  USE Buried treasure [AC only]
Treblinka (Poland : Concentration camp)
Tree farms (May add geog subd)
Tree frogs [AC only]
  UF Hylidae
       Tree toads
  NT Spring peeper [AC only]
Tree houses (May add geog subd)
Tree planting
  USE Trees—Planting [AC only]
Tree toads
  USE Tree frogs [AC only]
Treenware
  UF Woodenware
Trees [S] (May add geog subd)
  BT Plants
  NT Leaves
  SA the names of specific trees
  —Planting
       UF Tree planting
Trees in art [S]
Trees in winter (May add geog subd)
Trenary, Jill
Trent Affair, Nov. 8, 1861
Trenton (N.J.)
Trenton, Battle of, 1776
Trevino, Lee
Trials [S] (May add geog subd)
  RT Courts
       Jurisprudence
  NT Mock trials
  SA specific crimes, types of trials, and jurisdictions, and
       the subdivision —Trials, ligitation, etc.
Trials (Assasination) [S] (May add geog subd)
Trials (Espionage) [S] (May add geog subd)
  RT Espionage
Trials (Heresy) [S] (May add geog subd)
Trials (Libel) [S] (May add geog subd)
  UF Libel trials
Trials (Murder) [S] (May add geog subd)
  RT Murder
Trials (Political crimes and offenses) [S] (May add geog
  subd)
  RT Political crimes and offenses
Trials (Products liability) [S] (May add geog subd)
Trials (Sedition) [S] (May add geog subd)
Trials (Witchcraft) [S] (May add geog subd)
  RT Witchcraft

Triangle
Tricks [S]
  RT Magic tricks
Tricycles
  USE Bicycles and bicycling [AC only]
Trieste (Italy)
Trigonometry [S]
Trigonometry, Plane
  USE Plane trigonometry
Trillion (The number)
Trinidad and Tobago
  UF Trinidad
       Tobago
Trinity County (Tex.)
Triplets
Tripods (May add geog subd)
Trips
  USE Travel
  SA the subdivision —Journeys
Tristan (Legendary character)
Trojan War
Trolley car lines
  USE Street-railroads
Trollope, Anthony, 1815-1882
Trolls
Trombone [S]
Trompe l'oeil painting (May add geog subd)
  BT Painting
       Realism in art
       Still-life painting
Tropic-birds [S]
  UF Tropicbirds
  BT Birds
Tropical fish [S]
Tropical diseases
  USE Tropical medicine
Tropical medicine [S] (May add geog subd)
  UF Tropical diseases
Tropical plants (May add geog subd)
Tropical rain forests
  USE Rain forests
Tropics [S]
Trost, Henry C. (Henry Charles), 1860-1933
Trotsky, Leon, 1879-1940
Trousers (May add geog subd)
Trout [S] (May add geog subd)
Trout fishing (May add geog subd)
Troy (Extinct city)
TRS-80 (Computer)
Truck drivers
Truck driving (May add geog subd)
Trucking [S] (May add geog subd)
Trucks [S] (May add geog subd)
  SA the names of specific types of truck, e.g., Tractor trailors
Trucks in art [S]
Trudeau, Pierre Elliott
Trull, Patti
Truman, Harry S., 1884-1972
Trumpet [S]
Trumpet players
  BT Musicians
Trumpeter swan [S]
Trunks (Luggage) (May add geog subd)
Trust (Psychology)
Trusts and trustees (May add geog subd)
Truth [S]

Truth, Sojourner, d. 1883
Truthfulness and falsehood
   USE Honesty *[AC only]*
Tsimshian Indians
Tsunamis *[S] (May add geog subd)*
   UF Tidal waves
TSS
   USE Toxic shock syndrome
Tuaregs
   BT Berbers
   NT Ajjer (African people)
Tuberculosis *[S] (May add geog subd)*
Tubers
   BT Stems (Botany)
Tubman, Harriet, 1820?-1913
Tucker, Preston
Tudor, House of
Tudor, Owen, ca. 1400-1461
Tudor, Tasha
Tugboats *[S] (May add geog subd)*
Tule elk
Tulips *[S] (May add geog subd)*
Tulsa (Okla.)
Tumbleweeds *[AC only]*
   UF Russian thistle
Tumbling *[S]*
Tumors
   UF Neoplasms
   NT Cancer
Tumors, Radiation-induced *(May add geog subd)*
Tundra ecology *(May add geog subd)*
Tundras *(May add geog subd)*
Tunguses *(May add geog subd)*
   BT Arctic peoples
Tunica Indians
Tunisia
Tunnels *[S] (May add geog subd)*
Turkey
   —History
   — —Ottaman empire, 1288-1918
Turkey hunting *(May add geog subd)*
Turkey vulture *(May add geog subd)*
Turkeys *[S] (May add geog subd)*
Turner, J.M.W. (Joseph Mallard William), 1775-1851
Turner, Lana, 1921-
Turner, Morrie
Turner, Nat, 1800?-1831
Turner, Philip M., 1948-
Turner, Ted
Turow, Scott
Turquoise *(May add geog subd)*
Turtles *[S] (May add geog subd)*
Turtles as pets
Tuscarora Indians
Tuskegee Institute
Tusks
Tutankhamen, King of Egypt
Tutoring
   USE Tutors and tutoring
Tutors and tutoring *[S]*
   UF Tutoring
   BT Teachers
       Teaching
   RT Volunteer workers in education
Tuttle, Merlin D.
Tutu, Desmond

Twain, Mark, 1835-1910
Twain, Mark, 1835-1910.   Adventures of Huckleberry Finn
Twelve-step programs *[S] (May add geog subd)*
Twelfth century
   BT Civilization, Medieval
       Middle Ages
Twentieth century *[S]*
   SA *the subdivisions* —20th century *and* —History —20th century
   —Forecasts
Twenty-first century *[S]*
   —Forecasts
Twilight
Twilight Zone (Television show)
Twin Cities Metropolitan Area (Minn)
   USE Minneapolis Metropolitan Area (Minn.)
       Saint Paul Metropolitan Area (Minn.)
Twins *[S]*
Two (The number)
Two Trees, Joe
Tyler, John, 1790-1862
Tyler's Insurrection, 1381
Tyndale, William, d. 1536
Type A behavior *(May add geog subd)*
Type and type-founding *(May add geog subd)*
   UF Fonts
   BT Printing
Typewriters *[S]*
Typewriting *[S]*
   UF Typing
Typha
   USE Cattails
Typhoid fever *[S] (May add geog subd)*
   BT Diseases
Typhoons *[S] (May add geog subd)*
Typing
   USE Typewriting
Typography, Advertising
   USE Advertising layout and typography
Typology (Psychology)
Tyrannosaurus rex *[S]*
Tyrol (Austria)
Tz'u-hsi, Empress dowager of China, 1835-1908
U-2 Incident, 1960
U2 (Musical group)
U.S.
   USE United States
U.S. Air Force
   USE United States. Air Force
U.S. Army
   USE United States. Army
U.S. Army Air Forces
   USE United States. Army Air Forces
Ueberroth, Peter
UFOs
   USE Unidentified flying objects
Uganda
Ukraine
Ukrainian Americans
Ukrainians
Ulcers
Ullmann, Liv
Ulster (Northern Ireland and Ireland)
Ultralight aircraft *(May add geog subd)*
Ultrasonics *[S]*

Umbilicus
    USE Belly button [AC only]
Umbrellas and parasols [S]
    UF Parasols
Uncle Scrooge (Fictitious character)
    USE McDuck, Scrooge (Fictitious character) [AC only]
Uncles
Underachievers
Undercover operations (May add geog subd)
Undercover wildlife agents
Underground architecture [S] (May add geog subd)
Underground construction
    BT Construction industry
Underground electric power plants
    UF Electric power plants, Underground
Underground railroad [S]
    RT Slavery—Anti-slavery movements
    SA the subdivision —Underground movements
Underground utility lines (May add geog subd)
    BT Public utilities
Underground water
    USE Water, Underground
Undersea research stations
    USE Manned undersea research stations
Undertakers and undertaking [S]
Underwater archaeology (May add geog subd)
    BT Archaeology
Underwater exploration [S] (May add geog subd)
Underwater photography [S]
    NT Photography
Underwater research stations
    USE Manned undersea research stations
Underwear
Underwood, Barbara
Underwood, Betty
Unemployed [S]
Unemployment [S] (May add geog subd)
    RT Employment (Economic theory)
        Job hunting
Ungulata
    USE Ungulates [AC only]
Ungulates [AC, S] (May add geog subd)
    UF Ungulata
Unicorns
Unidentified flying objects [S]
    UF UFOs
Unification Church (May add geog subd)
Unincorporated societies (May add geog subd)
Uniforms, Military
    USE Military uniforms
Uniforms, Sports
    USE Sports uniforms
Union catalogs
    USE Catalogs, Union
Union Pacific Railroad
Unit method of teaching
    BT Teaching
Unitas, Johnny, 1933-
United Cerebral Palsy Associations
United Daughters of the Confederacy
United Farm Workers
United Nations [S] (May add geog subd)
    RT International cooperation
        League of Nations
United Service Organizations (U.S.)

United States [S]
    UF U.S.
—**Air National Guard**
—**Civilization** [S]
— —**1970-**
— —**20th century**
—**Constitution** [S]—**Amendments—1st-10th**
    UF Bill of rights (United States Constitution)
—**Constitutional law** [S]—**Amendments—1st-10th**
—**Description and travel** (no subd by date)
—**Economic conditions** [S]
— —**To 1865**
— —**1945-**
— —**1981-**
— —**20th century**
—**Economic policy** [S]
— —**1981-1993**
—**Foreign relations** [S] (May add geog subd)
— —**1945-1953**
— —**1989-**
—**History** [S]
— —**Colonial period, ca. 1600-1775**
— —**King William's War, 1689-1697**
— —**French and Indian War, 1755-1763**
— —**Revolution, 1775-1783**
— —**Confederation, 1783-1789**
— —**1783-1865**
— —**Constitutional period, 1789-1809**
— —**Tripolitan War, 1801-1805**
— —**War of 1812**
— —**1815-1861**
— —**Civil War, 1861-1865**
— — —**Afro-Americans**
— —**1865-1898**
— —**War of 1898**
— —**19th century**
— —**1913-1921**
— —**1919-1933**
— —**1933-1945**
— —**1945-**
— —**1945-1953**
— —**1953-1961**
— —**1961-1969**
— —**1969-1974**
— —**20th century**
—**History, Military**
— —**20th century**
—**History, Naval**
— —**20th century**
—**Insular possessions**
—**Politics and government** [S]
— —**To 1775**
— —**Revolution, 1775-1783**
— —**1783-1809**
— —**1783-1865**
— —**1789-1797**
— —**1815-1861**
— —**1829-1837**
— —**1853-1857**
— —**1857-1861**
— —**1877-1881**
— —**1885-1889**
— —**1893-1897**

United States *(Cont.)*
— —1897-1901
— —20th century
— —1901-1909
— —1919-1933
— —1921-1923
— —1923-1929
— —1933-1945
— —1945-1953
— —1945-1989
— —1953-1961
— —1961-1963
— —1969-1974
— —1974-1977
— —1981-1989
— —1989-
—Social conditions *[S]*
— —1945-
— —1960-1980
— —1980-
—Social life and customs *[S]*
— —Civil war, 1861-1865
— —To 1775
— —1783-1865
— —1865-1918
— —1865-1918
— —20th century
— —1945-1970
—Social policy *[S]*
— —1980-
United States. Air Force
United States. Army
—**History**
— —Civil War, 1861-1865
— —Punitive Expedition into Mexico, 1916
United States. Army. Cavalry
United States. Army. Infantry Regiment, 54th (1863-1865)
United States. Army. Signal Corps
United States. Army Air Forces
United States. Bureau of the Census
United States. Bureau of the Mint
United States. Central Intelligence Agency
United States. Civil Air Patrol
United States. Coast Guard
United States. Congress
  RT Legislators
United States. Congress. House
  RT Legislators
United States. Congress. House. Committee on the Judiciary
United States. Congress. Senate
  RT Legislators
United States. Continental Army
United States. Declaration of Independence
—**Signers**
United States. Dept. of Defense
United States. Dept. of Education
United States. Dept. of State
United States. Dept. of the Interior
United States. Environmental Protection Agency
United States. Federal Bureau of Investigation
United States. Forest Service
United States. Immigration Border Patrol

United States. Marine Corps
United States. National Aeronautics and Space Administration
  UF NASA
United States. National Park Service
United States. Naval Academy
United States. Navy
—**Aviation**
—**Submarine forces**
United States. Office of Strategic Services
United States. President, [dates]
  USE *name of individual, e.g.,* Fillmore, Millard, 1800-1874
United States. Secret Service
United States. Supreme Court
United States. War Dept.
United States Bill of Rights
  USE United States—Constitution—Amendments—1st-10th
United States Capitol (Washington, D.C.)
United States in art *[S]*
United States Lifesaving Service
United States Naval Expedition to Japan, 1852-1854
United States Naval Flight Demonstration Squadron
United States Navy Motor Torpedo Boat Squadrons
United States Navy Underwater Demolition Teams
United States Scientific Laboratory (Los Alamos, N.M.)
United States War Relocation Center (Manzanar, Calif.)
Universe *[S]*
  Use for works limited to the physical description of the universe. Works dealing with the general science or philosophy of the universe are entered under the heading Cosmology. *[AC only]*
  UF Cosmogony
       Cosmography
  NT Cosmology *[AC only]*
Universities and colleges *(May add geog subd)*
  UF Colleges and universities
  SA *the names of specific colleges and universities*
—**Admission**
  RT Scholastic Aptitude Test
—**Fiction** *[AC only]*
  UF College stories
—**Graduate work**
  UF Education, Graduate
       Graduate education
University extension *[S] (May add geog subd)*
University of Alabama
University of California, Berkeley
University of Texas at Austin
University of Virginia
Unmarried couples *[S]*
Unmarried fathers *[S]*
  BT Fathers
Unmarried mothers *[S]*
  BT Mothers
Unser, Bobby
Unser family
Untidiness
  USE Cleanliness *[AC only]*
       Orderliness *[AC only]*
Upholstery *[S] (May add geog subd)*
Upper class *(May add geog subd)*
Ur (Extinct city)
Uranium *[S]*
Uranus (Planet)

Urban animals *(May add geog subd)*
   UF   Animals, Urban
          Urban fauna
   BT   Animals
   SA   *names of specific animals likely to be found in the city*
Urban archaeology *(May add geog subd)*
Urban beautification *(May add geog subd)*
Urban climatology *(May add geog subd)*
Urban ecology (Biology) *(May add geog subd)*
Urban education
   USE   Education, Urban
Urban fauna
   USE   Urban animals *[AC only]*
Urban flora
   USE   Urban plants *[AC only]*
Urban plants *[AC only]*
   UF   Urban flora
Urban policy *(May add geog subd)*
Urban renewal *[S] (May add geog subd)*
Urban-rural migration *(May add geog subd)*
Urban sociology
   USE   Sociology, Urban
Urbanization *[S] (May add geog subd)*
Urinary incontinence
   NT   Bedwetting *[AC only]*
Urinary organs
Ursa Major
Ursulines
Uruguay
USA for Africa
Useful plants
   USE   Plants, Useful
Usonian houses *(May add geog subd)*
   BT   Organic architecture
Ustinov, Peter
Utah
Utah Jazz (Basketball team)
Ute Indians
Uterus *[S]*
Utilities
   USE   Public utilities
   RT   Underground utility lines
Utilities (Computer programs) *[S]*
Utopias *[S]*
Utopias in literature
Uttley, Alison, 1884-
V-1 bomb
V-2 rocket
Vacation Bible schools *[AC only]*
   UF   Vacation schools, Christian
Vacation homes
   UF   Summer homes
Vacation schools
   USE   Vacation Bible schools *[AC only]*
Vacations *[S] (May add geog subd)*
Vaccination *[S] (May add geog subd)*
   RT   Immunity
   SA   *the subdivision* —Vaccination
Vagabonds
   USE   Rogues and vagabonds
Vaganova Choreographic Institute
   USE   Kirov Ballet Academy *[AC only]*
Vagina
Valentine, Saint
Valentine decorations
Valentines

Valentine's Day *[AC, S]*
   UF   Saint Valentine's Day
          St. Valentine's Day
Valenzuela, Fernando, 1960-
Valets
Valium
   BT   Drugs
Vallejo, César, 1892-1938
Valley Forge (Pa.)
Valley of the Kings (Egypt)
Values *[S] (May add geog subd)*
Vampire films
   BT   Motion pictures
Vampires *[S]*
   RT   Werewolves
Vampires in literature
Van Buren, Martin, 1782-1862
Van der Weyden, Rogier, ca. 1399-1464
   USE   Weyden, Rogier van der, 1399 or 1400-1464
Van Devanter, Lynda
Van Dyck, Anthony, Sir, 1599-1641
Van Eyck, Jan, ca. 1390-1441
   USE   Eyck, Jan van, 1390-1440
Van Gogh, Vincent, 1853-1890
   USE   Gogh, Vincent van, 1853-1890
Van Halen (Musical group)
Van Leeuwenhoek, Anton, 1632-1722
Van Lew, Elizabeth L., 1818-1900
Van Ruisdael, Jacob, 1628?-1682
   USE   Ruisdael, Jacob van, 1628 or 9-1682
Van Zandt County (Tex.)
Vandalism *(May add geog subd)*
Vanderbilt, Gloria, 1924-
Vanderbilt family
Vans *[S] (May add geog subd)*
Variation (Biology) *(May add geog subd)*
   SA   *the subdivision* —Variation
Varicella
   USE   Chickenpox
Vasa (Warship)
Vase-painting
Vasectomy *[S] (May add geog subd)*
Vasovasostomy *(May add geog subd)*
Vásquez de Coronado, Francisco, 1510-1554
   USE   Coronado, Francisco Vásquez de, 1510-1554 *[AC only]*
Vatican Palace (Vatican City)
Vaudeville *[S] (May add geog subd)*
Vaughan family
Vector algebra
Vegetable gardening *[S] (May add geog subd)*
   BT   Gardening
          Vegetables
Vegetable juices
Vegetables *[S] (May add geog subd)*
Vegetarian cookery
Vegetarianism *[S]*
Vehicles *[S]*
   SA   *names of specific vehicles and types or uses of vehicles*
Vehicles, Military *[S] (May add geog subd)*
Vehicles in art *[S]*
Veils *(May add geog subd)*
Velazquez, Diego, 1599-1660
Velikaia Sibirskaia magistral
   USE   Trans-Siberian Railway *[AC only]*

Vendetta *(May add geog subd)*
    UF   Feuds
    RT   Revenge
Vendors and purchasers
    UF   Purchasers
    RT   Purchasing
Venereal diseases
    USE   Sexually transmitted diseases
Venezuela
Venice (Italy)
Venice (Los Angeles, Calif.)
Ventilation *[S]*
Ventriloquism *[S]*
Venture capital *(May add geog subd)*
Venus (Planet)
    —Exploration
Venus probes
    BT   Space flight
Venus's flytrap *[S] (May add geog subd)*
Verbal learning *[S]*
Verdi, Giuseppe, 1813-1901
Verdi, Giuseppe, 1813-1901.   Aida
Verdi, Giuseppe, 1813-1901.   Rigoletto
Verdun, Battle of, 1916
Vermeer, Johannes, 1632-1675
Vermont
Vernacular architecture *(May add geog subd)*
    BT   Architecture
Verne, Jules, 1828-1905
Vernon, Malcolm Graham, 1861-1936
Verrazano-Narrows bridge
Versailles (France)
Versification *[S]*
Vertebrates *[S] (May add geog subd)*
Vertebrates, Fossil *(May add geog subd)*
    UF   Fossil vertebrates
Vesey, Denmark, 1767 (ca.)-1822
Vespucci, Amerigo, 1451-1512
Vesuvius (Italy)—Eruption, 79
Veterans *[S]*
    SA   *the subdivision* —Veterans
Veterans Day *[S]*
Veterans of Foreign Wars of the United States
Veterinarians
    RT   Animals—Treatment
           Veterinary medicine
    NT   Women veterinarians
Veterinary hospitals *(May add geog subd)*
Veterinary medicine *[S] (May add geog subd)*
    RT   Veterinarians
Veterinary public health *(May add geog subd)*
Vice-Presidential candidates *(May add geog subd)*
Vice-Presidents *[S]*
Vices
Vicksburg (Miss.)
    —Siege, 1863
Victimless crimes
    USE   Crimes without victims
Victims of crimes *[S]*
    RT   Crime
Victoria, Queen of Great Britain, 1819-1901
Victorian literature
    USE   English literature—19th century
Victoriana *(May add geog subd)*
Victorio, Apache Chief, d. 1881

Video disc players
Video discs
Video games *[S] (May add geog subd)*
    NT   Nintendo video games
Video recordings *(May add geog subd)*
    —Production and direction
Video recordings for the hearing impaired
    UF   Closed captioned video recordings
    BT   Hearing impaired
Video tape recorders and recording *(May add geog subd)*
Video tapes
    RT   Motion pictures
    SA   *the subdivision* —Video catalogs
Video tapes in education
Videocassettes *(May add geog subd)*
Vidocq, Eugène François, 1775-1857
Vienna (Austria)
Vienna Congress
Vienna Convention for the Protection of the Ozone Layer (1985)
    USE   Diplomatic Conference on the Protection of the Ozone Layer (1985 : Vienna, Austria)
Vietnam
Vietnam Veterans Memorial (Washington, D.C.)
Vietnam War, 1961-1975
    USE   Vietnamese Conflict, 1961-1975
Vietnamese
Vietnamese Americans
Vietnamese Conflict, 1961-1975
Vietnamese language *(May add geog subd)*
    —Readers *[AC only]*
        Use for reading texts in Vietnamese containing materials for instruction and practice in reading that language.
        RT   Vietnamese language materials *[AC only]*
Vietnamese language materials *[AC only]*
    Use for works written in Vietnamese intended primarily for general information or recreational reading. Such works with text also given in English are further subdivided by the subdivision —Bilingual.
    RT   Vietnamese language—Readers *[AC only]*
    —Bilingual *[AC only]*
Vieux Carré (New Orleans, La.)
    USE   French Quarter (New Orleans, La.)
Vigilance committees *[S] (May add geog subd)*
    BT   Crime prevention
Viking Mars Program
Viking ships
Vikings *[AC, S]*
    UF   Northmen
Villa, Pancho, 1878-1923
Village communities *(May add geog subd)*
Villages *[S] (May add geog subd)*
    RT   Local government
Villagrá, Gaspar Pérez de, d. 1620
Villains in literature
Villains in mass media *(May add geog subd)*
Villaseñor family
Viola *[S]*
Violence *[S] (May add geog subd)*
    RT   Police shootings
    NT   School violence
           Shootings
Violence in mass media *(May add geog subd)*
Violence in television *(May add geog subd)*
Violent crimes *(May add geog subd)*
Violent deaths *(May add geog subd)*

Violets *(May add geog subd)*
Violin *[S]*
Violinists
Violoncellists
Violoncello *(May add geog subd)*
Viorst, Judith
Vipers
    USE   Snakes
Virgil. Aeneid *[AC only]*
    UF   Virgil. Aeneis
Virgil. Aeneis
    USE   Virgil. Aeneid *[AC only]*
Virgin Islands of the United States
Virginia
   —History
   — —Colonial period, ca. 1600-1775
   — —Revolution, 1775-1783
   —Politics and government
   — —1775-1783
Virginia (Boat)
Virginia City (Nev.)
Virgo (Astrology) *(May add geog subd)*
    BT   Astrology
Virologists
Virology *(May add geog subd)*
Virus diseases *(May add geog subd)*
Viruses *[S] (May add geog subd)*
    RT   Infection
Visas *(May add geog subd)*
Vision *[S]*
    UF   Seeing
Vision disorders *[S] (May add geog subd)*
    RT   Optometry
Visions *[S]*
Visits of state *(May add geog subd)*
Vista (Volunteers in Service to America)
Visual cortex
Visual learning *(May add geog subd)*
Visual literacy *[S] (May add geog subd)*
Visual perception
Visual training
Visualization
Visually handicapped
    RT   Blind
           Large type books
Vital force
Vitality
Vitamin C
Vitamin therapy
Vitamins *[S]*
Vitamins in human nutrition
    BT   Nutrition
Vivisection *[S] (May add geog subd)*
    BT   Biology, Experimental
Vlad III, Prince of Wallachia, 1430 or 31-1476 or 7
Vocabulary *[S]*
Vocation
    UF   Vocations
Vocational aptitude tests
    USE   Occupational aptitude tests
Vocational education *[S] (May add geog subd)*
    RT   Industrial arts
Vocational guidance *[S] (May add geog subd)*
    RT   Career education
    SA   *the subdivision* —Vocational guidance

Vocational interests *(May add geog subd)*
Vocational qualifications *(May add geog subd)*
Vocational school, Choice of
Vocations
    USE   Vocation
Voice *[S]*
Voice of America (Organization)
Voigt, Cynthia
Volcanoes *[S] (May add geog subd)*
    SA   *the subdivision* —Eruption, [date]
Volga River (Russia)
Volga River Region (Russian)
Volition
    USE   Will
Volkswagen automobile
Volleyball *[S] (May add geog subd)*
Voltaire, 1694-1778. Candide
Volume (Cubic content) *[S]*
Voluntarism *[S] (May add geog subd)*
Volunteer workers in education
    RT   Schools
           Tutors and tutoring
Volunteer workers in social service
Von Braun, Wernher, 1912-1977
Von Karajan, Herbert, 1908-1989
Von Neumann, John, 1903-1957
Vonnegut, Kurt
Vonnegut, Kurt. Slaughter house five
Voodooism *(May add geog subd)*
Voting *(May add geog subd)*
    RT   Suffrage
Votive offerings in art
Voyager (Airplane)
Voyager Project
Voyages and travels
    USE   Travel
    SA   *the subdivision* —Journeys
Voyages around the world *[S]*
    UF   World travel
Vulcan (Jet bomber)
Vultures *[S] (May add geog subd)*
Waco (Tex.)
   —Tornado, 1953
Waffles
    USE   Pancakes, waffles, etc.
Wage surveys *(May add geog subd)*
Wagers *(May add geog subd)*
    UF   Bets
Wagner, Richard, 1813-1883
    RT   Nibelungenlied (Musical work)
Wagons *(May add geog subd)*
Wah
    USE   Lesser panda *[AC only]*
Wahhabiyah
Wainwright, Jonathan Mayhew, 1883-1953
Waite, Terry
Waiters
    USE   Waiters and waitresses *[AC only]*
Waiters and waitresses *[AC only]*
    UF   Waiters
           Waitresses
Waitresses
    USE   Waiters and waitresses *[AC only]*
Wake Island, Battle of, 1941
Waldheim, Kurt
Wales

Walesa, Lech, 1943- *[AC only]*
Walker, Alice, 1944-
Walker, Amos (Fictitious character)
Walker, Herschel
Walker, John Anthony, 1937-
Walker, Maggie Lena
Walker family
Walking *[S]*
Walking (Sports)
Walking catfish *[S]*
Wall hangings *(May add geog subd)*
Wall Street (New York, N.Y.) *[S]*
Wallaby Creek (N.S.W.)
Wallace, Big-Foot, 1817-1899
    UF   Wallace, William Alexander (Bigfoot), 1817-1899
Wallenberg, Raoul
Waller, Fats, 1904-1943
Wallpaper *[S] (May add geog subd)*
Walls *[S] (May add geog subd)*
Walruses *[S]*
Walt Disney Productions
Walt Disney World (Fla.)
Walters, Barbara, 1931-
Walton, Bill, 1952-
Walton, Sam, 1918-
Wampanoag Indians
Wanamaker, John, 1838-1922
Wandering albatross *(May add geog subd)*
Wang, Ya-ni, 1975-
Wankel engine
Wapner, Joseph A.
War *[S]*
    SA   *the names of specific wars and the subdivision* —Wars
   —Fiction *[AC only]*
    UF   War stories
War correspondents
    BT   Reporters and reporting
War crime trials *[S] (May add geog subd)*
    BT   Trials
War crimes *[S]*
War criminals
War films *[S] (May add geog subd)*
War games
War memorials *(May add geog subd)*
War poetry *[S]*
War posters *(May add geog subd)*
War songs *[S] (May add geog subd)*
Warbeck, Perkin, 1474-1499
Ward family
Warhol, Andy, 1928-
Warm Spring Apache Indians
Warner, Lenn Scobey, 1871-1954
Warner, Malcolm-Jamal
Warren, Earl, 1891-1974
Warsaw (Poland)
   —History
Warsaw Treaty Organization
Warships *(May add geog subd)*
    BT   Ships
Wart hog
Warts *(May add geog subd)*
Washing-machines
Washington (D.C.)
    As a geographic subdivision, this heading is used directly.
Washington (D.C.) in art
Washington (State)

Washington (Tex.)
Washington, Booker T., 1856-1915
Washington, George, 1732-1799
Washington, Harold, 1922-1987
Washington, Martha, 1731-1802
Washington Bullets (Basketball team)
Washington Metropolitan Area
Washington Post (Newspaper)
Washington Redskins (Football team)
Washington Region
    As a geographic subdivision, this heading is used directly.
Washington's Birthday
Washo Indians
Wasps *[S] (May add geog subd)*
Wasserstein, Wendy
Waste disposal sites *(May add geog subd)*
Waste in government spending *(May add geog subd)*
Waste paper *(May add geog subd)*
Waste products *[S] (May add geog subd)*
    UF   Trash
    RT   Refuse and refuse disposal
Watch fobs *(May add geog subd)*
Watchdogs
Water *[S] (May add geog subd)*
   —Pollution *(May add geog subd)*
   —Purification
Water, Underground
    UF   Underground water
Water birds *[S] (May add geog subd)*
Water buffalo *[S] (May add geog subd)*
Water bugs *[AC, S]*
    UF   Naucoridae
           Belostomatidae
           Hebridae
Water conservation *[S] (May add geog subd)*
    UF   Conservation of water
Water gardens *(May add geog subd)*
Water in the body
Water moccasin *[AC, S]*
    UF   Agkistrodon piscivorus
           Cottonmouth
Water in art
Water power *[AC, S]*
    UF   Water-power
Water quality *(May add geog subd)*
Water quality management *(May add geog subd)*
Water resources development *(May add geog subd)*
Water rights *[S]*
Water skiing *[S]*
    BT   Skis and skiing
Water sports
    USE Aquatic sports
Water supply *[AC only]*
    UF   Water-supply
    RT   Saline water conversion
           Waterworks
Watercolor painting *[S] (May add geog subd)*
Waterfalls *(May add geog subd)*
Waterfowl *(May add geog subd)*
Waterfowl shooting *(May add geog subd)*
Watergate Affair, 1972-1974
Waterloo, Battle of, 1815
Waters, Alford, 1919-
Waterworks *(May add geog subd)*
    RT   Water supply *[AC only]*

Watie, Stand, 1806-1871
Watkins, Yoko Kawashima
Watkins Glen Grand Prix Race
Watson, James D.
Watson, J.S. (John Selby), 1804-1884
Watt, James, 1736-1819
Watteau, Antoine, 1684-1721
Watts (Los Angeles, Calif.)
Watts, Heather
Watts Riot, Los Angeles, Calif., 1965
Waves [S]
Wax modeling [AC only]
 UF Wax-modeling
Waxberg, Joseph D., 1922-
Wayne, Anthony, 1745-1796
Wayne, John, 1907-1979
We Are the World
Wealth [S] (May add geog subd)
Weapons (May add geog subd)
 SA the names of specific weapons or types of weapons,
   e.g., Pistols
Wearable art (May add geog subd)
Weasels (May add geog subd)
Weather [S]
Weather control [S] (May add geog subd)
Weather forecasting [S] (May add geog subd)
 RT National Weather Service
Weather in art
Weather vanes (May add geog subd)
Weaverbirds [AC only]
 UF Weaver-birds
Weaving [S] (May add geog subd)
Webb, Sheyann
Webb, Walter Prescott, 1888-1963
Webber, Andrew Lloyd. Phantom of the opera
Webelos
 BT Cub Scouts
Weber, Max, 1881-1961
Webster, Daniel, 1782-1852
Webster, Noah, 1758-1843
Wedding etiquette
 BT Etiquette
Wedding music
Weddings [S] (May add geog subd)
 RT Marriage
 NT Marriage service
Weeds [S] (May add geog subd)
Wedgwood ware
Week [S]
Weight control [AC only]
 UF Reducing
 RT Diet [AC only]
Weight lifting [S] (May add geog subd)
Weight throwing
 BT Track and field [AC only]
 RT Javelin throwing
Weight training (May add geog subd)
 RT Physical fitness
Weight Watchers International
Weightlessness [S]
Weights and measures [S] (May add geog subd)
Weil, Lisl
Weinstein, Frida Scheps
Weisse Rose (Resistance group)
 USE White Rose (German resistance group) [AC only]
Weizman, Chaim, 1874-1952

Welch, Bob, 1956-
Welch, Jack (John Francis), 1935-
Welding [S]
Welfare
 USE Public welfare
Welfare state
Welfare recipients
Welles, Orson, 1915-
Welles, Orson, 1915- . War of the worlds
Wellington (Ohio)
Wellington, Arthur Wellesley, 1st Duke of, 1769-1852
Wells, H.G. (Herbert George), 1866-1946
Wells Fargo & Company
Welsh Americans
Welty, Eudora, 1909-
Wenceslaus, Duke of Bohemia, ca. 907-929
 UF Wenceslaus, Saint, Duke of Bohemia, 907?-935
Wenceslaus, Saint, Duke of Bohemia, 907?-935
 USE Wenceslaus, Duke of Bohemia, ca. 907-929
Wendy's International
Wenzek family
Werewolves (May add geog subd)
 BT Superstition
 RT Vampires
Wesker, Arnold, 1932-
Wesley, John, 1703-1791
West, Benjamin, 1738-1820
West, Jerry, 1938-
West, Mae
West (U.S.) [S]
 —Fiction
  UF Western stories [AC only]
West (U.S.) in art
West (U.S.) in literature
 —Description and travel (Not subd by date)
 —History
 — —1848-1860
West Africans
West Bank
West Indies
West of the Imagination (Television program)
West Virginia
Westchester County (N.Y.)
Westerbork (Netherlands : Concentration camp)
Western Europe
 USE Europe
Western films (May add geog subd)
 BT Motion pictures
Western States
 USE West (U.S.)
Westinghouse, George, 1846-1914
Westminster (London, England)
Westminster Abbey
Wetland animals [AC only]
 UF Wetland fauna
Wetland conservation (May add geog subd)
Wetland fauna
 USE Wetland animals [AC only]
Wetland ecology (May add geog subd)
Wetlands [S] (May add geog subd)
 RT Marshes
   Swamps
Wetzon, Leslie (Fictitious character)
Wexford, Inspector (Fictitious character)

Weyden, Rogier van der, 1399 or 1400-1464
    UF   Van der Weyden, Rogier, ca. 1399-1464
Whale shark *[S] (May add geog subd)*
Whale watching *(May add geog subd)*
Whalers (Persons)
Whales *[S] (May add geog subd)*
    NT   Narwhal
           Sperm whale
Whales in art *[S]*
Whaling *[S] (May add geog subd)*
Wharton, Edith Newbold Jones, 1862-1937
Wheat *[S] (May add geog subd)*
Wheat-free diet
Wheatley, Phillis, 1753-1784
Wheelchairs *(May add geog subd)*
Wheeler family
Wheels *[S] (May add geog subd)*
Whipper family
Whirligigs
    BT   Toys
Whiskey Rebellion, Pa., 1794
Whistler, James McNeill, 1834-1903
Whistles *[AC only]*
Whistling
Whitbread Round the World Race
White, Danny, 1952-
White, E.B. (Elwin Brooks), 1899-1985
White, George, b. 1764
White, Theodore Harold, 1915-
White collar crimes *[S] (May add geog subd)*
    BT   Crime
White collar workers
White familly
White-footed mouse *[AC only]*
    UF   Peromyscus
White House (Washington, D.C.)
White Mountains (N.H. and Me.)
White pelican
White rhinoceros *(May add geog subd)*
White Rose (German resistance group) *[AC only]*
    UF   Weisse Rose (Resistance group)
White shark *[S] (May add geog subd)*
White stork *(May add geog subd)*
White supremacy movements *[S] (May add geog subd)*
White-tailed deer *[S] (May add geog subd)*
White-water canoeing *(May add geog subd)*
    BT   Canoes and canoeing
Whitechapel (London, England)
Whitehead, Mary Beth
Whites
Whitman, Marcus, 1802-1847
Whitman, Narcissa Prentiss, 1808-1847
Whitman, Walt, 1819-1892
Whitney, Eli, 1765-1825
Whittier, John Greenleaf, 1807-1892
Whittington, Richard, d. 1423
Whitworth, Jerry
Whitworth, Kathy
Who (Musical quartet)
Whole language approach in education
    USE Language experience approach in education
Wholesale trade *(May add geog subd)*
    BT   Selling
Whooping cough *(May add geog subd)*
Whooping crane *(May add geog subd)*
Whyte, William

Wichita County (Kan.)
Wichita County (Tex.)
Wichita Falls (Tex.)
Wicker furniture *(May add geog subd)*
    BT   Furniture
Widows *[S]*
Wied, Maximilian, Prinz von, 1782-1867
Wiesel, Elie, 1928-
Wiesenthal, Simon
Wife abuse *[S] (May add geog subd)*
    BT   Family violence
Wiggin, Kate Douglas Smith, 1856-1923
Wigginton, Eliot
Wigs *[S] (May add geog subd)*
Wilbarger County (Tex.)
Wild, Jonathan, 1682?-1725
Wild animals
    USE Feral animals
Wild boar *(May add geog subd)*
Wild cats
    USE Feral cats
Wild children
    USE Feral children
Wild dogs *(May add geog subd)*
    NT   Dingo
Wild flower gardening *(May add geog subd)*
Wild flowers *[S] (May add geog subd)*
Wild flowers in art
Wild horse adoption *(May add geog subd)*
Wild horses *(May add geog subd)*
Wild plants, Edible *(May add geog subd)*
Wild turkeys *(May add geog subd)*
Wild west shows
Wildcats
    USE Felidae
Wilde, Oscar, 1854-1900
Wildenhain, Marguerite
Wilder, Almanzo
Wilder, Laura Ingalls, 1867-1957
Wilder, Thornton, 1897-1975
Wilder, Thornton, 1897-1975.   Our town
Wilderness, Battle of the, Va., 1864
Wilderness areas *[S] (May add geog subd)*
Wilderness Road
Wilderness survival *[S] (May add geog subd)*
Wildflowers
    USE Wild flowers
Wildlife
    USE Animals
           Zoology
Wildlife and pesticides
    USE Pesticides and wildlife
Wildlife art *(May add geog subd)*
    UF   Art, Wildlife
Wildlife attracting *(May add geog subd)*
Wildlife cinematography *(May add geog subd)*
Wildlife conservation *[S] (May add geog subd)*
Wildlife diseases *(May add geog subd)*
Wildlife management *(May add geog subd)*
Wildlife pests *(May add geog subd)*
Wildlife refuges *[S] (May add geog subd)*
Wildlife rescue *(May add geog subd)*
Wildlife veterinarians
Wildlife watching *(May add geog subd)*
    BT   Nature study
Wilkes, Charles, 1798-1877

Will
> *UF* Volition

Will in literature
Willard, Frances Elizabeth, 1839-1898
Willard, Nancy
William I, King of England, 1027 or 8-1087
William II, King of England, 1056?-1100
William III, King of England, 1650-1702
Williams, Edward Bennett
Williams, Hank, 1923-1953
Williams, John
Williams, Mike
Williams, Roger, 1604?-1683
Williams, Ted, 1918-
Williams, Tennessee, 1911-1983
Williams, Tennessee, 1911-1983.   Glass menagerie
Williams, William Carlos, 1883-1963
Williamsburg (Va.)
Williamson, David
Williamson, Jack, 1908-
Williamson County (Tex.)
Willig, George
Willows *(May add geog subd)*
> *BT* Trees

Wills *[S] (May add geog subd)*
> *NT* Holographic wills

Wilson, Cheryl Landon, 1953-
Wilson, Edith Bolling Galt, 1872-1961
Wilson, Edward Adrian, 1872-1912
Wilson, Elizabeth, 1820-1902
Wilson, Nancy
Wilson, Woodrow, 1856-1924
Wimsey, Peter, Lord (Fictitious character)
Winchell, Walter, 1897-1972
Winchester Repeating Arms Company
Winchester rifle
Wind instruments *[S]*
Wind power *[S] (May add geog subd)*
Windmills *[S] (May add geog subd)*
Window gardening *[S] (May add geog subd)*
Windows *[S] (May add geog subd)*
Winds *[S] (May add geog subd)*
Windsor, Edward, Duke of, 1894-1972
Windson, House of
Windsor, Merrill, 1924-
Windsor, Wallis Warfield, Duchess of, 1896-
Windsurfing *[S] (May add geog subd)*
Wine and wine making *[S] (May add geog subd)*
Wine tasting
Winfield, Dave, 1951-
Winfrey, Oprah
Winkler, Henry, 1945-
Winning and losing *[AC only]*
> *UF* Losing and winning

Winter *(May add geog subd)*
> *NT* Jack Frost *[AC only]*
> *SA* the subdivision —Wintering

Winter Olympic Games (15th : 1988 : Calgary, Alta.)
Winter Olympics
> *BT* Olympics

Winter sports *[S] (May add geog subd)*
Winter storms *(May add geog subd)*
> *BT* Storms

Winthrop, Elizabeth Fones, b. 1610
Wire craft
> *BT* Handicraft

Wire fencing
Wirehaired dachshund
Wirsig, Jane
Wisconsin
Wisdom
Wishes *[S]*
Wit and humor *[AC, S]*
> *UF* American wit and humor
>   English wit and humor
> *RT* Literature *[S]*
> *NT* Jokes *[AC only]*
>   Parody *[S]*
>   Satire *[S]*
> *SA* the subdivisions —Humor *and* —Wit and humor

Witch World (Imaginary place)
Witchcraft *[S] (May add geog subd)*
> Use for works on those practicing or accused of practicing sorcery or witchery. *[AC only]*
> *RT* Trials (Witchcraft)
>   Witches

Witches *[AC, S]*
> Use for works on Halloween witches and other witches of fantasy.
> *RT* Witchcraft *[AC only]*

Witez II (Horse)
Witnesses
Witte, Kaaren
Wittgenstein, Paul von
Wives *[S]*
Wizards
Wojciechowska, Maia, 1927-
Wok cookery
Wolfe, James, 1727-1759
Wolfe, Nero (Fictitious character)
Wolfe, Thomas, 1900-1938
Wolff, Tobias, 1945-
Wolstenholme Towne (Va.)
Wolves *[S] (May add geog subd)*
Wombats
Women *[S]*
> *NT* Businesswomen *[AC only]*
> *SA* the subdivision —Women

> **—Mythology**

Women, Black
> *UF* Black women

Women, Jewish
> *USE* Jewish women

Women, Prehistoric
Women air pilots *[S]*
> *BT* Air pilots

Women and literature *(May add geog subd)*
> *UF* Literature and women
> *RT* Women in literature
> *SA* the subdivision —Women authors

Women and religion
> *USE* Women in religion *[AC only]*

Women architects
> *BT* Architects

Women artists
> *BT* Artists

Women astronauts
> *BT* Astronauts

Women astronomers
> *BT* Astronomers

Women athletes
> *BT* Athletes

Women authors *[S]*
  BT Authors
  SA *the subdivision* —Women authors
Women basketball players
  BT Basketball players
Women biologists
  BT Biologists
Women chemists
  BT Chemists
Women college teachers
  BT College teachers
Women conservationists
  BT Conservationists
Women costume designers
  BT Costume designers
Women consumers
  BT Consumers
Women costume designers
  BT Costume designers
Women detectives
  BT Detectives
Women dramatists
  BT Dramatists
Women entrepreneurs
  USE Businesswomen *[AC only]*
Women evangelists
  BT Evangelists
Women executives
  BT Executives
Women explorers
  BT Explorers
Women farmers
  BT Farmers
Women fashion designers
  BT Fashion designers
Women gardeners
  BT Gardeners
Women geologists
  BT Geologists
Women heads of households
  BT Heads of households
Women heads of state
  BT Heads of state
Women healers
  BT Healers
Women historians
  BT Historians
Women in aeronautics
Women in astronautics
Women in business
  USE Businesswomen *[AC only]*
Women in Christianity
Women in horse racing
Women in journalism
Women in Judaism
Women in labor unions *[AC only]*
  UF Women in trade-unions
Women in literature *[S]*
  RT Women and literature
Women in medicine
  RT Women medical scientists
        Women physicians
Women in motion pictures *[S]*
Women in politics
Women in public life

Women in religion
  UF Women and religion
Women in science
  RT Women scientists
Women in the Bible
Women in the professions
Women in trade-unions
  USE Women in labor unions *[AC only]*
Women inventors
  BT Inventors
Women journalists
  BT Journalists
Women judges
  BT Judges
Women lawyers
  BT Lawyers
Women mathematicians
  BT Mathematicians
Women medical scientists
  BT Scientists
  RT Women physicians
Women mountaineers
  BT Mountaineers
Women murderers
  BT Murderers
Women musicians
  BT Musicians
Women orators
  BT Orators
Women-owned business enterprises
Women painters
  BT Artists
Women physicians
  BT Physicians
Women pioneers
  BT Pioneers
Women poets
  BT Poets
Women prime ministers
  BT Prime ministers
Women primatologists
  BT Primatologists
Women publishers
  BT Publishers
Women revolutionaries
  BT Revolutionaries
Women rock musicians
  BT Rock musicians
Women sailors
  BT Sailors
Women scholars
  BT Scholars
Women scientists
  BT Scientists
Women silversmiths
  BT Silversmiths
Women slaves
  BT Slaves
Women social reformers
  BT Social reformers
Women social workers
  BT Social workers
Women soldiers
  BT Soldiers
Women spies
  BT Spies

Women stunt performers
    BT Stunt performers
Women surgeons
    BT Surgeons
Women teachers
    BT Teachers
Women textile workers
    BT Textile workers
Women track and field athletes
    BT Track and field athletes
Women veterinarians
    BT Veterinarians
Women's Air Service Pilots (U.S.)
Women's dreams
Women's encyclopedias and dictionaries
Women's rights *(May add geog subd)*
Women's studies
Wonder, Stevie
Wood *[S] (May add geog subd)*
    NT Driftwood *[AC only]*
Wood, Allen Tate
Wood, Grant, 1891-1942.   American gothic
Wood, Natalie
Wood-carved figurines
Wood carvers *[AC only]*
    UF Wood-carvers
Wood carving *[AC, S]*
    UF Wood-carving
Wood-engraving *(May add geog subd)*
Wood finishing *[S]*
Wood lice (Crustaceans) *[AC only]*
    UF Pill bugs
          Sow bugs
    BT Isopods
Wood lice (Crustaceans) as pets *[AC only]*
    BT Isopods as pets *[AC only]*
Wood stork
Woodard, Lynette
Woodburning
    USE Pyrography
Woodbury County (Iowa)
Woodchuck *[AC, S]*
    UF Groundhog
    BT Marmots *[AC only]*
Wooden-frame buildings *(May add geog subd)*
Wooden toys *(May add geog subd)*
Woodenware
    USE Treenware
Woodland Indians
Woodpeckers *[S] (May add geog subd)*
Woodpile animals
    UF Woodpile fauna
Woodpile fauna
    USE Woodpile animals *[AC only]*
Woodworking industries *(May add geog subd)*
Woodworking tools
Woods, Donald, 1933-
Woods Hole Oceanographic Institution
Woodstock Festival, Bethel, N.Y., 1969
Woodward, Bob
Woodwork *[S] (May add geog subd)*
    RT Handicraft
          Industrial arts
    NT Marquetry

Woodworking machinery *[S] (May add geog subd)*
Woody plants *(May add geog subd)*
Wool *[S] (May add geog subd)*
    RT Yarn
Woolf, Virginia, 1882-1941
Woollcott, Alexander, 1887-1943
Woolley, Leonard, Sir, 1880-1960
Woolly monkeys
Woolly rhinoceros *(May add geog subd)*
Worcester Art Museum
Worcester porcelain
Word (Linguistics)
Word games *[S]*
    RT Puns and punning
    NT Palindromes
          Play on words
          Rhyming games
          Tongue twisters
Word problems (Mathematics)
Word processing *[S] (May add geog subd)*
    BT Computer programs
Worden, Alfred Merrill
WordPerfect
    BT Word processing
Words, New *[S]*
WordStar
    BT Word processing
Wordsworth, William, 1770-1850
Work *[S]*
    UF Employment
    RT Labor
    NT Summer employment
Work and family *(May add geog subd)*
Work ethic *(May add geog subd)*
Workaholics
Workers' compensation *[S] (May add geog subd)*
Working animals *[S] (May add geog subd)*
Working class *(May add geog subd)*
    UF Labor and laboring classes
    RT Labor
Working dogs *(May add geog subd)*
    BT Dogs
Working mothers
    BT Mothers
Workshop recipes
    BT Chemistry, Technical
Workshops *(May add geog subd)*
World Bank *(May add geog subd)*
World government
    USE International organization
World health
World history *[S]*
World maps
World politics *[S]*
    —1945-
    —1945-1965
    —20th century
World records *[S]*
World series (Baseball)
World Trade Center (New York, N.Y.)
World travel
    USE Voyages around the world
World War, 1914-1918 *[S] (May add geog subd)*
    UF World War I

World War, 1939-1945 *[S] (May add geog subd)*
　UF　World War II
　—Displaced persons
　　USE　World War, 1939-1945—Refugees *[AC only]*
　—Refugees *[AC only]*
　　UF　World War, 1939-1945—Displaced persons
World War I
　USE　World War, 1914-1918
World War II
　USE　World War, 1939-1945
World War III *[S]*
　—Fiction
　　BT　World politics
Worms *[S] (May add geog subd)*
Worry *[S]*
Worship *[S]*
　BT　Religion
Worsley, Gump
Wound healing *(May add geog subd)*
Wounded Knee (S.D.)
Wounded Knee Creek, Battle of, 1890
　USE　Wounded Knee Massacre, S.D., 1890
Wounded Knee Massacre, S.D., 1890
Wounds and injuries *[S] (May add geog subd)*
　UF　Injuries
　RT　Accidents
Wovoka, ca. 1856-1932
Wreaths *(May add geog subd)*
Wrecking
Wren, Christopher, Sir, 1632-1723
Wrestling *[S] (May add geog subd)*
Wrestling in art *[S]*
Wright, Frank Lloyd, 1867-1959
Wright, John M. (John MacNair), 1916-
Wright, Orville, 1871-1948
Wright, Peter
Wright, Richard, 1908-1960
Wright, Wilbur, 1867-1912
Writing *[S]*
　UF　Handwriting
　RT　Blind—Printing and writing systems
　　　Penmanship
　SA　*individual forms of writing and the subdivision* —Writing
　　　and the heading Written communication
　—Materials and instruments
Writing (Composition)
　USE　Composition (Language arts)
Writing, Italic
Written communication *(May add geog subd)*
　　Use for works about written language as a form of communication
　or discourse. Use Writing for works on the process or result of
　literally recording visible marks or graphic signs on a surface.
　UF　Written discourse
　　　Written language
　BT　Communication
　　　Language and language arts
　RT　Composition (Language arts)
　　　English language—Composition and exercises
　　　Report writing
Written composition
　USE　Composition (Language arts)
Wyandot Indians
　UF　Huron Indians
Wyeth, Andrew, 1917-
Wyeth, N.C. (Newell Convers), 1882-1945
Wynette, Tammy, 1942-

Wyoming
Wyoming Valley (Pa.)
X-ray lasers
X rays *[AC, S]*
　UF　X-rays
　RT　Radiography
X, Malcolm, 1925-1965
　UF　Malcolm X
Xerography *[S]*
Xerox Corporation
Xerxes I, King of Persia, 519-465 or 4 B.C.
XIT Ranch (Tex.)
Yachting *(May add geog subd)*
Yachts *(May add geog subd)*
Yakama Indians *(May add geog subd)*
Yale University
Yalow, Rosalyn S. (Rosalyn Sussman), 1921-
Yamaha motorcycle
　BT　Motorcycles
Yana Indians
Yangtze River (China)
Yangtze River Delta (China)
Yankee Doodle (Dance)
Yaqui Indians
Yarborough, Ralph Webster, 1903-
Yardley, Jonathan
Yarn *[S]*
　RT　Wool
Ya'sodhar⁻a, wife of Gautama Buddha
Yates, Elizabeth, 1905-
Yavapai Indians
Yeager, Chuck, 1923-
Yeager, Jeana
Yearbooks
Yeast *[S]*
Yeats, William Butler, 1865-1939
Yellow fever *[S] (May add geog subd)*
Yellow River (China)
Yellow ware
　BT　Pottery
Yellowstone National Park
Yeoman, Cushla, 1971-
Yep, Laurence
Yeti *[S]*
Yevtushenko, Yevgeny Aleksandrovich, 1933-
Yezierska, Anzia, 1880?-1970
Yiddish fiction *(May add geog subd)*
Yiddish language *[S] (May add geog subd)*
　—Readers *[AC only]*
　　　Use for reading texts in Yiddish containing materials for in-
　　struction and practice in reading that language.
　　RT　Yiddish language materials *[AC only]*
Yiddish language materials *[AC only]*
　　Use for works written in Yiddish intended primarily for general
　information or recreational reading. Such works with text also given
　in English are further subdivided by the subdivision —Bilingual.
　RT　Yiddish language—Readers *[AC only]*
　—Bilingual *[AC only]*
Yo-yos
　BT　Toys
Yoga *[S]*
Yoga, Hatha *(May add geog subd)*
　UF　Hatha yoga
Yoknapatawpha County (Imaginary place)
Yolen, Jane
Yom Kippur *[S]*

Yoni, 1946-1976
York, House of
York, Sarah Mountbatten-Windsor, Duchess of, 1959-
Yorkshire (England)
Yorktown (Va.)
Yoruba (African people) *[S]*
   —Folklore
      USE Folklore, Yoruba *[AC only]*
Yosemite National Park (Calif.) *[S]*
Young, Andrew, 1932-
Young, Carrie
Young, John W. (John Watts), 1930-
Young adult drama
Young adult fiction
Young adult literature
Young adult literature, English *(May add geog subd)*
Young adult poetry *(May add geog subd)*
Young adults
Young adults' libraries *(May add geog subd)*
   UF Libraries, Young people's
      Young adults' library services
   —Book selection
Young adults' library services
   USE Young adults' libraries
Young American Medal for Bravery
Young County (Tex.)
Young men *[S]*
Young women *[S]*
Younger, Cole, 1844-1916
Younger, James, 1848-1902
Youth *[S]*
   NT Teenagers
   SA the subdivision —Youth
Youth in literature *[S]*
Youth movement *[S] (May add geog subd)*
   —Germany
      NT Hitler Youth *[AC only]*
Yucatán Peninsula
Yucatán (Mexico : State)
Yugoslavia
Yukon River (Yukon and Alaska)
Yukon Territory
Yuma Indians
Yupik Eskimos
Zaharias, Babe Didrikson, 1911-1956
Zaire
Zambia
Zane, Elizabeth, 1759?-1847?

Zapata, Emiliano, 1879-1919
Zapotec Indians
Zar, Rose, 1923-
Zavala, Lorenzo de, 1788-1836
Zeami, 1363-1443
Zebras *[S]*
Zen Buddhism *[S] (May add geog subd)*
   BT Buddhism
Zephyr (Tex.)
Zero (Fighter planes)
Zero (The number)
Zeus (Greek deity)
Ziemian, Joseph
Zigas, Vincent
Zimbabwe
Zindel, Paul
Zinsser, William Knowlton
Zion National Park (Utah)
Zionism *[S] (May add geog subd)*
Zionists
Zip code *[S] (May add geog subd)*
Zippers
Zodiac *[S]*
   RT Astrology
Zola, Emile, 1840-1902
Zolotow, Charlotte, 1915-
Zoo animals *(May add geog subd)*
Zoo keepers
Zoo veterinarians
Zoogeography
   USE Animal distribution *[AC only]*
Zoological illustration *(May add geog subd)*
Zoological models
Zoological Society of London
Zoological specimens *(May add geog subd)*
Zoologists
Zoology *[S] (May add geog subd)*
   RT Animals
Zoos *[S] (May add geog subd)*
   RT National Zoological Park (U.S.)
   NT Petting zoos
Zorza, Jane
Zulu (African people)
   —Folklore
   USE Folklore, Zulu
Zulu War, 1879
Zulu War, 1879
Zululand (South Africa)
Zuni Indians